Stress and Mental Health

Contemporary Issues and Prospects for the Future

The Plenum Series on Stress and Coping

Series Editor:
Donald Meichenbaum, *University of Waterloo, Waterloo, Ontario, Canada*

Current Volumes in the Series:

COMBAT STRESS REACTION
The Enduring Toll of War
Zahava Solomon

COPING WITH WAR–INDUCED STRESS
The Gulf War and the Israeli Response
Zahava Solomon

INFERTILITY
Perspectives from Stress and Coping Research
Edited by Annette L. Stanton and Christine Dunkel-Schetter

INTERNATIONAL HANDBOOK OF TRAUMATIC STRESS SYNDROMES
Edited by John P. Wilson and Beverley Raphael

PSYCHOTRAUMATOLOGY
Key Papers and Core Concepts in Posttraumatic Stress
Edited by George S. Everly, Jr. and Jeffrey M. Lating

THE SOCIAL CONTEXT OF COPING
Edited by John Eckenrode

STRESS AND MENTAL HEALTH
Contemporary Issues and Prospects for the Future
Edited by William R. Avison and Ian H. Gotlib

THE UNNOTICED MAJORITY IN PSYCHIATRIC INPATIENT CARE
Charles A. Kiesler and Celeste G. Simpkins

WOMEN, WORK, AND HEALTH
Stress and Opportunities
Edited by Marianne Frankenhauser, Ulf Lundberg, and Margaret Chesney

---

A Continuation Order Plan is available for this series. A continuation order will bring delivery of each new volume immediately upon publication. Volumes are billed only upon actual shipment. For further information please contact the publisher.

Stress and Mental Health

Contemporary Issues and Prospects for the Future

Edited by

William R. Avison

The University of Western Ontario
London, Ontario, Canada

and

Ian H. Gotlib

Northwestern University
Evanston, Illinois

PLENUM PRESS • NEW YORK AND LONDON

Library of Congress Cataloging-in-Publication Data

Stress and mental health : contemporary issues and prospects for the
future / edited by William R. Avison and Ian H. Gotlib.
       p.   cm. -- (Plenum series on stress and coping)
    Includes bibliographical references and index.
    ISBN 0-306-44687-1
    1. Stress (Psychology) 2. Adjustment (Psychology) 3. Stress
(Psychology)--Research. 4. Adjustment (Psychology)--Research.
5. Mental health--Research.   I. Avison, William R. II. Gotlib, Ian
H. III. Series.
RC455.4.S87S763   1994
155.9'042--dc20   94-21336
                                                                   CIP

ISBN 0-306-44687-1

©1994 Plenum Press, New York
A Division of Plenum Publishing Corporation
233 Spring Street, New York, N.Y. 10013

Printed in the United States of America

Contributors

William R. Avison, Centre for Health and Well-Being, Department of Sociology, The University of Western Ontario, London, Ontario, Canada N6A 5B9

Andrew Baum, Department of Medical Psychology, School of Medicine, Uniformed Services University of the Health Sciences, Bethesda, Maryland 20814-4799

Ian H. Gotlib, Department of Psychology, Northwestern University, Evanston, Illinois 60208

Charles J. Holahan, Department of Psychology, University of Texas at Austin, Austin, Texas 78712

Ronald C. Kessler, Department of Sociology and Institute for Social Research, University of Michigan, Ann Arbor, Michigan 48106-1248

Naomi Lester, Department of Medical Psychology, School of Medicine, Uniformed Services University of the Health Sciences, Bethesda, Maryland 20814-4799

Bruce G. Link, Department of Epidemiology, Columbia School of Public Health, Columbia University, and Epidemiology of Brain Disorders, New York State Psychiatric Institute, New York, New York 10032

William J. Magee, Department of Psychiatry, University of Wisconsin, Madison, Wisconsin 53706

v

Diane E. McLean, Harlem Center for Health Promotion and Disease Prevention, Columbia School of Public Health/Harlem Hospital Center, New York, New York 10037; Division of Epidemiology, Columbia School of Public Health and Gertrude H. Sergievsky Center, Columbia University, New York, New York 10032

John R. McQuaid, Department of Psychology, University of Oregon, Eugene, Oregon 97403-1227

Elizabeth G. Menaghan, Department of Sociology, Ohio State University, Columbus, Ohio 43210-1353

John Mirowsky, Department of Sociology, Ohio State University, Columbus, Ohio 43210-1353

Scott M. Monroe, Department of Psychology, University of Oregon, Eugene, Oregon 97403-1227

Rudolf H. Moos, Department of Veterans Affairs, and Stanford University Medical Centers, Palo Alto, California 94304

Linda E. Nebel, Department of Medical Psychology, School of Medicine, Uniformed Services University of the Health Sciences, Bethesda, Maryland 20814-4799

Gregory R. Pierce, Department of Psychology, Hamilton College, Clinton, New York 13323

Patricia Roszell, Department of Sociology, University of Toronto, Toronto, Ontario, Canada M5S 1P9

Barbara R. Sarason, Department of Psychology, University of Washington, Seattle, Washington 98195

Irwin G. Sarason, Department of Psychology, University of Washington, Seattle, Washington 98195

R. Jay Turner, Department of Sociology, University of Toronto, Toronto, Ontario, Canada M5S 1P9

Blair Wheaton, Department of Sociology, University of Toronto, Toronto, Ontario, Canada M5S 1P9

Preface

A fundamental task of mental health researchers has been to understand the nature of the association between stress and mental health. It is abundantly clear that this task presents a formidable challenge. Investigators have become aware of the vast array of different experiences that constitute the universe of stressors. Similarly, they have recognized that stressors manifest themselves in a wide range of different mental health outcomes. Moreover, stress researchers have identified a substantial number of diverse factors that mediate the effects of stressors on mental health. Consequently, stress researchers have recognized that there is substantial complexity to be understood. This has been made all the more complicated by the large number of studies that have demonstrated how individuals' positions in the social structure and their personal predispositions further influence the experience of stressors and their effects on mental health.

Given the complex layers of these associations that characterize the stress process, mental health researchers now face several challenges. First, the wealth of information concerning the stress process has encouraged investigators to think along and pursue new lines of inquiry. Thus researchers have been challenged to develop new conceptual and theoretical formulations concerning the relation between stress and mental health. Second, there is a clear need to identify the most important research questions to be studied. With the vast body of stress research that now exists, this is an appropriate time for experts in the field to express their views concerning those questions that deserve major consideration. A third challenge follows logically from the first two: Theoretical advances and new research questions typically require new and innovative research designs and methods.

With these challenges in mind, we invited a group of prominent stress researchers to consider specific topic areas and to suggest what they believe are promising new directions for theoretical, empirical, and methodological development. The contributors to this volume were mandated to focus less on reviews of previous work and more on identifying emerging conceptual issues, formulating promising research questions, and specifying new methodological techniques to address important empirical problems.

In our introductory chapter, we briefly review the stress process paradigm and describe the organization of this volume. The contributions in this book are organized around various components of the stress process: stressful life events, chronic strains, mediators, vulnerability to stress, and mental health outcomes. We conclude the volume with a chapter in which we attempt to identify emergent themes that are common to many of the other chapters. In addition, we highlight controversies and differing points of view that constitute intriguing and potentially fruitful research issues for subsequent investigation.

The chapters that make up this book reflect a wide range of different disciplines and research interests. All of the contributors have raised important and compelling questions that are certain to generate substantial advances in the study of the stress process. We wish to extend to them our gratitude for their efforts, insights, and patience. We also wish to acknowledge Donald Meichenbaum, editor of this series, and Eliot Werner, Executive Editor at Plenum Publishing Corporation, for their advice and guidance on this project.

WILLIAM R. AVISON

London, Ontario, Canada

IAN H. GOTLIB

Evanston, Illinois

Contents

PART I. INTRODUCTION

Chapter 1. Introduction and Overview **3**

William R. Avison and Ian H. Gotlib

The Stress Process Paradigm 4
Organization of the Volume 7
References 10

PART II. STRESSFUL LIFE EVENTS

Chapter 2. Unraveling Complexity: Strategies to Refine Concepts, Measures, and Research Designs in the Study of Life Events and Mental Health **15**

Diane E. McLean and Bruce G. Link

Conceptual and Methodological Considerations: Stressors 17
Conceptual and Methodological Considerations:
    Outcome and Causal Inference 34
Future Directions for Research 35
References 38

Chapter 3. Measuring Life Stress and Assessing Its Impact on Mental Health **43**

Scott M. Monroe and John R. McQuaid

The Assessment of Life Events 45
Stressful Life Events and Mental Health:
  Etiology and Other Influences 59
Concluding Remarks 68
References 70

PART III. CHRONIC STRAINS

Chapter 4. Sampling the Stress Universe **77**

Blair Wheaton

Life Events: The Making of a Concept 78
The Origins of the Stress Concept Reconsidered 80
Event versus Chronic Stressors 81
The Stress Continuum 83
The Cumulative Effects of Stressors 95
Concluding Comments 111
References 113

Chapter 5. The Daily Grind: Work Stressors, Family Patterns, and Intergenerational Outcomes **115**

Elizabeth G. Menaghan

Workplace Stressors: Effects on Individual Workers 117
Gender Differences in Effects of Occupational Conditions
  on Family Interaction 119
Intergenerational Effects of Adult Work and Family Stressors:
  An Example 125
Conclusions 141
References 143

PART IV. PSYCHOSOCIAL RESOURCES AND MEDIATORS

Chapter 6. General and Specific Perceptions of Social Support 151

Irwin G. Sarason, Gregory R. Pierce, and Barbara R. Sarason

The Concept of Social Support 153
The Assessment of Social Support 156
Continuing Lines of Social Support Research 158
A New Approach: Social Support in the Context
 of Relationships 164
An Interactional-Cognitive View of Social Support 168
References 173

Chapter 7. Psychosocial Resources and the Stress Process 179

R. Jay Turner and Patricia Roszell

Some Preliminary Considerations 179
Personal Agency ...,....................................... 181
Self-Esteem 190
Other Relevant and Promising Constructs 196
Social Stress and Personal Resources 200
Closing Comments 202
References 204

PART V. VULNERABILITY TO STRESS

Chapter 8. Life Stressors and Mental Health: Advances in Conceptualizing Stress Resistance 213

Charles J. Holahan and Rudolf H. Moos

Review of Stress Resistance Research 214
Emerging Research Directions 218
Conclusions 232
References 234

Chapter 9. The Disaggregation of Vulnerability to Depression as a Function of the Determinants of Onset and Recurrence **239**

Ronald C. Kessler and William J. Magee

Conceptual Issues 242
Empirical Illustrations 247
Discussion 252
References 255

PART VI. THE DEPENDENT VARIABLE IN STRESS RESEARCH

Chapter 10. The Advantages of Indexes over Diagnoses in Scientific Assessment **261**

John Mirowsky

Indexes Clarify What Diagnoses Confound 261
Efficient Assessment 274
Minimizing Attenuation and Preconception 276
Implications for Stress Research 283
Appendix A: Data 285
Appendix B: Short Indexes 287
References 289

Chapter 11. Psychophysiological and Behavioral Measurement of Stress: Applications to Mental Health **291**

Naomi Lester, Linda E. Nebel, and Andrew Baum

Measurement of Stress 292
Stress and Mental Health 298
Conclusions 309
References 310

PART VII. CONCLUSION

Chapter 12. Future Prospects for Stress Research **317**

William R. Avison and Ian H. Gotlib

Emergent Themes 318
Emergent Issues 327
References 330

Index **333**

I

Introduction

1

Introduction

1

Introduction and Overview

WILLIAM R. AVISON and IAN H. GOTLIB

For more than two decades, researchers in several disciplines have been interested in understanding how socially induced stress manifests itself in psychological distress, in symptoms of psychiatric disorder, or in other types of social dysfunction or health problems. Various models of the stress process have been developed to address these issues (e.g., Billings & Moos, 1982; Cronkite & Moos, 1984; Finney, Moos, Cronkite, & Gamble, 1983; Lazarus & Folkman, 1984; Lazarus, Kanner, & Folkman, 1980; Pearlin, Lieberman, Menaghan, & Mullan, 1981). All of these models have as their primary focus the nature of the association between sources of stress and their manifestations. All of them also postulate the existence of at least three critical groups of mediators—social supports, psychosocial resources, and coping resources—that alter the effects of stressors on illness or dysfunction. More recently, stress models have also been elaborated through a consideration of social characteristics of individuals and the effects of prior functioning. The result of this work has been the development of a stress process paradigm that is used widely in the study of health and illness outcomes.

There now exists a sizable body of investigations that have tested various aspects of the stress process paradigm. Indeed, it is no exaggeration to state that this perspective has been a major driving force for

WILLIAM R. AVISON • Centre for Health and Well-Being, Department of Sociology, The University of Western Ontario, London, Ontario, Canada N6A 5B9. **IAN H. GOTLIB** • Department of Psychology, Northwestern University, Evanston, Illinois 60208.
Stress and Mental Health: Contemporary Issues and Prospects for the Future, edited by William R. Avison and Ian H. Gotlib. New York, Plenum Press, 1994.

scientists from diverse disciplines who are interested in the nature of the association of social and psychosocial processes with mental health and illness. There is now little doubt that life stressors and chronic strains represent important etiological risk factors for mental health problems, and that this stress-distress relationship is mediated by various psychosocial resources.

At present, however, research that examines the stress process appears to have reached an impasse. At this point it is not at all clear what future directions are most promising, and there has been disappointingly little discussion among stress researchers concerning the next generation of studies that are needed. Rather, the most recent research has focused either on the development of more sophisticated methods for measuring components of the stress process or on the application of the paradigm to a broader range of disorders or dysfunctions.

There is clearly a need for researchers to take stock of the progress that has been made thus far on the stress process and to suggest new directions to be pursued. In this volume, we bring together the views of prominent stress researchers who identify critical issues that have emerged regarding the stress process and offer what they believe are promising future paths for research in this area.

THE STRESS PROCESS PARADIGM

As we have indicated, various models of the stress process have been formulated by researchers interested in understanding how various sources of stress translate into symptoms of health problems. Although there is some variation in the specific content of these different stress models, all of them begin with the proposition that social and psychological sources of stress influence health outcomes. Indeed, there have been hundreds of empirical reports of the association between stressful life events and health outcomes, variously measured (see Aneshensel, 1992; Monroe, 1992, for excellent reviews of this literature). Furthermore, several investigators have documented the important roles played by ongoing stressors or chronic strains in affecting mental health outcomes (e.g., Avison & Turner, 1988; Eckenrode, 1984; Link, Dohrenwend, & Skodol, 1986). Where early work in this area focused primarily on stressful life events and chronic strains as the major sources of stress, more recent investigations have examined such other dimensions of stressful experience as daily hassles and life traumas. Regardless of the type of stressor studied, there is consensus among researchers that these sources of stress are potentially interactive in their effects on health outcomes. For example, Pearlin et al. (1981) have suggested that stressful life events might affect mental health by generating new chronic strains or by changing the meaning of existing strains. Indeed, Pearlin and Lieberman (1979) concluded that "to an appreciable extent the impact of events is channelled through relatively durable problems impinging on the lives of people" (p. 240). Similar conclusions have been reached by Brown and Harris (1978) and Paykel (1978). More recently, Wheaton (1990) has presented a particularly compelling exposition of the ways in which preexisting chronic stressors condition the effects of subsequent life events on distress.

Another central postulate of all stress process formulations is the existence of factors that mediate the experience of stressors and the expression of symptoms of illness or dysfunction. These mediating factors either intervene between stress and illness or have interactive or buffering effects that moderate the impact of stressors on distress and disorder. Social resources or social supports, coping resources or psychosocial resources, and coping responses or behaviors are three critical groups of mediating factors. Several important books and reviews of the literature on social support have been published over the last decade (e.g., Cohen & Wills, 1985; Cohen & Syme, 1985; Gottlieb, 1988; House, Landis, & Umberson, 1988; Sarason & Sarason, 1985; Sarason, Sarason, & Pierce, 1990; Turner, 1983). These reviews have provided incontrovertible evidence on the important role played by social support in the stress process. Moreover, they have demonstrated that the study of social supports must take into account the multidimensional nature of the construct, including considerations of the structure of social networks, the functions of social support, and an awareness of the distinctions between perceived and actual support.

Individuals' psychosocial resources constitute a second important domain of mediators in stress process formulations. Research has demonstrated that self-efficacy and self-esteem are especially important resources that have important effects on the ways in which stressors manifest themselves as distress or disorder. Under the rubric of self-efficacy, numerous studies have demonstrated that personal constructs such as locus of control, mastery, helplessness, and fatalism have significant effects on individuals' mental health. Similarly, there is a substantial body of research documenting the benefits of self-esteem with respect to positive mental health.

Third, variations in coping abilities and differences in the use of specific coping strategies are also central elements of stress process models. Early work on coping behaviors by Lazarus (1966), Pearlin and Schooler (1978), and Antonovsky (1979) stimulated considerable interest among stress researchers. Subsequent research efforts have provided significant insights into the ways in which situational contexts and cognitive appraisals influence the choice of coping responses by individuals who experience stressful circumstances (Eckenrode, 1991; Kessler, Price, & Wortman, 1985; Lazarus & Folkman, 1984; Menaghan, 1983; Moos, 1986). This large body of research attests to the complexity involved in understanding how individuals cope with socially induced stressors.

In addition to specifying the various linkages among sources, mediators, and manifestations of stress, researchers have also become aware that social contexts and other antecedents may condition the entire stress process. For example, Finney et al. (1983) and Cronkite and Moos (1984) have argued that these models should be elaborated by including the effects of individuals' social characteristics and the effects of prior functioning or psychopathology. Cronkite and Moos argue that predisposing factors are likely to be correlated both with stress and with later illness or dysfunction. In a similar vein, Monroe and Simons (1991) have contended that certain kinds of stress may be influenced by specific cognitive diatheses or individual predispositions. Finally, Pearlin (1989) has argued persuasively that stress research has not consistently attended to the social structures that mold or condition the stress process. Pearlin maintains that the structure of social life, as reflected in status and social roles, has important implications for the kinds of stressors experienced by people, the kinds of mediators that are available to them, and the ways in which stressors manifest themselves.

The result of this work has been the development of a stress process model that is widely used in the study of illness outcomes. Although various authors have modified it, variations in the stress process model typically involve the measures that are used to index the various constructs.

The application of this model to the study of mental health, psychological distress, and other dysfunctions has a number of advantages. First, the model is dynamic, and it explicitly considers changes in functioning over time. Second, the model integrates principles from a variety of diverse disciplines, including psychology, sociology, and psychiatric epidemiology. Consequently it provides a more comprehensive, multidimensional approach to understanding the stress process. Third, the model is generalizable to a broad range of functional outcomes. Though its major applications have been to the study of psychological distress and depressive symptomatology, it has also been applied successfully in the exploration of factors associated with symptoms of physical illness and determinants of alcohol consumption. Finally, the stress process model explicitly recognizes that individuals' functioning is importantly influenced by others in their social world. Many of the eventful stressors and chronic strains experienced by individuals are the result of illness, accidents, or difficulties experienced by their family and friends. Social resources that mediate the stress–illness relationship include emotional support (such as one experiences in a warm marital and family milieu) or instrumental support (from friends and coworkers).

ORGANIZATION OF THE VOLUME

We have organized this book around five major topic areas that have been central to investigations of the stress process:

- the etiological significance of stressful life events for psychological distress and psychiatric disorder
- the role of ongoing stressors or chronic strains in the stress process
- the role and significance of mediators such as social support and psychosocial resources in the stress process
- the concept of vulnerability to stressors
- the nature of the dependent variable in stress process research

Our selection of these issues was based in large part on our assessment of the issues and debates that appear to have engaged stress researchers in recent years. Certainly there are other contemporary issues that we might have chosen to highlight in this volume. In our view, however, those that we have selected represent the major substantive components of the stress process formulation. Moreover, an array of other pertinent issues has been addressed in each chapter of this volume.

For each of these topic areas, we invited internationally respected experts to contribute chapters that would not only assess the current state of research but, more importantly, suggest new directions for research that would advance our understanding of the links between stress and mental health. For each area, we solicited two chapters. We also attempted to invite contributors from different scientific specialities so that this volume would benefit from a multidisciplinary approach to the study of stress and mental health. The result of this collaborative endeavor is a collection of chapters that should generate considerable discussion and stimulate a new generation of studies of the stress process.

The book begins with two chapters that focus on stressful life events and mental health, perhaps the most widely studied area in stress process research. Diane McLean and Bruce Link consider a number of

problems that face stress researchers in unraveling the complex relationship between stressors and their mental health effects. They begin by
discussing a number of conceptual and methodological issues, including
what should be considered as stress; whether we should measure
stressors that occur to others in the respondent's social network; how
social context should be incorporated into these measures; and how
problems such as timing of events, event linkage and redundancy, and
recall can be addressed most effectively. In the second section of their
chapter, McLean and Link consider issues related to the range of outcomes that might be included in stress research.

In the second chapter, Scott Monroe and John McQuaid raise questions on two grounds concerning the validity of the existing literature on
the health consequences of increased levels of life events. Monroe and
McQuaid suggest that contemporary methods for measuring life events
may not adequately control for biases that are inherent in the subjective
reporting of life events by respondents. They also argue that life stress
may have effects on individuals that go beyond the onset of a particular
disorder. In making these arguments, Monroe and McQuaid eloquently
raise a series of issues concerning the specificity of both direct and
indirect effects of stress on mental health.

The next section focuses on the concept of chronic strain. Blair
Wheaton provides a comprehensive framework for conceptualizing the
"stress universe." He begins with a consideration of models of stress
from the social and physical sciences and discusses the fundamental
distinction between eventful and continuous forms of stress. Wheaton
then describes the evolution of stress concepts, including chronic stress,
daily hassles, macroevents, nonevents, and traumas, and presents a
scheme for placing these different kinds of stressors in relation to one
another. He concludes by presenting results of his research assessing the
independent effects of these different types of stressors on mental
health outcomes, and by developing a model that takes into account the
cumulative effects of these stressors over the life course.

In the second chapter in this section, Elizabeth Menaghan argues
that the competing demands of work and family constitute significant
ongoing stressors for many families. She argues that lack of self-
direction or control in the workplace and the number of hours on the
job represent chronic strains that affect individuals' marital relationships
and parenting activities. Menaghan also presents empirical results that
document the intergenerational repercussions of these work–family
strains. She demonstrates how such problems have implications for the
emotional well-being of children. Moreover, Menaghan discusses how

gender differences in workplace experiences are associated with differences in children's outcomes.

The third section of the book is devoted to a consideration of social support and psychosocial resources. Irwin Sarason, Gregory Pierce, and Barbara Sarason begin their chapter by reviewing different approaches that focus on the structure of social networks and social support, the functions of support, and the distinction between the receipt of support and the perception of available social support. They then discuss several issues concerning the assessment of social support, emphasizing the need to consider more explicitly both the role of support as a stress buffer and the complexity of social support processes. Sarason et al. conclude with a theoretical discussion that draws attention to the potential importance of personality characteristics of the receiver of support, relationships between support providers and receivers, and the context in which supportive activity occurs.

R. Jay Turner and Patricia Roszell then review the roles of psychosocial resources in the stress process. They begin by assessing the importance of personal agency or efficacy for mental health and the ways in which social structure appears to condition self-efficacy. Turner and Roszell then examine the role of self-esteem as a mediator in the stress process. They offer some intriguing suggestions about the potential impact of other psychosocial constructs, such as psychological centrality and identity accumulation. Their chapter concludes with a consideration of the ways in which stressful life experiences may condition individuals' levels of psychosocial resources.

Concepts such as invulnerability, resilience, and stress resistance have occupied a central place in recent stress process investigations. These issues are the focus of the fourth section of the book. Charles Holahan and Rudolf Moos examine how personal and social resources and different types of coping strategies in the face of stressful experience constitute resistance to stress. They begin with a historical review of the evolution of the concept of stress resistance. Holahan and Moos report the results of their research in which they constructed their Life Stressors and Social Resources Inventory to develop a more comprehensive assessment of the interplay among stressors and resources. They describe their program of research on recovery from psychological disorder, the interdependence among family members, and the psychological growth of individuals who have experienced stress. Holahan and Moos conclude with a consideration of the theoretical and clinical implications of their approach to stress resistance.

Ronald Kessler and William Magee then discuss vulnerability in the context of factors that buffer the effects of stressful life events on clinical depression. Specifically, they argue that the use of diagnostic measures allows for the decomposition of stress and stress-buffering effects into components that affect initial onset and recurrence of episodes. Kessler and Magee contend that differentiating predictors of lifetime occurrence of disorder from the predictors of recent onset and recent recurrence can clarify some of the causal pathways that make up the stress process paradigm.

The final section of this volume consists of two chapters that discuss issues concerned with the choice of the dependent variable or mental health outcome in stress process research. First, John Mirowsky argues for the superiority of indexes over diagnoses as the most appropriate measures of mental, emotional, or behavioral problems. Mirowsky begins with an overview that distinguishes between indexes and diagnoses. He then illustrates how results based on the former differ from those derived from the latter. Mirowsky concludes with a discussion of the implications of these considerations for stress process research.

In the second chapter in this section, Naomi Lester, Linda Nebel, and Andrew Baum examine advances in the development of models that assess different levels of response to stress. They review approaches that partition responses to stress into self-report, behavioral, physiological, and biochemical levels. They then eloquently discuss the implications of this multilevel approach for the study of substance abuse, anxiety disorders (including posttraumatic stress disorder), and depression.

We contribute a concluding chapter that identifies emergent themes that may guide future stress research. Though the contributors to this book come from diverse disciplines and focus on distinctly different research issues, it is interesting to find considerable agreement among these authors about the future of stress research. At the same time, a reading of these chapters reveals a number of ongoing debates that have not been resolved. These, too, constitute new research questions that investigators may wish to examine.

REFERENCES

Aneshensel, C. S. (1992). Social stress: Theory and research. *Annual Review of Sociology, 18,* 15–38.

Antonovsky, A. (1979). *Health, stress, and coping.* San Francisco: Jossey-Bass.

Avison, W. R., & Turner, R. J. (1988). Stressful life events and depressive symptoms: Disaggregating the effects of chronic strains and eventful stressors. *Journal of Health and Social Behavior, 29,* 253–264.

Billings, A. G., & Moos, R. H. (1982). Stressful life events and symptoms: A longitudinal model. *Health Psychology, 1*, 99–117.

Brown, G. W., & Harris, T. O. (1978). *Social origins of depression: A study of psychiatric disorder in women.* London: Tavistock.

Cohen, S., & Syme, L. S. (Eds.). (1985). *Social support and health.* Orlando, FL: Academic Press.

Cohen, S., & Wills, T. A. (1985). Stress, social support, and the buffering hypothesis. *Psychological Bulletin, 98*, 310–357.

Cronkite, R. C., & Moos, R. H. (1984). The role of predisposing and moderating factors in the stress–illness relationship. *Journal of Health and Social Behavior, 25*, 372–393.

Eckenrode, J. (1984). Impact of chronic and acute stressors on daily reports of mood. *Journal of Personality and Social Psychology, 46*, 907–918.

Eckenrode, J. (Ed.). (1991). *The social context of coping.* New York: Plenum.

Finney, J. W., Moos, R. H., Cronkite, R. C., & Gamble, W. (1983). A conceptual model of the functioning of married persons with impaired partners: Spouses of alcoholic patients. *Journal of Marriage and the Family, 45*, 23–34.

Gottlieb, B. H. (1988). Social support and the study of personal relationships. *Journal of Social and Personal Relationships, 2*, 351–375.

House, J. S., Landis, K. R., & Umberson, D. (1988). Social relationships and health. *Annual Review of Sociology, 14*, 293–318.

Kessler, R. C., Price, R. H., & Wortman, C. B. (1985). Social factors in psychopathology: Stress, social support, and coping process. *Annual Review of Psychology, 36*, 531–572.

Lazarus, R. S. (1966). *Psychological stress and the coping process.* New York: McGraw-Hill.

Lazarus, R. S., & Folkman, S. (1984). *Stress, appraisal, and coping.* New York: Springer.

Lazarus, R. S., Kanner, A. D., & Folkman, S. (1980). Emotions: A cognitive-phenomenological analysis. In R. Plutchik & H. Kellerman (Eds.), *Theories of emotion* (pp. 189–217). New York: Academic Press.

Link, B. G., Dohrenwend, B. P., & Skodol, A. (1986). Socio-economic status and schizophrenia: Noisome occupational characteristics as a risk factor. *American Sociological Review, 52*, 96–112.

Menaghan, E. G. (1983). Individual coping effects: Moderators of the relationship between life stress and mental health outcomes. In H. B. Kaplan (Ed.), *Psychosocial stress: Trends in theory and research* (pp. 157–191). New York: Academic Press.

Monroe, S. M. (1992). Life events assessment: Current practices, emerging trends. *Clinical Psychology Review, 2*, 435–453.

Monroe, S. M., & Simons, A. D. (1991). Diathesis–stress theories in the context of life stress research: Implications for depressive disorders. *Psychological Bulletin, 110*, 406–425.

Moos, R. H. (Ed.). (1986). *Coping with life crises.* New York: Plenum.

Paykel, E. S. (1978). Contribution of life events to causation of psychiatric illness. *Journal of Psychosomatic Research, 27*, 341–352.

Pearlin, L. I. (1989). The sociological study of stress. *Journal of Health and Social Behavior, 30*, 241–256.

Pearlin, L. I., & Lieberman, M. A. (1979). Social sources of emotional stress. In R. Simmons (Ed.), *Research in community and mental health, vol. 1* (pp. 217–248). Greenwich, CT: JAI Press.

Pearlin, L. I., Lieberman, M. A., Menaghan, E. G., & Mullan, J. T. (1981). The stress process. *Journal of Health and Social Behavior, 22*, 337–356.

Pearlin, L. I., & Schooler, C. (1978). The structure of coping. *Journal of Health and Social Behavior, 19*, 2–21.

Sarason, B. R., Sarason, I. G., & Pierce, G. R. (Eds.). (1990). *Social support: An interactional view.* New York: Wiley.

Sarason, I. G., & Sarason, B. R. (Eds.). (1985). *Social support: Theory, research, and applications.* Dordrecht, Netherlands: Martinus Nijhoff.

Turner, R. J. (1983). Direct, indirect, and moderating effects of social support on psychological distress and associated conditions. In H. B. Kaplan (Ed.), *Psychosocial stress: Trends in theory and research* (pp. 105–155). New York: Academic Press.

Wheaton, B. (1990). Life transitions, role histories, and mental health. *American Sociological Review, 55,* 209–233.

II

Stressful Life Events

2

Unraveling Complexity
Strategies to Refine Concepts, Measures, and Research Designs in the Study of Life Events and Mental Health

DIANE E. McLEAN and BRUCE G. LINK

Despite literally thousands of research reports on the relationship between stressful circumstances and the onset or exacerbation of illness (Holmes, 1979), controversy remains about their importance. Some investigators claim that there is no compelling evidence for a causal association between stressful circumstances and illness outcomes. In his award-winning lecture to the American Psychopathological Association, Leonard Heston (1988) put these sentiments in strong terms, claiming that "the facts make it clear that searches for specific environmental factors external to the body juices are likely to prove dead ends. Such research has been done too long and too intensely with no result" (p. 212). According to Heston, we need to reorient the direction of our research towards a major redistribution of "human and material resources to hard ball biology" (p. 212).

DIANE E. McLEAN • Harlem Center for Health Promotion and Disease Prevention, Columbia School of Public Health/Harlem Hospital Center, New York, New York 10037; Division of Epidemiology, Columbia School of Public Health and Gertrude H. Sergievsky Center, Columbia University, New York, New York 10032.   **BRUCE G. LINK** • Division of Epidemiology, Columbia School of Public Health, Columbia University, and Epidemiology of Brain Disorders, New York State Psychiatric Institute, New York, New York 10032.
Stress and Mental Health: Contemporary Issues and Prospects for the Future, edited by William R. Avison and Ian H. Gotlib. New York, Plenum Press, 1994.

Even investigators who have worked within the life-events tradition have expressed grave reservations about the strength and interpretability of associations between measures of stressful circumstances and illness. For example, Rabkin and Struening (1976, p. 1015) found that correlation coefficients between life-events measures and illness are typically quite low, hovering around .12. Criticism of the interpretability of even these modest associations as causes of psychopathology rather than consequences or confounds has also been strenuous. Dohrenwend and colleagues have been the most persistent in reminding investigators of serious problems in this area (Dohrenwend & Dohrenwend, 1969; Dohrenwend, Dohrenwend, Dodson, & Shrout, 1984; Link, Mesagno, Lubner, & Dohrenwend, 1990). In order to address this issue directly, Barbara Dohrenwend et al. (1984) asked clinical psychologists to rate the items in several putative measures of stress as to whether they were symptoms of psychopathology. They found that many of the items in the most commonly used measures of stress (the Holmes and Rahe SRE and the Kanner et al. measure of daily hassles) and the Lin, Dean, and Ensel measure of social support were rated as more likely to be psychological symptoms than measures of environmental circumstances.

Finally, though focused specifically on the Holmes and Rahe SRE, Brown (1974, 1989) has challenged the accuracy and thus the effectiveness of the list approach to measuring stressful life events. Specifically Brown noted the following flaws: (a) the vagueness of some items (e.g., "revision of personal habits"); (b) empirical evidence of low reliability and validity; (c) the insensitivity of the list method's "dictionary" nature, which equates all experiences that occur within a specific life-event category (e.g., all job losses are assumed to be similarly stressful); and (d) the practice of adding events that are very different qualitatively (e.g., divorce and personal injury). Because the vast majority of studies of life events and illness use the list method, Brown's critique applies to almost all research that has been conducted under the life-events rubric.

Does all of this mean that inquiry into life stress processes must be abandoned because of the inherent flaws it entails? Should new investigators redirect their efforts to Heston's "hard ball biology"? Hardly. Significant advances in the measurement of life stress processes have occurred that respond to the major criticisms mentioned above (Brown & Harris, 1978; McGonagle & Kessler, 1990; McLean, 1991; Shrout et al., 1989; Wheaton, 1990). These improvements have expanded the scope of phenomena considered, the precision of measurement of those phenomena, and the interpretability of associations uncovered. Such advances have been highly productive and suggest that more, not less, attention be directed to life stress processes. At the same time, though, the widespread adoption of most of these improvements has been delayed; older, far less satisfactory life-event list approaches are still standard fare.

The goal of this chapter is to raise the salient issues that we feel must be considered in a serious study of the health effects of stressful circumstances and to discuss advances that have been made in each of them. We begin by discussing five broad areas:

1. What experiences should be included in an assessment of stressful circumstances?
2. Which, if any, of the stressful circumstances occurring to people other than the respondent should be included in the assessment?
3. How should the context in which the stressful circumstance occurs be incorporated?
4. What information about the timing of the stressful circumstance needs to be included?
5. How can measurement issues such as redundancy (the same event being reported twice under different event categories), linking (one event causing another creating a sequence), and recall problems be addressed most effectively?

The complexity of an inquiry into stressful circumstances will be apparent after considering these issues. The second section of the chapter raises two issues that are crucial in making effective choices about assessment procedures within this complex terrain. The first issue concerns the outcome or the range of outcomes (Aneshensel, Rutter, & Lachenbruch, 1991; Cassel, 1974) that one is interested in explaining; the second concerns theoretical questions about the mechanism through which stressful circumstances affect outcomes. If one is seriously concerned with understanding the social sources of stressful circumstances in the lives of individuals and the ways in which these stressful circumstances produce illness, we propose that the nature of the theoretical explanation being investigated and the key alternatives to that theoretical explanation should dictate the stressor assessment strategy chosen.

CONCEPTUAL AND METHODOLOGICAL CONSIDERATIONS: STRESSORS

Content of Life-Event Inventories: What to Measure

Stressors can be divided into two general classes: stressful life events and chronic strains. We will focus our discussion on life events, although we will note particular points of convergence and overlap between events and strains. Stressful life events can themselves be separated into two broad categories: recent stressors (usually considered to be those experiences that have occurred within the past year) and remote stressors. A few investigators have considered the psychological effects of such childhood stressors as early loss of or separation from a mother (Brown & Harris, 1978; Kendler, Neale, Kessler, Heath, & Eaves, 1992), and the literature on the long-term mental health effects of such traumatic childhood events as sexual or physical abuse is rapidly growing (Beitchman et al., 1992). The influence of other remote stressors (childhood or otherwise), however, has not been systematically investigated. As there is evidence to support the occurrence of physiological adaptation to chronic stressors and evidence of differential physiological responses to current stressors based on exposure to remote stressors (Van der Kolk & Greenberg, 1987), the development of reliable and valid assessment strategies appropriate for remote stressors is clearly needed. Investigation of exposure to a range of remote stressors and an understanding of the psychosocial and physiological pathways through which they may exert their effects on mental and physical health is likely to be a fruitful avenue for further study.

Conceptual Development of Event Inventories

Our focus here is largely on the effect of recent stressors. Research on the impact of recent life events has developed from two related, but inherently different theoretical conceptualizations of what is or is not a "life event." As a consequence, the content of instruments measuring life events has been determined in large part by these different conceptions of the construct of stressfulness. The first is that life events consist of recent experiences that lead to life change, experiences that require some type of readjustment or behavioral change in routine (Dohrenwend, Krasnoff, Askenasy, & Dohrenwend, 1978; Holmes & Rahe, 1967; Monroe, 1982; Thoits, 1983). The second is that life events consist of recent experiences that are likely to arouse strong emotion, regardless of the specific emotion produced (Brown, 1974, 1989; Brown & Harris, 1978). Although these two formulations have a great deal of overlap, their differences have implications for the populations of events studied, the outcomes considered, and the methods chosen to study them. As noted by Dohrenwend et al. (1978), "The decisions we make in the construction of [a] list [of events] will determine the kinds of inferences and generalizations that we can make" (p. 207).

Life Events and Change. From the early work of Cannon and Selye, it has been clear that exposure to experimental stressful stimuli produces an adaptive physiological response in animals and humans. The initial effort of Holmes and Rahe (1967) in the field of life stress research was an inquiry into recent life events that clustered at the time of illness onset; it extended the notion of an adaptation response to stressful stimuli to postulate an adaptation response to psychosocial stressors. These authors' Schedule of Recent Experiences (SRE) and Social Readjustment Rating Scale (SRRS) ranked a list of 43 life experiences in terms of the average amount of life change expected as a consequence of that experience (Holmes & Masuda, 1973). The amount of life change associated with each recent experience was then summarized to give a total life change score.

Although there has been substantial development in the field since then, persistent criticisms have remained about the adequacy of coverage of important life experiences on checklists. The summary by Thoits (1983) of critiques of the content areas covered in life-event inventories is still broadly applicable today. First, the SRE and many other checklists leave out socially controversial events (e.g., abortion, infidelity). Second, most checklists emphasize the events of young adulthood, thereby leaving out events associated with other periods in the life cycle. Third, most checklists underrepresent or leave out entirely events that are more common to women, to particular ethnic groups, or to a particular social class (Rabkin & Struening, 1976). Fourth, "non-events," or "events that are desired or anticipated but do not occur," are also usually omitted (Gersten, Langner, Eisenberg, & Orzek, 1974). Using such restricted lists of events may lead investigators to miss important variations in the impact of recent life experiences within different social or ethnic groups or between men and women; omission of important events will certainly lead to lower correlations between life events and illness. Unfortunately, the last decade has seen little substantial change in the content covered by inventories of life events.

In addition, most event inventories contain both positive and negative experiences, stemming from the original theoretical framework that the occurrence of *any* life change requires readjustment. The literature on the events–illness relationship has shown that negative events, not positive ones, are associated with increased risk of psychological disorder. Taken at face value this would seem to challenge the change-per-se notion about the impact of stress. Life-event checklists, however, do not include equal numbers of events of each type. Thus it has not been possible to test uniformly the interrelationship of positive and negative events to either psychological distress, psychiatric disorder, or physical illness. This has serious implications for our ability to understand the overall impact of recent life experiences on illness. For instance, the simultaneous occurrence of positive events may exert a "neutralizing" effect on the relationship of negative events to disorder (Gersten et al., 1974; Kellam, 1974; Monroe & Roberts, 1990). The occurrence of positive events may buffer physiological change associated with the occurrence of negative events, again with implications for investigation of the effects of life events on mental and physical health outcomes, especially as exposure to positive and negative events is likely to vary by social class, gender, and ethnicity, as well as by other social factors. Additionally, most life events are neither entirely positive nor negative but have both positive and negative characteristics (Cassel, 1974; Dohrenwend, Link, Kern, Shrout, & Markowitz, 1987).

In fairness, once we recognize the enormous complexity of human experience, we can see that criticizing any particular list for failure to capture all such experience is an easy undertaking. Still, when large domains relevant to major population groups are underrepresented (Thoits, 1983) or experiences relevant to alternative theories about how life events affect health are left out, an important problem of coverage exists. In the next section we will see how an alternative theory about how life events affect health can lead to new ideas about what should be covered in life-events inventories.

Life Events and Psychological Meaning. The work of Brown and Harris in the United Kingdom, and of those investigators who have used their instruments and measures, begins with a different view of life events than the concern with change that guided Holmes and Rahe in the United States. Whereas Holmes and Rahe based their theoretical framework on a physiological understanding of the consequences of adaptation and change, Brown and colleagues concentrate on the psychological meaning of life events and the strong emotion they produce, rather than adaptation as such (Brown, 1974, 1989; Brown & Harris, 1978). Change and adaptation are not absent from their formulation, but change is theoretically important only insofar as it relates to the psychological meaning of an event:

> With change we risk, at least temporarily, losing the sense of life's reality. . . . Crises may raise fundamental questions about our lives. They focus our attention on the present and since this is the visible outcome of our past—our choices, commitments and mistakes—we may come to question what our life might have been, what it is about and what it will become.
>
> Changes are important in so far as they alter assumptions a person has made about the world: about personal material possessions, the familiar world of home and place of work and the individual's own body and mind. . . . The importance of such a formulation is that it makes clear how we can lose what we have never had: ideas of what we might possess or become—hope of a promotion, a child, someone's

love. Indeed a crisis or change is probably only ever significant if it leads to a change in thought about the world. (Brown & Harris, 1978, pp. 84–85)

Within this formulation, these investigators list 40 types of events, falling into the following eight categories (Brown & Harris, 1989):

1. Changes in a role for the respondent (e.g., changing a job, losing or gaining an opposite-sex friend)
2. Changes in a role for close relatives of the respondent
3. Major changes in health of the respondent
4. Major changes in health for close relatives of household members
5. Forecasts of change (e.g., respondent told about being rehoused)
6. Residence changes and any marked change in the amount of contact with close relatives and household members
7. Valued goal fulfillments or disappointments
8. Other dramatic events involving respondent, close relative or family member (e.g., brother being arrested)

These, then, are events that involve change in an activity, a role, life circumstances, or an idea (Brown & Harris, 1989). Many of these events appear on the checklist inventories reviewed earlier, but many do not. Specifically, such "nonevents" as forecasts of change (5) and loss of valued goals or disappointments (7) are not usually considered on checklist inventories.

Criticisms of the methodology used by Brown and colleagues have come from several directions. The interview method attempts to separate the occurrence of events from vulnerability factors and the occurrence of disorder; nevertheless, it does not entirely succeed (Shrout et al., 1989; Tennant & Bebbington, 1978; Tennant, Bebbington, & Hurry, 1981). Measures of contextual threat incorporate measures of vulnerability factors, especially aspects of the social situation of the respondent, thus rendering understanding of the isolated etiological role of life events impossible. Although the conceptual underpinning of Brown's research program on life events and illness is appealing and many of the measures of intraevent variability developed by Miller and colleagues (Miller et al., 1986; Miller & Ingham, 1983) are intuitively meaningful, it is not possible to determine whether the striking associations found between life events and depression in these studies are attributable to (a) sampling of a different population of events from those in the studies focused on change (some of which may be confounded with psychological state), or (b) differences in method that combine indices of events with measures of the social situation. It is possible that a combination of both is at work. The research of Kessler and colleagues that incorporates

Brown's concept of emotional loss (loss of a cherished idea) into a check-list methodology is unusual among research on life events that relies on checklists (Kessler & Wethington, 1986; McGonagle & Kessler, 1990; McLean, 1991). To date, however, Kessler and colleagues have not analyzed these events separately from the events usually found on a check-list inventory.

Intraevent Variability

We have just considered breadth of coverage in measures of life events from two different conceptualizations of the mechanism through which life experiences are stressful. Given a broad set of events, as noted earlier, many checklist approaches treat all events the same, even though measurement of intraevent differences is crucial in order to test alternative mechanisms adequately (e.g., change versus meaning). Several investigators who rely on the checklist approach have developed innovative strategies to measure characteristics of events that cut across specific experiences, such as the amount of behavioral change associated with the event, its magnitude, its degree of anticipation or control, or its degree of undesirability (Shrout et al., 1989). The SEPRATE, a structured approach to measurement of intraevent variability recently developed by Dohrenwend, Raphael, Schwartz, Stueve, and Skodol (1993), uses narrative probes to elicit information on event characteristics, with a particular focus on factors leading up to the occurrence of the event.

In the methodologic approach of Brown and Harris, trained interviewers conduct open-ended interviews, using systematic probes about experiences and feelings leading up to and following each event. The interviewers then use this information to rate severity and 28 contextual scales covering many characteristics of the events, or intraevent variability. The most significant of these contextual scales has been a measure of the "threat" or the psychological meaning of the event. Only those life events with moderate or severe long-term threat (i.e., the threatening implications of the event lasted at least 1 week) were significantly associated with depression or such physical health disorders as multiple sclerosis. Once contextual threat was taken into account, events associated only with behavioral change in routine were not related to depression (Brown & Harris, 1978, 1989). Building upon these contextual scales, Miller and Ingham (1983) rated severe events along dimensions of emotional loss (excluding material loss or loss of a cherished idea), threat, antisocial action, hopelessness, uncertainty of outcome, and need for future action, concluding that combinations of these dimensions were particularly likely to be associated with depression.

In a manner similar to Dohrenwend's approach to fateful events, other investigators have restricted analyses to severe events that are independent of the respondent's condition as a strategy to unconfound events and disorder (Brown & Harris, 1978; Miller et al., 1986; Surtees et al., 1986). While identification of "independent" events helps to separate events from disorder, there is disagreement on how to define independence, and consequently there have been varying results.

Chronic Strains

The study of stress and psychopathology has been mainly concerned with the effects of acute life events. In the last few years, however, a growing body of research attests to the substantial impact of persistent life strains on depressive symptoms and disorder (Avison & Turner, 1988; Brown & Harris, 1978, 1989; McGonagle & Kessler, 1990; Miller et al., 1986; Pearlin, Lieberman, Menaghan, & Mullan, 1981; Wheaton, 1990). In fact, the "acute events" reported on checklist inventories may often represent long-standing difficulties, and thus research that relies on a checklist methodology may be actually measuring a composite of acute and chronic stressors (Avison & Turner, 1988; McLean, 1991). The intermixture of chronic and acute stressors as reported in life-event inventories makes the ascertainment of a clearly ordered temporal association between life events and disorder quite complicated. As the separation of these chronic and acute stressors seems an essential first step in clarifying further the association of life stressors and psychopathology, we briefly discuss concepts and measures of chronic stressors as part of our discussion of life events (although our colleagues will address this issue in greater detail in following chapters).

Chronic strains can be conceptualized to fall into four broad areas: (a) persistent life difficulties or chronically stressful situations that can be considered as corollaries of life events; (b) role strain, including the strain within specific roles as well as the strain of holding multiple roles; (c) chronic strains that derive from societal responses to characteristics of a person that include him or her as part of a class of persons, such as racism or sexism; and (d) chronic communitywide strains that may operate at an ecological level, such as the chronic strain of residence in a high crime area or residence near an environmental threat. We will briefly review each of these constructs of chronic strain in turn. A fifth type of chronic strain, frequency of such daily hassles as waiting too long in line or being stuck in traffic, has also been considered to be a source of chronic strain (Kanner, Coyne, Schaefer, & Lazarus, 1981). Difficulties of measurement and the substantial problems of confounding with personality disposition, psychological state, and social situation make the unique contribution of exposure to daily hassles extremely difficult to interpret in relation to health outcomes (Dohrenwend et al., 1984).

Persistent Life Difficulties. Investigators within each theoretical framework on the nature of life events have considered the role of persistent life difficulties, either as a unique contributor to disorder or in combination with acute life events. By persistent life difficulties, we refer to stressors either perceived to be chronic or quantitatively assessed to be chronic, using the duration of the stressor as a measure of chronicity. As persistent difficulties are often the source of acute life events, the interrelationship of these two sources of life stress is complicated to untangle. The temporal association between life events and disorder is often difficult to establish; the temporal relationship between persistent difficulties and disorder is even more so. Yet persistent situations are pervasive in human lives; to ignore their existence and possible contributions to the onset, maintenance, and remission of illness would be to ignore what might turn out to be the most etiologically important component of recent life experience. For example, in a study of pregnant women, once the effects of chronic concerns were taken into account, acute events were only minimally related to depressive symptomatology (McLean, 1991).

The measurement and consideration of persistent life difficulties has been an integral part of Brown's conceptualization of the construct of life stress. All recent experiences within the forementioned eight categories that last for more than 4 weeks are treated not as life events but as ongoing "difficulties." All the contextual ratings used for events, particularly those on short-term and long-term threat, are used also for difficulties; "marked" difficulties are those that are rated moderate or high on long-term threat. In Brown's model, where "provoking agents" in the context of vulnerability and symptom-formation factors are causally related to depression, severe events and major difficulties are each considered as provoking agents and evaluated simultaneously.

The impact of persistent difficulties has also been of interest to those investigators interested in the importance of life change following life events. The work of Wheaton, Pearlin, and other investigators provides strong evidence that both acute stressors and persistent life difficulties are related to psychological distress (McGonagle & Kessler, 1990; Monroe & Roberts, 1990; Moos & Swindle, 1990; Pearlin & Lieberman, 1979; Pearlin et al., 1981; Wheaton, 1990). Avison and Turner (1988) were the first to operationalize measures of the duration and recency of events on an event checklist to separate acute events from chronic strains. A general limitation to an overall synthesis of findings on persistent difficulties, however, aside from the pervasive problem of determining time order between difficulties and psychopathology, is that these experiences have been considered to include both events that are perceived to be chronic and events that have lasted an arbitrary length of time (usually 10 to 12 months). Perhaps both the perception of stressors as persistent and their duration are independent predictors of outcome; it would be useful to separate the two.

Role Strain. Pearlin and other investigators have suggested that role strain is another important source of chronic strain related to psychological distress (Pearlin et al., 1981). Domains of role strain include work strain (House, 1974; Karasek, Triantis, & Chaudy, 1982; Kessler, House, & Turner, 1987; Pearlin & Schooler, 1978), relationship strain with a partner or strain in other important relationships with friends or family members (Pearlin & Schooler, 1978), caretaking strain (e.g., as in parenting or care of a loved one with Alzheimer's disease or AIDS), or the breadwinner strain of financial responsibility for extended family members. There is chronic strain associated with simultaneously inhabiting multiple roles; such strain may have particular importance for women. One would also anticipate that the likelihood of exposure to multiple sources of role strain will differ by race/ethnicity, class, and age. There is conflicting evidence, however, on the joint effects of life events and role strains. The occurrence of role strains has been shown both to increase the effects of stressful life events on psychological distress (Monroe & Roberts, 1990; Moos & Swindle, 1990; Pearlin & Lieberman, 1979; Pearlin et al., 1981) and to decrease these effects (Wheaton, 1990).

Chronic Strain of Discrimination. A third category of chronic strain results from the response of one social group to another in which all individuals within that group are identified primarily as members of a class of persons; the discriminatory behaviors and attitudes of racism and sexism on the part of individuals as well as institutions are examples of factors leading to this type of chronic strain. These characteristics of persons can be mutable or immutable; as income and social standing can change, so can discrimination due to class bias. Characteristics of race, ethnicity, disability, sexuality, and gender are for the most part immutable, and bring with them chronic strains that are likely to affect health (Dressler, 1990; Krieger, 1990; Link, 1987). Discrimination can lead to an increased frequency of many types of stressors (e.g., unemployment) including such discrimination-specific stressors as hate mail, lewd remarks, or racial epithets. In addition, cultural stereotypes can have powerful effects if an individual internalizes them, thereby leading to negative self-evaluations. For example, Link and colleagues (Link, 1987; Link, Cullen, Struening, Shrout, & Dohrenwend, 1989; Link et al., 1990) have shown that people who are officially labeled mentally ill and who believe that such a label leads to rejection by "most people" suffer severe consequences. Specifically, they are more likely to be unemployed, to feel demoralized, and to have constricted social support networks than either labeled persons who do not expect such rejection or people who have never been officially labeled. More strategies like this one are needed to describe and measure exposure to the chronic strains of stigmatization and to measure discrimination-specific stressors in order to understand the extent of their psychological and physiological effects.

Chronic Strain in Communities. Both persistent life difficulties and acute events have been found to be associated with increased risk of psychological symptoms. Communities as well as individuals, however, can be exposed to acute and chronic stressors. For example, the occurrence of natural or man-made disasters can expose a community to periods of acute stress as well as ongoing strain (Bachrach & Zautra, 1985; Bromet, 1989; Bromet, Parkinson, & Dunn, 1990; "Disaster Epidemiology," 1990; Dohrenwend, 1983; Logue, Melick, & Hansen, 1981; Shore, 1986; Toole & Waldman, 1990). These studies report that physical and mental health effects vary by the type of disaster (e.g., natural, technological, regional conflict), by its "length" (floods may occur over an extended period of time, technological disasters such as Three Mile Island may entail long periods of cleanup, and regional conflicts may continue for years without resolution), and also in terms of both the objective losses created by the disaster and the community's perception of it.

Although individual lives are always lived within a broader social, political, and environmental context, research on chronic strain has considered exposure to chronic community strain usually through consideration of such broad social variables as urban or rural residence. It is plausible, although untested, that exposure to sources of chronic strain on a community level (including social and health disasters, e.g., communities in long-standing poverty or with a high prevalence of AIDS or substance abuse) might modify the observed relationships of individual-level chronic and acute stressors to psychological symptoms. Using ecological indicators of the social well-being of a community (divorce rates, mortality rates, employment rates, etc.), Linsky and colleagues have developed indices of "community stressors" analogous to a list of life events for an individual. Measures of exposure to these stressors can then be compared across communities (Linsky, Straus, & Colby, 1985). Strategies such as this one and small-area analysis are needed to measure the impact of exposure to community strain and its interaction with sources of stress on an individual level.

Focus of Stressors: Whom to Include

Most studies of life events restrict events to those that happen to the respondent, usually for one of two reasons. First, events that happen to oneself clearly have a direct impact on one's mental well-being. Second, events that happen to others are more likely to be underreported and/or unreliably reported than those that happen to oneself. Studies of the reliability of event reporting support this assumption (Neugebauer, 1981), although these studies are often comparisons of reports by spouses or other informants and are not thus strictly tests of reliability. Although there has been little systematic exploration of the impact of specific network events, there is evidence that events that occur to other people in a respondent's close social network may be particularly important for women and may partly account for their higher levels of depression (Aneshensel et al., 1991; Kessler & McLeod, 1984; Turner & Avison, 1989).

Understanding the impact of events on network members is a compromise between investigating the range of experiences that happen to important others and a realistic evaluation of the reliability and validity of reporting. Nonetheless, events that happen to important others may be significant stressors. Thus we advocate inclusion of network events in the measurement of stressors and the testing of their absolute and relative importance, given careful consideration of issues of measurement.

Because we propose that the impact of network events needs further investigation, we raise several broad questions for consideration. First, whom do we include as part of the network whose experiences are hypothesized to have a substantial impact on the respondent? There needs to be a clear theoretical justification for the choice of particular network members to include. Events to family members seem particularly important to assess. Nevertheless, it is likely that underreporting and unreliability increases with increasing relational distance of a network member from a respondent; events that happen to a spouse are more likely to be reliably reported than those that happen to a distant cousin. Household members also make up a close network that may include both family members and others. Events to household members may be more likely to be reliably reported than events to nonhousehold family members. Events that happen to close friends, however, may be just as accurately reported as those that happen to close family members. Though there is evidence that gender is associated with differential knowledge of events to network members (Kessler & McLeod, 1984; Kessler & Wethington, 1986), knowledge of the occurrence of network events may also differ by social class, race, and ethnicity, as well as by stage in the life cycle.

Next, we need to decide which events to consider. Do we probe events for network members within each of the life domains in which we consider events to the respondent, including chronic stressors? Do we consider positive as well as negative events? These may be important contributors to a respondent's sense of self-esteem or feelings of control that could be overlooked. For example, the success of a brother's new job may raise important issues for a respondent who is out of work; the birth of a friend's new baby may be particularly stressful for a woman trying to get pregnant. As a caution, however, there is evidence that major events (e.g., job loss, death, marriage) are more likely to be reliably reported for network members than minor events such as illnesses (Kessler & Wethington, 1986; Neugebauer, 1981).

In our view, network events can have either direct or indirect effects on a respondent. For instance, a spouse's job loss affects a respondent's household income directly; a friend's job loss does not. As one possible strategy to choose network events to consider, do we restrict consideration to only those network events with direct effects? In addition, network events may have single or multiple sources of impact. In the above example, the spouse's job loss is likely to carry with it multiple sources of stress (the psychological meaning of the job loss as well as behavioral changes related to decreased family finances), whereas the friend's job loss may carry only the single stressor associated with meaning.

It is also plausible that the relative importance of network events and events to self may vary at different stages in the life cycle. For example, events that happen to a woman's partner and children may be particularly important during her pregnancy; events involving the pregnancies of close friends and family members might also have special salience for this group of women. Young children may perceive events that happen to themselves or to immediate family members as much more important than those that affect peers, whereas events that happen to peers may be most important for adolescents. We can speculate that the relative importance of network/self events may vary by gender as well as age and stage in the life cycle. These are important issues to consider as we begin to develop and test hypotheses about the impact of network events. If specific network events are included in an inventory of recent stressors, such hypotheses can then be tested empirically, as in the study of stressors and depressive symptoms in pregnant women mentioned earlier (McLean, 1991). Certainly the choice of network events needs to be considered within the framework of a larger study question, as in the example given above of the impact of events during pregnancy.

Context of Stressors: How to Assess Social Circumstances

There is striking evidence to suggest that the context in which an event occurs matters. First, taking account of context has been shown to reveal much stronger associations between life events and various outcomes. This is evident in the strong associations that Brown and Harris find by explicitly considering context, compared to the very modest associations that characterize the list approach (Rabkin & Struening, 1976). The point is made most explicitly in a study by Shrout et al. (1989) that compares a straight list approach to one that probes the context of the event and makes judgments about the magnitude of change based on verbatim information gathered about the event. Shrout et al. show no association between a simple count measure of life events and depression but a relatively strong association (an odds ratio of 3.22) for a measure of disruptive fateful events based on probes about the event context.

Second, studies that use event lists and measures of distress have shown that the association between events and distress varies for people with different social statuses. Specifically, many studies have found that the association between life events and distress are stronger among women and people of lower socioeconomic status than they are among men and people of higher socioeconomic status (e.g., Langner & Michael, 1963; McLeod & Kessler, 1990; Turner & Noh, 1983). The term *vulnerability* has been used to describe this pattern of association, a decision that has lead to considerable controversy (Aneshensel et al., 1991; Turner & Avison, 1989).

But how does one assess the context of events? While the answer may seem to be obvious, there are in fact several important choices that an investigator must make. In order to understand some of these, we begin by sketching two measurement approaches to the assessment of context: the separation approach and the combination approach. In the separation approach one conceptualizes and measures aspects of a person's social context, or his or her location in social space, and measures these separately from life events. Then one can examine whether the impact of events differs according to socioeconomic status, age, gender, marital status, ethnicity, parental status, and so on. In the combination approach one gathers detailed information about the event, including aspects of the social context and the target person's location within that social context. The stressfulness or "threat" of the event can then be rated by taking that unique combination of circumstances into account.

These two approaches have different strengths and weaknesses. The strength of the separation approach is that the measurement of the context is kept separate from the measurement of the stressful circumstance, so that one can empirically examine whether context does in fact modify the stressor. The problem with the separation approach is that it misses many of the intricacies and subtleties that constitute the context of a stressful circumstance. For example, because of the nature of his or her occupation, a musician may loses 3 to 4 jobs a year because of shifts to different "gigs." Knowing the context in which the events occur makes it clear that these "job losses" may not be nearly as severe as the disruptions others with more structured work situations experience.

It is hard to imagine, however, fully specifying this and all other variables that would be needed to assess the true complexity of the event context in a sample of respondents whose life circumstances vary greatly. In fact, the typical analysis conducted using the separation approach simply ignores this kind of complexity. The weakness of the separation approach is relevant to the previously mentioned issue of the vulnerability of women and people of low socioeconomic status (SES). Because list measures of events gather little or no information about context, it is difficult to know whether the apparently greater impact of events for women and low SES persons is attributable to an individual vulnerability (genetic, personality, etc.) or whether these events would actually be judged more severe if we knew more about the context in which they occurred. If the latter is the case, the term *vulnerability* is truly a misnomer. The apparent reactivity of women and people of low SES might instead be the result of more severe exposure.

But what about the approach that gathers details about context and combines these into the measurement of the severity of the stressor? This combination approach offers the opportunity to consider the specific, even unique circumstances surrounding an event and to build these circumstances into a rating of how stressful the situation is. It has the intuitive appeal of being less abstracted from the subject's real experience and simultaneously makes the measure of stressful circumstances far more powerful. At the same time the strategy, by its very nature, confounds the measurement of the stressor with the measurement of the context. Consider, for example, events falling under the rubric of "person moves out of the household." According to the combination approach, the measure of the stressfulness or threat that these events entail would include such considerations as whether the respondent was left totally isolated or whether he or she was left responsible for the full rent while unemployed. When this approach is used, the stressfulness rating of the event is then powerfully influenced by the availability of social support and the co-occurrence of the chronic stressor of unemployment. By allowing aspects of the context to affect one's rating of the stressfulness or threat caused by an event, one introduces ambiguity about whether it is the event or the context that is responsible for an association with an outcome variable.

How does an investigator choose between these two measurement approaches? First, it is important to recognize that the choice is not an either-or decision. One can choose how much detail about context to incorporate into a measure of threat, as well as which contextual factors should be measured separately. What is critically important is that these decisions be made consciously and that the interpretation of associations take into account the decisions that have been made.

The foregoing discussion focused exclusively on the issue of the measurement of events. We now consider a separate issue relating to the choice of study design. Because exposure to specific types of life events is likely to depend on an individual's social situation (Clark, Aneshensel, Frerichs, & Morgan, 1981; Thoits, 1987) and stage in the life cycle (Kellam, 1974; Schultz & Rau, 1985; Susser, 1968, 1981), restriction of the study sample to respondents at a single point in the life cycle or to those in a common social situation holds them at approximately equal risk of experiencing similar life stressors, unlike the more heterogeneously exposed samples used in most population studies of stress and mental health. A similar distribution of recent events across respondents can then be expected, allowing better isolation of the relationship of specific characteristics of events to psychological and psychiatric symptomatology. The similar physical and psychosocial context of a single stage in the life cycle or of a common social situation is also likely to impart similar psychosocial meaning to concurrent life stressors across study participants. Examples of such design strategies include research on stressors among children (Gersten et al., 1974), among the elderly, and during pregnancy (McLean, 1991).

Timing of Stressors: When Do Events Occur?

The relative timing of stressors is clearly important to consider in relationship to the relative timing of measurement of psychopathology, but it is also important in consideration of the timing of individual stressors in relationship to each other. Most of the attention to timing of events has been in an effort to specify the causal ordering of events in relation to outcome (Depue & Monroe, 1986). We add to this evidence supporting the possibility that many events exert their strongest effects only from a few weeks to a few months after they occur (Andrews, 1981; Brown & Harris, 1978; Tennant et al., 1981). Additionally, in a four-wave panel study of the relationship of life events to distress, events that occurred more than 4 months prior to an interview were found to be unrelated to distress (Andrews, 1981).

That the impact of life events is restricted to recent events may be partly an artifact of the timing of outcome measurement. McGonagle and Kessler (1990) propose two possible interpretations for their finding that chronic stress is a more powerful predictor of depressive symptoms than acute stress: (a) The change per se associated with acute events is not an important dimension of life experience, but the persistence of a difficult situation is stressful; and (b) because chronic stressors are more likely than acute events to be ongoing at the time of the assessment of symptomatology, the impact of chronic stressors may simply reflect the more powerful effect of ongoing stressors relative to resolved stressors. Findings from a study of pregnant women add evidence to support their second hypothesis. In this study, completed or resolved stressors were largely unrelated to depressive symptoms; most of the relationship of stressors to symptoms was carried by stressors ongoing at the time of symptom assessment, particularly those that had begun within the 3 months prior to symptom assessment (McLean, 1991).

The timing of events is critical to consider from another perspective as well. Surtees and colleagues have proposed a decay model for the lingering impact of events that begins to provide a theoretical framework for measurement of events in time. In order to consider the effects of event clustering, Surtees and Ingham (1980) proposed a model to take into account the potentially additive effects of events over time, particularly to assess whether the occurrence of many minor events in the presence of a severe event was related to depression. By incorporating weights for both the focus of the event (respondent or other) and the severity of long-term threat, and assuming a constant rate of decay for the stressful effect of a severe event, they tested the hypothesis that in relation to depression, events have a "stressful lifetime" not usually taken into account in analyses of rates of event occurrence (Surtees, 1989).

As we see it, in any particular stretch of time, the stressful lifetime of an individual event is layered on top of other events. The length of this time period may be related to several of the dimensions of intra-event variability and context discussed earlier, and it is likely to be a combination of the actual duration of the stressor, its psychological meaning and degree of contextual threat, and the amount of accompanying behavioral change. We propose that the overall amount of stress experienced by an individual at any one point in time is partly a reflection of these factors, as well as of the positive or negative valence of the individual stressors. Through consideration of these factors, we can modify the assumption of a constant rate of decay for the effect of stressful events.

Because there is growing evidence that knowledge of the duration and timing of an event is important, there is a growing need to develop ways of accurately specifying the timing of events, their dates of onset and resolution, and their positive or negative valence in order to understand the layering of stressors in time and the specific mechanisms through which they affect mental health. To ignore these characteristics of events leads to a misspecification of exposure that is highly likely to weaken tests of the apparent effect of stressors on mental health.

Measurement of Stressors: How to Ask the Question

Events reported on checklists or in interviews are not always independent of each other. First, an event can trigger a whole chain of linked events, as in the case of a job loss that leads to financial difficulties, which in turn cause a move to a new city. These are separate events, but they are linked to each other in a causal sequence. Within any particular sequence, there are also multiple minor events that occur between the more major ones. Moreover, events differ in their likelihood of being linked to other events. Explicit consideration of this lack of independence, criteria for the magnitude of events to be included in a linked sequence, and the development of appropriate assessment strategies may offer additional clues to event severity and will help to reduce misspecification in the measurement of exposure to stressors. In the extreme case, two events may be so closely linked that they are essentially redundant. Strategies need to be developed to determine which events are so closely linked that they should be considered to be a single event.

In addition, an investigator evaluating sets of events that are not usually included on checklists must ensure that these events are not redundant with the usual items. For instance, if a category of "disappointments" was added to an event checklist, a respondent might report "not receiving an expected wage or salary increase" (an item on some checklists) and report it again as experiencing "anything you were hoping for or expecting that didn't work out the way you wanted" (i.e., a disappointment; McLean, 1991). A priori analytic strategies for dealing with event linking and redundancy need to be developed. The possibility of event redundancy within and across all event categories suggests that it may be a particularly serious problem for some studies, in particular those that rely on self-report versions of life-event inventories.

Attention must also be paid to strategies used to elicit events. Kessler and Wethington (1986) suggest that recall can be improved if life-event items are administered in short lists after sections of an interview that cohere to a particular theme, rather than as a single long list of items. This approach may also prove less boring and burdensome to the respondents than the use of a long list and may be less likely to result in a "no" response set. For example, items on events relating to love and marriage can be asked after questions on the respondent's marital status, and items on events relating to work can be asked after questions on the respondent's occupational status. The multiple-list method attempts to encourage memory recall by generating contextual clues. Because memories are organized in units, or schemas, asking a respondent to focus attention on a particular area of his or her life and then to recall recent experiences relevant to that area may improve event recall (Kessler & Wethington, 1986).

CONCEPTUAL AND METHODOLOGICAL CONSIDERATIONS: OUTCOME AND CAUSAL INFERENCE

Just as decisions are required concerning which stressors to measure and how to measure them, one must decide which mental or physical health outcome to focus on or include. We consider two issues. The first involves considerations about how broad the outcomes need to be and the pitfalls of making the range too narrow. The second concerns the strategic value that including multiple outcomes can have for causal inference.

Considerations Concerning the Breadth of Outcomes

If one's primary interest begins with stress, either a particular type of stressor (e.g., job loss, sexual abuse) or psychosocial stress more generally, one must consider which of a range of potential outcomes to include as a consequence of exposure to stress. As epidemiologist John Cassel (1974) observed some time ago, examining only one outcome per study severely limits the assessment of stress effects, because stressful circumstances can contribute to many different outcomes. Thus, in order to ensure a sound test of an hypothesis about the effects of a stressor, an investigator needs to consider a range of mental *and* physical outcomes. Current research concerned with stress often focuses narrowly on distress or depression (for exceptions, see Brown & Harris, 1989; Dohren-wend et al., 1992). Moreover, as Aneshensel et al. (1991) have pointed out, inferences about the reactivity of population subgroups can be bad-ly misleading if the range of outcomes considered is narrow. For exam-ple, men and women may respond differently to stress, one displaying elevated levels of depression when under stress while the other displays elevated levels of alcohol use. A researcher who examines only one of these outcomes runs the risk of inappropriately concluding that either men or women are more affected by stressful circumstances, when in fact they simply express the effects of stressors differently (see Cullen, 1984, for a theoretical argument supporting this possibility). In addi-tion, some individuals may express the effects of stressors primarily through physical symptoms (e.g., ulcers, headache) and not through psychological symptoms.

Considerations Concerning Causal Inference

Although we have just pointed out that stressors can affect many conditions, there are times when this may not be so. Stressors may have specific effects, determining one outcome but not another. If such pat-terns cohere with relevant theory, confidence in causal inference is en-hanced. For example, Link, Dohrenwend, and Skodol (1986) studied the potential impact of noisome occupational conditions on schizophrenia. Theory and research suggested that people with schizophrenia are af-fected by overstimulation in a way that people without the condition are not. Consistent with this Link, Dohrenwend and Skodol showed that noisome occupational conditions—conditions likely to be overstimulat-ing—were related to schizophrenia but not to major depression. Cases of major depression were much like controls with respect to exposure to noisome occupations. Other examples of specific effects are Silver and Wortman's (1980) finding that rape is more likely to lead to anxiety than depression and Finlay-Jones and Brown's (1981) demonstration that events involving loss are likely related to depression, whereas events involving danger are more likely to be associated with anxiety. The main point here is that if theory leads to a prediction of specific effects, it makes sense to include multiple outcomes so that the theory can be tested.

FUTURE DIRECTIONS FOR RESEARCH

It is probably safe to say that attention to the details of measurement in the stress process area has expanded greatly in recent years. Indeed, the issues outlined in this chapter remind us that the many central issues involved in the measurement of events have greatly expanded to reflect recent developments in research on chronic strains, social support, coping, personality, and so on. With such rich possibilities before us, how do we deal with the realities of limited budgets, respondent tolerance, and the knowledge that even our best efforts to "cover it all" will prove inadequate when yet another expansion or more detailed specification is forcefully proposed by an esteemed colleague?

The answer we propose calls for theoretically guided investigations directed at particular questions. The questions might involve social sources of stressful circumstances, mechanisms linking events to outcomes, the relative plausibility of stressful circumstances (as opposed to rival hypotheses) as the true cause of an outcome, or some combination of these three. Once the question is set, then the relative importance of various aspects of stress process measurement become more apparent; one has a basis for making reasoned choices about just what needs measuring most. Before returning to this proposed approach, we will outline below a different one that we believe is bound to fail, but which enjoys considerable implicit support among stress process researchers.

The approach we believe to be doomed to failure can be characterized as follows. In an initial step, one conceptualizes a comprehensive package that includes all viable components of the stress process and develops operational measures of these components. These components are then specified according to theory, and an appropriate analysis (complicated, if possible) will reveal the true impact of stressful circumstances on health outcomes.

There are two related reasons that this approach is doomed to failure. First, comprehensiveness is impossible because the list of candidates for inclusion is too long. There are social structural factors, recent life events, remote life events, chronic strains, hassles, scores of personality measures, value orientations, social support, environmental factors that are not directly social (e.g., noise), genetic factors, and biological factors (e.g., catecholamines, measures of immune function). Moreover, this list does not mention important subcomponents of many of these factors and certainly excludes factors that have not yet been conceptualized and measured.

Second, the analytic specification one chooses in order to organize this massive compendium of measures is certain to be vulnerable to alternative specifications that would support radically different theoretical explanations than the one that motivated the initial specification. Moreover, because the list includes concepts that are partially overlapping in ways that we do not fully understand at this point in the development of life stress research, control for one component might inappropriately strip another component of its power to relate to an outcome.

The approach we advocate is one that is focused on a central theoretical explanation and uses designs, measures, and analysis in a strategic fashion to test the power of the theoretical explanation against alternatives. There are two main differences between this approach and the one we just described: the notion of strategy, and the emphasis on testing a hypothesis against alternatives. Under our approach one looks for strategic circumstances that will allow tests of competing theoretical explanations. The strategic circumstances might involve sampling particularly informative populations—for example, people exposed to the aftermath of the Three Mile Island nuclear accident and a comparison population in order to assess the relative contributions to psychological symptoms of acute stressors, persistent strains, and a chronic communitywide stressor (McLean, 1991), or workers unemployed because of circumstances beyond their control in order to assess the impact of unemployment on symptoms independent of an individual's prior psychological state (Kessler, 1987)—or focusing attention on a particular measure, such as fateful loss events as a specific subpopulation of acute stressors (Shrout et al., 1989) or the inclusion of "nonevents," chronic concerns, and spouse events in an inventory of stressors in order to assess their relative contributions to symptomatology (McLean, 1991). It might also involve longitudinal research, although this is often believed to be more of a panacea for problems of causal inference than it probably is, at least where panel studies are concerned (Link & Shrout, 1992). In any case, the chosen strategy would be dictated by the nature of the theory competition, with the goal of collecting data that optimizes the chances of validly choosing one theoretical explanation over another.

If one adopts this strategic approach, the key issues of assessment that we identified and discussed above become useful because they flesh out the possibilities for testing theoretical explanations against one another. Once a possible test has been identified, the nature of the theory competition will dictate where the greatest attention should be directed in terms of assessing stress process variables. For example, if one were interested in testing meaning versus behavioral change as the mechanism linking events to outcomes, one might focus on a special set of events. Events that radically change meaning but involve little behavioral change, and those that involve a great deal of behavioral change but alter meaning very little, would become particularly important. For these events, one would make different predictions about associations with outcomes from the two perspectives. Special effort would be invested in these events, with care focused on assessing behavioral change and meaning surrounding them.

Though one would still want to measure other stress process variables (probably as many as possible), one would have a rational means of deciding which ones were more and which ones were less important for solving the theoretical issue at hand. Thus, from this perspective, the approach to the assessment of stressful circumstances should begin with focused questions and, when possible, clearly identified competing explanations. Decisions about the assessment package to be collected would then be made based on the constraints imposed by the research question(s).

A theoretically grounded approach to understanding the relationship of stress to adverse health outcomes becomes even more necessary as stress process researchers expand their focus of outcomes to include physical health status and causes of chronic disease. In order to be fruitful, research to understand the relationship of stressors to such physical health outcomes as cardiovascular disease, cancer, and preterm delivery (as well as to a spectrum of mental health outcomes), to incorporate advances in the rapidly expanding field of psychoneuroimmunology, and to understand further the physiology of the stress process requires careful attention to the methodological and conceptual issues we have raised for the study of stressful circumstances. It is clear to us that, by itself, the redistribution of resources to "hard ball biology" as Heston (1988) suggested is unlikely to lead far toward new developments in understanding the behavioral, neuroendocrine, and immunological pathways through which psychosocial stressors exert their effects on mental and physical health. In this regard, the possibility for innovation in strategies to refine concepts, measures, and research designs in the study of life experiences and health holds great promise. Through thoughtful consideration of the methodological issues we discuss in this chapter, we are certain (unlike Heston) that investigators searching for specific environmental risk factors will not find dead ends but will provide important contributions to the further understanding of causes of disease and the development of new ways to improve mental and physical well-being.

REFERENCES

Andrews, G. (1981). A prospective study of life events and psychological symptoms. *Psychological Medicine, 11*, 795–801.

Aneshensel, C., Rutter, C., & Lachenbruch, P. (1991). Social structure, stress and mental health: Competing conceptual and analytic models. *American Sociological Review, 56*, 166–178.

Avison, W. R., & Turner, R. J. (1988). Stressful life events and depressive symptoms: Disaggregating the effects of acute stressors and chronic strains. *Journal of Health and Social Behavior, 29*, 253–264.

Bachrach, K. M., & Zautra, A. J. (1985). Coping with a community stressor: The threat of a hazardous waste facility. *Journal of Health and Social Behavior, 26*, 127–141.

Beitchman, J. H., Zucker, K. J., Hood, J. E., daCosta, G. A., Akman, D., & Cassaria, E. (1992). A review of the long-term effects of child sexual abuse. *Child Abuse and Neglect, 16* (1), 101–118.

Bromet, E. (1989). The nature and effects of technological failures. In R. Gist & B. Lubin (Eds.), *Psychosocial aspects of disaster* (pp. 120–139). New York: Wiley.

Bromet, E. J., Parkinson, D. K., & Dunn, L. O. (1990). Long-term mental health consequences of the accident at Three Mile Island. *International Journal of Mental Health, 19*, 48–60.

Brown, G. W. (1974). Meaning, measurement and stress of life events. In B. S. Dohrenwend & B. P. Dohrenwend (Eds.), *Stressful life events: Their nature and effects* (pp. 217–244). New York: Wiley.

Brown, G. W. (1989). Life events and measurement. In G. Brown & T. Harris (Eds.), *Life events and illness* (pp. 3–45). New York: Guilford.

Brown, G. W., & Harris, T. (1978). *Social origins of depression*. New York: Free Press

Brown, G. W., & Harris, T. (1989). Depression. In G. Brown & T. Harris (Eds.), *Life events and illness* (pp. 49–93). New York: Guilford.

Cassel, J. (1974). Psychosocial processes and "stress": Theoretical formulation. *International Journal of Health Services Research, 4*, 471–481.

Clark, V. A., Aneshensel, C. S., Frerichs, R. R., & Morgan, T. M. (1981). Analysis of effects of sex and age in response to items on the CES-D scale. *Psychiatry Research, 5*, 171–181.

Cullen, F. T. (1984). *Rethinking crime and deviance theory: The emergence of a structuring tradition*. Totowa, NJ: Rowman & Allenheld.

Depue, R. A., & Monroe, S. M. (1986). Conceptualization and measurement of human disorder in life stress research: The problem of chronic disturbance. *Psychological Bulletin, 99*, 36–51.

Disaster epidemiology. (1990). *Lancet, 336*, 845–846.

Dohrenwend, B. P. (1983). Psychological implications of nuclear accidents: The case of Three Mile Island. *Bulletin of the New York Academy of Medicine, 59*, 1060–1076.

Dohrenwend, B. P., & Dohrenwend, B. S. (1969). *Social status and psychological disorder: A causal inquiry*. New York: Wiley.

Dohrenwend, B. P., Levav, I., Shrout, P., Schwartz, S., Naveh, G., Link, B., Skodal, A., & Stueve, A. (1992). Socioeconomic status and psychiatric disorder: The causation–selection issue. *Science, 255*, 946–952.

Dohrenwend, B. P., Link, B., Kern, S., Shrout, P., & Markowitz, J. (1987) Measuring life events: The problem of variability within life events categories. In B. Cooper (Ed.), *Psychiatric epidemiology: Progress and prospects*. London: Croon Helm.

Dohrenwend, B. P., Raphael, K. G., Schwartz, S., Stueve, A., & Skodol, A. (1993). The structured event probe and narrative rating method for measuring stressful life events. In L. Goldberger & S. Bresnitz (Eds.), *Handbook of Stress: Theoretical and Clinical Aspects* (pp. 174–199). New York: Free Press.

Dohrenwend, B. S., Dohrenwend, B. P., Dodson, M., & Shrout, P. E. (1984). Symptoms, hassles, social supports and life events: Problem of confounded measures. *Journal of Abnormal Psychology, 93*, 222–230.

Dohrenwend, B. S., Krasnoff, L., Askenasy, A. R. & Dohrenwend, B. P. (1978). Exemplification of a method for scaling life events: the PERI life events scale. *Journal of Health and Social Behavior, 19,* 205–229.

Dressler, W. W. (1990). Lifestyle, stress and blood pressure in a southern black community. *Psychosomatic Medicine, 52,* 182–198.

Finlay-Jones, R., & Brown, G. W. (1981). Types of stressful life events and the onset of anxiety and depressive disorders. *Psychological Medicine, 11,* 803–815.

Gersten, J. C., Langner, T. S., Eisenberg, J. G., & Orzek, L. (1974). Child behavior and life events: Undesirable change or change per se? In B. S. Dohrenwend & B. P. Dohrenwend (Eds.), *Stressful life events: Their nature and effects* (pp. 159–170). New York: Wiley.

Heston, L. (1988). What about environment? In D. Dunner, E. Gershon, & J. Barrett (Eds.), *Relatives at risk for mental disorder* (pp. 205–213). New York: Raven.

Holmes, T. H. (1979). Development and application of a quantitative measure of life change magnitude. In J. Barrett (Ed.), *Stress and mental disorder* (pp. 37–53). New York: Raven.

Holmes, T. H. & Masuda, M. (1973). Life change and illness susceptibility. In J. P. Scott & E. C. Senay (Eds.), *Separation and depression* (pp 161–186). Washington, DC: American Association for the Advancement of Science.

Holmes, T. H., & Rahe, R. H. (1967). The social readjustment rating scale. *Journal of Psychosomatic Research, 11,* 213–218.

House, J. S. (1974). Occupational stress and coronary heart disease: A review and theoretical investigation. *Journal of Health and Social Behavior, 15,* 12–27.

Kanner, A. D., Coyne, J. C., Schaefer, C., & Lazarus, R. S. (1981). Comparison of two models of stress measurement: Daily hassles and uplifts versus major life events. *Journal of Behavioral Medicine, 4* (1), 1–39.

Karasek, R. A., Triantis, K. P., & Chaudy, S. S. (1982). Coworker and supervisor support as moderators of associations between task characteristics and mental strain. *Journal of Occupational Behavior, 3,* 181–200.

Kellam, S. (1974). Stressful life events and illness: A research area in need of conceptual development. In B. S. Dohrenwend & B. P. Dohrenwend (Eds.), *Stressful life events: Their nature and effects* (pp. 207–214). New York: Wiley.

Kendler, K. S., Neale, M. C., Kessler, R. C., Heath, A. C., & Eaves, L. J. (1992). Childhood parental loss and adult psychopathology in women. *Archives of General Psychiatry, 49,* 109–116.

Kessler, R. C., House, J. S., & Turner, J. B. (1987). Unemployment and health in a community sample. *Journal of Health and Social Behavior, 28,* 151–159.

Kessler, R. C., & McLeod, J. D. (1984). Sex differences in vulnerability to undesirable life events. *American Sociological Review, 49,* 620–631.

Kessler, R. C., & Wethington, E. (1986). *Some strategies for improving recall of life events in a general population survey.* Unpublished manuscript.

Krieger, N. (1990). Racial and gender discrimination: Risk factors for high blood pressure? *Social Science and Medicine, 30,* 1273–1281.

Langner, T. S., & Michael, S. T. (1963). *Life stress and mental health.* New York: Free Press.

Link, B. (1987). Understanding labeling effects in the area of mental disorders: An assessment of the effects of expectations of rejection. *American Sociological Review, 52,* 96–112.

Link, B., Cullen, F., Struening, E., Shrout, P., & Dohrenwend, B. P. (1989). A modified labelling theory approach to mental disorders: An empirical assessment. *American Sociological Review, 54,* 400–423.

Link, B., Dohrenwend, B. P., & Skodol, A. (1986). Socio-economic status and schizophrenia: Noisome occupational characteristics as a risk factor. *American Sociological Review, 51,* 242–258.

Link, B., Mesagno, F. P., Lubner, M., & Dohrenwend, B. P. (1990). Problems in measuring role strains and social functioning in relation to psychological symptoms. *Journal of Health and Social Behavior, 31,* 354–369.

Link, B., & Shrout, P. (1992). Spurious association in longitudinal research. In J. Greenley & P. Leaf (Eds.), *Research in community and mental health* (pp. 301–321). Greenwich, CT: JAI Press.

Linsky, A. S., Straus, M. A., & Colby, J. P. (1985). Stressful events, stressful conditions and alcohol problems in the United States: A partial test of Bales's theory. *Journal of Studies of Alcohol, 46,* 72–80.

Logue, J. N., Melick, M. E., & Hansen, H. (1981). Research issues and directions in the epidemiology of health effects of disasters. *Epidemiology Reviews, 3,* 140–162.

McGonagle, K. A., & Kessler, R. C. (1990). Chronic stress, acute stress, and depressive symptoms. *American Journal of Community Psychology, 18,* 681–706.

McLean, D. E. (1991). Psychosocial stress and depressive symptoms in pregnant women: Strategies for refinement of measures of life events. *Dissertation Abstracts International,* 53-03B. (University Microfilms No. 92-09871)

McLeod, J. D., & Kessler, R. C. (1990). Socioeconomic status differences in vulnerability to undesirable life events. *Journal of Health and Social Behavior, 31,* 162–172.

Miller, P., Dean, C., Ingham, J. G., Kreitman, N. B., Sashidharan, S. P., & Surtees, P. G. (1986). The epidemiology of life events and long-term difficulties, with some reflections on the concepts of independence. *British Journal of Psychiatry, 148,* 686–696.

Miller, P., & Ingham, J. G. (1983). Dimensions of experience. *Psychological Medicine, 13,* 417–429.

Monroe, S. M. (1982). Life events assesment: Current practices, emerging trends. *Clinical Psychology Review, 2,* 435–453.

Monroe, S. M., & Roberts, J. E. (1990). Conceptualizing and measuring life stress: Problems, principles, procedures, progress. *Stress Medicine, 6,* 209–216.

Moos, R. H., & Swindle, R. W. (1990). Stressful life circumstances: Concepts and measures. *Stress Medicine, 6,* 171–178.

Neugebauer, R. (1981). The reliability of life-event reports. In B. S. Dohrenwend & B. P. Dohrenwend (Eds.), *Stressful life events and their contexts* (2nd ed., pp. 85–107). New Brunswick, NJ: Rutgers University Press.

Pearlin, L. I., & Lieberman, M. A. (1979). Social sources of emotional distress. *Research in Community and Mental Health, 1,* 217–248.

Pearlin, L. I., Lieberman, M. A., Menaghan, E. G., & Mullan, J. T. (1981). The stress process. *Journal of Health and Social Behavior, 22,* 337–356.

Pearlin, L. I., & Schooler, C. (1978). The structure of coping. *Journal of Health and Social Behavior, 19,* 2–21.

Rabkin, J. G., & Struening, E. L. (1976). Life events, stress and illness. *Science, 194,* 1013–1020.

Schultz, R., & Rau, M. T. (1985). Social support through the life cycle. In S. Cohen & S. L. Syme (Eds.), *Social support and health.* New York: Academic Press.

Shore, J. H. (Ed.). (1986). *Disaster stress studies: New methods and findings.* Washington, DC: American Psychiatric Press.

Shrout, P., Link, B., Dohrenwend, B. P., Skodol, A., Stueve, A., & Mirotznik, J. (1989). Characterizing life events as risk factors for depression: The role of fateful loss events. *Journal of Abnormal Psychology, 98,* 460–467.

Silver, R. L. & Wortman, C. B. (1980). Coping with undesirable life events. In J. Garber & M. E. P. Seligman (Eds.), *Human helplessness: Theory and applications* (pp. 279–375). New York: Academic Press.

Surtees, P. G. (1989). Adversity and psychiatric disorder: A decay model. In G. Brown & T. Harris (Eds.), *Life events and illness* (pp. 49–94). New York: Guilford.

Surtees, P. G., & Ingham, J. G. (1980). Life stress and depressive outcome: Application of a dissipation model to life events. *Social Psychiatry, 15,* 21–31.

Surtees, P. G., Miller, P. M., Ingham, J. G., Kreitman, N. B., Rennie, D., & Sashidharan, S. P. (1986). Life events and the onset of affective disorder: A longitudinal general population study. *Journal of Affective Disorders, 10,* 37–50.

Susser, M. W. (1968). *Community psychiatry.* New York: Random House.

Susser, M. W. (1981). The epidemiology of life stress: A commentary. *Psychological Medicine, 11,* 1–8.

Tennant, C., & Bebbington, P. (1978). The social causation of depression: A critique of the work of Brown and his colleagues. *Psychological Medicine, 8,* 565–577.

Tennant, C., Bebbington, P., & Hurry, J. (1981). The role of life events in depressive illness: Is there a substantial causal relation? *Psychological Medicine, 11,* 379–389.

Thoits, P. A. (1983). Dimensions of life events that influence psychological distress: An evaluation and synthesis of the literature. In H. B. Kaplan (Ed.), *Psychosocial stress* (pp. 33–103). New York: Academic Press.

Thoits, P. A. (1987). Gender and marital status differences in control and distress: Common stress versus unique stress explanations. *Journal of Health and Social Behavior, 28,* 7–22.

Toole, M. J., & Waldman, R. J. (1990). Prevention of excess mortality in refugee and displaced populations in developing countries. *Journal of the American Medical Association, 263,* 3296–3302.

Turner, R. J., & Avison, W. R. (1989). Gender and depression: Assessing exposure and vulnerability to life events in a chronically strained population. *Journal of Nervous and Mental Disease, 177,* 443–455.

Turner, R. J., & Noh, S. (1983). Class and psychological vulnerability among women: The significance of social support and personal control. *Journal of Health and Social Behavior, 24,* 2–15.

Van der Kolk, B. A., & Greenberg, M. S. (1987). The psychobiology of the trauma response: Hyperarousal, constriction and addition to traumatic reexposure. In B. Van der Kolk (Ed.), *Psychological trauma* (pp. 63–87). Washington, DC: American Psychiatric Press.

Wheaton, B. (1990). Life transitions, role histories, and mental health. *American Sociological Review, 55,* 209–223.

3

Measuring Life Stress and Assessing Its Impact on Mental Health

SCOTT M. MONROE and JOHN R. McQUAID

Men and women throughout the ages have often felt overwhelmed by life's demands. They have long ruminated about the implications these adversities have for their physical health and mental well-being (Rosen, 1959). Interestingly, the words of people expressing such concerns across the different ages portray similar themes of "stress, distress, and dis-ease" (Rees, 1976; see also Hinkle, 1977; Lazarus & Folkman, 1984; Monroe & Johnson, 1992). Overall, it seems clear that people are prone to perceive their worlds as filled with almost constant, if not excessive, demands, and that they frequently employ such perceptions to explain a great variety of psychological and physical phenomena.

The early writings of Cannon (1932) and Selye (1936) formed the basis for the more modern interests in life stress. These investigator formally introduced, defined, and measured stress with stringent operational methods, and they studied it with respect to many types of adaptive failures. The initial emphasis of stress research was upon the physiological mechanisms of responses that laboratory animals demonstrated to diverse sets of circumstances. It did not take long, however, for inves-

SCOTT M. MONROE and JOHN R. McQUAID • Department of Psychology, University of Oregon, Eugene, Oregon 97403-1227.

Stress and Mental Health: Contemporary Issues and Prospects for the Future, edited by William R. Avison and Ian H. Gotlib. New York, Plenum Press, 1994.

tigators to generalize the concepts of stress to humans and to include psychological processes as well (Pollock, 1988; Sarason, de Monchaux, & Hunt, 1975). These ideas about human stress were operationalized using life-event checklists, such as the Schedule of Recent Experiences (Holmes & Rahe, 1967). As a consequence, the popular but loosely formulated subjective perspectives on human stress were linked with the more esoteric but rigorously investigated laboratory study of stress.

Since the development of life-event assessment procedures, a very large literature has emerged in general support of the proposition that increased levels of life events predispose individuals to a wide variety of physical and mental health problems (Brown & Harris, 1989b; Dohrenwend & Dohrenwend, 1981; Harris, 1989; Miller, 1989). Although such pervasive effects are consonant with the early theory on stress effects, there are at least two major reasons why we question the validity of the existing empirical literature. The first concern is primarily methodological. Specifically, current methodologies may not provide adequate constraint over potential sources of bias or error, given the entrenched and enduring human tendency to perceive stress as ubiquitous and to use stress to explain away all sorts of ills. Consequently, most people possess their own subjective models of what constitutes stress, and these models draw heavily from cultural beliefs about the pernicious effects of stress. Existing life-event assessment methods may not be sophisticated enough to control these potentially pervasive biases (see also Monroe & Johnson, 1990; Pollock, 1988).

The second concern we raise about the existing literature involves the many effects stress has on a person's thought and behavior. Most research to date has been concerned with the onset of various problems in relation to prior life events (i.e., etiology of disorder). Yet it is clear that stress can influence a person's life in many other ways—directly or indirectly—that also have a bearing on their psychological functioning. For example, stress may influence the availability of social support (Monroe & Steiner, 1986), the amount of time to enter treatment following onset of acute episodes of disorder (Monroe, Simons, & Thase, 1991), response to treatment (Monroe, Kupfer, & Frank, 1992), recovery from untreated episodes (Brown, Bifulco, & Andrews, 1990), and the chronicity of psychopathology (Monroe & Roberts, 1991). These findings suggest that life stress has effects that include but also go well beyond the onset of a particular disorder. These effects may be of crucial importance for developing a broader understanding of stress in relation to mental health.

The purpose of this chapter is to explore these two issues in greater detail. First, we will examine the methodological issues involved with the assessment of life events. How might our subjective views of stress distort our scientific approach to measuring the construct? Second, we will examine stress in relation to broader models of its influences on thought and behavior. In particular, we will be concerned with ideas of specificity of stress effects, both in terms of direct influences on mental health and in terms of influences on other matters that bear upon mental health. This will help to outline for future research correlates of stress that can influence psychological functioning and that may sharpen our understanding of stress in relation to disorder.

THE ASSESSMENT OF LIFE EVENTS

In a sense, the idea of "measuring" people's lives appears both doubtful and daunting. The worlds of different individuals appear so diverse, and the dimensions along which they might be compared so numerous and varied, that systematic comparison can seem next to impossible. It is in this context that the introduction of the life-events inventories for capturing relatively distinctive, time-bound, and concrete life experiences received enthusiastic reception. The Schedule of Recent Experiences (SRE; Holmes & Rahe, 1967) represented a conceptual and methodological advance that introduced the idea that features of people's recent lives could be assessed in a scientific manner as relatively specific life events.

The checklist approach to assessing life stress clearly has gained rapid acceptance in the research community. For example, Holmes (1979) reported that approximately 1,000 studies had used the SRE alone to study stress associations with diverse mental and physical health outcomes. Considerable research since this time has continued to employ the SRE. As use of checklist measures has spread, however, so have concerns over methodological flaws. A second generation of life-events measures has been developed in response to these concerns and received widespread use. Although these newer instruments possess some methodological advances, for the most part they suffer from many of the shortcomings of their predecessors.

Could it be that our individual subjective beliefs concerning the phenomenology of stress blind us to some of the methodological inadequacies of this approach? We examine this issue, based on recent research along with anecdotal evidence from our own research program, to clairfy some broader limitations of the checklist approach to assessing life stress. Once we have presented both specific and general reasons for the inadequacy of checklist approaches, we will outline major issues sur-

rounding the development of more scientifically sound assessment instruments for life stress based on recent developments. Finally, to substantiate our position regarding the utility of these different approaches
to assessing life stress, we will review some data directly comparing the
two approaches.

The Life-Events Checklists

Perhaps the major problem with the checklist approach to measuring life stress was its immediate, and essentially uncritical, acceptance:
"The assessment procedures appear to have been accorded instant validity, having seemingly sprung from the minds of the creators much like
Minerva sprung from the brain of Zeus: instantly, fully, and perfectly
formed" (Monroe, 1990, p. 465). Thus there was little further conceptual or psychometric refinement of the SRE before its initial widespread
application. Only after the early wave of studies and several years of use
did more skeptical perspectives begin to appear in the literature (Brown,
1974; Dohrenwend, 1974). There are many reasons why these methods
were, and continue to be, inadequate for developing a scientifically
sound approach to the measurement and study of life stress.

Measurement Limitations

When investigators turn to traditional psychometric methods for
evaluating the adequacy of the SRE and related measures, it becomes
quite clear that such basic requirements as test–retest reliability for assessments covering the same time period are inadequately met (Jenkins,
Hurst, & Rose, 1979; McQuaid et al., 1992; Monroe, 1982a,b; Yager,
Grant, Sweetwood, & Gerst, 1981). For example, respondents do not
report the same checklist items consistently when they are asked again,
at a later point in time, to report events occurring for the same time
period. Other important issues have been raised, such as the confounding between items that represent actual symptoms as opposed to life
events (e.g., "major change in sleeping habits"), or events that are a
consequence—as opposed to a cause—of mental or physical illness (e.g.,
"major change is social activities"; Brown, 1974, 1981; Dohrenwend,
1974; Thoits, 1982).

Still other questions arise that suggest the greater complexity of the
task involved. How are intrinsically related events to be treated? For
example, a marital separation typically also involves a move by one of the
partners, possible changes in income, potential legal contacts, and so on.
Should this be coded as one event, or multiple events? The core concern
at the outset is not so much *which* approach is adopted, but that the

approach be consistent and standardized across individuals. Since investigators themselves had not at the time reached a consensus on this complicated issue, it seemed imprudent to leave the decision to the individual interpretations of the respondents. Finally, it is also evident that there are diverse practices across studies in terms of the operationalization of the events endorsed by subjects (different time periods for summing events, different types of events used to produce composite scores, different weights for events, etc.; see also Alloy, Hartlage, & Abramson, 1988; Monroe, 1982b, 1989).

Overall, the construct of stress has been inconsistently operationalized by researchers as a result of the diversity of theories and interpretations of life stress. Though this limitation is substantial, to our mind it represents only one of the potential problems in the assessment of life stress. Other problems arise from more subtle biases people harbor that stem from their subjective models of stress and its believed impact. The following section more fully details these less obvious concerns that we propose underlie considerable problems with the self-report life-event checklists.

Clinical Anecdotes

Following our early studies on life stress and psychological functioning (Monroe, 1982a; Monroe, Bellack, Hersen, & Himmelhoch, 1983), we began to complement the self-report checklist approach with follow-up interviews. Specific probe questions were developed for each checklist item to allow the respondent an opportunity to detail more fully the nature of the experience involved. Essentially, we wanted to ensure that the subject's definition of an event corresponded with our definition. The results were quite often instructive.

We soon discovered the interpretation of an event varied greatly between subjects. For example, one subject reported her daughter's recent bout with the flu under the category "serious illness in close family member." In contrast, another subject whose spouse had suffered a heart attack 3 months previously failed to endorse any items, because the previous event was not stressful any longer and had actually led to a better current situation (the spouse had recovered nicely and was living a healthier existence as a result of changes in diet, smoking, and exercise). Although one could argue the viewpoint that stress is in the eyes of the beholder, it is clear from such examples that dramatically different environmental circumstances are being reported by respondents. Without a better procedure for separating idiosyncratic interpretations from actual environmental circumstances, the roles of external sources of stress and of subjective perceptions of stress are hopelessly confounded (see also Dohrenwend, Link, Kern, Shrout, & Markowitz, 1990, on "variability within categories"; Monroe & Simons, 1991).

Another problem became especially salient with subjects who really had very little stress—at least in terms of the more objectively defined major life events—to report in their lives. These people would often spontaneously note how "boring" their lives appeared, and how disappointed the research assistant must be at the subject's inability to provide what the latter viewed as the desired data. Often these individuals would lower their thresholds for reporting minor experiences as events, apparently to placate the experimenter (e.g., very minor arguments or work problems could achieve the status of major altercations). Subjects inferred their task was to detail stress, and some of them may have stretched their reporting to be "good" subjects.

Perhaps most interesting has been our experience with research involving individuals who have a lifetime history of recurrent depression (Monroe, Kupfer, & Frank, 1992). Because of their multiple experiences with depression (3 or more episodes), many of these people are astute observers of their transitions into clinical episodes, and they are articulate chroniclers of the forces that they perceive to influence their mental well-being. We have found some individuals with multiple episodes who indicate that stress is not related to their depressions, particularly their later episodes. (This, of course, is consonant with the many reports of depression that appears to arise "out of the blue"; see Monroe & Depue, 1991.) For example, one patient indicated that although it appeared that stress may have been influential in her first or second episodes, it was not related to the onset of her later episodes. Most interestingly, she also emphasized that she had to manufacture stress-related explanations to assuage her inquiring family and friends; other people simply would not accept that her psychological misery was unrelated to her life circumstances!

This social drive to attribute depression to life stress also was apparent in our prospective research on life stress and recurrent depression. Interviewing patients every 12 weeks, we were able to track major stress factors in a fairly detailed manner. When one patient suffered a recurrence and we probed for "hidden" stressors, she calmly indicated that there were absolutely no relevant stressors before her recent onset. She also politely reminded us that she had been very candid in previous interviews and would not now purposefully mislead us. Yet when we interviewed her mother for corroboration, the latter insisted that work stressors had been paramount (but she could not provide specific events or details—she simply "knew" that it was work that "did it"). Although one could argue who was right, we believed that the patient—with her extensive prior experiences with us and previous candid reporting—was the most accurate in her reporting. Again, we witness the possibility that stress is easily invoked to assuage anxieties about our ignorance concerning the etiology of mental and physical disorders, which we believe seriously tarnishes our measures of the actual forms of adversity faced by the individuals we study (Pollock, 1988).

Conclusions

We have detailed several "hard" issues involving the assessment of life stress, as well as "softer" anecdotes bearing on the matter. Many serious problems become readily apparent after probing the possible discrepancies between subjects' reports and the implicit metrics of the investigators. Although further method developments might improve life-event checklists (e.g., clearer instructions), we believe that such efforts at this point are probably not worth undertaking. Nonetheless, there are many who disagree with this view (Oei & Zwart, 1986; Zimmerman, Pfohl, & Stangl, 1986). To clarify our position further, we will outline below some fundamental requirements for developing adequate measurement systems of life stress.

Interview- and Rater-Based Methods

Self-report checklist procedures for the assessment of life stress are still the most common instruments employed in the literature. Approaches based on interview methods, however, are gaining wider acceptance. Ideally the latter forms of assessment comprise two components. First, a semistructured interview probes the basic domains of potential stressors. Second, the interviewer presents the information gleaned from the interview to one or more raters trained in the specific definitions and rules of the particular system for defining events and rating different dimensions of theoretical relevance. (Depending upon the particular system used, raters may or may not be blind to the psychological status of the subject.) There are many research groups who have reported studies based on such general interview- and rater-based methodologies (e.g., Brown & Harris, 1989b; Dohrenwend et al., 1990; Hammen, 1991; Miller et al., 1986; Monroe et al., 1991; Paykel, 1982).

Although it is our opinion that the development of these interview-based procedures is to be encouraged, one must also maintain a skeptical eye toward the likely problems accompanying such measurement systems. Interestingly, as a whole the measurement limitations of these approaches are not yet well spelled out. There are two features of the procedures that need to be addressed: the adequacy of the interview, and the adequacy of the rating procedures. We will discuss each of these in turn.

Considerations Pertaining to Interviews

The first question involving the adequacy of an interview-based method concerns whether the interview elicits the necessary information for the rating procedure. How thoroughly does the interview probe the various areas of possible stressors in the individuals life? This particular issue has not been systematically examined, and there is consequently no information available (to our knowledge) on which comparisons have been made across interview-based systems. One problem with attempting such comparisons is that the interview instruments are generally not readily available in the literature, and the contents can only be surmised through the brief descriptions provided in publications. Thus the adequacy of specific interviews, as well as the comparative adequacy of different interviews, is an open question.

.A related concern is the degree to which the interview facilitates the subject's recall or admission of past stressful experiences. This is partially dependent upon the nature of the interview protocol and the skill of the interviewer; multiple probes, interviewer perceptiveness, and interviewer rapport can influence the degree to which such information may be accessed. Basic assumptions, though, are (a) that respondents are capable of recalling at least the more significant events in their recent lives, and (b) that they are willing to discuss the experiences with the interviewer. For particular types of experiences (e.g., abuse or other illegal or morally questionable activities, or traumatic experiences), respondents may be reluctant or unwilling to provide the information (Kessler & Wethington, 1991). For some potentially stress-related types of disorders (e.g., posttraumatic stress disorder, dissociative disorders) subjects may be reluctant to provide, or incapable of providing, the requisite information. Thus interview-based procedures may be hampered by a subject's willingness or ability to report events. Note, that these are not unique problems for such assessment methods. Though it might be argued that the potential anonymity of self-report checklists for assessing life stress could afford greater ease of divulging sensitive information (Oei & Zwart, 1986), one could as easily argue that skilled interviewing and sensitive rapport would provide an even likelier context for eliciting the information. Further, the multiple probes and questioning involved with interview-based methods would most likely work in favor of the interview approach for stimulating recall of forgotten information.

A final possible concern—though one that is not commonly

raised—is that subjects may fabricate events. Although we have already noted how study participants may "stretch" experiences to have them count as an event, we have not suspected that subjects will frankly make up stressors. To our knowledge, there is no suggestion that this constitutes a problem from the research of other investigators. Obviously, though, we have no alternative source of information on which to substantiate such impressions. Although this remains a possibility, we believe that there are other problems that require more immediate attention.

Considerations Pertaining to Rating Procedures

Once the basic information is obtained from the semi-structured interview, the next step concerns the processing of the raw material. How are decisions made about what does and does not constitute an event, and how are various dimensions of stress or severity of stress assigned? Again there are subtle, yet very basic, problems at this level of analysis. People tend to have prototypic events in mind that fit with their subjective models of stress, and they do not ponder the more subtle questions of what constitutes an event: How are related events to be differentiated and distinguished, and how are ratings to be influenced by successive events or calamities that cascade from one area of life into others? We emphasize that these are issues that frequently arise in rating meetings. The core information on life stress involves many delicate decisions concerning how the raw information is to be standardized across study participants. This is because life tends to be more a process of interrelated experiences and activities than a set of readily definable, discrete, and apparently quantal events. Consequently the adequacy of the system for structuring this task is crucial for judging its potential merit. We will discuss a few of the concepts that a system needs to consider for evaluating life experiences, including valence (positivity/negativity), severity, focus (who is the most involved in the stressor), independence (whether the event is caused by the respondent or his or her psychological state), time dimensions of the experience, and relationships between different experiences. The goal of this section is only to highlight some of the requirements for adequately operationalizing life stress, not to outline exhaustively the full array of considerations or details involved.

Even those dimensions that would seem the easiest to define can hold pitfalls. For example, determining whether an event is positive or negative can be a surprisingly difficult task. Is taking out a major loan positive or negative? It can be a positive experience for someone taking out a loan for his or her dream house, a negative experience when borrowing from loansharks, and ambiguous when a loan allows a positive purchase but puts a severe financial strain on the respondent. Experiences can also have more than one aspect that affects valence. For example, participants in a study on alcohol abuse sometimes described being arrested for drunk driving as a positive experience, because it led to treatment for their alcohol problems (Brown et al., 1990). Should the immediate experience of the event define its valence, or should longer-term impact be considered?

The severity of the event (i.e., how likely it is to cause problems) is another seemingly clear concept. A divorce is obviously more severe than a parking ticket, and a death of a loved one more severe than a cold. But differences in severity are not always so clear cut. Is a broken arm as severe as a broken leg? Is a getting fired as severe as being laid off? The researcher needs some means of answering these questions. The researcher also needs to determine how fine a gradation in severity may be needed to adequately describe life experiences. Do two levels of severity (presence or absence of a stressor) effectively do the job, or some 500? Life stress research has encompassed both numbers of levels (Brown, 1989; Dohrenwend, Krasnoff, Askenasy, & Dohrenwend, 1978; Holmes & Rahe, 1967).

The focus of the event is another dimension that is often ambiguous (Brown & Harris, 1978). Though it would seem that by definition life events are centered on the respondent, events that occurred to other people are often reported. Examples include a spouse losing a job, a child being arrested, or a close friend undergoing a relationship crisis. Events often involve both the respondent and another person, such as a marital fight. What aspects of the experience (participation in the event, emotional or psychological reaction to it) make it the respondent's experience? For example, is it an event for a mother when her 5-year-old son breaks his arm? Is it an event if the son is 25, no longer living at home, and covered by his own health insurance? The rater must determine to what degree the experience needs to be focused on the subject for it to be considered a life event for him or her.

Another crucial issue that raters need to deal with in life-events assessment is detecting possible influences of the disorder on the occurrence of the life experience. In other words, the investigator must determine whether the disorder caused the event, rather than the other way around. It is critical to determine the independence of events from the disorders they are thought to predict, especially in relation to disorders such as major depression, anxiety, and alcohol and drug abuse, where the pathology can easily bring about adverse events (e.g., being laid off for being drunk on the job, having child behavior problems when one is too depressed to supervise the child). This problem takes on added complexity if indirect effects are considered. For example, an alcohol abuser arrested for driving while intoxicated clearly has experienced a disorder-caused event. But at what point do the repercussions of the arrest cease to be alcohol related: after being jailed, or appearing in court, or paying a fine? Would getting fired from a job because of time off for court appearances be alcohol related (even if one has been sober since the arrest)? In this hypothetical case later events are less determined by the disorder, yet they may be following from a similar initial cause. The decision as to where to draw the line simply is not clear.

Life experiences that are related to each other (as in the alcohol example above) raise the dimension of time as an important consideration for classifying stress. When does one event end and another begin? In the case above, is it more informative to describe each court appearance, each visit to the lawyer, and each fine that has to be paid as a separate event; the entire complex of experiences as one superordinate major event; or the continuing experiences as an ongoing "arrest" chronic stressor? For systems distinguishing acute from chronic forms of stress, additional concerns arise. How are changes in severity across time dealt with? How are the interactions between the difficulty and related events (either as a cause or result) treated? The investigator needs to determine how to answer these questions.

The task of assessing life stress is further complicated by the fact that life is not experienced as a series discrete events and difficulties. There is a continual interaction of different experiences that can modify the impact of each one on the individual. For example, a person may be involved in a car accident, be hospitalized, miss work, and subsequently incur financial difficulties. Are these all separate experiences, or should they be considered subcomponents of an overarching event? If physical pain attributable to the car accident continues to interfere with work and there are increased confrontations with the employer, how is the relationship of these experiences to each other and to the original accident to be represented?

Assessment Requirements

The foregoing discussion of considerations for rating procedures outlines many of the background issues involved with the assessment of life stress. As we have attempted to illustrate, these are often subtle yet pervasive concerns that are not readily apparent and are often ignored. They are crucial to confront, however, if one wishes to measure life stress with scientifically sound, replicable procedures.

To address these issues, methods that follow the same logic as those for diagnosis and classification of psychopathology are useful. Explicit rules and operational criteria are required to define what constitutes events and ongoing stressors, as well as how to handle the interrelations among events and between events and difficulties. It should be clear by now that this is not a simple or straightforward task; it involves an extensive set of rules, guidelines, and criteria to cover the many ways in which life's adversities may conspire against the individual. In addition, life-events evaluation can be enhanced by providing case exemplars that investigators can use to guide their ratings. Different systems will vary in regard to the degree to which such rules and criteria are general in application rather than specific and differentiated. Thus there will be trade-offs in terms of relative ease of implementation versus specificity of ratings obtained.

Brown and Harris (1989b) emphasize the use of the context in which the experience occurs to help tailor ratings of impact to the particular respondent's life circumstances. For example, when rating the birth of a baby, it is the context (e.g., stable finances, adequate medical care, and supportive family versus poverty, no health care, and no support) that determines the severity of the event rating. By eliciting information about a respondent's life that may influence the impact of the event, the investigator can take these moderating aspects of the subject's life into account without leaving the task to the subjective beliefs of the respondent. This allows the investigator to use a much more individualized yet complex set of rules for evaluating events and difficulties, and it helps to ensure consistent ratings of events across subjects with differing biographical circumstances.

The system with which we are most familiar is the Bedford College Life Events and Difficulties Schedule (LEDS; Brown & Harris, 1978). The manuals for rating life stress with this approach have been developed since the early 1970s, and they incorporate general guidelines and criteria for defining events and ongoing difficulties, as well as specific guidelines and criteria for particular types of experiences. The manual also provides approximately 5,000 case examples that can be used to guide ratings of life event or difficulty severity. These examples allow raters to "anchor" their rating of an event with standardized ratings, thereby serving to increase reliability and standardization across research settings. The LEDS system consequently represents a very carefully developed, thoroughly documented, and comprehensive system that addresses most of the issues raised in a very detailed and specific manner.

Psychometric Data Base

Given the lack of data bearing directly on these issues (i.e., coverage of interview questioning, adequacy of respondent compliance, respondent fabrication, and rating procedures issues), one must turn to more indirect sources of information to judge the utility of the overall approach as well as of its respective embodiments. The work of Brown and Harris in the development of the LEDS provides the strongest empirical record for justifying such approaches (Brown, 1989), although research by other investigators has provided promising leads (Dohrenwend et al., 1990; Hammen, 1991). With respect to severe types of life events, Brown and Harris have reported little falloff in reporting over a period of at least 1 year (Brown, 1989). This suggests that such experiences can be reliably recalled and reported when employing the LEDS procedures.

In terms of predictive validity, there have been many studies using the LEDS that have substantiated the strong predictive power of severe life stress for an episode of clinical depression. These findings essentially have been replicated in at least nine investigations performed by several different investigators employing LEDS methodology. The samples for these studies have included women from working-class homes, inner-city environments, rural settings, and general medical practice patients. In all, almost 2,000 women between 18 to 65 years of age have been studied. Across these studies, the occurrence of at least one severe event or major difficulty before onset ranged for cases between 62% to 94% (average 82%), for noncases between 25% to 39% (average 33%; Brown & Harris, 1989a, p. 55; Monroe & Simons, 1991). It appears that the LEDS has received the greatest attention in the existing literature, and it has considerable empirical support for both its reliability and its validity as a comprehensive measure of life stress.

Comparisons among different interview-based systems are difficult owing to the lack of information readily available on the topic. The nature of the training for raters, as well as the guidelines and criteria used in most life stress assessment approaches, are typically not delineated well in the different reports. An exception to this lack of adequate detail, as noted above, is the LEDS system. The LEDS embodies a comprehensive manual explicitly detailing decision rules and operational criteria for defining events and chronic difficulties, as well as guidelines for distinguishing between related events and repeated incidents of events. It will be useful to learn more of the other approaches that are now appearing in the literature, for there may be considerable benefit to these alternatives. In the interim, it appears that the LEDS system provides an excellent working example of the requirements involved for providing reliable and standardized ratings of life stress.

Conclusions

A system for assessing and rating life stress needs to deal with the complexity and potential biases involved with measuring life's adversities. Such a system needs to extract information from an individual by providing appropriate memory cues and probes, yet do this without biasing the information that is produced. It must provide a consistent, objective quantification of stress that describes each stressor on several key dimensions (e.g., severity, focus, relationship to disorder, duration). The ratings must reflect the impact of the event within the context of the person's life without being biased by the respondent's personal beliefs about the nature of stress and its relationship to his or her disorder.

Several research groups have begun to undertake such procedures seriously. We are most familiar with the LEDS system developed by Brown and Harris (1978), which serves as an excellent reference system in terms of the detail and sophistication of the documented procedures. Other rigorous approaches, though, are important at the present stage of research to provide alternative methods of addressing the phenomena involved and to provide potentially different perspectives on the construct of stress. Optimally, the rules used in ratings for a system would be based upon empirical evidence regarding the impact of each dimension on particular disorders. More commonly, the procedural guidelines and dimensional ratings at present are based upon clinical observation, investigator intuition, or reasoned convention. As research with life stress continues with the LEDS and other related approaches, these arbitrary and clinically based distinctions can be tested empirically to improve both methodology and our understanding of life stress.

Comparative Findings: Interview and Checklist Procedures

There have been relatively few attempts to compare checklist and interview procedures. Zimmerman et al. (1986) found that the mean number of events reported on an interview and a checklist were nearly identical. However, 41.3% of the items elicited in an interview procedure had not been reported on a checklist, whereas 38.8% of the items reported on the checklist were not reported during the interview. The authors noted that of all the items reported on the checklist, about one sixth were errors (e.g., outside of time frame or mislabeled). In addition, approximately half of the events reported on the checklist but not on the interview were errors. The authors concluded that as an overall measure of life stress, a checklist may be useful, but if a researcher required more detailed information, an interview-based approach was more appropriate.

In a different study, Oei and Zwart (1986) found that there was a significantly different number of events reported on a checklist as compared to an interview, depending on the type of event (e.g., related to work, health, or education). Specifically, subjects reported significantly more work problems, education events, personal illnesses, and marital problems on a questionnaire, and significantly more deaths during the interview. The authors implied that the personal nature of the events reported more frequently on the checklist made them difficult to discuss in an interview. Their interpretation of the results suggested that each type of instrument had advantages: The checklist gave the respondent some anonymity in reporting personal events, whereas the interview provided the researcher a chance to use clinical observations to gain important information. The authors concluded that both instruments should be used.

The previous two studies provided some information about the relationship between interviews and checklists. The interviews used in the comparisons, however, did not use a contextual rating system such as the LEDS. Katschnig (1986) compared life events reported by depressed patients using Holmes and Rahe's SRE with life events elicited from those patients using the LEDS. The findings showed a relationship between both types of measurement and symptomatology for the overall sample. A closer analysis, though, found that an individual's global stress scores on the SRE and LEDS were unrelated. Katschnig concluded that either the two instruments were measuring different phenomena or the SRE was producing spurious results. He also suggested that care had to be taken in drawing any conclusions from the checklist type of measure.

The previous studies examined the relationship between the summary variables (i.e., the score or number of life events) produced by the instruments in question. As Katschnig pointed out, however, it was unclear as to whether these differences were attributable to theoretical discrepancies between the instruments or to the unreliability of the checklist in comparison to the interview. We examined life events assessed using the modified self-report Psychiatric Epidemiology Research Interview (PERI) Life Events Scale, subsequently interviewed patients about the endorsed events, and then rated the information in accord with the LEDS rating system (McQuaid et al., 1992). We found that more than 60% of the events reported on the checklist did not match with the LEDS events. We then attempted to determine what aspects of the instruments caused the discrepancies.

The LEDS has stringent criteria for what is included as an event, whereas the PERI constrains the definition of life stress by what appears on the inventory and what the respondent decides to include as an event. For example, 15.1% of events reported on the PERI (e.g., vacation) did not meet the criteria for LEDS events. The LEDS differentiates events from difficulties (ongoing stressors that last more than 4 weeks), whereas the PERI does not; more than 22% of the events reported on the PERI were classified as difficulties on the LEDS. In total, nearly 42% of reported events met one system's definition of a life event, but not the other's. In general, it appeared that the two measures were measuring related, but different experiences.

There were also clear errors in reporting on the PERI that were detected by the LEDS. Individuals endorsed the same event twice under different headings (e.g., endorsing "trouble with boss" and "trouble at work" in reference to the same fight at work) 4.5% of the time. The interview also found that some events that were reported (7.6%) fell outside of the relevant time period. These errors suggest that the self-report checklist method alone is unreliable. Overall, 19.9% of events were outside the time period, mislabeled, elicited in the interview, or a combination of these errors. These results suggest that both of Katschnig's conclusions may be correct: Self-report checklists measure different constructs than interviews (at least the LEDS interview), and they include high rates of error variance.

Conclusions

The SRE (Holmes & Rahe, 1967) was a significant step toward understanding the impact of stress on the individual. Since its development, researchers have continued to improve the methodology. The advent of investigator-based measures employing structured interviews and standardized rating systems allow the researcher greatly increased control in gathering and categorizing information. These latter approaches have greatly improved the amount of relevant information a researcher can gain from a subject. Systematic rating techniques, guided by extensive operational rules and criteria, assist raters in attaining high levels of reliability.

The next step for researchers interested in life-events methodology is systematic comparisons between different operationalizations of life stress based on these more reliable methodologies. For example, Brown and Harris (1989) have found an essentially dichotomous division of stress to be the most predictive of the onset of depression. Individuals with one or more severe events are most vulnerable to depression; individuals with other types of more minor events—even if highly frequent—but without a severe event are not at increased risk. Other researchers, such as Dohrenwend and colleagues, have found "fateful loss" events (i.e., events that are beyond the influence of the person and entail some form of important loss; Shrout et al., 1989) to be most highly related to depression. Other approaches to operationalizing life stress treat it as a continuous construct where all forms of adversity, from minor hassles through major events, are included (Alloy et al. 1988). This latter approach is probably the most commonly invoked view of stress.

It is no surprise that different studies often lead to different results, given that different instruments have different definitions of a "life event." The general concept of life stress is treated in the literature as a unitary concept, however, when in fact the term refers to a variety of related yet distinct experiences. Future research should attempt to determine which psychological disorders, or which aspects of different psychological disorders, may be influenced by general or different forms of stress (Monroe & Simons, 1991). We address these considerations in greater detail next.

STRESSFUL LIFE EVENTS AND MENTAL HEALTH: ETIOLOGY AND OTHER INFLUENCES

Having clarified important procedural bases for assessing life events, we can now turn to the issues involved with stress impact. If the consequences of stress are as extensive as we suspect they may be, we need more differentiated perspectives on the ways in which forms of stress might be involved with different aspects of thought and behavior, as well as with different psychological problems. For example, particular types of stress may be related to particular types of disorders (Monroe & Johnson, 1990). Furthermore, stress may influence the onset and/or the clinical course of disorder, as well as the likelihood of recurrence. In other instances stress may affect other variables—such as the probability of receiving treatment (Ginsberg & Brown, 1982) or the timing of treatment entry (Monroe et al., 1991)—that then affect the onset, course, and outcome of the disorder. Each of these possibilities raises a host of concerns for conducting research and for developing broader models of stress consequences (Monroe & Depue, 1991; Monroe & Simons, 1991), and each complicates the task of separating the direct effects of stress on disorder from the effects of stress on other relevant variables.

Onset Considerations

There are several concerns that should be taken into account with regard to investigating the onset of psychological disorder. These concerns, in turn, raise a number of other considerations for the investigator interested in understanding the potential influences of life stress.

Type of Disorder

As we have already indicated, research on human stress and psychological functioning drew upon the early animal laboratory studies on the physiology of the stress response (Selye, 1936). The theoretical focus of the early animal work was upon nonspecific stress; that is, the type of stress did not matter as much as the degree of stress. Positive and negative stressors were viewed as predisposing an organism to pathology by taxing its adaptive resources. Most of the available information on life events and mental health, however, demonstrates that nonspecific principles are less important than specific ones. The current literature suggests that relatively specific forms of life stress predispose individuals to relatively specific forms of psychopathology (Monroe & Johnson, 1990).

The distinctions between the types of stressors and the respective disorders they give rise to may be dramatic. For example, it appears that particularly severe forms of stress precede the onset of clinical depression, whereas more minor types of events precede the onset or exacerbation of schizophrenia (see Brown & Harris, 1989b, for further examples of stressor–disorder specificity). Furthermore, particular types of severe events may predispose toward depression (i.e., those with strong "loss" components) and other toward anxiety disorders (i.e., those with strong "danger" components; Brown & Harris, 1986; Monroe, 1990). Thus investigators should be guided by theoretical as well as empirical leads when operationalizing particular forms of adversity with regard to the onset of particular forms of psychopathology.

Given the current state of diagnostic uncertainties, more differentiated analyses of life stress also may help inform important nosological distinctions. There may be classes of disorder that "cut across" current diagnostic divisions (Abramson, Alloy, & Metalsky, 1989). The role of life stress, or specific forms of life stress, may be very helpful in elucidating such potential diagnostic distinctions (Monroe, 1990). For example, Abramson et al. (1989) have suggested that the interaction of life stress with cognitive vulnerabilities may produce "hopelessness" depression, a type of depression that could cut across current categories of depression, anxiety, and perhaps other syndromes.

It is also plausible to think of life stress in terms of the expression of symptoms (a role that may or may not be related to the etiological role of the stressors; Brown & Harris, 1978; Monroe, 1990). Particular types of events, or perhaps chronic stressors, may influence the development of particular symptoms or constellations of symptoms, but not necessarily the development of the underlying disorder. For example, depressed patients with melancholic profiles may have different ambient life stress circumstances from depressed patients with agitated depressions. In a sense, the current social environment might "pull" for particular types or combinations of symptoms that are part of the spectrum of possibilities associated with the expression of a particular type of disorder. Although there are few data bearing on this issue, it appears to be one that is of promise for clarifying the different effects stress has in terms of mental health.

Timing of Disorder

A second major issue pertains to the timing of onset and the timing of stress. With regard to the initiation of disorder, it is certainly optimal that stressors be found to precede the actual onset of the disorder. Yet in practice this distinction is less clear-cut than it might seem. For example, it is well known that many people who incur depression have elevated baselines of depressive symptoms, and that some qualify as dysthymia and thereby have at least 2 years of subsyndromal symptomatology (Keller, Shapiro, Lavori, & Wolfe, 1982). How should the timing issue be resolved in such cases?

A related question pertains to the temporal characteristics of onset. Not all onsets are acute; many involve somewhat protracted prodomes (albeit less drawn out than for the dysthmic example just cited). During the period of being brought down into their depression, such individuals may incur serious forms of life stress. Indeed, their lack of adaptive coping—essentially synonymous with their emerging depression—may be a significant factor contributing to the incidence of the negative events. People who perform poorly at work or are hostile or withdrawn in personal relationships because of low-level depression may be at greater risk for severe events (Monroe, 1990). Again, how should such timing issues be resolved?

In both of these examples, there is strong suspicion that the individual brings about the stressors. This has led to a certain methodological unease, with one interpretation being that the stressors are simply a consequence of the emerging depression (and perhaps were even irrelevant to the etiology of the disorder). To control for such concerns, it is often recommended that researchers not include such "nonindependent" types of events or only include events that are clearly beyond the individual's control (e.g., unemployment caused by office closing). We believe the issue is a difficult one to solve, but it seems that discarding of the nonindependent forms of stress is unduly restrictive. First, most of the severe events found to precede depression are not entirely independent of the person's actions or control (Hammen, 1991). Second, it may be that it is the occurrence of such events *during periods of psychological vulnerability* that is critical for movement into a full-blown episode. And it makes some sense that the risk factors (i.e., elevated depression and severe events) may not be entirely independent as they conspire to produce a clinical episode of the disorder (Monroe & Simons, 1991). Both independent and nonindependent events may have important (and different) effects. Both types of events should be identified and evaluated.

Finally, little is known about the time interval between stress and onset of the disorder. The available information suggests that onset of depression occurs most often within 38 weeks of the occurrence of at least one severe event (Brown & Harris, 1978, 1989a), yet there may be an effect up to 1 year prior to onset. It is of interest to know what happens during these interim periods between severe event and disorder onset. Why do some individuals succumb almost immediately, and others much more belatedly? Could it be that the factors modulating celerity of onset also hold important clues for the factors that differentiate those who succumb under severe stress from those who do not? These are intriguing possibilities for future studies to address.

Recurrence of Disorder

People who have suffered from a psychological disorder are at increased risk for future episodes of disorder. For example, Belsher and Costello (1988) concluded that approximately 50% of individuals who recover from an episode of depression experience a relapse or recurrence within 2 years. This means that many individuals typically studied in research on life stress are not truly first-onset cases, but rather relapses or recurrences of the disorder. Kraepelin (1921) noted that one of his patients became depressed "after the death first of her husband, next of her dog, and then of her dove" (p. 179). As Kraepelin suggests, life stress may play a different role in recurrence than it does in first onset. Future work should be attentive to the possible importance of such distinctions based on the lifetime history of mental disorder.

Clinical Course Considerations

A number of studies have begun to examine the consequences of life stress for the course of disorder once begun (Brown, Bifulco, & Andrews, 1990; Monroe & Depue, 1991; Monroe, Kupfer, & Frank, 1992). This research has been an extension of treatment outcome studies, and probably the largest available literature deals specifically with treatment response for depression in relation to life events occurring either prior to treatment entry or during treatment. This literature nicely portrays some general principles to be considered for similar types of research on the clinical course of other mental health outcomes.

Overall, results have suggested the importance of this approach to studying stress effects (see Monroe & Depue, 1991). The available work is important for delineating the many challenges confronting researchers interested in attaining a better understanding of the role of stress in the course of depression. In particular, several issues should be borne in mind.

Patient Characteristics

Most investigations vary greatly with respect to the types of depressed patients included (e.g., endogenous versus nonendogenous; recurrent versus nonrecurrent; anxious versus nonanxious depressives). Stress may be differentially associated with depression as a function of either severity or subtype. For example, life stress has been found to predict better outcomes primarily for patients exhibiting endogenous profiles (Monroe, Thase, Hersen, Bellack, & Himmelhoch, 1985). Another issue of importance again concerns recurrent depressions (Kupfer & Frank, 1987; Monroe & Depue, 1991). Recent findings suggest that the role of life stress may differ depending upon patients' history of depression. For example, recurrent depressives with life stress have been found to respond more poorly to treatment, whereas patients not selected for a history of recurrence may do better (Monroe, Kupfer, & Frank, 1992).

In addition to differences between subtypes or symptoms of depressed individuals, other nonclinical patient characteristics that could be related to the impact of life stress include marital status, age, and gender. Gender is a particularly important issue for examining research using the LEDS, given that a large proportion of reported studies that use the LEDS to examine depression and life stress include only female depressives (Brown & Harris, 1989a). It would seem wise at the current stage of knowledge to be quite clear about the composition of the patient samples to help clarify potential differential associations with life stress and to protect against unwarranted assumptions and generalizations (Depue & Monroe, 1986).

Treatment Outcome, Recovery, and Recurrence

Clearly remission rates vary according to type and adequacy of intervention. The implications of life stress for the treatment course of depressed patients need to take into account this broader context of treatment efficacy. Variations in treatments across the studies (pharmacotherapies with different dosages and trial durations; psychotherapies with different trial durations), as well as in treatment settings (inpatient versus outpatient), further limit the inferences one may draw from this body of work. To examine the role of stress one must be able to hold constant the main effects of treatment, or at least to examine their possible influence on the associations between stress and the clinical course of the disorder.

In theory there are many ways in which life stress could influence the treatment course of depression, and there has been little systematic portrayal of the corollaries embedded within the overarching hypothesis that stress influences treatment course. One possibility is that the nature and severity of the presenting clinical picture is related to stress. Patients with heightened life stress prior treatment entry may present with more severe symptoms (e.g., Reno & Halaris, 1990). Second is the question of symptom course. Do patients with greater pretreatment stress show greater (e.g., Monroe et al., 1983) or lesser (Zimmerman, Pfohl, Coryell, & Stangl, 1987) response during the course of treatment? Finally, do patients with greater *concurrent* life stress have a poorer prognosis?

Perhaps most importantly, definitions of response have varied substantially across studies in examining treatment effects. Most investigations simply employ final symptom scores or percentage reductions in symptoms from intake status. Because few studies use clear criteria to ensure both the degree of symptom reduction and stability of response, this suggests that outcome comparisons are based largely upon unstable estimates of depressive symptomatology. Lastly, it would be of interest to know if the timing of recovery varied systematically in relation to either pretreatment or concurrent stress (e.g., patients with severe stress may take longer to recover relative to nonstressed counterparts).

The vast majority of research on the clinical course of psychological disorders is confined to questions of a relatively short-term nature. The focus is primarily upon who remits and who does not over relatively circumscribed periods of time, and what factors correlate with differential outcome. Yet the most prevalent forms of mental disorder (e.g., anxiety disorder and depressive disorders) are known have a high likelihood of being repeated over time; for instance, many treatment "successes" for depression relapse within 6 months of their recovery (Belsher & Costello, 1988). Furthermore, even after sustained recovery many people with prior anxiety or depressive experiences are at heightened risk for future episodes of these disorders (Monroe, 1990). Thus investigations of life stress and the course of disorder would profit from enlarging the temporal scope to include both relapse and recurrence of such problems over prolonged periods of time (Monroe & Depue, 1991; Reno & Halaris, 1990).

Overall, it appears that life stress occurring prior to and during treatment may predict important clinical considerations during treatment (see also Pollard, Pollard, & Corn, 1989; Ventura, Nuechterlein, Lukoff, & Hardesty, 1989). Further evidence suggests that future work examining the lifetime course of disorder, and specifically relapse and recurrence following recovery, may also help to enlarge the picture of life stress implications for mental health.

Correlates of Stress

Only recently have investigators begun to be concerned with a variety of other possible stress effects that could have important mental health implications. These possibilities suggest that stress may subtly distort our understanding of its effects, and that it may have many other indirect influences upon mental health and the likelihood of developing more severe forms of disorder.

Treatment Seeking and Entry

Much of the work on life stress and psychopathology has been performed with patient samples. Although such individuals provide a convenient and very relevant sample for studying stress, they may also harbor particular problems. In particular, because many people in the community who develop clinical levels of psychopathology never come into treatment with formal mental health agencies (roughly 19%; Robins, Locke, & Regier, 1991), stress may be instrumental in determining who gains access to such treatment. In a descriptive study examining barriers to entering treatment, Ginsberg and Brown (1982) studied a sample of 45 depressed mothers who typically never received treatment. These investigators reported that the woman's family, friends, and general practitioners tended to interpret symptoms as "natural" reactions to recent stress, and therefore believed the symptoms did not warrant formal intervention. Based on such information, it might be hypothesized that life stress preceding onset retards entry into treatment. Another idea on this issue is that life stress occurring *after* the disorder begins might play a role in hastening seeking of formal help. For example, such stress may foster recognition of the severity of the problem and the need for additional help (Monroe et al., 1991). In either case, stress may lead to a clinical population that is unrepresentative of the overall population with the disorder.

Recently we found life stress to be very influential in determining the time period between onset of symptoms in depression and the patient's entry into treatment (Monroe et al., 1991). Life stress occurring prior to onset of depression was highly predictive of the time it took for patients to enter into treatment. In marked contrast, stress occurring after onset was not associated with any delay. Further analyses indicated different mechanisms of association between different stress variables and the time until treatment entry. In general, acute severe stressors hastened one's entry into treatment; for example, there was mean difference of more than 100 days between times of entry for the patients with a severe event and for those without one. If there were two or more severe events *and* severe chronic stressors, however, there was a considerable delay in seeking treatment. Overall, the results add to the emerging literature on life stress and depression, enlarging the scope to include forces operative in the determination of seeking formal treatment.

These findings speak strongly to the other roles stress may play in the overall context of people's lives that can influence our understanding of life events and mental health. Such research indicates that existing patient studies need to be complemented with studies of nonpatient (but disordered) samples to clarify the implications of life stress—occurring before onset or during the symptomatic phase—for onset and remission of psychopathology.

Attrition

Not all patients remain in treatment for the full course of prescribed intervention. This is true for general practice as well as for formal treatment outcome studies. With increasing sophistication in research on treatment outcome, the time period of coverage has expanded considerably. For example, follow-up periods now span years, and investigators are increasingly focusing on the issues of maintenance of treatment gains, relapse, and recurrence (e.g., Frank et al., 1990). Much of the research base that underlies future clinical practice thus is predicated upon prolonged studies wherein many patients, for a variety of reasons, drop out over time.

Hollon, Shelton, and Loosen (1991) have noted that there is approximately a 20% to 40% attrition rate, and a 60% to 75% response rate, during acute treatment with cognitive and pharmacotherapy interventions in depression. They point out that if different types of patients are more likely to remain in and to respond to treatment, then the acute treatment period acts as "a differential sieve, producing systematic differences in the sets of patients entering the follow-up from the different modalities" (p. 97). This, of course, would alter the generalizability of the findings and would suggest that different theoretical mechanisms may be operating. A parallel argument can be mounted in relation to the possible influences of life stress. Thus, if patient attrition or treatment response is in part a function of life stress, then the results for treatment outcome must be qualified accordingly. Finally, if the effects of stress continue to influence who remains in the treatment protocol over more protracted periods of follow-up, further caveats are in order.

At least for recurrent depression, we have found preliminary support to suggest that this is an important concern. For example, we found that a significantly greater proportion of patients with severe life stress prior to treatment entry dropped out during a 3-year period of maintenance treatment (following initial treatment response) compared to patients without such forms of stress (Monroe, Roberts, Frank, & Kupfer, 1992). Combined with the findings noted before from this sample for a relatively poor treatment response for patients reporting severe stress prior to treatment entry (Monroe, Roberts, et al., 1992), this indicates that such life events play an influential role in determining the composition of the sample over time. Based on these findings, one should be cautious about the progressive filtering of patients from such research protocols as a function of life stress. The population of patients who tend to complete such long-term studies—and consequently upon whom treatment efficacy estimates are ultimately based—may be biased toward the exclusion of patients for whom stress plays an important role in their pathology. Thus there is the clear possibility that although stress may influence the recurrence of disorder, it may also influence the probability of dropping out of the protocol. If the latter is an especially prominent effect, then the former would not be detectable. This represents on clear instance in which the multiple effects of stress should be taken into account to understand the more specific effects of interest with respect to mental health.

Moderating Variables: Social Support and Coping

Because not all people who experience major forms of life stress develop mental or physical problems, it has become increasingly common to develop more sophisticated models of the process via which stress may eventuate in disorder. A great amount of interest has been generated in vulnerability factors: aspects about the individual or the individual's social world that may increase the likelihood of problems in the face of stress. These are also often referred to as *buffering* hypotheses, wherein the lack of a vulnerability factor or the presence of a buffering factor mitigates the effects of stress. Two particularly topics in this area of inquiry are social support and coping (Coyne & Downey, 1991; Kessler, Price, & Wortman, 1985).

There has been little systematic study of the effects of stress on such buffering or vulnerability factors. Yet it is clear that the effects of stress might influence the availability or quality of social support or coping capabilities. For example, stress may erode social support over time through taxing the individual and his or her support system. Thus the support network may be incapable of meeting heightened demands, it may weary of continued demands, or the individual simply may not be able to maintain supportive ties (Monroe & Steiner, 1986). In addition, life stress and social support are often confounded (Thoits, 1982); life events such as marriage, the death of a spouse, and a best friend moving away clearly can be characterized as both stressors and changes in social support.

Mitchell and Moos (1984) reported that increases in life strains lead to decreases in perceived family support (see also McFarlane, Norman, Streiner, & Roy, 1983; Monroe & Steiner, 1986). Thoits (1982) demonstrated that social support appeared to buffer the impact of life stress on the onset of depression; however, closer analysis exposed a direct effect of life stress on social support (i.e., people with elevated life stress were less likely to stay married). When the effect of stress on social support was controlled for, the buffering effect was not found. Brown, Andrews, Harris, Adler, and Bridge (1986) found that efficacy of crisis support— support from someone whom the person expected would be supportive in time of need—was especially important for predicting the onset of depression. Women in this prospective study who expected support but were "let down" by a confidant in the face of a crisis were especially prone to develop depression. It is possible that stress had wearied past confidants, causing them to be less supportive. If so, then stress could eliminate supports that protect against depression, as well as have a direct effect on the subject.

Stress also may influence vulnerability to depression through its impact on the person's capabilities for coping with major life events. In this sense, then, particular forms of stress may deplete the person's coping resources for dealing with other stressful life events. Once again, it is apparent that the many possible consequences of stress could operate very differently in producing changes in mental health. Without models incorporating such possibilities, though, it will be very hard to gauge the nature of the influences stress has on psychological well-being and psychopathology.

CONCLUDING REMARKS

It should not be surprising that research bearing on the interrelations between life stress and mental health present many challenging issues in terms of theory and method. Beneath the surface of the seemingly obvious fact that life stress promotes psychological distress, more complicated and subtle considerations arise. The purpose of this chapter has been to illuminate some of these more elusive influences on our understanding of life stress, and to provide a more differentiated perspective on how life stress may be related to mental health. Thus we have tried to demonstrate why particular methodologies may be inadequate for measuring life stress, to specify some of the requirements for adequate assessment, and to outline the several pathways by which life stress may influence psychological well-being. In concluding, we will discuss the implications of these issues for understanding current estimates of the overall importance of stress in relation to mental health.

It is commonly reported that the magnitude of the association between life stress and psychological disorder is typically quite small. Many if not most reviews have emphasized this relatively weak statistical relationship (Rabkin & Struening, 1976; Sarason et al., 1975; Tennant, Bebbington, & Hurry, 1981). Following this line of reasoning, it is typically concluded that greater emphasis be placed upon factors that moderate stress impact in order to provide stronger risk estimates (social support, coping, etc.). Though we are in agreement that expanded models may prove quite useful, we also believe that the rationale of a weak association between stress and disorder is premature. Past estimates of the effects of stress are predicated on data that do not adequately reflect the nature of life stress.

There are three considerations that deserve concluding commentary. First, there are many forms of life stress and many forms of mental disorder. There are also many approaches to operationalize stress, and these differ in their validity and their associations with disorder. Finally, there are many ways in which life stress may influence psychological and behavioral functioning with respect to mental disorder. Consequently, general statements concerning the magnitude of effect for life stress on mental health only represent crude averages across different types of stress, measures of stress, and forms of disorder. From this perspective, it does not appear particularly surprising that more robust relations typically have not been reported.

Second, traditional procedures for determining the magnitude of effect attributable to life stress represent poor statistical measures of the effect. For example, although a large number of people under stress do not develop any disorder, most people who become depressed have been exposed to serious forms of stress prior to onset (Brown & Harris, 1978, 1989a). Other indices of risk may be more appropriate to convey the statistical importance of the association (e.g., attributable risk; see also Cooke, 1987). It is also noteworthy that recent advances in clarifying the characteristics of specific forms of stress have led to greater precision in predicting the onset of depression as indicated by such alternative measures of the association (see Brown & Harris, 1989a).

As a final note, though, we suggest that it seems unlikely that stress is predictive of *all* psychological and physical problems. Although we cannot discount the possibility of nonspecific stress effects, there is evidence that some psychological problems occur relatively independent of life stressors. For example, it has long been reported that some people become depressed without any external cause (Jackson, 1986; Monroe & Depue, 1991). We emphasize again that an obstacle to demonstrating a lack of association between stress and pathology stems from the cultural and subjective emphasis on stress. Very few people do not readily resonate to the idea of stress and cannot provide ardent accounts detailing the stressors in their lives. It is only with relatively rigorous and specific measures of the experiences people endure, rated in standardized and replicable ways, that we will begin to discover how stress may or may not be related to mental health.

REFERENCES

Abramson, L. Y., Alloy, L. B., & Metalsky, G. I. (1989). Hopelessness depression: A theory-based subtype of depression. *Psychological Review, 96*, 358–372.

Alloy, L. B., Hartlage, S., & Abramson, L. Y. (1988). Testing the cognitive diathesis–stress theories of depression: Issues of research design, conceptualization, and assessment. In L. B. Alloy (Ed.), *Cognitive processes in depression* (pp. 31–73). New York: Guilford.

Belsher, G., & Costello, C. G. (1988). Relapse after recovery from unipolar depression: A critical review. *Psychological Bulletin, 104*, 84–96.

Brown, G. W., Andrews, B., Harris, T. O. Adler, Z., & Bridge, L. (1986). Social support, self-esteem and depression. *Psychological Medicine, 16*, 813–831.

Brown, G. W., Bifulco, A., & Andrews, B. (1990). Self-esteem and depression: IV. Effect on course and recovery. *Social Psychiatry and Psychiatric Epidemiology, 25*, 244–249.

Brown, G. W. (1974). Meaning, measurement, and stress of life events. In B. S. Dohrenwend & B. P. Dohrenwend (Eds.), *Stressful life events: Their nature and effects* (pp. 217–243). New York: Wiley-Interscience.

Brown, G. W. (1981). Life events, psychiatric disorder, and physical illness. *Journal of Psychosomatic Research, 25*, 461–473.

Brown, G. W. (1989). Life events and measurement. In G. W. Brown & T. O. Harris (Eds.), *Life events and illness* (pp. 3–45). London: Guilford.

Brown, G. W., & Harris, T. O. (1978). *Social origins of depression: A study of psychiatric disorder in women.* New York: Free Press.

Brown, G. W., & Harris, T. O. (1986). Establishing causal links: The Bedford College studies of depression. In H. Katschnig (Ed.), *Life events and psychiatric disorders: Controversial issues* (pp. 107–187). Cambridge, England: Cambridge University Press.

Brown, G. W., & Harris, T. O. (1989a). Depression. In G. W. Brown & T. O. Harris (Eds.), *Life events and illness* (pp. 49–93). London: Guilford.

Brown, G. W. & Harris, T. O. (1989b). *Life events and illness.* London: Guilford.

Brown, S. A., Vik, P. W., McQuaid, J. R., Patterson, T. L., Irwin, M. R., & Grant, I. (1990). Severity of psychosocial stress and outcome of alcoholism treatment. *Journal of Abnormal Psychology, 99*, 344–348.

Cannon, W. B. (1932). *The wisdom of the body* (2nd ed.). New York: Norton.

Cooke, D. J. (1987). The psychological significance of life events as a cause of psychological and physical disorder. In B. Cooper (Ed.), *Psychiatric epidemiology: Progress and prospects* (pp. 67–80). London: Croon Helm.

Coyne, J. C., & Downey, G. (1991). Social factors and psychopathology: Stress, social support, and coping processes. *Annual Review of Psychology, 42*, 401–425.

Depue, R. A., & Monroe, S. M. (1986). Conceptualization and measurement of human disorder in life stress research: The problem of chronic disturbance. *Psychological Bulletin, 99*, 36–51.

Dohrenwend, B. P. (1974). Problems in defining and sampling the relevant population of stressful life events. In B. S. Dohrenwend & B. P. Dohrenwend (Eds.), *Stressful life events: Their nature and effects* (pp. 275–310). New York: Wiley-Interscience.

Dohrenwend, B. P., Krasnoff, L., Askenasy, A. R., & Dohrenwend, B. S. (1978). Exemplification of a method for scaling life events: The PERI life events scale. *Journal of Health and Social Behavior, 19*, 205–229.

Dohrenwend, B. P., Link, B. G., Kern, R., Shrout, P. E., & Markowitz, J. (1990). Measuring life events: The problem of variability within event categories. *Stress Medicine, 6*, 179–188.

Dohrenwend, B. S., & Dohrenwend, B. P. (1981). *Stressful life events and their contexts.* New York: Prodist.

Frank, E., Kupfer, D. J., Perel, J. M., Cornes, C., Jarrett, D. B., Mallinger, A. G., Thase, M. E., McEachran, A. B., & Grochocinski, V. J. (1990). Three-year outcomes for maintenance therapies in recurrent depression. *Archives of General Psychiatry, 47*, 1093–1099.

Ginsberg, S. M., & Brown, G. W. (1982). No time for depression: A study of help-seeking among mothers of preschool children. In D. Mechanic (Ed.), *Symptoms, illness behavior, and help-seeking* (pp. 87–114). New York: Prodist.

Hammen, C. (1991). Generation of stress in the course of unipolar depression. *Journal of Abnormal Psychology, 100*, 555–561.

Harris, T. O. (1989). Physical illness: An introduction. In G. W. Brown, & T. O. Harris (Eds.), *Life events and illness* (pp. 199–212). New York Guilford.

Hinkle, L. E., Jr. (1974). The concept of "stress" in the biological and social sciences. *International Journal of Psychiatry in Medicine, 5*, 335–357.

Hollon, S. D., Shelton, R. C., & Loosen, P. T. (1991). Cognitive therapy and pharmacotherapy for depression. *Journal of Consulting and Clinical Psychology, 59*, 88–99.

Holmes, T. H. (1979). Development and application of a quantitative measure of life change magnitude. In J. E. Barrett, R. M. Rose, & G. L. Klerman (Eds.), *Stress and mental disorder* (pp. 37–53). New York: Raven.

Holmes, T. H., & Rahe, R. H. (1967). The social readjustment rating scale. *Journal of Psychosomatic Research, 11*, 213–218.

Jackson, S. W. (1986). *Melancholia and depression.* New Haven, CT: Yale University Press.

Jenkins, C. D., Hurst, M. W., & Rose, R. M. (1979). Life changes: Do people really remember? *Archives of General Psychiatry, 36*, 379–384.

Katschnig, H. (1986). Measuring life-stress—a comparison of the checklist and the panel technique. In H. Katschnig (Ed.), *Life events and psychiatric disorders: Controversial issues* (pp. 74–106). Cambridge, England: Cambridge University Press.

Keller, M. B., Shapiro, R. W., Lavori, P. W., & Wolfe, N. (1982). Relapse in major depressive disorder: Analysis with the life table. *Archives of General Psychiatry, 39*, 689–694.

Kessler, R., Price, R. H., & Wortman, C. B. (1985). Social factors in psychopathology: Stress, social support, and coping processes. *Annual Review of Psychology, 36,* 531–572.

Kessler, R. C., & Wethington, E. (1991). The reliability of life event reports in a community survey. *Psychological Medicine, 21,* 723–738.

Kraepelin, E. (1921). *Manic-depressive insanity and paranoia.* Edinburgh: Livingstone.

Kupfer, D. J., & Frank, E. (1987). Relapse in recurrent depression. *American Journal of Psychiatry, 144,* 86–88.

Lazarus, R. S., & Folkman, S. (1984). *Stress, appraisal, and coping.* New York: Springer.

McFarlane, A. H., Norman, G. R., Streiner, D. L., & Roy, R. G. (1983). The process of social stress: Stable, reciprocal, and mediating relationships. *Journal of Health and Social Behavior, 24,* 160–173.

McQuaid, J. R., Monroe, S. M., Roberts, J. R., Johnson, S. L., Garamoni, G., Kupfer, D. J., & Frank, E. (1992). Toward the standardization of life stress assessment: Definitional discrepancies and inconsistencies in methods. *Stress Medicine, 8,* 47–56.

Miller, P. M., Dean, C., Ingham, J. G., Kreitman, N. B., Sashidharan, S. P., & Surtees, P. G. (1986). The epidemiology of life events and long-term difficulties, with some reflections on the concept of independence. *British Journal of Psychiatry, 148,* 686–696.

Miller, T. W. (1989). *Stressful life events.* Madison, CT: International Universities Press.

Mitchell, R. E., & Moos, R. H. (1984). Deficiencies in social support among depressed patients: Antecedents or consequences of stress? *Journal of Health and Social Behavior, 25,* 438–452.

Monroe, S. M. (1982a). Assessment of life events: Retrospective versus concurrent strategies. *Archives of General Psychiatry, 39,* 606–610.

Monroe, S. M. (1982b). Life events assessment: Current practices, emerging trends. *Clinical Psychology Review, 2,* 435–453.

Monroe, S. M. (1990). Psychosocial factors in anxiety and depression. In J. D. Maser & C. R. Cloninger (Eds.), *Comorbidity of mood and anxiety disorders* (pp. 463–497). Washington, DC: American Psychiatric Press.

Monroe, S. M., Bellack, A. S., Hersen, M., & Himmelhoch, J. M. (1983). Life events, symptoms course, and treatment outcome in unipolar depressed women. *Journal of Consulting and Clinical Psychology, 51,* 604–615.

Monroe, S. M., & Depue, R. A. (1991). Life stress and depression. In J. Becker & A. Kleinman (Eds.), *Psychosocial aspects of depression* (pp. 101–130). New York: Erlbaum.

Monroe, S. M., & Johnson, S. L. (1990). The dimensions of life stress and the specificity of disorder. *Journal of Applied Social Psychology, 20,* 1678–1694.

Monroe, S. M., Kupfer, D., & Frank, E. (1992). Life stress and treatment course in recurrent depression: I. Response during index episode. *Journal of Consulting and Clinical Psychology, 60,* 718–724.

Monroe, S. M., & Roberts, J. R. (1991). Psychopathology research. In M. Hersen, A. E. Kazdin, & A. S. Bellack (Eds.), *The clinical psychology handbook* (2nd ed., pp. 276–292). New York: Pergamon.

Monroe, S. M., Roberts, J. E., Kupfer, D. J., & Frank, E. (1992). *Life stress and treatment course in recurrent depression: II. The maintenance of recovery and of treatment participation over 3 years.* Unpublished manuscript.

Monroe, S. M., & Simons, A. D. (1991). Diathesis–stress theories in the context of life stress research: Implications for the depressive disorders. *Psychological Bulletin, 110,* 406–425.

Monroe, S. M., Simons, A. D., & Thase, M. E. (1991). Onset of depression and time to treatment entry: Roles of life stress. *Journal of Consulting and Clinical Psychology, 59,* 566–573.

Monroe, S. M., & Steiner, S. C. (1986). Social support and psychopathology: Interrelations with preexisting disorder, stress, and personality. *Journal of Abnormal Psychology, 95,* 29–39.

Monroe, S. M., Thase, M. E., Hersen, M., Bellack, A. S., & Himmelhoch, J. M. (1985). Life events and the endogenous–nonendogenous distinction in the treatment and post-treatment course of depression. *Comprehensive Psychiatry, 26,* 175–186.

Oei, T. I., & Zwart, F. M. (1986). The assessment of life events: Self-administered questionnaire versus interview. *Journal of Affective Disorders, 10,* 185–190.

Paykel, E. S. (1982). Life events and early environment. In E. S. Paykel (Ed.), *Handbook of affective disorders.* New York: Guilford.

Pollard, C. A., Pollard, H. J., & Corn, K. J. (1989). Panic onset and major events in the lives of agoraphobics: A test of continuity. *Journal of Abnormal Psychology, 98,* 318–321.

Pollock, K. (1988). On the nature of social stress: Production of a modern mythology. *Social Sciences and Medicine, 26,* 381–392.

Rabkin, J. G., & Struening, E. L. (1976). Life events, stress, and illness. *Science, 194,* 1013–1020.

Rees, W. L. (1976). Stress, distress disorder. *British Journal of Psychiatry, 128,* 2–18.

Reno, R. M., & Halaris, A. E. (1990). The relationship between life stress and depression in an endogenous sample. *Comprehensive Psychiatry, 31,* 25–33.

Robins, L. N., Locke, B. Z., & Regier, D. A. (1991). An overview of psychiatric disorders in America. In L. N. Robins & D. A. Regier (Eds.), *Psychiatric disorders in America: The Epidemiologic Catchment Area study* (pp. 328–366). New York: Free Press.

Rosen, G. (1959). Social stress and mental disease from the eighteenth century to the present: Some origins of social psychiatry. *The Millbank Memorial Fund Quarterly, 37,* 5–32.

Sarason, I. G., de Monchaux, C., & Hunt, T. (1975). Methodological issues in the assessment of life stress. In L. Levi (Ed.), *Emotions: Their parameters and measurement* (pp. 499–509). New York: Raven.

Selye, H. (1936). A syndrome produced by divers nocuous agents. *Nature, 138,* 32.

Shrout, P. E., Link, B. G., Dohrenwend, B. P., Skodol, A. E., Stueve, A., & Mirotznik, J. (1989). Characterizing life events as risk factors for depression: The role of fateful loss events. *Journal of Abnormal Psychology, 98,* 460–467.

Tennant, C., Bebbington, P. E., & Hurry, J. (1981). The role of life events in depressive illness: Is there a substantial causal relation? *Psychological Medicine, 11,* 379–389.

Thoits, P. A. (1982). Conceptual, methodological, and theoretical problems in studying social support as a buffer against life stress. *Journal of Health and Social Behavior, 23,* 145–159.

Ventura, J., Neuchterlein, K. N., Lukoff, D., & Hardesty, J. P. (1989). A prospective study of stressful life events and schizophrenic relapse. *Journal of Abnormal Psychology, 98,* 404–411.

Yager, J., Grant, I., Sweetwood, H. L., & Gerst, M. (1981). Life event reports by psychiatric patients, nonpatients, and their partners. *Archives of General Psychiatry, 38,* 343–347.

Zimmerman, M., Pfohl, B., & Stangl, D. (1986). Life events assessment of depressed patients: A comparison of self-report and interview formats. *Journal of Human Stress, 11,* 13–19.

Zimmerman, M., Pfohl, B., Coryell, W., & Stangl, D. (1987). The prognostic validity of DSM-III Axis IV in depressed inpatients. *American Journal of Psychiatry, 144,* 102–106.

III

Chronic Strains

4

Sampling the Stress Universe

BLAIR WHEATON

The word *stress* has many connotations. There are two quite distinct areas of ambiguity surrounding this term. One has to do with the stage of the stress process at which stress occurs. Some use *stress* to refer to the problems people face (the stimulus), others to refer to the generalized response to these problems (as in "psychological stress"), and still others to refer to a mediating state of the organism in response to threat that may or may not generalize (the black box between stimulus and generalized response). It may be helpful, therefore, to distinguish at the outset among *stressors, stress,* and *distress*—the stimulus problem, the processing state of the organism that remains unmapped in the psychosocial approach, and the generalized behavioral response. The term *strain* is also sometimes used to refer to stressors, but I use it, following its original meaning, to refer to the response side of the model.

The second area of ambiguity in using the term *stress* has to do with the content of stressors themselves. There are life change events (Holmes & Rahe, 1967), daily hassles (Kanner, Coyne, Schaefer, & Lazarus, 1981), role strains (Pearlin, 1983), ongoing difficulties (Brown & Harris, 1978), nonevents (Gersten, Langner, Eisenberg, & Orzeck, 1974), and various forms of childhood and adult traumas (Garmezy, 1983; Langner &

BLAIR WHEATON • Department of Sociology, University of Toronto, Toronto, Ontario, Canada M5T 1P9.
Stress and Mental Health: Contemporary Issues and Prospects for the Future, edited by William R. Avison and Ian H. Gotlib. New York, Plenum Press, 1994.

Michael, 1962) to consider as variations in the type of life problems referenced by the term *stressors*. This variation in the content of stressors is the subject of this chapter.

What is striking about the stress literature is its collective ability to use the term *stress* in a variety of ways, without apparent need for clarification of the relationships among types of stressors (discussions such as in Pearlin, 1989, being more an exception than the rule). When distinctions are made, inevitably it is to distinguish a type of stressor from the presumed core of the social stress concept: stressful life changes (Brown & Harris, 1978; Kanner et al., 1981). In fact, the differentiation in stress concepts has reached the point at which some clarification is crucial. Part of this clarification necessarily involves the notion that different stress concepts share certain core themes in common, yet occupy different parts of the overall realm of stress. Part implicitly involves the setting of boundaries for the stress concept.

It should be clear that the study of stress has been dominated by the thinking and specific examples of the life-events inventory approach. When the word *stress* is used in research circles, the most common operational link that gives expression to this word is the life change event, a discrete, observable, and (it is thought) objectively reportable event that requires some social and/or psychological adjustment on the part of the individual. Despite this association between life events and stress, however, it has always been true that certain more chronic, less discrete stressors have traditionally been included on life-events inventories, thus standing for the indirect measurement of a rather different type of stressor (Avison & Turner, 1988). These items often include the term *problems* in their wording, denoting an ongoing open-ended issue in the person's life. This kind of heterogeneity is a clue to the fact that there really are different kinds of stressors at work, with rather different modis operandi. An inappropriate conclusion would be that these items simply act as "noise" in the measurement of life events and thus get in the way of measuring stress properly.

LIFE EVENTS: THE MAKING OF A CONCEPT

A basic historical question is this: Where does the modern stress concept come from? From the many important publications of Bruce and Barbara Dohrenwend, we can focus on two that discuss the antecedents of their understanding of the concept of stress (Dohrenwend & Dohrenwend, 1970, 1974). Given the paramount importance of this work in the history of stress research, we see historical clues as to why stress has usually been restricted to the notion of life change events. They trace the intellectual lineage of their work on stress (1974, pp. 2–4) to the experiments of Cannon (1929) on the effects of pain, hunger, and emotions on bodily changes. The basic lesson of this work is that stimuli associated with emotional arousal cause changes in basic physiological processes.

This approach was formalized in Selye's (1956) classic work on stress. The biological stress model involves four components: (a) stressors, in Selye's approach both discrete (electric shock) and continuous (noise) in form; (b) conditioning factors that alter the impact of the stressor on the organism; (c) the adaptation syndrome, an intervening state of stress in the organism; and (d) responses, whether adaptive or maladaptive. Note that Selye's model is not exclusively focused on identifying stressors as changes in the environment. In applying this model, Dohrenwend and Dohrenwend (1970) then utilize a crucial distinction from Koos (1946) between "troubles" and exigencies of daily life—the former referring to situations that block the usual patterns of daily activities and call for new ones, the latter referring to the patterns that persist over time. At this point in the discussion, however, the notion of stress is restricted to issues which reflect change in the usual patterns of daily life. As Dohrenwend and Dohrenwend (1970) frankly state, "We limit the term stressor to objective events" (p. 115).

In a sense, the easily verifiable nature of events was a very attractive feature in the search for an operationalization of the concept of stress. The life events inventory of Holmes and Rahe (1967) provided a relatively easy to use, clear-cut, and objectively defined list of events that were also bound to the notion of stress as a traumatic insult to the organism in the classic Selye biological stress model. The life events inventory was a starting point for decades of research on stress; it made the concept of stress easy to incorporate into research plans, and it also conformed to a known theoretical model. In effect, one could say there was a happy marriage between model and measure. In fact, this inventory became so popular that it began to define the limits of the assumed concept. This subtle reversal of historical causation, in which the measure begins to imply the boundaries of the concept, has had the effect of limiting the legitimacy of other stress concepts. At the same time, it is clear that part of the concept of stress originally in the Selye model has been left behind—the part that focuses on continuous rather than event forms of stress. We often assume that stress implies change, but change is not a necessary condition of stress in the biological model.

THE ORIGINS OF THE STRESS CONCEPT RECONSIDERED

Warren K. Smith (1987) appropriately traces the original meaning of stress to physical mechanics, not biology. His discussion supports the idea that we have unintentionally excluded a large component of the stress concept. Smith notes that Selye borrowed the term *stress* from engineers but "neglected to take along its definition." (p. 215). This is not entirely true; rather, sociologists and psychologists applying the Selye model neglected to take along the complete definition. The important point often forgotten here is that Selye himself based his model on the definitions and distinctions of this earlier stress model.

In the engineering model, stress is defined as a force on a resisting body that may or may not operate within normative limits. To be precise, stress is defined as load in relation to capacity to resist, but the application of the stress concept in the human sciences has more often than not rejected this notion because it potentially confounds stress with coping capacity. The preferred approach is to consider coping capacity as a separate factor in the stress process model so that we may *discover* how it combines with stress loads.

Smith also notes that confusing stress with strain is, from the perspective of his model, confusing the input problem with the output response. The analogue in our models for strain is in fact distress (or disorder), the mental health response to the stressor. In metallurgy, elongation and compression of a material constitute instances of strain caused by excessive loads applied to the material. There is also temporary strain, which results from "usual forces" on the material. The distinction here is that usual forces occur within the elastic limit of the material—that is, the material is able to bounce back to its original shape. This in turn allows for a distinction between normative and excessively stressful pressure: A permanent strain response appears when forces exceed the elastic limit strength of the material. The analogy is that individuals have an elastic limit, perhaps varying over time, but distress/illness will occur when stress levels exceed the elastic limit of the individual at any given point in time.

This brings us to an essential distinction of the engineering model: a distinction between catastrophic forces and continuous forces as two kinds of stress loads. This distinction is not offered to distinguish between stressors and other kinds of force; rather, it is a distinction between subclasses of stressors. The utility of this distinction derives from the fact that catastrophic forces act as sudden impacts on the resisting material, whereas continuous forces act as an insidious, wearing force that slowly but increasingly challenges the capacity of the material. To paraphrase another metaphor for this distinction, if catastrophic forces act like a hammer, then continuous forces act like a slow poison (Wheaton, 1983). To blur this distinction is to obscure the fact that very different kinds of coping are called for. Of course, the catastrophic force of mechanics maps easily to life events, and the continuous force maps easily to another kind of stress: chronic stressors.

If we believe that this original stress model more fully represents the concept of stress, then a shift away from the more historically proximal work of Selye to the physical stress model is in order when citing a logic for the concepts and measures of stress we use. This model is more than an analogy: it provides a basis for definition, and for articulation of the boundaries of the stress concept.

EVENT VERSUS CHRONIC STRESSORS

Gersten et al. (1974) use arousal theory to suggest the need for the specification of stressors beyond the notion of an "event." They note that some "arousal is necessary for the maintenance of efficient behavior; the well-documented inverse U-shaped function between arousal and behavior efficiency attests to this. . . . Accordingly, maladaptive behavior would occur either at levels of extremely low arousal (change) or extremely high arousal (change)" (p. 167). Although unaware of this particular rationale for expansion of the realm of stress beyond an event-based logic, I echoed these thoughts in a later paper: "Stress can result either from too much change or too little change—in the former case, when an individual is exposed to a number of difficult or undesirable life changes, and in the latter case, when an individual is exposed to continuously difficult or demanding environments that do not change" (Wheaton, 1983, pp. 209–210).

These statements make clear that a large part of what is stressful remains both unspecified and unmeasured. The main component left out involves stressors that are inherently more continuous, ongoing, and insidious in onset than discrete life events. These stressors (a) do not necessarily start as an event but develop as continuing problematic conditions in our social environments and roles, and (b) typically have a longer time course than life events from onset to resolution. Among a large set of alternative possibilities, I choose to use the term *chronic stressors* to refer to the missing part of the realm.

The distinction at issue refers to characteristics of stressors as stimuli and does not imply anything about how long-term or serious the consequences may be. The crux of the distinction between event stressors and their more continuous counterpart is the time course of the stressor, but there is more involved, including differences in the ways in which the stressor develops, exists, and ends. The term *chronic* has been applied less to designate a time course presumptuously than to designate the fact that this subclass of stressors will have a typical time course very unlike that of an event. Chronic stressors are continuous stressors in an approximate sense, standing for problems and issues that are either so regular in the enactment of daily roles and activities, or so defined by the nature of daily role enactments or activities, that they behave as if they are continuous for the individual.

Chronic stressors are less self-limiting in nature than the typical life event. A life event almost by definition will end, but chronic stressors are typically open-ended, using our resources in coping without promising resolution. Although chronic stress is most often associated with the problem of overload, it is more than that. Most generally, it arises from one of an array of problems: not only excessive task or role demand but also excessive complexity, uncertainty, conflict, restriction of choice, underreward, or personal threat. These are "the enduring problems, conflicts, and threats that many people face in their daily lives" (Pearlin, 1989, p. 245).

A typical chronic stressor is represented in Figure 1, along with a typical discrete event stressor. The onset of the chronic stressor is gradual, the course long-term and continuous (not a string of events), and the offset problematic and often unpredictable. If we were to envision the perfect opposite of this kind of stress (also in Figure 1), we would have a traumatic event that occurs suddenly, without warning, reflecting a clear and discretely defined onset. The actual length of the stressor would be short-term, followed by a definite resolution.

There is, of course, the inevitable fact that some life events will be more chronic than others, and some chronic stressors will act more like discrete problems. This overlap in phenomenology is not at issue. Event and chronic stressors represent two large and distinct classes (i.e., the trajectories in Figure 1 represent modal patterns).

If we imagine a spliced curve in Figure 1, starting like the event but continuing like the chronic stressor, we would have the perfect borderline case. But in many cases this situation will actually be describing two stressors, not one. The distinction between event and chronic stressors allows us to distinguish the effects of *getting* divorced from *being* divorced. Stressors are confounded if we think of this only as "getting a divorce." The process of living as a single parent after the divorce is a distinct issue to be faced. The entry into the single parent role causes, for many but not all, a corresponding increase in the level of demand on

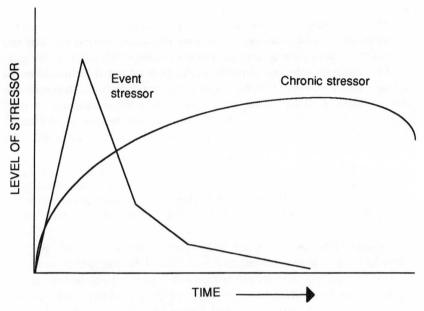

Figure 1. The natural history of event versus chronic stressors.

the person's daily functioning capacities: The task levels stay the same, but it is spread across fewer persons. This is the stressor in this case, not the divorce. Keeping the stressors separate allows one to distinguish between the problems of identity loss and identity adjustment, on the one hand, and the problems of continual vigilance and pressure, on the other. Put another way, one is distinguishing between the loss of a spouse and the abstract absence of a partner as two stressors.

THE STRESS CONTINUUM

The Evolution of Stress Concepts

There are a number of coexisting concepts in the current stress literature. The distinction between events and continuous stressors is fundamental, however, because it allows the classification of other stress concepts along a continuum describing the phenomenology of the stressor. First, however, we must make clear the distinguishing features of each type of stress concept as it has been articulated in the literature.

Chronic Stress

There are many sources for the notion of chronic stress within the stress literature. Two obviously formative discussions are in Brown and Harris (1978) and Pearlin and Schooler (1978).

The former refer to chronic stressors as life "difficulties" to be distinguished from events. Their approach to this distinction is straightforward: life events are problems that occur at a "discrete point in time" (Brown & Harris, 1978, p. 130), but this cannot be the only kind of adversity people face. This other kind of stress is described with the following scenario:

> A woman living for three years in two small damp rooms with her husband and two children would not have been picked up by our measure of events unless her situation has led to some kind of crisis in the year. . . . There clearly is no theoretical justification for dealing with such situations only when they give rise to a crisis. (p. 130)

This observation leads Brown and Harris to consider a set of "ongoing difficulties" such as an increase in a husband's drinking (which can occur slowly over time), a partner's chronic health problem, a son's drug taking, and sexual unfulfillment. Brown and Harris find that such ongoing difficulties have importance independent of life events in predicting depression.

Pearlin (1983) outlines a series of components of "role strain" that point to a number of foundations for chronic stress. He argues convincingly for the importance of roles as "potent sources of stress" (p. 5), in part because people organize their daily activities in terms of role boundaries and attach importance to their role identities. Pearlin outlines six types of role strain, many of which are central to what we think of as chronic stress. They include (a) the nature of role tasks and role demands (e.g., externally imposed overload); (b) inequity in role resources or rewards (e.g., the level of reward in a role in relation to effort or skills invested); (c) failure of reciprocity in roles, frequently the basis for interpersonal conflict; (d) role conflict resulting from inconsistencies of the demand structure of different roles; (e) role captivity, focusing on the problems of desiring exit from a role situation when it is not possible; and (f) role restructuring, including the effects of reallocations of responsibilities and expectations within existing roles. This last feature of role strain may or may not be a feature of chronic stress, depending on whether one focuses on the restructuring per se (an event) or the fact that restructuring often results in higher demand loads on individuals or expectations that do not match the individual's skills.

It should be clear by now that the term *chronic stress* is not coextensive with the term *role strain*, although the two are often used inter-changeably. In a later discussion, Pearlin (1989) explicitly uses the term *chronic stress* to include not only role strains but also "ambient strains" that cannot be attached to any one role situation. The importance of this point cannot be overstated. If chronic stress is tied only to the notion of role strain, then role occupancy becomes conceptually confounded with, and a necessary condition of, the experience of chronic stress. This is unfortunate insofar as selection into major roles in which strain is measured—marital, parental, work, and so forth—is partly based on social competence. This social-competence component could act as a suppressor in assessing the effects of total role strain.

This point can be elaborated to suggest that there are in fact four subcomponents of chronic stress (Wheaton, 1991). There are (a) stressors attributable to role occupancy, as in the classic work on role strains, but there are also (b) stressors attributable to role inoccupancy, as in the problems resulting from not having children when you want to, or not being in a relationship when you want to. In addition, there are stressors that are best called (c) role-defining strains, stressors that do not result from role engagement but precipitate it, as in the appearance of a chronic illness or the entry into an intrinsically difficult social role situation (e.g., a single parent). Finally, there are (d) ambient strains, stressors that are not role bound but instead are socially diffuse and general in origin (e.g., a recession, residential living space difficulties, time pressure, or social complexity). I have developed an instrument to measure chronic stress in which all of these possibilities are represented (Wheaton, 1991). Typical items include "You're trying to take on too many things at once" (ambient–overload), "You don't have enough money to buy the things you or your kids need" (role strain), "You have a lot of conflict with your boss or coworkers" (role strain–interpersonal conflict), "You don't get paid enough for what you do" (role strain–underreward), "Your relationship restricts your freedom" (role strain–role captivity), "You find it is too difficult to find someone compatible with you" (strain attributable to role inoccupancy–complexity; asked of singles only), "You cannot see your children enough due to divorce or separation" (parental role strain–restriction of choice), "You are often afraid you will be mugged, assaulted, or robbed" (ambient–threat), and "Someone in your family has an alcohol or drug problem" (role strain).

Daily Hassles

A concept that is often mistaken for chronic stress is daily hassles (Kanner et al., 1981). Judging what daily hassles are at the core can be difficult, because the measure of daily hassles includes a number of indicators of both mediators and outcomes in the stress process model (Dohrenwend, Dohrenwend, Dodson, & Shrout, 1984). The rationale for considering daily hassles, however, starts with the same concern of this chapter: the emphasis in the stress literature on events and crises as the sole basis for defining stress.

The alternative focus for Kanner et al. (1981) is on "the relatively minor stresses . . . that characterize everyday life" (p. 2). Here we see the introduction of another important dimension that has often been used to distinguish stressors but at the same time crosscuts the distinction between discrete and chronic: namely, a distinction between micro- and macro-level stressors. Hassles are defined as "the irritating, frustrating, distressing demands that to some degree characterize everyday transactions with the environment" (p. 3). The qualifying phrase "to some degree" is important. It is possible to argue that there is considerable variability in the degree to which the daily hassles used in measures are regular features of daily life. Interestingly, the examples of daily hassles given by Kanner et al. as examples—work overload, status incongruity between spouses, noise—*are* chronic stressors, but significantly, they are not at all typical of what is measured in the Daily Hassles Scale.

This scale itself has been the subject of some controversy. Complaints that a significant number of items are really measures of other concepts in the stress process model, including outcomes such as distress, seem all too valid (Dohrenwend et al., 1984). Items such as "thoughts about death," "use of alcohol," "trouble making decisions," "being lonely," "not getting enough sleep," "not enough personal energy," and "nightmares" are very clearly measures of distress or related concepts—many of these items existing in almost the same form on well-known distress scales. Other items sound very much like life events and should not be included as daily hassles per se (e.g., "laid off or out of work," "problems with divorce or separation"), while a large number indeed reflect standard chronic stress items but have little to do with the stated definition of daily hassles as daily minor stresses (e.g., "not enough money for basic necessities," "difficulties getting pregnant," "overload with family responsibilities," and "prejudice and discrimination from others").

The problem with this measure, then, is that it attempts to be too inclusive while starting from a clear but more delimited conceptual mandate—the minor but regular annoyances of day-to-day life. In the research to be reported later, I include a highly edited version of the Daily Hassles Scale, focusing on the 25 out of the original 117 hassles that seemed to me to operationalize the thinking behind daily hassles most straightforwardly. These include such items as "troublesome neighbors," "misplacing or losing things," "inconsiderate smokers," "care for a pet," "planning meals," "repairing things around the house," "having to wait," "too many interruptions," "preparing meals," "filling out forms," "the weather," and "traffic problems." It may be that distress causally increases the perception of such hassles, but that is not at issue: What is at issue here is the problem of measurement confounding per se. Causal confounding is a separate issue and should not be a consideration in deciding whether an item is indeed an operationalization of a concept.

I believe that daily hassles as operationalized in the reduced scale stand for a unique and important area of stress that is not tapped by the more general conceptualizations for chronic and event stressors. What is unique about this concept, however, is not the measurement of nonevent stressors; rather, its contribution is the specification of a level of social reality at which other stressors are not usually specified. The concerns expressed in these items—grocery shopping, traffic jams, caring for a pet—nicely express the mundane realities of daily life that, when experienced cumulatively, may be annoying and stressful. But note that they do not consistently refer only to *regular* features of daily life. Some items clearly refer to the almost automatic or ritualized concerns of daily life and thus may be more chronic in their manifestations (e.g., troublesome neighbors, preparing meals, grocery shopping). Such issues are defined as chronic by the unavoidability of their enactment, which is only one of the themes in a more general chronic stress concept. At the same time, a number of these items refer to more episodic, irregular microevents that cannot be anticipated daily and only occur contingently (e.g., "misplacing or losing things," "having to wait," "the weather," "traffic problems"). In the case of each of these items, the usual scenario would be that the problem occurs at some times and not at others, and usually unpredictably. These items measure something that would be better termed micro-events than chronic daily stresses.

Analyzing the content of the least confounded daily-hassles items reveals an important characteristic of this measure: It contains references to stressors that span the realm of both events and more chronic problems. This means that daily hassles are not essentially a measure of one type of stressor or the other. Thus it is misleading to represent these stressors as an alternative to life events, because (a) they contain event-like stressors, and (b) when the stressors measured are more chronic, the level of social reality sampled by the items focuses on the mundane concerns of daily life.

A closely related approach to stress comes under the rubric of "daily diary" studies (Bolger, Delongis, Kessler, & Schilling, 1989; Stone & Neale, 1984). Here stresses are measured because they are observed daily, but again not because they are predominantly chronic concerns or daily events. Both types of stressors can be included in these studies. Stone and Neale (1984) identify a set of severe daily events, some of which *are* purely events (e.g., a child getting sick or injured) and some of which can be enactments of more general chronic stressors (e.g., an argument with a spouse). Bolger et al. (1989), in contrast, focus primarily on manifestations of more chronic stressors, specifically role overloads and conflicts and arguments. These daily problems may or may not be chronic, of course, but they are usually treated as problematic over time because they stand for the potential of daily enactments. Thus daily-diary studies also do not specify a *type* of stressor exclusively along the stress continuum: They can include sporadic or unusual events, as well as regularly enacted, feared, or expected events that reflect the presence of a chronic problem or role condition. This does not mean that these studies have nothing unique to offer. In fact, they offer a methodological platform for studying the effects of stress on mood that few studies can achieve, because they allow for detailed time series that can sort out the interplay of specific stressors and distress over time.

Macrostressors

If there are such things as microstressors, then there must be macrostressors as well. In the previous section, I refer to microstressors based on a time referent for dividing up the concerns of life, starting from daily, and implying issues that are conceived of in larger time chunks (e.g., bad work situation). Units of analysis can also be divided by level of social reality. *Daily hassles* refer to stressors that occur at the experienced juncture of daily life and microsocial routines. At the other extreme, we have what may be called *system stressors*. These are stressors that occur at the macro or social system level and, almost by nature, cannot be considered features of daily life at the interpersonal level. The predominant focus in this approach has been the issue of economic recessions, usually embodied in studies of the unemployment rate (Brenner, 1974; Dooley & Catalano, 1984). A number of other system stressors qualify and can be included, however, such as the divorce rate, infant deaths, high school dropout rate, and disasters (Linsky, Colby, & Straus, 1987). As a group, then, these stressors contain both event and chronic concerns.

The point here is the same as for microstressors. The stresses specified in this approach point to a level of analysis that uniquely identifies stressors that otherwise would not be identified, but they may be either events (disasters) or chronic (recessions) in their manifestation. It is important to add that the micro–macro distinction highlights stressors that are not studied enough in the stress literature.

Nonevents

As noted above, Gersten et al. (1974) use arousal theory to point out that lack of change can be as stressful as change. They use this point, however, to suggest the importance not of chronic stressors, but of a closely related kind of stressor that they term *nonevents*. They define a nonevent as an "event that is desired or anticipated and does not occur. . . . Alternatively, a nonevent could be seen as something desirable which does not occur when its occurrence is normative for people of a certain group" (p. 169). Thus an anticipated promotion that does not occur, or not being married by age 35 when you want to be, can be considered stressful nonevents. These examples raise the clear possibility that nonevents are a form of chronic stressor. But nonevents also have the strange quality of seeming like events at the same time; this is clearly stated in Gersten et al.'s definition. This quality is clearest in the case of nonevents that reflect the absence of specific expected events— like a scheduled promotion, or hoping to get pregnant but failing.

Nonevents that derive from nontransitions to desired roles, however, seem more clearly like classic chronic stressors. Even the absence of promotion can be seen as role captivity, the inability to leave or alter a given role situation. The primary issue in defining this set of stressors is dissatisfaction with things as they are. Seen from this perspective, they look very much like a type of chronic stressor.

In a recent study I asked respondents to report any desired and expected things that did not happen in the last year. A wide array of answers were given, many of which qualified as classic nonevents: a husband finishing his studies, a loan for low-income housing, an improved relationship with a parent, a planned trip, higher marks in school, and so forth. Many of these issues reflect chronic ongoing issues in which the person has problems with the current state of affairs, and thus the lack of change is stressful.

Traumas

There are stressors that are thought to be so overwhelming in their impact that we must give them separate status to distinguish them from the usual class of events that we designate as stressful. The most applicable term for these stressors is *traumas,* although this term has the unfortunate connotation of physical damage, which is not implied. These are the spectacular, horrifying, or just deeply disturbing experiences of life that a relative few experience, but most who do experience some impact, even if it is short-lived. There are many different forms traumas can take, including war stress (Laufer, Gallops, & Frey-Wouters, 1984), sniper fire (Pynoos, 1987), nuclear accidents (Kasl, Chisolm, & Eskenazi, 1981), natural disasters (Erickson, 1981), and sexual abuse during childhood.

The only truly distinguishing feature of traumas is the level of imputed seriousness of the stressor—an order of magnitude beyond what is included on life-event or role strain scales. Some events on life-event inventories (e.g., death of a child) would in fact qualify as traumas. There is no clear-cut division, only the obvious fact that many traumatic experiences are not measured in life-event approaches, presumably because they are too rare.

There are traumas that may be less rare, such as growing up with an alcoholic parent. It is clear, however, that it will often be difficult to assess the effects of individual traumas in general population studies unless the sample size is very large. Two strategies make the study of traumas more tractable: study of specialized samples selected for the experience of the trauma, or study of a number of traumas simultaneously so that cumulative exposure can be studied even if the effects of individual traumas cannot. In a recent study I used 8 questions with an open-ended follow-up to detect traumatic experiences in childhood. The questions asked about a range of issues, from hospitalization for more than a week during childhood to parental divorce, parental death, repeating a year of school, any terrifying event that caused the person to think about it for years after, and having parents with a drinking or drug problem. In addition, open-ended responses were coded for issues such as physical or sexual abuse, witnessing violence, natural disasters, and experience in a war or revolution zone while growing up.

As in previous cases, the actual stressors that qualify as traumas range widely from sudden events to chronic long-term issues. The Three Mile Island nuclear leak, a flood, a rape, and parental divorce are examples of event traumas. But regular physical abuse, living with an alcoholic spouse, and war combat are examples of chronic traumas.

Stage of Life Issues

One other distinction has been used to classify stressors that may be important in considering their impact: the stage of life at which they occur. Usually the main distinction used here is between childhood and adult life stage stress experiences. The rationale for this explicit consideration of certain stages of life is often that stressors in childhood will be particularly virulent in their long-term impacts because they occur at a formative and therefore vulnerable stage in the life course (Garmezy, 1983; Rutter, 1983). In the classic midtown Manhattan study, Langner and Michael (1962) used a cumulative stress score based on certain childhood conditions and experiences to predict eventual adult adjustment. They identified a set of crucial distinguishing features of individuals with worse versus better adult mental health: childhood "broken homes," poor physical or mental health of parents, economic deprivation, poor relations with parents, and marital discord between parents. Note that some of these refer to events, whereas others refer to chronic childhood problems. Standard measures of childhood stressors, however, often emphasize primarily discrete events as the souce of stress (e.g., the Life Events Schedule for Children; Coddington, 1984).

The notion that stage in the life course will alter the stress potential of events, traumas, or chronic problems is an idea that must be considered in stress research more regularly and more explicitly. The life-course perspective directs our attention to the fact that stress exposure accumulates in a biography over a lifetime. It is likely that the timing of stressors, their clustering, and the match in content of stressors over time will have a major influence on their cumulative impact on adult mental health.

The Mapping of Stressors

The preceding discussion identifies a basic continuum of level of discreteness that can be used to distinguish most types of stressors, often crosscutting other ways of dividing up the stress universe. It is also clear from the review that there are at least three other important dimensions to consider: (a) a macro–micro dimension, identifying the unit of analysis at which the stressor occurs; (b) a life-course dimension, focusing on the timing of stressors and the importance of developmental stage of life; and (c) a dimension of imputed seriousness of the stressor as a class. The discreteness issue is treated as fundamental, however, because it describes essential differences in the ways stressors operate as problems.

We can use the discreteness continuum as a way of initially classifying types of stressors along a single dimension. My purpose is to suggest an organization of stress concepts that makes clear their relationships to each other in a conceptual universe of stressors. My initial assumption is that we should keep different stress concepts separate in order to show how stress accumulates and how stressors are interrelated.

Figure 2 shows the stress continuum from the most discrete to the most continuous stressors, with typical stressors of each type placed at some point on this continuum. Stressors are represented at the average

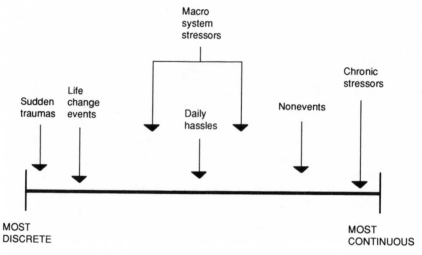

Figure 2. The stress continuum.

point of their operation as a class. Obviously, some of these types of stressors are more variable than others. At the most discrete end, we have sudden traumas. Although traumas come in many forms and with a variety of natural histories, I have used this subtype to specify what we can think as the most discrete form of stress. This class of stressor involves the kinds of single, unanticipated, overwhelming event experiences that seem particularly discrete because the onset and offset of the stressor are usually so short-term in nature. In this class of stressors I place natural disasters; sexual assaults; unexpected deaths of parents, children, or partners; victimization in a violent crime; and severe accidents.

Life events are represented as slightly less discrete on average than sudden traumas. This represents the fact that although many life events have a self-limiting time course with an inevitable resolution, they also take considerable lengths of time to reach this resolution. Individuals who rate the beginning and end points of events clearly see these events as occurring over a time period (Avison & Turner, 1988). The most obvious cases that qualify in this category are divorces, serious illnesses, unwanted pregnancies, being sued by someone, going on welfare, moving to a worse neighborhood, and having a child move back into the house. Some of the classic life events, it should be noted, are more like traumas in terms of discreteness; besides deaths, these include losing a home through fire or disaster, getting physically attacked, and getting fired from a job.

Daily hassles occupy an ambiguous middle ground on this continuum. They are the true borderline problem in this scheme. These problems seem best conceived as microevents built into the fabric of daily life, some occurring ritually and regularly and others episodically and contingently. At the same time, it is also clear that they do not refer to major chronic life problems or major life events. Their unique focus is on the accumulation of the mundane into something that may be important.

Macro or system stressors are represented as a particularly variable type of stressor, as they should be, given that the unit of analysis is their defining characteristic. Figure 2 shows this variability by centering the average discreteness in the middle, as for daily hassles, but representing this discreteness as occurring over a range around this midpoint. If we consider just two examples, war and recession, we will understand this representation: Both may be chronic (as in the Vietnam War and the Great Depression), but there are military and economic events that are system level and very acute in nature. A military coup is a system-level traumatic event; a stock market crash is the same thing in the economic sphere.

The continuous end of the continuum is occupied by nonevents and major chronic stressors, in that order. Nonevents are most simply understood as manifestations of chronic conditions that do not change, and thus are close to the continuous end. As a stressor, however, they do show one characteristic of events: Because they refer to expected or desired events, the nonevent is itself like an event—and thus nonevents are placed closer to the discrete end of the continuum than chronic stressors. Finally, chronic stressors are represented as the most consistently continuous form of stress. In the data I have analyzed evaluating a new measure of chronic stress (Wheaton, 1991), the estimated average chronicity of chronic stressors as a group is more than 5 years.

Although Figure 2 makes clear the relative chronicity of classes of stressors, the conceptual interrelationships among stressors could be clarified further by cross-classifying each class of stressor on two dimensions simultaneously. This is done in Figure 3. In Figure 3a, stressors are cross-classified by discreteness and unit of analysis. In Figure 3b, they are cross-classified by discreteness and stage in the life course. The classifications straightforwardly reflect the preceding discussion.

The discussion to this point suggests that stressors come in a variety of types and manifestations. The purpose of this discussion has been to clarify the conceptual relationships among stressors. But the discussion

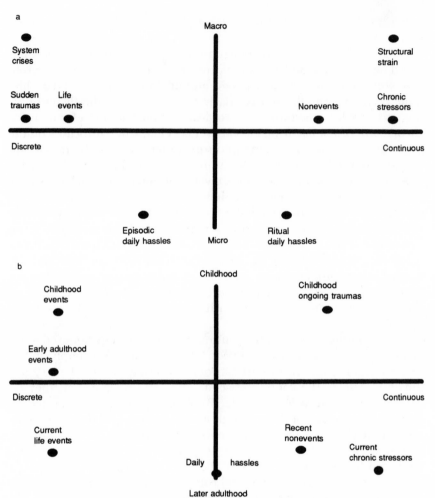

Figure 3. Cross-classifying types of stressors.

does raise two essential empirical questions. First, do stressors operate independently of each other in affecting health outcomes, or are the effects of some stressors spurious reflections of more basic and essential stress experiences? Second, how are stressors related to each other? Together, these questions can be characterized as a search for a possible "cornerstone" type of stress from which the effects of most other type of stressors flow.

THE CUMULATIVE EFFECTS OF STRESSORS

In this section I will assess the effects of six sources of stressors: (a) childhood traumas (in the available data a mix of primarily events and a few chronic childhood issues); (b) current chronic stressors, using a 90-item chronic stress inventory from Wheaton (1991); (c) life events in the last year, using a standard life-event list; (d) current daily hassles, using the 25-item edited list discussed above; (e) nonevents in the last year; and (f) earlier adulthood life events, reported as occurring after the person leaves home but before the most recent 2 years. The actual items for these measures were discussed by example in the previous section. This list of stressors does not exhaust all of the possibilities, but it nonetheless represents a more comprehensive list of sources of stress than is usually (perhaps ever) found in the stress literature.

Data

A study was conducted in two large Canadian cities and one smaller city in 1989 to assess the predictive validity of chronic stressors in relation to other types of stressors in predicting a range of health outcomes, with emphasis on distress, DSM-III-R diagnoses of depression and generalized anxiety disorder, drinking, smoking, drug use, and a wide range of physical health problems. The sample was a random cluster sample of each city, with the clusters defined by census subdivisions (CSDs) of Statistics Canada. Random start points within clusters were generated from a sample of blocks in each cluster, using an appropriate skip for households to generate a sample of 530. Within households, adults over the age of 18 were randomly selected after application of an algorithm for listing eligibility and random selection of a number within the listing. Sex was stratified so that successive cases alternated genders, resulting in an even number of men and women in the sample. After taking into account ineligible addresses, language barrier problems, and "no contacts," the response rate was a somewhat low 64%. This low rate is in part because the research organization did not encourage more than two callbacks or elaborate methods for converting refusals. The sample requirement was fulfilled within each cluster, however, and thus representativeness may have been maintained even in the face of sample loss. In fact, the sample shows no special characteristics in terms of demographic distributions when compared with Statistics Canada aggregate statistics for each CSD.

Measures

Other than standard demographics and family background measures, the following measures were included.

Outcomes

The interview included a wide variety of questions tapping mental health outcomes. A 37-item distress scale was used consisting of well-known items from various existing scales, including the Langner 22-item index (Langner, 1962), the CES-D (Radloff, 1977), and the SCL-90 (Derogatis, Lipman, Rickels, Uhlenhuth, & Covi, 1974). The purpose of this approach was to collect some of the central and most useful items from a number of scales, rather than accept the limitations of each, and to choose items that filled in content gaps and omissions in any one scale. The result is what appears to be a very effective measure of distress: It factor analyzes as one factor (with loadings varying smoothly from a high of .67 to a low of .40), it is very reliable (with an α of .93), and it acts essentially like other distress scales except that findings for well-known relationships appear to be a little stronger. The interview also included the DSM-III-R sections for depression and generalized anxiety, so that diagnostic measures could be derived.

There were also questions about frequency of smoking, quantity of alcoholic intake per week, and frequency of taking nonprescription drugs. Questions about physical health focused on 27 physical ailments and diseases that ranged from acute and nonserious to life-threatening to chronic but not life-threatening. A standard question about general health was also included, asking the respondent to rate his or her health on a scale from excellent to very poor.

Sources of Stress

Most of the measures of stress used here come from well-known sources. This is not true of the childhood traumas measure and the chronic stress measure. The measure of childhood traumas was derived from the discussions of Rutter (1983) and Garmezy (1983) on significant childhood stressors, as well as from the earlier work of Langner and Michael (1962). In addition, a few questions were developed specifically for this study. A follow-up open-ended question was used to ask about other traumatic events; these were coded and included when appropriate responses were given. The chronic stress measure is a 90-item chronic stress inventory discussed in detail elsewhere (Wheaton, 1991). The items fall into 12 areas: financial issues, general or ambient problems, work, marriage and relationship, parental issues, family, social life, residence, crime and legal matters, religion, schooling, and health.

The items are subjectively reported life conditions and situations. I have argued (Wheaton, 1991) that the subjective component in these stressors is an inherent part of what the stressors are, and thus measurement approaches should take this subjectivity into account rather than attempt to circumvent it. It is clear that some of the items on the chronic stress inventory have objective social referents, and others do not. The clearest case is in the work area; the item "Your work is boring and repetitive" can be validated by use of the Dictionary of Occupational Titles (DOT) by checking the descriptors attached to the person's occupation, as suggested by Kessler (1983). But there is no DOT for marriage types. A major task in this area is to attach subjective reports, where possible, to objective referents (e.g., living alone and reporting being alone to much). Ultimately, however, there are problems with many external referents for validation (living alone may be very desirable for some), and there are many areas in which it is difficult to imagine what the objective referent is or how it can be practically measured or observed (e.g., "Too much is expected of you by others," "Your spouse doesn't understand you," "Your family lives too far away"). For a young person who has had a problematic relationship with his or her parents while at home, moving 500 miles away may not be far enough, but for a young newlywed couple who are close to their families, 5 miles across town may be too far.

These problems suggest that the search for objective referents may not be as generally useful as one would hope. In contrast, the advantage of subjective reports of chronic stress is that they allow shorthand reference to a complex objective social reality, and more importantly, they probably do reflect realities that we would consider objectively stressful. Though such subjective reports cannot be considered to be veridical reflections of reality, it would just as misleading to reach the opposite conclusion (i.e., that they are illusions constructed simply to justify the rest of our psychological experience). To address the issues of subjectivity and the possibilities of measurement and causal confounding with outcomes, I conducted three analyses. First, I estimated a series of confirmatory factor analytic models to establish the relative plausibility of one- versus two-factor models for sets of distress and chronic stress items. In all cases, the two-factor model was clearly superior and justified, suggesting the measurement integrity of assuming separate concepts. In fact, in no case did the factor loading of a chronic stress item on a distress factor reach as high as .30.

Second, I estimated a series of models to detect reciprocal causation between chronic stress and distress, on the assuumption that the presence of distress would also either increase the perception of chronic stress or actually help produce higher levels of chronic stress in the environment. Reciprocal causation held for most types of chronic stress, but in all cases the effect of chronic stress on distress survived and was not attenuated compared to simpler models assuming unidirectional causation. Finally, I investigated relationships between individual items on the chronic stress scale and any external referent information that might help validate these reports: DOT job codes, other chronic stress scales in the survey (Pearlin & Schooler, 1978), associated life events, associated role statuses and conditions, and so forth. The evidence points to a widespread pattern of linkage between the subjective reports and other more objectively based referents.

How Many Stress Concepts Do We Need?

The theoretical discussions earlier, focusing on the distinctions among stressors, will be of little use if we find that one or a few stressors basically explain the effects of most others. In this section, I assess the empirical need to consider a variety of stress concepts, from childhood traumas to an adult life history of major life change events to current chronic stressors to daily hassles to recent nonevents. The empirical issue is simple: do stressors have independent effects on mental health outcomes, or are the effects of some stressors subsumed by the effects of others?

To assess the simultaneous effects of six sources of stress, I used a stepwise regression approach—a crude but direct competition among predictors. This only gets at the direct impacts of stressors, but we can elaborate our concerns later to include the *total* effects of stressors. In this approach, I considered as the six predictors a count of nonevents over the last year, a set of chronic stressors reported as currently ongoing, a count of life events in the last year, current daily hassles, life events reported as occurring before the last two years but during adulthood, and childhood traumas. Note that one could also consider these stressors in more disaggregated form, focusing on which stressors of each type are important. To see the overall patterns, however, I concentrate here primarily on aggregated specifications of each type of stressor.

This is to some degree a decision born of necessity. Individual childhood traumas are not very prevalent, and thus only a small minority report each experience. Totaling exposure in this area is done for essentially the same reason it is done with life events. Daily hassles only make sense in the aggregate, but chronic stressors and even subareas of life events might be considered separately. Because of the wide dispersion of issues addressed in the chronic stress inventory, I felt it was especially likely that a total count approach might not effectively represent the effects of chronic stress exposure. This practice might suppress some of the effect of these stressors because (a) some areas of stress may have much less of an effect on mental health than others, and (b) different kinds of stress issues will be important for different people. Thus I considered chronic stress as a set of stress indices in nine areas (pooling responses in major roles, for example) supplemented with a set of 18 chronic stress items that did not fit into these indices and looked potentially important to mental health outcomes in initial screening of effects. The individual measures of chronic stress are shown in Table 1.

To assess total chronic stress impacts, I expressed the individual effects as a weighted total, basing the weights on the relative effects of individual chronic stress measures on the mental health outcome under consideration. This is basically a way of stating the combined effects of the chronic stressors in the model. I found in all results that consideration of the weighted set of chronic stressors led to much more powerful prediction of outcomes than use of the traditional total count approach —an increase in predictive power of from 30% to 50%. This means, essentially, that chronic stressors need to be considered as a set of differentiated issues. At the same time, if one wants to get a sense of their total impact, as I did here, one can still combine their individual effects using the weighted-effects approach to express more fairly the total impact. Because I wanted to give all stressors equal opportunity in this regard, I also considered subsets of life events, divided among relationship losses, victimization, financial losses, work problems, abortions, moving to a worse residence, deaths, and criminal involvement. Although event stressors are often found to work as well as a total count as in disaggregated form, in this case I found for some outcomes that consideration of individual areas of events led to a notable increase in prediction.

Table 1 shows results from stepwise regressions for three outcomes: general distress, DSM-III-R depression in the last year, and DSM-III-R generalized anxiety in the last year. Models for the latter two outcomes were based on logistic regressions, and for the first on a normal OLS regression. All results shown are standardized coefficients (note that standardized coefficients in the logistic models are based on a *theoretical* standard deviation for the dependent variable, and thus are not comparable to the usual OLS standardized coefficients, only to each other).

Looking at the results for distress first in Table 1, and specifically at the aggregated effects of each variable, we see that five of the six mea-

Table 1. Sample Model Results for Distress and DIS Disorders: Best Predictors from All Sources of Stress

	Distress		Depression		General anxiety	
	Ind.	Total	Ind.	Total	Ind.	Total
Chronic stressors		.412^d		.976^d		.481^d
Financial	.063^b		.457^c			
Work					.131	
Relationship	.109^c					
Single; relationship uncertainty	.184^d		.518^d			
Social life			.231^b			
Residential					.126	
Chronic illness	.119^d				.152^b	
Pressure	.112^c					
Relationship conflict					.219^c	
Sexually unfulfilled	.059^a					
Can't have children			.182^c			
Not a good parent			.135^b			
Housewife; not appreciated	.070^b					
Friends bad influence	.058^b				.175^c	
Family too far/too close	.067^b		.211^b		.125	
Friend/family illness			.174^a			
Fear of assault/robbery	.055^b				.145^a	
Event stressors		.248^d		.141		.260^b
Relationship losses	.070^b				.132	
Crime victim	.055^b					
Financial losses	.052^a				.144^b	
Abortion	.181^d					
Moved to worse residence	.063^b				.123^a	
Daily hassles		.191^d				.163
Childhood traumas		.143^d		.225^b		
Earlier adult life events		.124^d				
Model R^2		.512		.551		.315

$^a = p < .10$
$^b = p < .05$
$^c = p < .01$
$^d = p < .001$

sures of stress had independent effects on distress. The only stressor that did not come into the stepwise model was nonevents, and to be fair, this could be because this stressor was measured by an open-ended question rather than a predesigned list. The predominant effect here is chronic stress, but this effect is by no means the only one. The size of the weighted chronic stress effect is large, given the history of the stress literature: The direct-effect β is .412, controlling for all other sources of stress. This effect, however, does not absorb the effect of life events; in fact, the β of .248 for recent life events is exactly within the expected range suggested by the life-events literature (Thoits, 1983). Thus life events and chronic stressors do operate somewhat independently.

Finding effects for chronic stress and life events may not be surprising, given that the literature is consistent with this finding (Brown & Harris, 1978; Pearlin, 1989). What may be more surprising is the fact that three other sources of stress have independent effects on distress after controlling for the effects of current life events and chronic stress. One may expect, for example, that daily hassles are just reflections of more general chronic stressors, but this is not the case. The importance of accumulated daily annoyances comes through as an independent influence on mental health. Further, one might not expect childhood trauma to have independent effects on adult mental health once accumulated stress exposure in adulthood is taken into account more comprehensively. As suggested by Garmezy (1983), Rutter (1983), and others, however, these stressors have long-term impacts for other reasons. We cannot tell which of these reasons—immediate effects on mental health that persist into adulthood, changes in development of coping resources and skills, shifts in achievement behavior in major social roles—apply, but the fact that there is a separate long-term effect that circumvents so many other stressors does suggest that one or more of these other reasons describe crucial consequences of childhood stress.

Finally, despite an impression in the stress literature that life events may have impacts that only last over a 1- to 2-year period, earlier adult life events do have an effect here that bypasses later life events and current chronic stress. This may be because the types of events reported are major and thus less self-limiting in terms of impact. A major question here, as in the case of childhood traumas, is whether current mental health colors the recall of events in earlier life. Recent research does suggest that individuals who are depressed, for example, are no less accurate or objective than others in recalling earlier life experiences (Brewin, Andrews, & Gotlib, 1992).

Note that stress explains over 50% of the variance in distress in this model. This amount of predictability is certainly higher than is often reported in stress studies, and it probably has to do with three factors: The distress index has 37 items and thus a wider range of content; it is also highly reliable; and this study in fact measures a wider array of sources of stress than most.

These results support the presumed need to measure an array of stressors in research on mental health. Rather than show that life events are not essential, these findings support continued work in this area.

Further, these findings suggest that research on variations in daily stress may be important as well, but not as a replacement for interest in other sources of stress.

The results in column 1 of Table 1 only speak to the prediction of distress. Is it necessary to consider various sources of stress in the prediction of actual psychiatric disorder as well? The results in columns 2 and 3 of Table 1 speak to this issue. Again, we find that multiple stressors must be considered. For depression, chronic stressors (predominantly) and childhood traumas have separate effects. The effect of life events just fails to reach a liberal significance level of .10. In the case of generalized anxiety, chronic stressors, events, and daily hassles have independent effects. Note that stressors have specific effects where one would expect: The long-term effect of childhood traumas is more on depression than anxiety, and the impact of current daily hassles is on anxiety, but not depression. In a separate analysis (Wheaton, 1991), I also show that the effects of stressors increase as the seriousness and extremity of the diagnostic outcome is increased from subdiagnostic threshold cut points to threshold-exact and superthreshold cut points. This means that stressors are not just important to the prediction of "common" mental health problems; in fact, they increase in importance as we approximate more clinically defined outcomes.

A final point in this table concerns the areas of chronic stress that are important. Certain themes surface in the results for individual chronic stress measures. First, relationship concerns are important, and in particular, relationship problems (e.g., transience, complexity, turnover) among the nonmarried have even more important effects than the traditional measure of relationship problems among those who are married or living together. This is a case of the importance of measuring "role inoccupancy" problems; in fact, relationship problems among the single constitute the largest source of stress among all chronic stressors —a major statement given the range of issues considered in this inventory. Second, financial stress is very important to extreme depression problems. Finally, note the importance of a number of issues that are not usually measured in stress scales: distance from family, fear of crime, the influence of friends, feeling unappreciated in the housewife role, not being able to have children, and a general sense of pressure, to name a few.

The results in Table 1 address the distinctiveness of stress effects on mental health outcomes, but not when physical health is at issue. Table 2 gives an idea of the need for heterogeneity in stress predictors for physical health. These results only give a taste of a large number of analyses that also included assessment of effects for specific illnesses or areas of physical illness. Here I present only the most general results.

Table 2. Stress Effects on Physical Health Problem Measures, Smoking, and Substance Use

	β				
	Physical health problem count	General health	Number cigarettes	Drinks per week	Frequency drug use
Chronic stressors (set)	.243[d]	.155[c]	.194[d]	.241[d]	.117[c]
Event stressors	.096[c]	.091[b]	.028	.012	.093[b]
Daily hassles	.199[d]	.150[d]	.058	.042	.064
Childhood traumas	.083[b]	.058[a]	.179[d]	.043	.046
Earlier adult life events	.072[b]	.107[c]	.039	.034	.083[b]
Nonevents	.085[b]	.094[b]	.034	.040	.005
Model R^2	.252	.112	.080	.064	.045

[a] $= p < .10$
[b] $= p < .05$
[c] $= p < .01$
[d] $= p < .001$

Note in Table 2 that all six sources of stress have separate effects on a total count of reported health problems and illnesses (from a list of 27). Again, the effects of stressors that vary by chronicity and stage in the life course must be considered. Here nonevents also have a separate impact, albeit a modest one. Chronic stressors (without the health area counted) are the single most important source of prediction again, but daily hassles are relatively more important for physical health issues than for mental health issues: Here they are close to chronic stressors in impact, whereas life events play a more modest role. The physical health problem count here includes such problems as hypertension, diabetes, viral illnesses, heart problems, allergies, emphysema and asthma, stomach diseases, skin rashes, gallbladder problems, muscle complaints, and gastrointestinal diseases. I also considered individual models for these problems, and though of course there is variation in the amount of relevance of each type of stressor, the essential conclusion remains the same: a variety of stressors are important.

Table 2 also shows results for a self-assessed general health measure. Results are very similar to the problem count. The last three outcomes focus on drinking, smoking, and drug use; the survey did not contain detailed measures in these areas, and thus frequency is all that is included. This may be especially problematic for drinking, because none of the problems that may accompany drinking are included and they may be relatively uncorrelated with quantity of intake. In the area of cigarette smoking, a clear health risk factor, both chronic stressors and childhood stressors are important predictors. The fact that only chronic stress predicts drinking suggests either that drinking is only sensitive to one kind of stress—and this is the kind most observers would predict *should* be related to drinking—or that the measure of alcohol use is not sensitive to important variations in drinking behavior. Finally, use of nonprescribed drugs is related to three kinds of stress: chronic, events, and earlier adult life events. Interestingly drug use seems more related to the occurrence of discrete forms of stress, indicating it may start when major events change the life course during adulthood.

These results reflect a number of important things about the specification of stress impacts. They suggest that the range of content in stressors is broad, and thus one cannot assume that one type of stress is a proxy for all types. They also suggest the importance of including stress experience over the life course. Perhaps most importantly, they suggest the importance of distinguishing stressors in terms of their natural discreteness as stressors (i.e., their chronicity). Rather than showing that our distinctions are unnecessary, the findings imply a fundamental heterogeneity of stress concepts.

A Causal Model of Stressors

Because various types of stress affect health independently, it becomes more important to understand how stressors are related to each other. The analyses above can only address the question of relative direct influences on health outcomes; they do not tell us anything about how stressors are related to each other over the life course, or how stress exposure builds and accumulates depending on earlier patterns of stress experience. Thus I turn my attention now to the interdependence among stressors.

Stressors are related to each other in some causal sequence. This causality could be complex, but there are clear leads in the literature about the expected ordering of certain types of stress, and we can specify a model that at least expresses these expectations without testing them. Further, we can take advantage of the implied ordering among stressors where information on stage in the life course or timing of occurrence is available. By proposing a model for lifetime stress exposure, we also achieve the ability to estimate not just the direct influences of stress, but also the indirect influences of stress on health over the life course. This is essential to the proper understanding of the roles of stressors, given that the direct effects of the previous section only tell us about a part of the effect of each stressor.

A reasonable beginning in the assessment of interrelationships is to

Table 3. Correlations among Stress Measures

	Traumas	Adult events	Life events	Chronic	Hassles	Nonevents
Childhood traumas	1.0					
Earlier adult events	.262	1.0				
Recent life events	.242	.168	1.0			
Chronic stressors	.334	.188	.227	1.0		
Daily hassles	.297	.211	.283	.437	1.0	
Nonevents	.115	.229	.168	.316	.232	1.0

look at the correlations among our aggregate measures of stress. These correlations, which are shown in Table 3, tell a story with two sides. On the one hand, they do not show such a high level of dependence among stressors that we would expect essentially confounded effects on health. Most of correlations in this table are in the .20 to .30 range. The main exception to this is in the expected area: The correlation of chronic stressors and current daily hassles is considerably higher (.437). Still, we have already seen that these stressors have separate impacts on health outcomes. On the other hand, the correlations show that there is a consistent pattern of interdependence across all of the stressors measured. Thus we should expect in a causal model to see widespread effects of stressors on each other, implying that stress exposure at any point both affects health and increases the chances for other kinds of stress experience.

Figure 4 shows a causal model that posits a specific sequence for causation among the six stressors measured in this study. This model considers childhood traumas as the starting point in the stress realm, earlier life events as intervening but subsequent to childhood stressors and prior to reports of stress impinging on the current point in time, and recent life events and current chronic stressors as prior to daily hassles and nonevents, in an "accumulation" model of stress experience.

According to the premises of the model, childhood traumas may have effects on the likelihood of most kinds of later stress experience. Presumably, experience of high levels of stress in childhood will alter the chances of successful performance in key social roles in that period, especially school, and will also affect the development of social competence. This may in turn affect educational attainments, transitions to marriage, and early job/career opportunities, which all affect the probability of stress exposure during the adult life course. The model shows earlier adult life events as prior to all current and recent stress measures. This is defined by the fact that these events are limited to a period up to

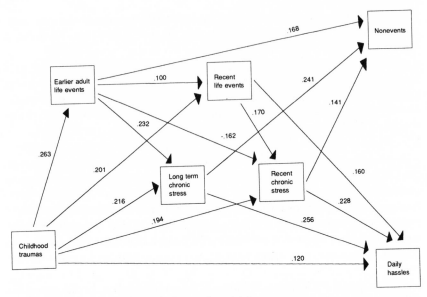

Figure 4. A causal model for stressors.

2 years before the interview. A commonly stated expectation in the literature is that life events may set in motion chronically stressful situations (e.g., unemployment may end, but the changes it brings to the family may not). If life-event occurrence increases the chances of other life events happening (Thoits, 1983), then earlier events will be related to recent event exposure as well.

Of all the relationships among stressors in this model, one seems significantly more likely to be causally reciprocal—the relationship between ongoing chronic stress and recent life events. It is likely that chronic stress will lead to events that are attempts to deal with the chronic stress, and it is also likely that life events will act as the starting point for more chronic stressors. In fact, the latter is a visible viewpoint in the literature, because when life events occur, they act like a necessary condition for the appearance of new chronic stressors. A divorce will, by definition, increase the chances greatly of experiencing stress as a result of being a single parent; similarly, a job loss will increase the chances of experiencing financial strain.

The data do allow for distinguishing the starting points of chronic stressors, a fact that will help separate causation of life events by longer-term chronic stressors from the causation of more recent chronic stressors by life events. Because we know, for each reported chronic stressor, the number of months of continuous presence of the problem, we can distinguish chronic stressors that started more than 12 months ago (and thus predated reported life events in the last year) from those that started within the last year. This allows for some assessment of a reciprocal relationship with life events, although an approach focusing on sequences of *specific* chronic stressors and events would tell us more.

The model represents both nonevents and daily hassles as basically epiphenomenal outcomes of current chronic stress. In addition, life events are seen as causally prior to the occurrence of hassles. This specification recognizes that daily hassles are not likely to be causally prior to any other stressor, in part because they tap aspects of daily life that seem unlikely to be powerful enough as causes to give rise to other stressors. Nonevents are also seen as an end point in the model, in part because I define nonevents to be the manifestation of basic ongoing chronic stressors, rather than vice versa. Finally, I leave the relationship between hassles and nonevents unspecified, as two coequal end points in the model.

The coefficients shown in Figure 4 are the standardized regression coefficients for each dependent variable at each stage of the model. Missing paths in the model reflect nonsignificant effects. The model shows that childhood traumas have implications for exposure to a number of different types of stressors in later life. These childhood experiences predict levels of early adulthood life events, later life events, both long-term and recently started chronic stress, and current daily hassles. This points to a process of cumulative disadvantage for individuals with childhood stress. Early adulthood life events, though not having a large direct impact on mental health, have a number of indirect impacts through other stressors, especially through long-term chronic stress. This effect reflects the common prediction that life events are the starting points of chronic stressors that follow from them. In contrast, earlier adult events are inversely related to more recent chronic stressors. This finding may reflect the fact that the stressors set in motion by earlier major adult life events tend to be long-term, difficult issues, whereas those set in motion more recently may be more likely to result from proximal and, on average, less serious life events.

The modified specification distinguishing the timing of chronic stressors proved to be very important to the results. Longer-term chronic stressors *have no effect on the occurrence of recent life events, but life events have a clear positive influence on the occurrence of chronic stressors that have started within the last year.* Thus, when the model is modified to allow for reciprocality, the results suggest that life events tend to be the starting point of chronic stressors, but not vice versa. It is important to note that the two chronic stress variables are practically uncorrelated ($r = -.034$), implying that the number of longer-term chronic stressors is unrelated to the number of new ones appearing.

At the final stage of the model, we see that both daily hassles and nonevents are largely affected by chronic stress, as expected. In addition, life events do increase at least the perception of daily hassles.

The importance of distinguishing the chronicity of chronic stressors may extend to the prediction of mental health outcomes as well. There are various hypotheses about how time may affect their importance for mental health. One viewpoint is that newer chronic stressors have not been habituated and thus may have a larger impact. Consistent with this viewpoint is the view that older chronic stressors lose their potency because they become normative. The opposite viewpoint, also possible, is that chronic stressors take time to surface as problems; like with a rusting bridge, the problem is not there until the elastic limit is exceeded. In this viewpoint, chronic stressors accumulate in impact, and thus we would observe stronger effects for longer-term stressors.

With the distinction between longer-term and recently started chronic stressors in mind, I return to the issue of the prediction of mental health. The results in Figure 4 show a strong pattern of interdependence among the set of stressors considered. In every analysis considered so far, we have seen the importance of consideration of a multiplicity of stressors. An important final step is to extend our model for stressors by reestimating the effects of these stressors on mental health in order to see how the total effects of stressors are distributed.

Decomposing the Effects of Stressors

Distress was used as the mental health outcome in an analysis of the full cumulative impact of all sources of stress. The results of the decomposition of the effects of all sources of stress are shown in Table 4. In this table, each stressor is shown as having a direct effect—the usual regression coefficient—plus a set of indirect effects through other stressors that are intervening. The total effect is then the sum of all indirect effects and the direct effect. This total effect represents the causal component of the correlation with distress; the rest is spurious (i.e., attributable to the dependence of each stressor on a prior stressor and the effect of that prior stressor on distress).

The direct effects show comparable regression coefficients to the analysis in Table 1, except that here chronic stress appears as two separate variables. Because these two variables are uncorrelated, one can add the two effects to get a sense of the aggregated effect of all chronic

Table 4. Decomposition of Effects of all Stressors on Distress

	Direct	Indirect						Total effect	Spurious	Correlation
		AD	CS (old)	CS (new)	LE	H	Total			
Childhood traumas	.160	.04	.07	.03	.06	.02	.230	.390	—	.390
Earlier adult life events	.069	—	.08	-0.03	.03	.02	.102	.171	.094	.265
Recent life events	.233	—	—	.03	—	.04	.067	.300	.096	.396
Long-term chronic	.285	—	—	—	—	.05	.051	.336	.113	.449
Recently started chronic	.117	—	—	—	—	.05	.046	.163	.053	.216
Hassles	.200	—	—	—	—	—	—	.200	.251	.451
Nonevents	—	—	—	—	—	—	—	—	.181	.181

stressors; here it is .402. The table only shows indirect effects where they are possible and contain significant effects as the intervening linkages.

Because nonevents do not have a direct effect on distress, all of the correlation of .181 is by definition spurious. Most of this spuriousness is attributable to the underlying influence of chronic stressors. The total causal effect and the direct effect of daily hassles are equal, because there are no intervening variables for daily hassles. Note that the correlation between daily hassles and distress is much higher than its total effect. This reflects the fact that more than 55% of its association with distress is spurious. Still, it does have some independent influence. The total effect of long-term and more recent chronic stressors together is a substantial .499 (.336 + .163). Much less of the association between chronic stress and distress is spurious (about 25%).

Table 4 shows that the direct effects significantly underestimate the total impact of both event stressors and, especially, childhood stressors. The direct effect of .233 for events becomes a total effect of .300 when intervening effects are taken into account. Because childhood stress is the starting point of the model, we should expect that a major portion of its total impact is hidden in indirect effects through other stressors. This is in fact the case. Childhood stressors have indirect effects on adult distress through early adult life events, through chronic stress, and especially through current life events. The result is a total effect of .390, as opposed to a direct effect of just .160. This is a case where the direct effect does not tell us nearly enough about the importance of a stressor. About 60% of the effect of childhood stress is expressed through adult stress experience in this model.

When we compare total effects, two kinds of stress emerge as primarily important. Current chronic stressors are clearly of preeminent importance, but childhood stress emerges as the next most important stress issue to consider over the entire life course. Its effects are broad and cumulative, in that childhood stress leads to increased exposure to a number of forms of stress in adulthood. Adult life events are also ultimately important, much more important than the single estimate of .233 in a direct-effects model would indicate. One way of interpreting the results in Table 4 is to aggregate effects of life events across adulthood by combining effects for current life events with previous adult life events. The resulting total effect of adult life events, after removing indirect effects of earlier events, is .441. This again is much higher than the "modest" association often assumed for life events (Rabkin & Streuning, 1976).

The lessons from these findings are simple. Overall, stressors have much higher impacts on mental health than is assumed in a literature that primarily depends on one or two stress concepts and typically only measures current (rather than lifetime) effects. In addition, no one stress concept is sufficient in understanding the relevance of stress for mental health.

CONCLUDING COMMENTS

The usual assumption in the stress literature over the last 20 years has been that stress comes in a single package. This package is organized around the concept of events. The implicit idea behind this approach is that it takes an event for change to occur, and some events denote challenging, threatening, or undesirable changes that require adjustment. Whereas we usually assume that the concept causes the measure, it is also historically the case that the measure can begin to cause the concept. This has happened in the area of stress. The life-events inventory was intended as an operationalization of a kind of stress, but its widespread application and predominance in the field insidiously produced the assumption that for something to be a stressor, it had to be an event of some sort.

At the same time, many stress researchers and theorists have long seen the necessity of having something more. Often, and interestingly, terms without a explicit reference to stress (e.g., *ongoing difficulties* or *role strain*) are used to describe these other problems. This choice of terminology may reflect the difficulty of establishing that there are other kinds of stress beyond life events, or it may reflect a belief that these other issues are not stressors because they are not events. Yet most would agree that there are many situations we would call stressful that do not begin as an event, do not exist as an observable event, and do not end with a self-limiting resolution. Rather, these stressors more typically just ebb and flow (or flow and ebb). I have used the term *chronic stressors* to refer to this type of stress.

In the area of stress research, we need to remember our roots. Both the stress models of biology and engineering allow for—indeed, point to—the need for a basic distinction between event and more continuous forms of stress. This distinction has not been entirely set aside, but it has been sometimes forgotten. The whole history of stress research has in fact, whether implicitly or unconsciously, been concerned with chronic stressors. The tradition of research on work stress has emphasized stressful *conditions* of the work environment—in other words, chronic stressors. Studies of the effects of the Great Depression, of caregiving of sick parents, and of the physically or sexually abused over extended periods of time are all looking at the consequences of chronic stressors.

And there are other types of proposed stress concepts to consider: daily stresses, childhood stressors, macro or system stressors, nonevents, and so on. In this chapter I have introduced the notion of a stress continuum to connect the existing stress concepts in the literature to each other along a single dimension of discreteness versus continuity. This discussion shows that many other stress concepts contain a mixture of chronic and event issues, especially childhood stressors, daily hassles, and system stressors. As long as these stressors are studied separately, there is no problem. But when they are collected into aggregate scores, there may be a problem in that the two types of stress may operate quite differently as stress problems.

When we elaborate the world of stress concepts, we also notice other basic dimensions. Here I have considered three: the stage of life at which the stressor occurs; the unit of analysis of the stressor; and the magnitude of the stressor—an issue that in the whole history of stress research has not really gone away. These organizing concepts place stressors in relation to each other in a multivariate dimensionality.

These distinctions are only potentially interesting if we also find that the effects of stressors do not reduce to an essential core of one or two kinds of stress. The findings I report here definitely point to a heterogeneity of stress effects. That is, stress is problematic nor for one reason but for a set of reasons corresponding to the kinds of problems each form of stress poses. If stress were more uniform as a problem, we would not expect to see a set of independent effects. Chronic stress, for example, may be problematic because resolution is uncertain; life events may be problematic because they require identity adjustment; daily hassles may be problematic because they drain off daily coping skills; and childhood stress may be problematic because it introduces blockages in developmental tasks that are necessary for successful attachments, achieved behavior, and the like. The problems are quite different. Thus assuming that stress comes in a single package may significantly miss the essentials of how stressors work and why they affect us.

The ultimate message of this chapter is that the stress universe is a differentiated set of stress concepts. In the elaborated stress universe, no one form or source of stress is sufficient to capture, even remotely, all that is stressful. If we are ultimately interested in a full representation and a fair evaluation of the relevance of stress in health—as we should be—we must consider stressors that vary in their typical time course, that occur at different levels of analysis, and that range in their timing from childhood through all phases of the adult life course. Unless we do this, we will never know how important stress is.

ACKNOWLEDGMENTS

The research reported in this chapter was supported by a grant from the National Health Research Development Program (Grant #6606-4396-46). I was also supported during this period by a Senior Research Fellowship from the Ontario Mental Health Foundation.

REFERENCES

Avison, W. R., & Turner, R. J. (1988). Stressful life events and depressive symptoms: Disaggregating the effects of acute stressors and chronic strains. *Journal of Health and Social Behavior, 29,* 253–264.

Bolger, N., DeLongis, A., Kessler, R. C., & Schilling, E. A. (1989). Effects of daily stress on negative mood. *Journal of Personality and Social Psychology, 57,* 808–818.

Brenner, M. H. (1974). *Mental illness and the economy.* Cambridge, MA: Harvard University Press.

Brewin, C. R., Andrews, B., & Gotlib, I. H. (1993). Psychopathology and early experience: A reappraisal of retrospective reports. *Psychological Bulletin, 113,* 82–98.

Brown, G. W., & Harris, T. (1978). *The social origins of depression: A study of psychiatric disorders in women.* New York: Free Press.

Cannon, W. B. (1929). *Bodily changes in pain, hunger, fear, and rage.* New York: Appleton.

Coddington, R. D. (1984). Measuring the stressfulness of a child's environment. In J. H. Humphrey (Ed.), *Stress in childhood* (pp. 97–126). New York: AMS Press.

Derogatis, L. R., Lipman, R. S., Rickels, K., Uhlenhuth, E. H., & Covi, L. (1974). The Hopkins Symptom Checklist (HSCL): A self-report symptom inventory. *Behavioral Science, 19,* 1–15.

Dohrenwend, B. S., & Dohrenwend, B. P. (1970). Class and race as status-related sources of stress. In S. Levine & N. Scotch (Eds.), *Social stress* (pp. 111–139). Chicago: Aldine.

Dohrenwend, B. S., & Dohrenwend, B. P. (1974). A brief historical introduction to research on stressful life events. In B. S. Dohrenwend & B. P. Dohrenwend (Eds.), *Stressful life events: Their nature and effects* (pp. 1–5). New York: Wiley.

Dohrenwend, B. S., Dohrenwend, B. P., Dodson, M., & Shrout, P. E. (1984). Symptoms, hassles, social supports, and life events: Problem of confounding measures. *Journal of Abnormal Psychology, 93,* 222–230.

Dooley, D., & Catalano, R. (1984). Why the economy predicts help-seeking: A test of competing explanations. *Journal of Health and Social Behavior, 25,* 160–175.

Erickson, K. T. (1976). Loss of community at Buffalo Creek. *American Journal of Psychiatry, 133,* 302–305.

Garmezy, N. (1983). Stressors of childhood. In N. Garmezy & M. Rutter (Eds.), *Stress, coping, and development in children* (pp. 43–84). New York: McGraw-Hill.

Gersten, J. C., Langner, T. S., Eisenberg, J. G., & Orzeck, L. (1974). Child behavior and life events: Undesirable change or change per se? In B. S. Dohrenwend & B. P. Dohrenwend (Eds.), *Stressful life events: Their nature and effects* (pp. 159–170). New York: Wiley.

Holmes, T. H., & Rahe, R. H. (1967). The social readjustment rating scale, *Journal of Psychosomatic Research, 11,* 213–218.

Kanner, A. D., Coyne, J. C., Schaefer, C., & Lazarus, R. S. (1981). Comparison of two modes of stress measurement: Daily hassles and uplifts versus major life events. *Journal of Behavioral Medicine, 4*, 1–39.

Kasl, S. V., Chisolm, R. F., & Eskenazi, B. (1981). The impact of the accident at Three Mile Island on the behavior and well-being of nuclear workers. Part II: Job tension, psychophysiological symptoms, and indices of distress. *American Journal of Public Health, 71*, 484–495.

Kessler, R. C. (1983). Methodological issues in the study of psychosocial stress: Measurement, design, and analysis. In H. B. Kaplan (Ed.), *Psychosocial stress: Recent developments in theory and research* (pp. 267–341). New York: Academic Press.

Koos, E. L. (1946). *Families in trouble*. New York: Kings Crowe.

Langner, T. S. (1962). A twenty-two item screening score of psychiatric symptoms indicating impairment. *Journal of Health and Human Behavior, 3*, 269–276.

Langner, T. S., & Michael, S. T. (1963). *Life stress and mental health*. London: Free Press.

Laufer, R. S., Gallops, M. S., & Frey-Wouters, E. (1984). War stress and trauma: The Vietnam veteran experience. *Journal of Health and Social Behavior, 25*, 65–85.

Linsky, A. S., Colby, J. P., Jr., & Straus, M. A. (1987). Social stress, normative constraints, and alcohol problems in American states. *Social Science and Medicine, 24*, 875–883.

Pearlin, L. I. (1983). Role strains and personal stress. In H. B. Kaplan (Ed.), *Psychosocial stress: Trends in theory and research* (pp. 3–32). New York: Academic Press.

Pearlin, L. I. (1989). The sociological study of stress. *Journal of Health and Social Behavior, 30*, 241–256.

Pearlin, L. I., & Schooler, C. (1978). The structure of coping. *Journal of Health and Social Behavior, 19*, 2–21.

Pynoos, R. S. (1987). Life threat and post-traumatic stress in children. *Archives of General Psychiatry, 44*, 1057–1068.

Rabkin, J. G., & Streuning, E. L. (1976). Life events, stress, and illness. *Science, 194*, 1013–1020.

Radloff, L. (1977). The CES-D scale: A self-reported depression scale for research in the general population. *Applied Psychological Measurement, 1*, 385–401.

Rutter, M. (1983). Stress, coping, and development: Some issues and some questions. In N. Garmezy & M. Rutter (Eds.), *Stress, coping, and development in children* (pp. 1–42). New York: McGraw-Hill.

Selye, H. (1956). *The stress of life*. New York: McGraw-Hill.

Smith, W. K. (1987). The stress analogy. *Schizophrenia Bulletin, 13*(2), 215–220.

Stone, A. A., & Neale, J. N. (1984). Effects of daily events on mood. *Journal of Personality and Social Psychology, 46*, 137–144.

Thoits, P. (1983). Dimensions of life events that influence psychological distress. In H. B. Kaplan (Eds.), *Psychosocial stress: Trends in theory and research* (pp. 33–103). New York: Academic Press.

Wheaton, B. (1983). Stress, personal coping resources, and psychiatric symptoms: An investigation of interactive models. *Journal of Health and Social Behavior, 24*, 208–229.

Wheaton, B. (1991, August). *Chronic stress: Models and measurement*. Paper presented at meeting of the Society for the Study of Social Problems, Cincinnati, OH.

5

The Daily Grind
Work Stressors, Family Patterns, and Intergenerational Outcomes

ELIZABETH G. MENAGHAN

Perhaps the most dramatic change in stress research since the early 1980s has been the enlarged understanding of what constitutes stressful circumstances. As has been reviewed elsewhere (see, e.g., Menaghan, 1991; Pearlin, 1989) much early stress research focused on discrete stressful events that had a clear onset. These events were sometimes clearly beyond the control of the individual (e.g., plant closings, floods, tornadoes, or earthquakes, national or local economic recession) and sometimes partially attributable to individual characteristics or actions (e.g., being fired from one's job, divorcing one's spouse, or being arrested); some were expectable, whereas others were not; and some were desirable, whereas others were not. But all of these events could be located in time. A researcher could compare well-being before and after their occurrence, and he or she could chart the duration of their effects.

Yet some of the most stressful conditions that humans face are not captured in this conceptualization. These are what have come to be referred to as chronic stressors, the demands and constraints that are an ineluctable part of social and economic arrangements. Primary—both in

ELIZABETH G. MENAGHAN • Department of Sociology, Ohio State University, Columbus, Ohio 43210-1353.

Stress and Mental Health: Contemporary Issues and Prospects for the Future, edited by William R. Avison and Ian H. Gotlib. New York, Plenum Press, 1994.

the strength of their effects and in recent research emphasis—are the relatively stable conditions associated with normatively expected adult occupational and family roles. It has become increasingly clear that the search for "socially induced stress," as Avison and Gotlib (Chapter 1) refer to it, must include the unremarkable, ordinary, repetitive challenges and setbacks that individuals face in the boardroom, behind the word processor, or on the assembly line, and it must consider their repercussions on everyday family interaction. Conversely, the search must also include the recurring emotional and instrumental tasks that adults face as spouses and as parents, and it must consider their effects on the individual well-being of all members of the family.

In this chapter I focus on workplace stressors and their implications for both parents and children. I review some of the emerging generalizations about the impact of these stressors on individuals and consider effects of individual work conditions on other family members, particularly spouses and children. As Aneshensel, Rutter, and Lachenbruch (1991) have eloquently argued, social scientific study of stress must be less concerned with tracing the antecedents of particular psychiatric disorders and more focused on a broad range of potential consequences of social structural arrangements. Aneshensel and her colleagues accordingly investigate not one specific disorder but an array of mental health indicators. I argue that the sociological study of stress must move still further—beyond individual mental health consequences—and consider the multiple social and intergenerational consequences of adults' socially structured stressors. In particular, the study of work stressors must consider their impact on workers' intimate marital relationships, on their parenting activities, and on their children's emotional well-being.

Tracing the intergenerational repercussions of structured occupational arrangements is an important developing area of study, in part because the steady increase in two-earner families has drawn greater attention to work–family linkages and to the new opportunities and stressors that working husbands and wives may encounter as they negotiate novel patterns of interaction and collaboration. Struggling with the competing demands of occupation and family now constitutes the typical situation for most American adults; this struggle is a significant chronic stressor in American lives (U.S. Bureau of the Census, 1990), and each spouse's work problems may readily erode their family lives. Some prior research on intergenerational effects of parents' occupational stressors has considered how fathers' occupational conditions affect their parental values and goals for their children. The expansion of women's employment has brought new energy to these questions as researchers pursue how mothers' employment experiences affect child socialization. The relatively recent development of large national data sets linking responses of parents and their children (e.g., the Child–Mother Data Sets of the National Longitudinal Surveys of Youth, the National Surveys of Children, and the National Surveys of Families and Households) has also fostered an explosion of empirical work on both academic and social outcomes for children. Further attention to family and intergenerational repercussions of occupational experiences can enrich more general stress models and help to develop models that predict wider, intergenerational repercussions of adult arrangements and experiences; it can also illuminate the gender dynamics underlying male and female occupational experiences and occupational effects on both adults and children. To contribute to these developments, I therefore draw some implications of parental work stressors for marital relationships and for children's family environments and emotional well-being, and I present some of my own research findings that are relevant to this issue.

WORKPLACE STRESSORS: EFFECTS ON INDIVIDUAL WORKERS

I focus particularly on two aspects of working conditions: the extent of self-direction and control permitted in the occupation, and the hours workers spend on the job. I also will discuss how men's and women's experiences in the workplace are likely to differ, to set the stage for discussion of how the effects of occupational experiences may also vary by gender.

Occupational self-direction refers to the extent to which jobs permit the individual worker to exercise judgment, make decisions, and solve problems. At one end of the continuum are jobs that are highly standardized and in which good performance involves applying a simple rule or taking a predictable action. Tasks in these jobs tend to be highly repetitive, so that the worker enacts the same response many times a day. He or she may be closely supervised to ensure standard response, or the workplace itself may be organized to constrain options and discourage innovation. There is no expectation that the worker will need to solve problems or experiment with alternative ways either to accomplish the task or to conceive it in the first place. In one sense, such jobs are easy to learn, easy to accomplish once learned, and easy to do without engaging one's full attention. Yet such work conditions have been repeatedly linked to negative psychological outcomes. At the other end of the continuum are jobs that defy easy description or prescription; the workday is filled with a varied range of activities, and much of the work does not have a "canned" solution. Tasks are complex, and they invite problem solving and experimentation. Such work carries a greater risk of failure and frustration, yet it also has many positive consequences. A man interviewed by Robert Weiss (1990a) captures some of the emotional meaning of such work: "It's making decisions, having options, going one way or the other, and seeing how that works out. . . . There's a sort of thrill in that. Just the self-satisfaction that you can juggle fourteen balls in the air at the same time without dropping one of them. . . . I really love the work" (p. 3).

Social stress arguments have generally emphasized such aspects of work as supportive or conflict-ridden workplace relations and work overload, considering their effects on individual emotions and mental health. In contrast, most work on the effects of occupational self-direction has emphasized effects on cognition and attitudes. When social stress theorists think of work stress, they are not likely to consider the degree of self-direction a job affords. Yet this is an aspect of work that is intimately tied to issues of control, challenge, and mastery. As Mirowsky and Ross (1986) have reviewed, low levels of such conditions produce a sense of powerlessness and alienation that colors beliefs about the possibility of control in other aspects of life and arouses psychological distress. Work socialization theorists argue that greater opportunity to exercise self-direction at work improves cognitive habits and skills (Kohn & Schooler, 1982, 1985; Miller, Slomczynski, & Kohn, 1985; Naoi & Schooler, 1985; Schooler & Naoi, 1988); workers think more flexibly and effectively off the job as well (Kohn, Naoi, Schoenbach, Schooler, & Slomczynski, 1990; see also O'Brien, 1986; Spenner, 1988) and spend their leisure time in more complex ways (Miller & Kohn, 1983). The degree of self-direction exercised on the job also shapes more general attitudes and values (Schooler, 1987), including such attitudes about the self as sense of self-worth and self-efficacy. Occupational self-direction also affects workers' overall emotional well-being (Gecas & Seff, 1989; Hibbard & Pope, 1987; Lennon, 1987; Menaghan, 1991; Mortimer & Borman, 1988; Mortimer, Lorence, & Kumka, 1986; Spenner & Otto, 1985). Stated more negatively, the persistent absence of opportunities for self-direction and autonomy at work constitutes a chronic stressor that erodes cognitive habits and skills, constrains leisure choice, undercuts positive self-attitudes, and negatively colors daily mood and overall emotional health.

Work by Karasek and others (Haynes & Feinleib, 1980; House, Strecher, Metzner, & Robbins, 1986; Karasek, 1979; Karasek, Baker,

Marxer, Ahlbom, & Theorell, 1981) suggests that the combination of high job demands with low decision latitude is particularly lethal, generating high levels of emotional and physical distress. Time pressures and long work hours have also been linked to greater overall anxiety and concerns about one's adequacy and competence (Miller, Schooler, Kohn, & Miller, 1979; Voydanoff & Donnelly, 1989). Rosenfield (1989) has investigated how high work and child-rearing demands may combine to reduce adults' sense of control; the resultant reductions in perceived control increase individual distress.

GENDER DIFFERENCES IN EFFECTS OF OCCUPATIONAL CONDITIONS ON FAMILY INTERACTION

Many of these studies discuss workers and parents without distinguishing them by gender, but men and women differ sharply in the average conditions they encounter at work (Parcel 1989). Occupations, and jobs within occupations, remain segregated by sex, and much female employment tends to be in such "female ghetto" occupations as secretarial and clerical work, retail sales, cashiering, beauty/cosmetics, and young children's education (see Bielby & Baron, 1984; Jacobs, 1989; Reskin & Roos, 1990). The combination of high job demands and low decision latitude that Karasek has identified as so negative is more characteristic of women's jobs than of men's jobs. The jobs that women typically hold also have lower average wages than those dominated by men, and despite popular opinion to the contrary, "women's jobs" do not offer compensating flexibility in work schedules or demands (see Glass, 1990; Glass & Camarigg, 1992). As a result, men and women are unlikely to gain equivalent economic or emotional rewards from their work. Although there has been some reduction in the last few decades in the extent of wives' economic dependency (Sorensen & McLanahan, 1987), employed wives' lower wages and fewer work hours keep even most full-time employed wives' contribution to family income below 50%. Thus, even when families are labeled dual-earner families, the couple are not likely to be equivalent earners.

Pervasive gender role beliefs, not merely objective differences, make men's occupations and men's wages more powerful in affecting family interaction. Bielby and Bielby (1992) note that even when wives are employed, their economic contribution tends to be downplayed and interpreted as secondary, by both husbands and wives as well as by the larger society. Husbands remain responsible for breadwinning (i.e., providing for the family), and this recognized role of provider carries privileges. It legitimizes greater attention to a husband's occupational requirements and to his career progress over his wife's, even when the two are similar in earnings and potential earnings. In contrast, viewing husbands and wives as coproviders changes spousal interaction and decision making. Bielby and Bielby cite Hood (1983), whose study suggested that such recognition makes a difference independent of the objective economic contributions of the two spouses and has substantial consequences for behavior: Spouses' bargaining power depends both on each person's relative resources and on mutually recognized rights or authority to exercise power in a given area (Hood, 1983, p. 7). Hood reports that husbands who view their wives as coproviders are more willing to take on shared responsibility for parenting and household work than are husbands who have employed wives but view themselves as primarily responsible for the provider role (see also Bielby & Bielby, 1992; Mincer, 1978; Potuchek, 1992).

If gender role beliefs affect the impact of occupational conditions, it is also true that occupational conditions may affect gender role beliefs and behavior. To the extent that workplace opportunities to exercise judgment and self-direction make both men and women less socially conservative and less tied to traditional solutions to problems, they may reduce the traditionality of gender role beliefs and behaviors, and such lessened traditionality may permit a more equitable arrangement of household and parenting responsibilities. Such changes should decrease work–family conflict and increase well-being for wives in dual-earner families. Effects for husbands—negative or positive—may be weak, given research findings that husbands' greater participation in household tasks does not have much emotional impact on them (Ross, Mirowsky, & Huber, 1983). In addition, as women increase their representation in higher-status positions, workplace interaction may provide greater male–female rehearsal of cooperative interaction among status equals, providing new models for more egalitarian spousal relationships within families (see Wharton & Baron, 1987, for a dissenting view).

But this picture may be too optimistic. Bielby and Bielby (1992) point out that the cultural assignment of provider roles to husbands, and the widespread acceptance of this assignment as legitimate by both spouses, leads wives to subordinate their job interests to those of their husbands without much explicit bargaining or overt conflict (see also Ferree, 1990). As allegiance to these gender roles weakens, however, husbands and wives may face greater overt conflict as they struggle to work out jointly satisfying occupational and family arrangements. Ironically, better jobs—defined in terms of higher wages and greater occupational complexity—may have negative consequences for marital quality, despite their positive individual psychological consequences. The reasons differ by gender. Wives with such jobs may be less willing to subordinate their own preferences and forego occupational opportunities; their challenge to taken-for-granted patterns may increase marital problems. Husbands with these jobs may feel more entitled to claim breadwinner privileges and be less willing to jeopardize their own occupational progress by accommodating their wives. In an innovative study of variations in willingness to take on responsibility for child care arrangements, Peterson and Gerson (1992) find that for both male and female workers, having a job that provides more scope for decision making increases investment in the job and reduces willingness to carry out domestic tasks. Typical male "underinvolvement" in domestic life may partially reflect their greater employment in such occupational settings.

If implications of parental occupational self-direction for marital relations are mixed, effects on children's well-being are more consistent. A long line of research has linked occupational self-direction to the values that parents hold for their children (Pearlin & Kohn, 1966; Pearlin, 1971; Kohn, 1977; Kohn & Schooler, 1983; Kohn, Slomczynski, & Schoenbach, 1986) and for the way that they interact with them. More substantively complex job conditions have been linked to valuing more self-directed qualities in one's children, as well as encouraging them to be more autonomous and intellectually flexible (Gottfried & Gottfried, 1988; Piotrkowski & Katz, 1982). Parents in such occupations put less emphasis on parental control and worry less about spoiling children by responsive and affectionate behavior; accordingly, they display more warmth and involvement, restrict the child's actions less frequently, and report less frequent spankings (Luster, Rhoades, & Haas, 1989). Mothers in jobs involving more substantively complex work also provide more cognitive stimulation and affective warmth to their young children (Menaghan & Parcel, 1991).

Such parenting approaches are expected to foster child socialization and reduce children's behavior problems. Better home environments are also associated, as expected, with better verbal development (Parcel & Menaghan, 1990) and fewer behavior problems (Rogers, Parcel, & Menaghan, 1991). Thus we would expect positive total effects of parental occupational self-direction on children's cognitive and social outcomes, with this effect operating in large part via the quality of children's home environments. Effects on marital interaction and family involvement may be weaker as a result of countervailing processes: Positive impacts on individual well-being should facilitate marital interaction, but to the extent that such conditions foster less traditional gender role attitudes for women but reinforce them for men, they may increase overt conflict.

Effects of economic factors are also likely to vary by gender. Whatever their source, wages from jobs are crucial in providing needed material resources for children. Low wages hamper parental efforts to provide adequate material resources for their children, and they produce feelings of distress that affect parent–child interaction. But among married-couple families, fathers' wages are probably particularly crucial for two reasons. First, because men generally earn higher wages than women, economically successful men can provide a firm foundation for family economic security even when their wives are not employed or earn meager wages. In contrast, when men are not economically successful, wives' employment is unlikely to be enough to compensate for the loss. Second, the emotional impact of poor earnings is greater when individuals see themselves as the primary breadwinners in families, and I have argued above that even in dual-earner families, both husbands and wives assign more responsibility for bread winning to husbands than to wives.

It is not surprising that married men's success or failure in economic provision powerfully shapes their own sense of well-being and contribution to family interaction: When fathers are demoralized by low earnings and economic shortfalls, they are more apt to be withdrawn, irritable, or explosive in interaction with their wives, and less likely to exhibit warmth and support. These negative changes in behavior tend to erode their wives' marital satisfaction and lead to increased thoughts of marital termination (Conger et al., 1990; see also Liem & Liem, 1990). Economic hardship also increases parental irritability and harsh treatment of children (Conger et al., 1992; Whitbeck et al., 1991; see also McLoyd, 1989, 1990, for extensive reviews of this literature, as well as Elder, 1974; Elder & Caspi, 1988; and Liker & Elder, 1983). Wives' wages are unlikely to have as powerful impacts as long as wives are not charged with equal responsibility for family earning.

I have noted that parental occupational wages and conditions may have differing effects for individuals than for family interaction, and that effects are likely to differ for husbands and wives. Effects of work hours are similarly complex. Much of the concern has focused on how longer maternal work hours may reduce mothers' interaction with children, but Nock and Kingston (1988) suggest that work hours affect fathers' time with children more readily than mothers' time (see also Grossman, Pollack, & Golding, 1988). Empirical studies of time use suggest that employed mothers try to protect time with children, but time in shared couple leisure activities diminishes under the constraints of wives' employment (Hill, 1988).

Work hours also affect both parents' availability and involvement at home. Within occupational constraints, workers may try to minimize or maximize their work hours. Part-time work is a more normatively permitted choice for married mothers than for married fathers, and in a given couple both spouses may prefer that wives work part-time. Fathers' working less than full-time hours, however, is more typically viewed as unwelcome underemployment; it typically signifies an important failure of normative expectations and has an unambiguously negative impact.

Very long work hours also have differing meanings for mothers and fathers. For mothers, for whom any work involvement tends to be discussed in terms of maternal absence from the home and potential child neglect, schedules with routine overtime are interpreted as particularly worrisome. For fathers, similar work schedules may be interpreted as signifying their commitment to their family's economic well-being. Despite these differences in interpretation, I would argue that very long work hours for fathers may also present problems, particularly when their wives are also employed. Such heavy time investments may absorb attention and energy that might otherwise be devoted to family needs, increasing the burden on other family members and carrying costs for the overall family environment. Similarly, heavy involvement in work tasks and long hours on the job may be an investment of time and energy aimed at producing long-term gains in family resources, but one that produces shortfalls in parental attention and involvement with their young children.

Though workers in low-paying jobs may work longer hours to increase earnings, many high-wage occupations also demand extensive time commitments. It is also difficult to assess the extent to which preoccupation with occupational triumphs and troubles decreases emotional and interpersonal availability even though the employed person is physically present at home. Both highly ego-enhancing and highly frustrating occupations are likely to remain salient for the worker even away from the workplace (see Piotrkowski, 1979). Thus more satisfying work may entail both longer work hours and greater work preoccupation, which undercut its emotional benefits. Occupations high in challenge and opportunities for self-direction may also absorb time, energy, and attention that might otherwise be available to family interaction (see also Peterson & Gerson, 1992). Such occupational conditions may be gratifying to the individual worker yet have less positive implications for family life.

Other work conditions also affect family interaction in gendered ways. Repetti's (1989) study of air traffic controllers suggested that a hard day in terms of workload appeared to reduce overall social and emotional responsiveness: Both positive and negative behaviors went down. Crouter, Perry-Jenkins, Huston, and Crawford's (1989) study of employed fathers reported similar patterns. Repetti speculates that an individual worker's withdrawal from interaction with family members may promote recovery from negative work experiences, and that such withdrawal is one avenue for individual recovery from occupational stressors and protection of family interaction from negative job stressor effects. Such withdrawal is only possible, though, if other family members are willing and able to pick up the slack. Given widely accepted gender differences in cultural responsibility for family well-being, wives may be more apt to support temporary withdrawal for husbands than vice versa. Bolger, DeLongis, Kessler, and Wethington (1989) found that when a spouse experienced work overload, respondents' work load at home increased whereas that of their spouses decreased, suggesting that respondents were shouldering more of the work for a weary spouse. This effect was stronger for wives than for husbands, so that husbands were more likely to gain some breathing space at home after a bad day at work.

Such effects would suggest that couples are aware of each other's work experiences and take them into account. Ironically, however, many couples do not communicate accurately with their spouses concerning the work stressors they may encounter. Weiss (1990a, b) finds that husbands facing difficult job conditions often fail to share their concerns with their wives because they do not want their wives to offer advice or tactical assistance. The husbands do not want their wives to doubt that they can deal with the problems. Pearlin and McCall (1990) also document this dynamic: Workers who have suffered workplace assaults on their self-esteem and competence are reluctant to reveal their problems because they fear the loss of their spouse's esteem and admiration. Unfortunately, this leaves their spouses annoyed at their unexplained moodiness, hostility, or withdrawal and puzzled about its origins. To the extent that couples are able to attribute problems to the negative residue of a bad day at work, they may be better able to sustain a positive and optimistic view of their partners and of the potential for future interaction to be more harmonious (see Bradbury & Fincham, 1990). Evidence suggests, however, that there are powerful countervailing forces limiting such attributions.

Children may be even less able to discern the workplace origins of their parents' behavior, but they are affected nevertheless. Downey and Coyne (1989) suggest that mothers worn down by occupational overload and economic pressures resemble clinically depressed mothers. These mothers display less total positive affect and less contingent positive affect. When they have to deal with their children's misbehavior or noncompliance, they use strategies that require a minimum of cognitive effort or interpersonal negotiation: They may simply enforce obedience without negotiation or persuasion, or withdraw or give in if a child resists. Such mothering strategies provide a flawed and inadequate model for children to use in resolving problems or conflicts with teachers or age peers, so that children may develop such behavior problems as excess reliance on coercion and/or tendencies to withdraw from the fray.

Thus effects of substantive complexity and work hours are likely to vary depending on the gender of the worker, both because individual workers' gender role beliefs make a difference and because gender-segregated occupational structures shape experience. There are still pervasive expectations that men will make more money, in different kinds of jobs, than women do; that they will assume primary breadwinning responsibility for their families; and that they will be more committed to work roles than women. To what extent are such differences diminishing? Ross and Mirowsky argue that assumptions about men's and women's relative responsibilities are becoming less stereotyped, and that "new look" couples who share breadwinning and child-rearing/ homemaking roles and view this as a valid arrangement are psychologically advantaged (Ross & Mirowsky, 1988; Ross et al., 1983). But such couples are rare. Men's employment is still done *for* the family, while women's employment is viewed as competing against their family responsibilities. Even men who believe that they support their wives' employment tend not to view women as equally responsible to be family breadwinners (see Thompson & Walker, 1989).

INTERGENERATIONAL EFFECTS OF ADULT WORK AND FAMILY STRESSORS: AN EXAMPLE

I have argued that we need to move beyond measures of individual adult well-being and consider the intergenerational consequences of workplace stressors. Although there is not sufficient space or data to investigate all of the issues raised here, I can investigate some key hypotheses regarding how parental working conditions—particularly opportunities for self-direction, earnings, and hours—affect marital interaction and the family environments that parents are able to provide for their children. In turn, these changes in family interaction affect children's social and cognitive well-being. Figure 1 outlines the major con-

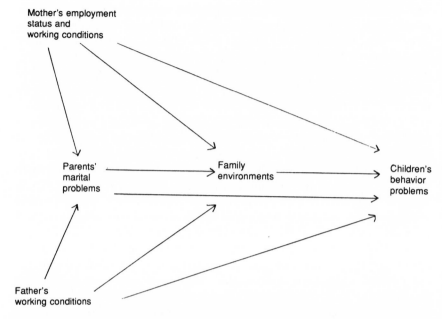

Figure 1. Intergenerational repercussions of adult work stressors: A conceptual model. (Note: Demographic variables, parents' personal resources, and family size effects not shown.)

cepts and linkages investigated here. To illustrate this approach, I draw on data from the national Longitudinal Surveys of Youth (NLSY), a large longitudinal data set containing information about both parents and children, and investigate how both parents' working conditions affect marital quality, family environments, and children's behavior problems. I focus on young married parents and examine how occupational and family circumstances may affect their children's socioemotional well-being.

As discussed more fully elsewhere (see Menaghan, 1991), studies of occupational stressors and their effects face many difficulties in establishing causal patterns. Conventional cross-sectional studies typically examine socially structured differences in requirements among occupations that would be expected to produce enduring differences among job incumbents in the extent of distress produced at work. In such studies, it is difficult to disentangle the unique effects of jobs from the characteristics of individuals that may select them into those jobs and/or into differing marital and family situations. Long-term panel designs provide an opportunity to control for selection into occupations and increase our understanding of the cumulative effects of relatively stable workplace conditions on individual and family outcomes.

The measurement of workplace requirements also typically involves self-reports regarding opportunities and demands, and such reports may be biased by emotional well-being. An alternative that I use here is to match Census Bureau codes of occupations with Dictionary of Occupational Titles data of occupational characteristics. Because individual jobs vary within a single occupational code, such data are also imperfect, and the imprecision of these measures makes it likely that they result in underestimates of effects of occupational conditions; measurement error, though, is likely to be independent of individual or family characteristics.

These analyses build on prior work investigating the effects of mothers' working conditions on their children's development (Menaghan & Parcel, 1990, 1991; Parcel & Menaghan, 1990; Rogers et al., 1991). The earlier analyses have demonstrated that the quality of home environments affects both cognitive and social outcomes; mothers' occupational complexity affects the quality of home environments, and both mothers' wages and mothers' work hours also have direct effects on child outcomes. In this analysis I focus on married mothers with young (5 to 8 years old) children; I consider effects of both parents' working conditions and investigate how those conditions affect marital quality as well as home environments and children's behavior.

Obviously, one cannot consider the effects of work and family stressors without taking into account the differing levels of psychosocial resources that parents bring to bear on their situations. These function as coping resources that enable parents to offset some of the stressful potential of difficult work and family circumstances. In addition, stronger resources may have interactive effects, enabling parents to deal more effectively with the stressful complexities of occupational and family demands; I investigate such interactive effects in this analysis. The number of children at home also affects marital interaction, parents' abilities to provide adequate home environments, and children's social development. I argue that increasing numbers of children constitute a stressor that may increase parental marital disagreement and reduce the investments of time and affection that parents can make in any one child. Family size is therefore controlled in all equations.

Thus I hypothesize that parental work stressors—particularly long work hours, low wages, and employment in occupations that offer little opportunity for self-direction—as well as parental cognitive and psycho-social resources, including self-esteem and mastery affect parents' marital interaction, the family environments that they provide for their children, and their children's socioemotional outcomes. The impact of parents' occupational conditions on the quality of husband–wife relations and the quality of the family environment that parents provide is particularly crucial, because these are important pathways by which parents' social experiences and position affect the intergenerational transmission of socially structured stress.

Study Sample

I use data from women in the National Longitudinal Surveys of Youth (NLSY), born between 1958 and 1965, who were interviewed each year from 1979 (when they were between 14 and 21) through 1988, as well as information collected in 1988 about the children who had been born to these women (see Baker & Mott, 1989; Mott & Quinlan, 1991). I select married women with at least one child aged 5 to 8 years in 1988; I exclude the very few mothers whose husbands were not currently employed, but permit mothers' employment status to vary. As the descriptive data in Table 1 show, nearly two thirds of these married mothers are employed, consistent with national data (U.S. Bureau of the Census, 1990). Most parents average a high school education, and occupational complexity is below the average for all U.S. occupations. Fathers' work is on average higher than mothers' in opportunities for self-direction and in hourly wages. Father's workweek is also longer, with only 10% of mothers but nearly half of fathers typically working more than 40 hours a week. Conversely, part-time work schedules are common for mothers but very rare for fathers.

Though the sample captures a large segment of American occupational and family experience, it is important to realize that the families studied are not representative of the full range of U.S. married-couple families in the late 1980s. All include mothers who are only aged 23 to 30 but have at least one child who is 5 to 8 years old, so that they must necessarily have begun childbearing at relatively early ages. Relatively few have gone beyond high school. The NLSY sample does not include representative numbers of higher-earning "career" occupants or dual career couples, whose more advantaged statuses take considerable education to acquire and who tend to delay childbearing. The young and relatively disadvantaged families I study are particularly likely to face problems of male underemployment and low female occupational opportunities, and their overall economic resources are fairly low.

Table 1. Variables in the Analysis: Description and Basic Statistics, NLSY Mothers Married to Employed Husbands and Living with Child Aged 5 to 8 in 1988 (unweighted n = 782)

Variable	Mean	Standard deviation	Description
MARRPROB	−.45	5.49	Mothers' report of frequency of arguments about chores, children, money, affection, religion, leisure, drinking, other women, relatives; calm discussion (R), laugh together (R), conversation (R). Items standardized and summed (alpha = .78).
HOME88	.54	0.78	Frequency of cognitive stimulation, verbal responsiveness/warmth, and safe, orderly physical surroundings. Items standardized and summed (alpha = .71).
BEHPROB	−2.26	12.46	Frequency of 28 behavior problems tapping aggressive, hyperactive, depressed, withdrawn behavior. Items standardized and summed (alpha = .81).
Parental resources			
MOMEDU88	12.08	1.73	Years of education completed.
MOMAGE88	27.84	2.03	Age in years.
SPSED88	12.29	2.12	Years of education completed.
SPAGE88	31.44	5.50	Age in years.
MOMAFQT	68.85	19.96	Armed Forces Qualifying Test administered in 1980 to obtain standard measure of cognitive skills.
SELF	−.04	.82	Average of 4-item locus of control scale and 10-item Rosenberg self-esteem scale.
Ethnicity			Maternal ethnicity dummy coded; white is the reference category in regressions.
BLACK	.10	.30	
WHITE	.82	.38	
MEXSPAN	.06	.23	
OTHSPAN	.02	.15	
Mothers' occupational conditions			
MESTAT88	.63	.48	Mother's employment status (1 = employed).
MOMSC88	−4.05	10.30	Sum of 19 items from Dictionary of Occupational Titles descriptors attached to U.S. Census codes for mother's current occupation (alpha = .94).

(*continued*)

Table 1. (*Continued*)

Variable	Mean	Standard deviation	Description
MWAGE88	6.66	3.82	Hourly wage rate of mothers' job.
MWKHRS88	34.98	12.26	Usual work hours per week.
Categorized work hours			
MHR88A	.15	.36	Dummy variables categorizing mother's usual
MHR88B	.18	.38	work hours: less than 20 hours (*A*), 20 to 34
MHR88C	.53	.50	hours (*B*), 35–40 hours (*C*, the reference cat-
MHR88D	.14	.35	egory), and more than 40 hours (*D*).
		Father's occupational conditions	
DADSC88	−3.64	10.24	See MOMSC88 above.
SPSWG88	10.88	6.27	Hourly wage rate of father's job.
SPSHRS88	45.12	12.19	Usual work hours per week.
Categorized work hours			
SHR88A	.04	.21	Dummy variables categorizing father's work
SHR88B	.55	.50	hours per week as less than 35 hours (*A*), 35
SHR88C	.41	.49	to 40 hours (*B*, the reference category), and more than 40 hours (*D*).
		Family size	
NUMKID88	2.33	.90	Number of children living with mother in 1988.
		Child characteristics	
CHLTH88	.03	.17	Health problem limits school or play (1 = yes/0 = no).
LOBRTHWT	.06	.23	Birth weight below 5.5 lb. (1 = yes/0 = no).
MALE	.53	.50	Gender (1 = male/0 = female).
AGE	85.21	12.42	Age of child in months.

Measures

The measures used in the analysis are listed and briefly described in Table 1. Behavior problems are measured by 28 items tapping mothers' reports of child behavior problems that had been included in the 1982 Child Health Supplement to the National Health Interview Survey (Zill, 1988). These items were drawn primarily from the larger Child Behavior Checklist (CBCL) developed by Achenbach and Edelbrock (1981, 1983). The items include difficulties in interaction with other children and at home, difficulties in concentration, having a strong temper, and being argumentative, as well as questions about being anxious or fearful, feeling sad or depressed, being withdrawn, being too dependent/clingy, and feeling worthless/inferior. Rogers et al. (1991) provide additional information regarding this measure of behavior problems.

Home environments are assessed using an abridged version of the age-specific HOME scales developed by Bradley and Caldwell (Bradley & Caldwell 1977; 1979; 1984; Bradley, Caldwell, Rock, Hamrick, & Harris, 1988). The items include both maternal report and interviewer observations; they tap both maternal contributions to family home environments and the contributions of other family members, but they give greater emphasis to actions of the mother. Exploratory factor analyses using the 1986 data and all age-appropriate children (see Parcel & Menaghan, 1989), as well as confirmatory factor analyses with the 1988 data, identified three major dimensions that were common to both the preschool and school-age factor structures and were consistent with the original Bradley and Caldwell conceptualization: cognitive stimulation, maternal responsiveness, and good physical environment. Because items varied somewhat for children 3 through 5 and those 6 and older, scales were standardized within these age groups and combined across the two groups to create the global measure of home environments used in this analysis. For additional detail regarding the measure of home environments, see Menaghan and Parcel (1991) and Parcel and Menaghan (1989).

Marital problems are measured by a series of questions asking about the frequency of arguments with the spouse and the frequency of positive interactions (see Table 1). To construct the measure of overall marital problems used here, the positive items are reflected and a sum of the standardized items is computed. Thus, the more frequent and the more widespread the conflicts, and the less frequent any offsetting positive interactions, the greater the marital problems.

I focus on occupational complexity, wage levels, and work hours as key aspects of both parents' work experiences. These measures of occupational conditions are constructed for all employed parents. Measures of parental occupational complexity are constructed from Dictionary of Occupational Titles (DOT) data compiled by the U.S. Department of Labor and matched to the detailed Census Bureau occupational code for parents' current jobs. The measure of occupational substantive complexity (see Parcel, 1989) includes 19 DOT items describing occupational content in terms of direction, control, and planning; influencing people; complexity of working with data and people; numerical and verbal aptitudes required; and low extent of repetitive or continuous processes. Reliability for the scale is .94. The extent of employment is measured in terms of usual hours worked per week for both mothers and fathers in 1988. For fathers, dummy variables differentiate part-time (1–34 hours) from overtime hours (41 or more hours), with full-time work hours (35–

40 hours) serving as the omitted category. Dummy variables for maternal hours also differentiate low part-time hours (1–20) from moderate part-time hours (21–34) to tap the greater variation in these hours. Hourly wages are measured directly for mothers, and estimated for fathers by using mothers' reports of spouse earnings in the preceding calendar year.

Analyses

I examine 1988 marital quality, family environments, and child behavior problems. In each case I estimate multivariate models to predict 1988 outcomes as a function of occupational and family circumstances, both parents' background and educational statuses, and initial maternal resources. I assume that the quality of children's family environments has significant protective effects on the level of children's behavior problems. Marital quality affects children's behavior in part via its effects on the quality of family environments that children experience, and in part via other unmeasured aspects of family interaction (see Figure 1). All analyses control for parental age and ethnicity; analyses of child outcomes also control for child characteristics (age, gender, low birth weight, and current health problems). The data are weighted to correct for the initial oversampling of minority and low-income youths in the sampling frame; these weights are adjusted so that the total weighted number of cases is identical to the unweighted number of cases.

For all three dependent variables, I estimated straightforward additive models, then examined nonadditive models including interaction terms to test three interactive arguments. First, I investigated whether fathers' occupational conditions had more powerful effects when mothers were not employed than when mothers were also employed. Second, when mothers were employed, alternate models tested whether the effects of mothers' occupational conditions varied depending on their own cognitive or psychosocial resources. Finally, analyses also examined whether effects of marital problems and home environments on children's behavior problems varied depending on either parent's occupational conditions. Additional models explored whether effects varied depending on the joint combination of occupational conditions for mothers and fathers, but there were no significant interactions of maternal and paternal occupational complexity or wages on any of the dependent variables. Other models also tested effects of total family earnings or total family hours; these had no effects that differed from the models that treated each spouse's earnings and hours separately. Tables 2, 3, and 4 display additive and interactive models for the three basic equations predicting marital problems, family environments, and children's behavior problems. All interactive tests that were statistically significant in final equations are shown.

Findings

Marital Problems

I had expected that parents' occupational conditions would affect their marital interaction. As the first two columns of Table 2 show, in straightforward additive models neither parent's occupational conditions has significant effects. In addition, mothers who were not employed at all reported *fewer* marital problems than employed mothers (evaluated at average levels of employed mothers' working conditions).

Interactive tests for differences by employment status and by initial resources modify these conclusions, however, and reveal that both mothers' and fathers' occupational self-direction have significant beneficial effects under certain conditions. The equation, including all significant interactive terms, is shown on the right-hand side of Table 2. First, there

Table 2. Parental Marital Problems: Effects of Parental Occupational Conditions, Married-Couple Families with Children Aged 5 to 8

	B	beta	B	beta
Maternal working conditions				
Occupational complexity	−.03	−.04	−.03	−.04
By mother's self-concept			.08	.11[b]
Hourly pay	.12	.07[d]	.10	.06
Work hours				
LT 20 hours/wk	.33	.02	.62	.03
20–34 hours/wk	.46	.03	.34	.02
35–40 hours/wk[e]				
GT 40 hours/wk	.57	.03	.71	.04
Employed (1 = yes)	.88	.08[c]	1.13	.10[b]
Spouse's working conditions				
Occupational complexity	−.02	−.04	−.06	−.12[c]
By mother employed			.08	.12[c]
Hourly pay	−.02	−.02	−.02	−.02
Work hours:				
LT 35 hours/wk	−1.35	−.05	−1.48	−.06
35–40 hours/wk[e]				
GT 40 hours/wk	−.15	−.01	−.10	−.01
R^2 (adjusted R^2)		.13 (.11)		.15 (.12)

Note: All equations control for parental age and education, maternal cognitive skills, maternal self-concept, family size, and ethnicity (African American, Mexican-Hispanic, and other Hispanic).
[a]$P < .001$, two-tailed test, $P < .0005$, one-tailed test. [b]$P < .01$, two-tailed test, $P < .005$, one-tailed test. [c]$P < .05$, two-tailed test, $P < .025$, one-tailed test. [d]$P < .10$, two-tailed test, $P < .05$, one-tailed test. [e]Reference category for categorical variable; unweighted $N = 782$.

is a significant interaction between maternal self-concept and maternal occupational complexity, such that occupational complexity effects are near zero for mothers at average or high levels of self-concept, but significantly protective for mothers initially low in self-esteem. Unstandardized regression coefficients at low (one standard deviation below the mean), average (mean), and high (one standard deviation above the mean) levels of self-concept are $-.10$, $-.03$, and $.03$, respectively. A similar pattern occurs for maternal wages, but the interaction falls just short of statistical significance. Thus mothers' great occupational opportunities do seem to protect against marital problems, but their role is limited to mothers whose initial low psychosocial resources would otherwise make them likely to register high marital problem levels.

Second, there is a significant interaction between mothers' employment status and fathers' occupational complexity. The effects of fathers' occupational complexity, nonsignificant overall, are significant and beneficial when mothers are not themselves employed ($B = -.06$, $P < .05$) but have virtually no effect on level of marital problems when mothers are also employed ($B = .06 + .08 = .02$, ns). It is interesting that the benefits of fathers' positive working conditions on marital quality are only significant when mothers are also employed. Most prior research on the benefits of men's occupational self-direction focused on fathers' values or child outcomes, not marital interaction, and this research was done at a time when lower proportions of employed men's wives were employed outside the home. Though a husband's better job conditions may continue to benefit his individual well-being, the current findings suggest that fathers' occupational complexity may have more mixed effects for marital quality when mothers are also employed.

The interaction between employment status and husband's substantive complexity is graphed in Figure 2 to show that there is not a uniform difference in marital problems between employed and unemployed mothers. Effects for employed mothers whose husbands have jobs of average complexity are set at zero, and other group effects are expressed relative to this group. This difference varies depending on the level of complexity in the husband's occupation: The more complex the husband's occupation, the more wives' employment is associated with greater marital complaints. Again, this pattern suggests that the effects of mothers' employment on their marriages depend in part on their husbands' occupational demands and opportunities. When husbands' occupational conditions are rewarding and absorbing, they may see less need for their wives to persist in their own occupational activities; her employment and the associated demands for greater husband participation in household routines may create greater conflict under these conditions.

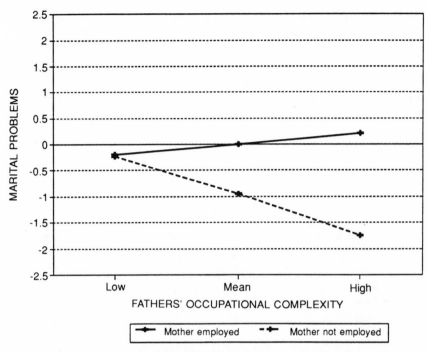

Figure 2. The effects of fathers' occupational complexity on marital problems: Variations by mothers' employment status. Effects shown are adjusted for parental age and education, maternal cognitive skills, maternal self-concept, family size, and ethnicity (African American, Mexican-Hispanic, and other Hispanic). Effects for employed mothers whose husbands have jobs of average complexity are set to zero.

Children's Family Environments

Table 3 displays additive and interactive equations for family environments. As expected, marital problems have significant adverse effects on the quality of children's home environments. Thus parental substantive complexity has indirect effects on home environments via its impact on marital quality. Fathers' occupational conditions also have direct effects: Fathers' substantive complexity predicts better home environments, and fathers' working less than normatively expected full-time schedules has strong negative implications for their children's home environments. Tests for interaction (see the right-hand equation in Table 3) show that these effects are stronger when mothers are not employed: Fathers' substantive complexity is more beneficial, and low father work hours are more negative, when fathers are the only family earner. Conversely, positive effects of mothers' employment are

Table 3. Children's Family Environments: Effects of Parental Occupational Conditions, Married-Couple Families with Children Aged 5 to 8

	B	beta	B	beta
Maternal working conditions				
Occupational complexity	.00	.03	.00	.04
Hourly pay	.00	.01	.00	.01
Work hours:				
LT 20 hours/wk	.04	.02	.07	.03
20–34 hours/wk	−.01	−.00	.02	.01
35–40 hours/wk[e]				
GT 40 hours/wk	.06	.02	.06	.02
Employed (1 = yes)	.00	.00	.03	.02
Spouse's working conditions				
Occupational complexity	.01	.07[c]	.01	.14[b]
By mother employed			−.01	−.09[b]
Hourly pay	.01	.05	.01	.05
Work hours:				
LT 35 hours/wk	−.26	−.07[c]	−.78	−.20[a]
By mother employed			.71	.15[b]
By marital problems			−.02	−.02
35–40 hours/wk[e]				
GT 40 hours/wk	−.01	−.00	.13	.08
By mother employed			−.20	−.11[d]
By marital problems			.03	.12[b]
Marital problems	−.02	−.13[a]	−.03	−.19[a]
R^2 (adjusted R^2)		.24 (.22)		.27 (.24)

Note: All equations control for parental age and education, maternal cognitive skills, maternal self-concept, family size, ethnicity (African American, Mexican-Hispanic, and other Hispanic), and child's age, gender, birth weight, and current health problems.
[a]$P < .001$, two-tailed test, $P < .0005$, one-tailed test.   [b]$P < .01$, two-tailed test, $P < .005$, one-tailed test.   [c]$P < .05$, two-tailed test, $P < .025$, one-tailed test.   [d]$P < .10$, two-tailed test, $P < .05$, one-tailed test.   [e]Reference category for categorical variable; unweighted $N = 782$.

stronger when husbands' work hours and substantive complexity are low.

I had argued that very long father work hours would have negative effects, particularly when their wives are also working, but I do not find this effect. If anything, fathers' heavy work schedules tend to be positive ($P < .12$) for male-earner families, although this effect is weaker when mothers are employed (interaction $P < .10$). In addition, interactive analyses suggest that when fathers work long work hours, marital problems have a *less* adverse impact on children's family environment. This finding is unexpected; it is possible that mothers who are dissatisfied with their marriages make a greater effort than other mothers to compensate for their husbands' absence, or that the greater absence of the father under conditions of high marital problems means that the child is exposed to less open conflict or disagreement between parents. It will be important to see whether this pattern is replicated in other data sets.

Children's Behavior Problems

Table 4 displays additive and interactive equations for children's behavior problems. As expected, both marital problems and family environments have significant effects on children's behavior. Because paren-

Table 4. Children's Behavior Problems: Effects of Parental Occupational Conditions, Married-Couple Families with Children Aged 5 to 8

	B	beta	B	beta
Maternal working conditions				
Occupational complexity	.11	.08[c]	.19	.13[b]
By family environments			−.17	−.11[c]
Hourly pay	−.15	−.04	−.24	−.06[d]
By marital problems			−.07	−.16[a]
Work hours				
LT 20 hours/wk	−.85	−.02	−.74	−.02
20–34 hours/wk	−.87	−.02	−.98	−.03
35–40 hours/wk[e]				
GT 40 hours/wk	−.76	−.06	−1.25	−.03
Employed (1 = yes)	.77	.03	.20	.01
Spouse's working conditions				
Occupational complexity	−.01	−.01	.06	.05
By family environments			−.11	−.09[c]
Hourly pay	−.03	−.02	−.08	−.04
Work hours:				
LT 35 hours/wk	5.14	.09[c]	15.07	.26[a]
By mother employed			−13.56	−.19[b]
35–40 hours/wk[e]				
GT 40 hours/wk	−.97	−.04	1.90	−.08
By mother employed			1.78	.06
Marital problems	.28	.13[a]	.56	.25[a]
Home environment	−2.30	−.15[a]	−2.86	−.19[a]
R^2 (adjusted R^2)		.16 (.13)		.19 (.16)

Note: All equations control for parental age and education, maternal cognitive skills, maternal self-concept, family size, ethnicity (African American, Mexican-Hispanic, and other Hispanic), and child's age, gender, birth weight, and current health problems.
[a]$P < .001$, two-tailed test, $P < .0005$, one-tailed test.   [b]$P < .01$, two-tailed test, $P < .005$, one-tailed test.   [c]$P < .05$, two-tailed test, $P < .025$, one-tailed test.   [d]$P < .10$, two-tailed test, $P < .05$, one-tailed test.   [e]Reference category for categorical variable; unweighted $N = 782$.

tal working conditions affect these intermediate outcomes, they have indirect effects on children's socioemotional outcomes. Fathers' low work hours also have direct adverse effects on children's behavior problems; again, the deleterious effects of fathers' low work hours are particularly powerful when mothers are not employed. Contrary to expectation, the direct additive effect of mothers' occupational complexity is positive, suggesting that children whose mothers have more complex and challenging occupations have *more* behavior problems.

Again, interactive tests qualify these findings: Both mothers' substantive complexity and fathers' substantive complexity interact with home environments, with occupational complexity effects slightly beneficial when home environments are good but having increasingly negative implications as home environments are less adequate. Conversely, of course, the generally protective effects of good home environments in reducing children's behavior problems are stronger when parents' occupational conditions are favorable, and more limited when parents' occupational complexity is lower. Figure 3 displays this interaction for mothers' occupational complexity. Effects for children whose mothers are in occupations of average complexity and providing average home environments are set to zero to serve as the reference group. It is clear that mothers' occupational complexity has little impact at average levels of home environments; increasing occupational complexity has favorable impacts as long as home environments are strong, but adverse effects when home environments are poor.

Interactive tests also show that employed mothers' wage levels quality the effects of marital problems on children's behavior problems, with benefits of better-wage jobs higher when marital problems are high. Conversely, the harsh implications of high marital conflict for children's behavior problems are strongest when employed mothers earn low wages. Figure 4 depicts this interaction.

A focus on occupational stressors has guided my presentation of findings, but it is important to note that family composition and parental resources also have significant effects on family and child outcomes. The strongest predictors of marital problems are large family size and poor maternal resources, including both poor initial self-concept and weak early cognitive skills. Echoing the findings for marital problems, both positive maternal self-concept and small family size have strong direct effects on the quality of home environments. Each parent's educational attainment also has a positive effect. Finally, maternal resources also affect children's behavior problems, with younger mothers and those with poorer initial self-concepts having children with higher levels of behavior problems.

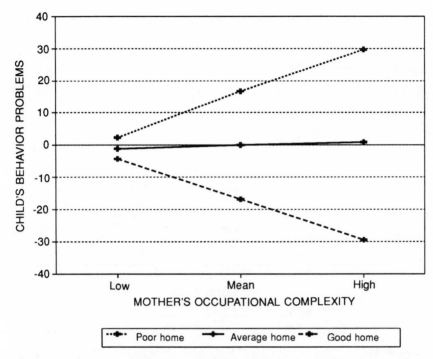

Figure 3. The effects of mothers' occupational complexity on child's well-being: Variations by quality of home environment. Effects shown are adjusted for parental age and education, maternal cognitive skills, maternal self-concept, family size, ethnicity (African American, Mexican-Hispanic, and other Hispanic), child's age, gender, birth weight, and current health problems. Effects for mothers in occupations of average complexity and providing average home environments are set to zero.

The Relative Contribution of Husbands and Wives

The models presented are limited in that they do not tap how various combinations of parental occupational conditions may shape family interaction and child outcomes. Again, a full examination of these issues is not possible in a brief space, but it is worth outlining how one might tap such combinations empirically to extend the analyses discussed here. One way of measuring this is to create summary measures of family wage levels and total family work hours, then calculate the relative contribution of husbands and wives to these family totals. Somewhat similarly, one can calculate the average direction of difference in spouses' substantive complexity. Although I do not present findings for such relative measures here, creating such variables for the subset of couples

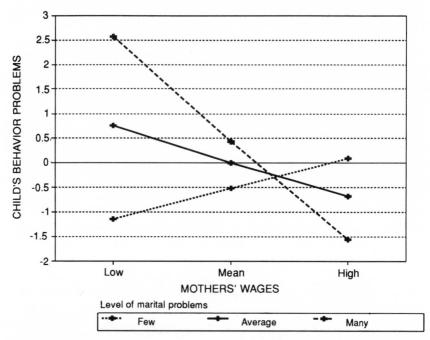

Figure 4. The effects of mothers' wages and marital problems on child's well-being. Effects shown are adjusted for parental age and education, maternal cognitive skills, maternal self-concept, family size, ethnicity (African American, Mexican-Hispanic, and other Hispanic), child's age, gender, birth weight, and current health problems. Effects for mothers with average wages and average marital problems are set to zero.

in which both spouses were employed provides additional insight into the characteristics of the sample studied. There were expectable gender differences in these relative measures, but it is noteworthy that the magnitude of the differences was not large: Husbands accounted for 56% of parental work hours and, on average, only slightly exceeded their wives' substantive complexity (mean difference is less than one twentieth of a standard deviation). At this early point in the life course and for this sample of early childbearers, differences between husbands and wives in occupational conditions and work hours are not as large as they may be later in the life course or in more inclusive samples of workers. Even at this early stage, however, and despite relatively small differences in work hours, husbands earned 66% of total family earnings, buttressing their claims to be considered the major breadwinners despite the significant contributions of their wives to the total family economic resources.

CONCLUSIONS

These illustrative analyses help to establish several conclusions and raise new questions. First, there is strong evidence that parents' occupational conditions have effects that reach beyond individual mental health and affect the emotional well-being and related behavior of the next generation. My findings support the argument that variations in parents' occupational and family conditions have theoretically interesting and socially important consequences not only for adults' own intellectual and emotional outcomes but also for the social development of their children.

Second, they suggest that the effects of parents' jobs are in part shaped by gender expectations regarding male and female responsibilities for economic provision and children's care. This is particularly striking with regard to work hours. Fathers' typical work hours are long—the mean hours are well above a full-time week of 40 hours—but extensive commitment has virtually no overt negative effects, suggesting that heavy work involvement of fathers does not violate parents' expectations or lead to marital conflict, negative home environments, or children with behavior problems. In contrast, when fathers are unable or unwilling to obtain full-time employment, negative effects are strong, and these are particularly powerful when these fathers are carrying the sole responsibility for earning. In contrast, variations in mothers' work hours are less pronounced, and they have no significant effects in these models.

Third, it is clear that the effects of occupational self-direction and complexity on family patterns and children's emotional well-being are complex and conditional. Effects vary depending on the resources parents bring to the situation, on the total employment configuration of the family, and on the overall family environment. It is striking to note the differences between conclusions based on the simple additive models and the final interactive equations here; future research on familial and intergenerational repercussions of workplace stressors must move beyond prevailing additive models.

Fourth, the results suggest that the increasingly common pattern of joint parental employment is creating new stressors as well as new opportunities for families. Mothers' employment and wages may compensate for husbands' occupational difficulties and shortfalls, but they may also increase conflicts when husbands are heavily involved in and relatively successful at their own occupational efforts. For such fathers, their wives' employment appears less necessary and less helpful, and they may prefer that their wives provide a more supportive backdrop to their own efforts. I speculate that their wives, however, are reluctant to give up their own occupational efforts and are pressing instead for greater male involvement at home.

It is also clear that there is not a single, unqualified effect of maternal employment on marriage or family outcomes. Maternal employment effects vary with fathers' occupational demands and mothers' resources; they are also very likely to vary depending on the gender role beliefs of both partners, although investigation of that possibility was beyond the scope of this analysis. The findings presented suggest that both parents' occupational conditions need to be considered simultaneously if we are to achieve an adequate understanding of their effects, both for the adults involved and for their families.

It is worth reiterating that the sample studied is not representative of all married-couple families with children in the early elementary years. Both mothers and fathers tend to have little educational attainment beyond high school, and they are unlikely to hold jobs that are high in occupational complexity or earnings. Some of the effects observed here may not hold for those who undertake parenting at later ages or with greater social resources. Additional research with more advantaged samples will illuminate these issues. Indeed, as the NLSY child–mother interviews are repeated, these questions can be investigated empirically.

At the outset I argued that parents' persistent exposure to better or worse occupational conditions constituted a set of chronic stressors that had implications beyond individual well-being. Both theoretical argument and the empirical findings presented bolster the claim that parental economic rewards, work hours, and opportunities for occupational self-direction have repercussions for parental marriage, the quality of home environments they provide their children, and their children's vulnerability to emotional and behavioral problems. These effects, moreover, are not simple extensions of effects on individual adult well-being. The effects of one spouse's occupational experiences on family outcomes are contingent in multiple ways that draw attention to deep-seated gender differences in both work experiences and the interpretation of those experiences. Incorporating these interpersonal and intergenerational contingencies into social stress theory is a task that provides an invigorating expansion of current research and a new challenge to researchers.

ACKNOWLEDGMENTS

Work on this paper was partially supported by grants from the National Institute of Child Health and Human Development (HD26047), and the Office of Population Affairs of the National Institutes of Health (PG00657), and by the Center for Human Resource Research at the

Ohio State University. I thank Lori Kowaleski Jones for research assistance.

REFERENCES

Achenbach, T. S., & Edelbrock, C. (1981). Behavioral problems and competencies reported by parents of normal and disturbed children aged four through sixteen. *Monographs of the Society for Research in Child Development, 46* (1, Serial No. 188).

Achenbach, T. S., & Edelbrock, C. (1983). *Manual for the child behavior checklist and revised child behavior profile.* Burlington: Department of Psychiatry, University of Vermont.

Aneshensel, C. S., Rutter, C. M., & Lachenbruch, P. A. (1991). Social structure, stress, and mental health: Competing conceptual and analytic models. *American Sociological Review, 56,* 166–178.

Baker, P., & Mott, F. L. (1989). *NLSY child handbook 1989: A guide and resource document for the National Longitudinal Survey of Youth 1986 child data.* Columbus: Center for Human Resource Research, Ohio State University.

Bielby, W. T., & Baron, J. N. (1984). A woman's place is with other women: Sex segregation within organizations. In B. F. Reskin (Ed.), *Sex segregation in the workplace: Trends, explanations, remedies* (pp. 27–55). Washington, DC: National Academy of Science.

Bielby, W. T., & Bielby, D. D. (1992). I will follow him: Family ties, gender role beliefs, and reluctance to relocate for a better job. *American Journal of Sociology, 97,* 1241–1294.

Bolger, N., DeLongis, A., Kessler, R. C., & Schilling, E. A. (1989). The effects of daily stress on negative mood. *Journal of Personality and Social Psychology, 57,* 808–818.

Bolger, N., DeLongis, A., Kessler, R. C., & Wethington, E. (1989). The contagion of stress across multiple roles. *Journal of Marriage and the Family, 51,* 175–183.

Bradbury, T. N., & Fincham, F. D. (1990). Attributions in marriage: Review and critique. *Psychological Bulletin, 107,* 3–33.

Bradley, R. H., & Caldwell, B. M. (1977). Home observation for measurement of the environment: A validation study of screening efficiency. *American Journal of Mental Deficiency, 81,* 417–420.

Bradley, R. H., & Caldwell, B. M. (1979). Home observation for measurement of the environment: A revision of the preschool scale. *American Journal of Mental Deficiency, 84,* 235–244.

Bradley, R. H., & Caldwell, B. M. (1984). The HOME inventory and family demographics. *Developmental Psychology, 20,* 315–320.

Bradley, R., Caldwell, B., Rock, S. L., Hamrick, H. M., & Harris, P. (1988). Home observation for measurement of the environment: Development of a home inventory for use with families having children 6 to 10 years old. *Contemporary Educational Psychology, 13,* 58–71.

Conger, R. D., Conger, K. J., Elder, Jr., Lorenz, F. O., Simons, R. L., & Whitbeck, L. B. (1992). A family process model of economic hardship and adjustment of early adolescent boys. *Child Development, 63,* 526–541.

Conger, R. D., Elder, G. H., Jr., Lorenz, F. O., Conger, K. J., Simons, R. L., Whitbeck, L. B., Huck, S., & Melby, J. N. (1990). Linking economic hardship to marital quality and instability. *Journal of Marriage and the Family, 52,* 643–656.

Crouter, A. C., Perry-Jenkins, M., Huston, T. L., & Crawford, D. W. (1989). The influence of work-induced psychological states on behavior at home. *Basic and Applied Social Psychology, 10,* 273–292.

Elder, G. H., Jr. (1974). *Children of the great depression.* Chicago: University of Chicago Press.
Elder, G. H., Jr., & Caspi, A. (1988). Human development and social change: An emerging perspective on the life course. In N. Bolger, A. Caspi, G. Downey, & M. Moorehouse (Eds.), *Persons in context: Developmental processes* (pp. 77–113). Cambridge, MA: Cambridge University Press.
Ferree, M. M. (1990). Feminism and family research. *Journal of Marriage and the Family, 52,* 866–884.
Gecas, V., & Seff, M. (1989). Social class, occupational conditions, and self-esteem. *Sociological Perspectives, 32,* 353–364.
Glass, J. (1990). The impact of occupational segregation on working conditions. *Social Forces, 90,* 779–796.
Glass, J., & Camarigg, V. (1992). Gender, parenthood, and job–family investment. *American Journal of Sociology, 98,* 131–151.
Gottfried, A. E., & Gottfried, A. W. (1988). *Maternal employment and children's development.* New York: Plenum.
Grossman, F. K., Pollack, W. S., & Golding, E. (1988). Fathers and children: Predicting the quality and quantity of fathering. *Developmental Psychology, 24,* 82–91.
Haynes, S. G., & Feinleib, M. (1980). Women, work, and coronary heart disease: Prospective findings from the Framingham study. *American Journal of Public Health, 70,* 133–141.
Hibbard, J. H., & Pope, C. R. (1987). Employment characteristics and health status among men and women. *Women and Health, 12,* 85–102.
Hill, M. S. (1988). Marital stability and spouses' shared time. *Journal of Family Issues, 9,* 427–451.
Hood, J. (1983). *Becoming a two-job family.* New York: Praeger.
House, J. S., Strecher, V., Metzner, H. L., & Robbins, C. A. (1986). Occupational stress and health among men and women in the Tecumseh community health study. *Journal of Health and Social Behavior, 27,* 62–77.
Jacobs, J. (1989). *Revolving doors: Sex segregation and women's careers.* Stanford, CA: Stanford University Press.
Karasek, R. A. (1979). Job demands, job decision latitude and mental strain: Implications for job redesign. *Administrative Science Quarterly, 24,* 285–308.
Karasek, R. A., Baker, D., Marxer, F., Ahlbom, A., & Theorell, T. (1981). Job decision latitude, job demands, and cardiovascular disease: A prospective study of Swedish men. *American Journal of Public Health, 71,* 694–705.
Kohn, M. L. (1977). *Class and conformity* (2nd ed.). Chicago: University of Chicago Press.
Kohn, M. L., Naoi, A., Schoenbach, C., Schooler, C., & Slomczynski, K. M. (1990). Position in the class structure and psychological functioning in the United States, Japan, and Poland. *American Journal of Sociology, 95,* 964–1008.
Kohn, M. L., & Schooler, C. (1982). Job conditions and personality: A longitudinal assessment of their reciprocal effects. *American Journal of Sociology, 87,* 1257–1286.
Kohn, M. L., & Schooler, C. (Eds.), with the collaboration of J. Miller, K. A. Miller, C. Schoenbach, & R. Schoenberg. (1983). *Work and personality.* Norwood, NJ: Ablex.
Kohn, M. L., Slomczynski, K. M., & Schoenbach, C. (1986). Social stratification and the transmission of values in the family: A cross-national assessment. *Sociological Forum, 1,* 73–102.
Lennon, M. C. (1987). Sex differences in distress: The impact of gender and work roles. *Journal of Health and Social Behavior, 28,* 290–305.
Lennon, M. C. (1991). The structural context of stress. *Journal of Health and Social Behavior, 30,* 261–268.

Liem, J. H., & Liem, G. R. (1990). Understanding the individual and family effects of unemployment. In J. Eckenrode & S. Gore (Eds.), *Stress between work and family* (pp. 175–204). New York: Plenum.

Liker, J. K., & Elder, G. H., Jr. (1983). Economic hardship and marital relations in the 1930s. *American Sociological Review, 48*, 343–359.

Luster, T., Rhoades, K., & Haas, B. (1989). The relation between parental values and parenting behavior: A test of the Kohn hypothesis. *Journal of Marriage and the Family, 51*, 139–147.

McLoyd, V. C. (1989). Socialization and development in a changing economy. *American Psychologist, 44*, 293–302.

McLoyd, V. C. (1990). The impact of economic hardship on black families and children: Psychological distress, parenting, and socioemotional development. *Child Development, 61*, 311–346.

Menaghan, E. G. (1991). Work experiences and family interaction processes: The long reach of the job? *Annual Review of Sociology, 17*, 419–444.

Menaghan, E. G., & Parcel, T. L. (1990). Parental employment and family life: Research in the 1980s. *Journal of Marriage and the Family, 52*, 1079–1098.

Menaghan, E. G., & Parcel, T. L. (1991). Determining children's home environments: The impact of maternal characteristics and current occupational and family conditions. *Journal of Marriage and the Family, 53*, 417–431.

Miller, J., Schooler, C. Kohn, M. L., & Miller, K. A. (1979). Women and work: The psychological effects of occupational conditions. *American Journal of Sociology, 85*, 66–94.

Miller, J., Slomczynski, K. M., & Kohn, M. L. (1985). Continuity of learning-generalization: The effect of job on men's intellective process in the United States and Poland. *American Journal of Sociology, 91*, 593–615.

Miller, K. A., & Kohn, M. L. (1983). The reciprocal effects of job conditions and the intellectuality of leisure-time activities. In M. L. Kohn & C. Schooler (Eds.), *Work and personality* (pp. 217–241). Norwood, NJ: Ablex.

Mincer, J. (1978). Family migration decisions. *Journal of Political Economy, 86*, 749–775.

Mirowsky, J., & Ross, C. E. (1986). Social patterns of distress. *Annual Review of Sociology, 12*, 23–45.

Mortimer, J. T., & Borman, K. M. (Eds.). (1988). *Work experience and psychological development through the life span.* Boulder, CO: Westview.

Mortimer, J. T., Lorence, J., & Kumka, D. S. (1986). *Work, family, and personality: Transition to adulthood.* Norwood, NJ: Ablex.

Mott, F. L., & Quinlan, S. (1991). *Children of the NLSY: 1988 tabulations and summary discussion.* Columbus: Center for Human Resource Research, Ohio State University.

Naoi, A., & Schooler, C. (1985). Occupational conditions and psychological functioning in Japan. *American Journal of Sociology, 90*, 729–752.

Newman, K. (1988). *Falling from grace.* New York: Free Press.

Nock, S. L., & Kingston, P. W. (1988). Time with children: The impact of couples' work-time commitments. *Social Forces, 67*, 59–85.

O'Brien, G. E. (1986). *Psychology of work and unemployment.* New York: Wiley.

Parcel, T. L. (1989). Comparable worth, occupational labor markets, and occupational earnings: Results from the 1980 census. In R. Michael, H. Hartmann, & B. O'Farrell (Eds.), *Pay equity: Empirical inquiries* (pp. 134–152). Washington, DC: National Academy Press.

Parcel, T. L., & Menaghan, E. G. (1989). *Child home environment as a mediating construct between SES and child outcomes.* Columbus: Center for Human Resources Research, Ohio State University.

Parcel, T. L., & Menaghan, E. G. (1990). Maternal working conditions and child verbal ability: Studying the transmission of inter-generational inequality from mothers to young children. *Social Psychology Quarterly, 53,* 132–147.

Pearlin, L. I. (1971). *Class context and family relations: A cross-national study.* Boston: Little Brown.

Pearlin, L. I. (1989). The sociological study of stress. *Journal of Health and Social Behavior, 30,* 241–256.

Pearlin, L. I., & Kohn, M. L. (1966). Social class, occupation, and parental values: A cross-national study. *American Sociological Review, 31,* 466–479.

Pearlin, L. I., & McCall, M. (1990). Occupational stress and marital support: A description of microprocesses. In J. Eckenrode & S. Gore (Eds.), *Stress between work and family* (pp. 39–60). New York: Plenum.

Peterson, R. P., & Gerson, K. (1992). Determinants of responsibility for child care arrangements along dual-earner couples. *Journal of Marriage and the Family, 54,* 527–536.

Piotrkowski, C. S. (1979). *Work and the family system.* New York: Free Press.

Piotrkowski, C. S., & Katz, M. H. (1982). Indirect socialization of children: The effects of mothers' jobs on academic behaviors. *Child Development, 53,* 409–415.

Potuchek, J. (1992). Employed wives' orientation to breadwinning: A gender theory analysis. *Journal of Marriage and the Family, 54,* 548–558.

Repetti, R. L. (1989). The effects of daily workload on subsequent behavior during marital interaction: The roles of social withdrawal and spouse support. *Journal of Personality and Social Psychology, 57,* 651–659.

Reskin, B. F., & Roos, P. (1990). *Job queues, gender queues: Explaining women's inroads into male occupations.* Philadelphia: Temple University Press.

Rogers, S. J., Parcel, T. L., & Menaghan, E. G. (1991). The effects of maternal working conditions and mastery on child behavior problems: Studying the intergenerational transmission of social control. *Journal of Health and Social Behavior, 32,* 145–164.

Rosenfield, S. (1989). The effects of women's employment: Personal control and sex differences in mental health. *Journal of Health and Social Behavior, 30,* 77–91.

Ross, C. E., & Mirowsky, J. (1988). Child care and emotional adjustment to wives' employment. *Journal of Health and Social Behavior, 29,* 127–138.

Ross, C. E., Mirowsky, J., & Huber, J. (1983). Dividing work, sharing work, and in-between: Marriage patterns and depression. *American Sociological Review, 8,* 809–823.

Schooler, C. (1987). Psychological effects of complex environments during the life span: A review and theory. In C. Schooler & K. W. Schaie (Eds.), *Cognitive functioning and social structure over the life course* (pp. 24–49). Norwood, NJ: Ablex.

Schooler, C., & Naoi, A. (1988). The psychological effects of traditional and of economically peripheral job settings in Japan. *American Journal of Sociology, 94,* 335–355.

Sorensen, A., & McLanahan, S. (1987). Married women's economic dependency, 1940–1980. *American Journal of Sociology, 93,* 659–687.

Spenner, K. I. (1988). Social stratification, work, and personality. *Annual Review of Sociology, 14,* 69–97.

Spenner, K. I., & Otto, L. B. (1985). Work and self-concept: Selection and socialization in the early career. In A. C. Kerckhoff (Ed.), *Research in sociology of education and socialization, vol. 5* (pp. 197–235). Greenwich, CT: JAI Press.

Thompson, L., & Walker, A. J. (1989). Gender in families: Women and men in marriage, work, and parenthood. *Journal of Marriage and the Family, 51,* 845–871.

U.S. Bureau of the Census (1990). *Statistical abstract of the United States* (110th ed.). Washington, DC: Government Printing Office.

Voydanoff, P., & Donnelly, B. W. (1989). Economic distress and mental health: The role of family coping resources and behaviors. *Lifestyles: Family and Economic Issues, 10,* 139–162.

Weiss, R. S. (1990a). Bringing work stress home. In J. Eckenrode & S. Gore (Eds.), *Stress between work and family* (pp. 17–37). New York: Plenum.

Weiss, R. S. (1990b). *Staying the course: The emotional and social lives of men who do well at work.* New York: Free Press.

Wharton, A. S., & Baron, J. N. (1987). So happy together? The impact of gender segregation on men at work. *American Sociological Review, 52,* 574–587.

Whitbeck, L. B., Simons, R. L., Conger, R. D., Lorenz, F. O., Huck, S., & Elder, G. H., Jr. (1991). Family economic hardship, parental support, and adolescent self-esteem. *Social Psychology Quarterly, 54,* 353–363.

Zill, N. (1988). Behavior, achievement, and health problems among children in step-families: Findings from a national survey of child health. In M. Hetherington & J. D. Arasteh (Eds.), *The impact of divorce, single parenting, and stepparenting on children* (pp. 325–368). Hillsdale, NJ: Erlbaum.

IV

Psychosocial Resources and Mediators

6

General and Specific Perceptions of Social Support

IRWIN G. SARASON, GREGORY R. PIERCE, and
BARBARA R. SARASON

This chapter is intended to serve several purposes. We begin by reviewing the concept of social support and its implications for assessment, an
activity that has preoccupied social support researchers for over a decade and a half. One conclusion we draw from this review is that research on social support, if it is to make significant advances, must focus
its attention on the mechanisms by which the various constructs of social
support lead to positive, and sometimes negative, psychological and
physical health outcomes. We then briefly describe several recent lines of
research on social support. Our aim is not to be exhaustive, but rather to
draw attention to what we believe are some intriguing pathways for
empirical inquiry. One of our major themes is that research on social
support needs to take more fully into account not only the role of social
support as a stress buffer, but also the complexity of social support
processes. The chapter ends with a theoretical perspective that builds on
available information and draws attention to several important variables
in the social support equation, including (a) the personality characteristics of the recipient, especially the recipient's general and specific expec-

IRWIN G. SARASON and BARBARA R. SARASON • Department of Psychology, University of Washington, Seattle, Washington 98195. GREGORY R. PIERCE • Department of Psychology, Hamilton College, Clinton, New York 13323.
Stress and Mental Health: Contemporary Issues and Prospects for the Future, edited by William R.
Avison and Ian H. Gotlib. New York, Plenum Press, 1994.

tations for social support; (b) the nature of the relationship between the recipient and the support provider, as well as other key members in the recipient's network; and (c) the situational context in which supportive efforts take place.

A major challenge to stress researchers has been the frequent finding of marked differences in how people respond to particular types of challenges. Whereas some people seem to deteriorate rapidly under stress, others show only minimal or moderate deterioration, and still others seem unaffected. For some people stress is a catastrophe, whereas for others it appears to be an opportunity for personal growth.

A historical example of human variability under stress is the ill-fated Donner party, which in 1848 became trapped for the winter in heavy California mountain snows. The party was headed by wagon train from Illinois to California's Sacramento Valley when fierce, deep winter snows hit, stranding them. From late October to the following April, when the ragged remnant of the party was rescued, they ate their draft animals, pets, "soup" made from boiling hides and fur rugs, and ultimately their own dead companions to keep from starving. What is striking about the Donner party is the wide variability in its members' responses to stress. Age and sex seemed to be important factors in the survival of its members. Of the 16 children in the party under age 5, 10 died, and of the 5 adults between 49 and 69, none survived. Though this result is perhaps not surprising, less expectable is the fact that approximately 57% of the party's males died, compared to only 29% of the females. A number of factors might account for this difference, including the tendency of a woman's core body temperature to stay warmer, women being more temperamentally suited to survival in situations calling for long-term endurance, or the tasks each group was called upon to undertake. Of particular relevance to this chapter is yet another factor, social support, which seems to have played an important role in determining which members of the party survived. Survivors belonged to family groups that averaged twice the size of the nonsurvivors' families. Almost 90% of the single men traveling alone in the party perished. In contrast, all nine members of one family, including a 1-year-old girl, lived through the ordeal.

This difference between those who were alone and those who were socially embedded provides an anecdotal example of the role social support plays in how people cope with stress. This example is in line with a common focus of much early work on support as a resource that moderates stress. In the initial work that sparked interest in the role of social support in health, its presence was operationalized in a simple, direct way, usually as the presence of a spouse or confidant or embeddedness in a social group (Berkman & Syme, 1979).

Anecdotal findings such as those concerning the Donner party, together with a considerable body of formal research results, suggest the importance of social support in moderating stress. But they also raise some important questions: What role does social support play in how people handle stress? Is social support a stress buffer, and/or is it a reducer of vulnerability to stress? Is stress coping facilitated by support available in the stressful situation or by prior or continuing support that strengthens a person's coping repertoire? We will review the current status of theory and research concerning these and other questions related to social support.

THE CONCEPT OF SOCIAL SUPPORT

Several general approaches to social support can be discerned from the literature. They include attention to the structure of a person's social network (interpersonal connectedness, as discussed above), the functions of social support, and the distinction between the perception of social support availability and the perception of receipt of support.

Structure versus Functions

Structural Support
Definitions that emphasize interpersonal connectedness lead to inquiries concerning the structure of individuals' social networks, including such characteristics as network size (Berkman & Syme, 1979; Gottlieb, 1985). In investigations of personal adjustment and health, network analysts often base their studies on the assumption that structural features of a social network (for example, the density or interconnectedness of members) influence the impact that social interactions have on network members. This approach calls attention to differences in the patterns of social interaction characterizing different support networks. In addition, network analysts have proposed several important distinctions among categories of network members, including those who are family members, confidants, spouses, and sources of conflict. An especially important finding stemming from this perspective is that certain types of networks are associated with poor outcomes under some circumstances (Hirsch & Rapkin, 1986; Thoits, 1983). We believe that these theoretical and empirical contributions outweigh the frequent observation that measures of

network characteristics have not always been found to be related to
psychological adjustment and health status (Kaplan & Hartwell, 1987;
Wethington & Kessler, 1986).

Functions of Support

A functional approach seeks to specify those aspects of social support that are beneficial to individuals who are experiencing specific
types of stressful events (Cutrona & Russell, 1987). This approach was
stimulated by Weiss's (1974) hypothesis that there are six specific provisions of social relationships: attachment, social integration, opportunity
for nurturance, reassurance of worth, sense of reliable alliance, and
guidance. Cohen and Wills (1985) have theorized that the buffering
effect of social support, which serves to insulate or partially protect
those who are vulnerable to the effects of stress, is a function of the
match between the particular need engendered by the stressor and the
type of support given. This approach suggests that mismatched support
may explain why many research efforts have produced conflicting findings concerning the buffering effects of social support. Cutrona and
Russell (1990) have proposed a theoretical model that categorizes life
events in terms of the challenges they pose as well as the types of social
support that are likely to play especially positive roles in individuals'
responses to life challenges.

Support Receipt versus Perception of Available Support

Another way of categorizing approaches to measuring social support is whether they are focused on support given or support potentially
available.

Support Receipt

Typically, information on support, given by others is gathered from
the self-report of the recipient. In using this information it is important
to note that the agreement between givers and recipients on the support
given may be only moderate (50% to 60%; Antonucci & Israel, 1986;
Shulman, 1976). It would probably be a mistake, however, to view this
finding as an indication simply of a lack of validity regarding received
support measures. Instead, this result underscores the need to consider
the evaluative aspects of social support (i.e., recipients' appraisals of
supportive activity) in addition to objective measures of supportive
transactions. We will return to this point later in the chapter when we
review research making use of behavioral observation strategies. Re-

ceived support measures, by themselves, may provide a confounded picture of the social support process.

A person's exposure to stressful life events may trigger supportive actions by those in the person's social network because these others are aware of the negative event, because they see the person as in need of help, or because the stressed person actively solicits support. The last two contingencies may have an implication different from that of the first. They may imply a failure in coping, either because of the person's ineffective skills or because of the event's overpowering nature (Dunkel-Schetter & Bennett, 1990; Graham & Barker, 1990). Thus, although measures of received support have to date yielded mixed results, they have led to important theoretical developments, particularly recognition of the complexity of social support processes. Recognition of this point has led researchers to focus attention on the potential recipient's subjective estimates of support availability, his or her apparent coping skills, and the degree of severity of life stress that he or she is perceived by others to be experiencing.

Perceived Support

The finding that a recipient's evaluation of supportive activity does not necessarily match the reports by others involved suggests that an individual's report of social support reflects at least two elements: objective properties of supportive interactions, and the respondent's interpretation of the interactions. The importance of the subjective side of social support is evidenced in the highly consistent finding that it is the perception of social support that is most closely related to adjustment and health outcomes (Antonucci & Israel, 1986; Blazer, 1982; Sandler & Barrera, 1984; Wethington & Kessler, 1986).

A focus on perceived social support meshes with and its reinforced by the current emphasis in psychology on cognitive appraisal and the influence over behavior of cognitive schemata. It also fits well with the early conceptualizations of social support by Cobb (1976) and Cassel (1976). Cobb hypothesized that social support's major role is to convey information to the individual that others care about and value him or her; thus the support emanates not so much from what is done but from what that indicates to the recipient about the relationship. In a similar vein, Cassel argued that conveying caring and positive regard to the recipient is more responsible for positive outcomes than is any specific behavior. A number of studies have shown that support perceived to be available is consistently related to outcome measures. Support that is actually received may affect outcome measures not as a result of this support per se but through its impact on perceptions of support. Results concerning perceived support suggest the need to consider both the intrapersonal and the interpersonal contexts in which supportive provisions become available. The intrapersonal context refers to the individual's perceptions of social relationships; internal cognitive representations of self, important others, and the nature of interpersonal relationships influence perceptions of social support. The interpersonal context refers to the social qualities of relationships (e.g., to what degree they are marked by conflict).

Strengths and Weaknesses of Multiple Support Concepts

The variety of approaches that have influenced social support research have proved to be both a blessing and a curse. As we have tried to emphasize, each approach focuses attention on different, yet promising, aspects of the social support equation. The available findings are often lumped together without regard for methodology, however, and they can appear inconsistent and even contradictory. As a number of researchers have observed, differences in the operationalization and assessment strategies associated with each approach have probably contributed to this apparent difficulty. For example, one important difference in assessment strategies concerns whether instruments focus on objective events (e.g., supportive transactions) versus subjective evaluations (e.g., perceptions of others' willingness to help). For this reason, we now review some of the prominent approaches to social support assessment with an eye toward highlighting important *and consistent* findings yielded by the various perspectives.

THE ASSESSMENT OF SOCIAL SUPPORT

Concepts such as social support need operationalization and assessment. In order to identify people who vary along the social support continuum, methods are needed for accurately measuring the relevant social resources. As mentioned in the previous section, however, one source of confusion concerning social support is that the term has been defined by some researchers as objective events (actual availability of others) and by others as subjective estimates (perceptions of others' willingness to help).

In line with one of the original conceptions of social support as helping behavior, some measures have been constructed to assess how much help a person recalls having received from others in a specified time period. These received support measures assess various types of support the individual reports having experienced. This approach reflects the assumption that social support is a social activity in which providers do something specific (e.g., offer advice) to the recipient in response to a stressful situation. One of the most frequently used of these measures is the Inventory of Socially Supportive Behaviors (ISSB; Barrera, Sandler, & Ramsey, 1981).

In contrast to assessment of receipt of support, perceived support measures assess subjective appraisals of support availability. This perspective can itself be divided into two views; one focuses on the belief that others, in general, care for and value the individual, whereas the other focuses on the perceived availability of a wide range of specific types of support (e.g., emotional support, information, instrumental aid). These two approaches to perceived social support share a common emphasis on social support as a cognitive appraisal.

The Social Support Questionnaire (SSQ; Sarason, Levine, Basham, & Sarason, 1983) and its more recent 6-item short form of the SSQ (Sarason, Sarason, Shearin, & Pierce, 1987) might be regarded as aggregate or global measures of social support. They emphasize the importance of feeling loved and cared about by others as the central element in the protective effect of social support. The idea reflected in this view is that if a person has close and caring relationships, these relationships can be counted on to provide support or, if that is not possible, to assist the person in finding others to provide the necessary support.

Whereas the SSQ is focused on perceptions of support availability and satisfaction, another group of perceived social support measures have grown out of the functional approach described earlier that emphasizes the need for the support available to fit what is needed. Examples of instruments designed to measure the functional components of support are the Interpersonal Support Evaluation List (ISEL; Cohen, Mermelstein, Kamarck, & Hoberman, 1985); and the Social Provision Scale (SPS; Cutrona & Russell, 1987).

It is of both practical and theoretical interest to assess the relationship between measures that define social support differently. Research comparing measures of these different types suggests that perceived social support is quite distinct from measures of social network characteristics or received social support (Sarason, Shearin, Pierce, & Sarason, 1987). In contrast, measures of perceived support used in this same study were found to be reasonably well correlated with each other. Another study that compared the overall factor structure of received support (as assessed by the ISSB) and perceived available support (as assessed by the SSQ) found that these two aspects of support were distinct and separate (McCormick, Siegert, & Walkey, 1987). This suggests a need to consider social support in terms of both objective social interactions and participants' evaluations of these interactions.

CONTINUING LINES OF SOCIAL SUPPORT RESEARCH

Measures of social support stemming from each of these approaches have been related to a wide variety of behaviors in a large number of populations. Because of the many ways in which social support has been assessed and the distinctive characteristics of most of the samples that have been studied, it is sometimes difficult to draw broad generalizations from the empirical work that has been carried out.

Running through most of the research on social support is the belief that connections with significant others and with the community have positive effects on personal adjustment and health. Although social support does seem to be associated with mental and physical health, neither causality nor causal mechanisms have been agreed upon.

Perceived Support Availability and Mental Health

A host of factors (including temperament, heredity, and physiological processes) no doubt contribute to individual differences in the perception of social support. Self-reports concerning the availability of social support are stable over many months and even years. Positively correlated with these stable perceptions of social ties is an equally stable set of personality characteristics that include high self-esteem, low anxiety, and a positive approach to social relationships (Sarason et al., 1983). Evidence is mounting for the view that perceived support is a part of the individual's personality (Sarason, Sarason, & Shearin, 1986). Lakey and Heller (1988) have concluded that the generalized appraisal that one is cared for and valued is not necessarily anchored in any specific relationship or particular helping transaction but instead is integrated into personality.

People high in perceived support generally believe that they are accepted by others. They have a sense of acceptance that is not just a mater of confidence that others will be responsive in times of need; it also reflects the person's belief that he or she is an interesting, worthy person and an appropriate stimulus for the attention of others. Viewed in this way, the sense of acceptance is related to the individual's beliefs concerning personal control in significant areas of life. People feel in control when they have options and wherewithal. The sense of control comes from histories of successful experiences in which people learn that they are effective in influencing the course of events.

The sense of acceptance that grows out of perceptions of social support seems to be a product of a history of positive social interactions. In this regard, it is interesting that when college students differing in SSQ scores were asked to describe their parents as they remembered them while growing up, both men and women with low SSQ scores described their parents as having had less interest in them and as having had less fun with them than other subjects higher in the SSQ score distribution (Sarason et al., 1987).

Whereas positive interactions seem to be associated with a strengthened sense of acceptance, negative interactions appear to be linked to depressed mood. Schuster, Kessler, and Aseltine (1990) found that negative interactions are predictive of depressed mood. Abbey, Abrams, and Caplan (1985) found that negative interactions with "the person closest to you" were by far the most important inducers of depressed mood and that, among pregnant adolescents, both self-ratings and informant ratings of social support were negatively related to postpartum depression. This study also found that the informant ratings were better predictors of 6-week postpartum depression than the self-ratings. In a study of the relationship between social support and depression in women caring for frail family members, depressed caregivers reported a higher incidence of negative interactions with other people (Rivera, Rose, Futterman, Lovett, & Gallagher-Thompson, 1991). There were no differences in overall satisfaction with received support in comparisons between depressed and nondepressed caregivers.

These results suggest the need in future research to attend not only to the positive interactions that contribute to a sense of acceptance, but also to negative interactions that are associated with conflict, anger, and other arousing experiences and emotions. We need to know as much about negative interactions that produce depression, anxiety, and other symptoms as we do about the positive interactions that make for a sense of being supported. This is true not only because of the potential "main effect" of negative interactions, but also because these negative interactions may influence the impact of positive interactions. For example, a recipient might discount potentially positive interactions that occur in the context of relationships marked by high levels of conflict. In addition, the ratio of positive to negative interactions may be linked with how people respond to stress and adjust to life's problems.

There is some evidence suggesting that the relationship between social support and depression depends upon who is providing the support. May and Revicki (1985) examined the effects of occupational stress and social support on depression among family physicians. They found support provided by the family, but not by peers, to moderate the relationship between occupational stress and depressive symptomatology. In a study of the determinants of the performance and attrition of Marine Corps recruits, the supportiveness of the training unit environment created by the supervising drill instructor was found to be a highly significant salutary factor (Cook, Novaco, & Sarason, 1982). Whereas in some situations an individual's generalized sense of support may mediate stress coping, in other situations the key factor may be the support of a particular person.

The link between social support on the one hand, and adjustment and mental health on the other, may be related to the role social support plays in the acquisition of coping skills. Bowlby (1969) has argued that a supportive environment contributes to exploration of the environment and reasonable risk taking that strengthens a child's coping repertory. Subjects with high social support scores are consistently rated as being more interesting and socially skilled than low scorers (Sarason, Sarason, Hacker, & Basham, 1985; Sarason et al., 1983). An important question about social support concerns whether its absence is in a sense inflicted upon the individual or is a function of either maladaptive personal attributions or a lack of social skills that elicit it. Are people with low levels of support unlucky in the support available to them, or do they drive other people away? If poor social skills are important factors in low support levels, training strategies to help people alter their social interaction patterns might be useful in increasing the sense of support and personal happiness (Sarason & Sarason, 1986).

Health and Illness

After reviewing the literature on social relationships and health, House, Landis, and Umberson (1988) concluded that there is both a theoretical and an empirical basis for hypothesizing a causal impact of social relationships on health. They found that prospective studies that control for baseline health status consistently demonstrate an increased risk of death among persons with a low quantity and sometimes low quality of social relationships. Other evidence from studies of humans and animals also suggests that social isolation is a major risk factor in mortality from widely varying causes. Schwarzer and Leppin (1991) have pointed out that several factors may interact with social support in influencing health and that it may be important to specify a person's perception not only of the general availability of support but also of specific people who are providing support. The relationship between social support and health may depend upon circumstances as yet unexplored by researchers. For example, mobilization of support may be weaker for chronic or gradual onset conditions in which caregiver burnout plays an important role than for accidents or sudden-onset diseases.

The complexity of the relationship between psychological factors such as stress and social support on the one hand, and illness on the other, has been well documented by Cohen and Williamson (1991). After reviewing the literature they concluded that social skills and social support were negatively related to illness. Though negative life events have been linked to illness, the presence of social support seems to moderate this effect. Research is needed to determine whether it is social support per se that moderates the stress–illness relationship or certain personality characteristics, such as intraversion or extroversion, that relate to support-eliciting skills. In a study of immune system function among spouses of cancer patients, Baron, Cutrona, Russell, Hicklin, and Lubaroff (1990) found that social support, but not stressful life events and depression, we related to immunocompetence. As Schwarzer and Leppin (1991) noted in their meta-analysis of social support–illness relationships, the role of social support in immune function may be moderated by a number of interacting variables. The importance of this point is illustrated by Coyne and Smith's (1991) study of couples coping with a husband's myocardial infarction. Wives' ability to help their husbands cope with a heart attack depended on the character of the infarction, the couples' interactions with medical personnel, and the quality of their marital relationship. In a study of recovery from coronary artery surgery, King, Reis, Porter, and Norsen (1991) found that patients' perception of general esteem support was the only type of support that consistently accounted for a unique share of the relationship between social support and surgery outcome. These researchers concluded that the influence of general esteem support on feelings of well-being most probably derived from its enabling the person to feel valued, loved, and competent.

The evidence concerning the relationship between social support and mental health, physical health, and recovery from illness suggests that although social support alone may play an important role, it also may interact with other individual difference and environmental variables that need to be identified and evaluated. Finally, the conceptualization and operationalization of social support represent significant influences over the findings of research studies. Later in this chapter we will discuss an interactional framework for social support that incorporates both individual difference and environmental factors.

Support Provision

Much research on social support has been directed toward two topics: social support as a stress moderator, and the assessment of social support. If the lack of social support is a factor in negative health and adjustment outcomes, more needs to be known about how support is or can be provided in an effective manner. Surprisingly, the topic of the provision of social support (how it is provided, by whom, and under what circumstances) has been barely touched on. The provision of support has been widely discussed in terms of its role in personal development, clinical processes, and behavior observed in laboratory settings; however, we need much more empirical information about support provision in everyday life. What types of support are most helpful? Do some have negative side effects? Is the outcome of support the same for all individuals (e.g., those high and low in perceived support)? Should interventions be directed mainly at high-risk groups? More knowledge is also needed about how to help individuals raise their own overall support level, as well as how they might obtain support in particular types of situations.

All of these questions lend themselves to inquiry within or outside of the laboratory. Lehman, Ellard, and Wortman (1985) have investigated the evaluations by bereaved individuals of the kinds of supportive comments offered to them. Gottlieb (1985) has studied the effective elements of group interventions on children of divorcing parents and the effects of supportive involvements on both members of adult child–elderly dependent parent duos. I. G. Sarason (1981) successfully manipulated social support so that it positively influenced subjects' performance in an evaluative situation. Heller and his coworkers (Heller, 1979; Heller & Swindle, 1983; Procidano & Heller, 1983) investigated the effects of the presence of others, either intimates or strangers, on performance in stressful laboratory situations in which overall support was analyzed as an individual difference variable.

When the social support concept first became of interest, its preventive or curative potentials were recognized. Support can be provided at various levels ranging from the community as a stabilizing force in a troubled individual's life to the empathy a loved one feels and expresses toward someone facing real or imagined difficulties. Rather than sapping self-reliance, strong ties with others—particularly family members—seem to encourage it. Reliance on others and self-reliance are not only compatible but complementary to one another. Though many examples could be given of social support's role as a buffer against stress, how to communicate support in a way that does not unduly tax the communicator and nurturer needs to be better understood. Lehman, Ellard, and Wortman's (1986) findings concerning the counterproductive effects of friends' "supportive" utterances to bereaved parents underlines the importance of this need.

Supportive interventions exist for a variety of problems, including bereavement in adults and children, divorce, cancer, and unemployment (Gottlieb, 1988). It is important to analyze the experience or situation concerning which an individual needs support. For example, Jacobson (1990) analyzed stress and support in stepfamily formation and found that a central task in the process is family members' review and reorganization of their assumptions concerning family interactions and responsibilities and the structure of meaning they entail. The process of remarriage calls for revision and disassembly of the microculture of the first marriage and the creation of a new social system. From this perspective, support includes information that enables individuals to undertake a process of cognitive restructuring. Such support offers feedback that alters the way in which a person views and experiences the world as meaningful, enabling him or her to achieve a better fit between the assumptive world and the self or environment. Self-help groups provide contexts in which individuals can reflect on the ideas that shape their behavior and then begin developing alternative perspectives from which to evaluate and establish the meaning of the circumstances in which they find themselves.

Understanding the Social Support Process through Laboratory Studies

Supportive processes such as those that occur in self-help groups, psychotherapy, and the support people provide each other in everyday life are not easily approached from a research standpoint. The effectiveness of support depends on the context in which it is provided, the nature of the problem, and the relationship between the supporter and the recipient of support. A worthwhile line of research might involve analogues of support provision that could be carried out in the laboratory. An example of what can be learned in laboratory research is Sarason and his coworkers' studies of the effects of manipulations intended to provide support (Lindner, Sarason, & Sarason, 1988; Sarason & Sarason, 1986). The manipulation in each case was the experimenter's offer of help, if needed, to students who were about to work on problem-solving tasks. The experimenter told the subjects that she would be available to them throughout their work and would answer any questions that might come up. Although no subject requested help, those who were low in social support satisfaction as assessed by the SSQ performed significantly better after receiving the supportive communication than a comparable group of those low in social support satisfaction who did not receive this communication. The performance of low-satisfaction subjects who were given this intervention did not differ from the performance of subjects high in satisfaction. The supportive condition did not raise the performance of those high in support satisfaction as compared with that of an untreated group with high satisfaction scores. Thus there was an interactive effect attributable to the intervention: Support was helpful only to groups whose self-evaluated support was low.

In another of the few examples of laboratory investigations of social support, Kamarck, Manuck, and Jennings (1990) investigated the effects of a nonevaluative social interaction on the cardiovascular response to psychological challenge. In one condition, a friend accompanied a college student who participated in two laboratory tasks. In the other condition, the subject came to the laboratory unaccompanied. Subjects who were accompanied by a friend showed reduced heart-rate reactivity to both tasks relative to the alone condition. The results suggested that interpersonal support reduces cardiovascular responsivity.

There is a need for intensive study of operationally defined supportive interventions and their effects. In addition to obtaining answers to questions concerning whether particular interventions are effective under controlled conditions, it is important to carry out research designed to increase understanding of the process by which a supportive intervention has a positive effect. Both psychological and physiological processes may play important roles in the support process. Empirical investigation of the support process will require attention to (a) the nature of interventions intended to be supportive, (b) the outcome variables to which interventions are directed, and (c) the effects of the intervention on self and social perception, physiological responsivity, and relevant attributions.

A NEW APPROACH: SOCIAL SUPPORT IN THE CONTEXT OF RELATIONSHIPS

As with research employing measures of received support, the development and use of general or global measures of perceived social support have led to recognition of the complexity of social support processes. Implicit in the aggregate view of social support is the idea that feeling loved and cared about enhances the individual's own self-efficacy, realistic appraisal of threat, and coping repertory. In other words, measures of perceived support such as the SSQ appear to tap the extent to which the individual is a part of and is capable of making use of a supportive social environment. To some extent, this view reflects Bowlby's (1969, 1979, 1980) attachment theory, which emphasizes the working models people develop about themselves and about interpersonal relationships. In a sense, this approach also presents a confounded picture of social support processes. Recent studies of adult children and their parents suggest the importance of objective properties of respondents' social environments in addition to their cognitive appraisals. For example, subjects who report high levels of perceived social support (as assessed by the SSQ) have relationships with their parents that are described by both parents and children as highly supportive, sensitive and warm (Sarason, Pierce, Bannerman, & Sarason, 1993). They are also described by their parents in more positive terms.

An analysis is needed of the objective and subjective events involved in the supportive process. What behaviors are intended by the provider to be supportive? Which of the provider's behaviors are used by the recipient in making attributions about the support he or she receives from the provider? What other factors influence the recipient's appraisals of the supportive interaction? What happens when one person tries to help another? Recent advances in the assessment of social support have come from attempts to understand the meaning of the association between the presence of a close relationship on the one hand, and personal adjustment and health on the other. Efforts have been made to conceptualize social support in terms of the various functions relationships fulfill. In everyday life, support—especially under stressful circumstances—usually occurs between people who share some type of close relationship. For this reason and because of our own research findings, we have come to believe that close relationships provide an excellent setting for the study of support processes as well as of events that might negatively influence support provision. The family is a particularly important group in which to study the support process because it provides many opportunities to examine the effects of supportive and countersupportive experiences that occur over the life course.

We have conducted a series of laboratory investigations in which a college student interacts with one or both parents (Keeker, Sarason, & Sarason, 1992; Pierce, 1990; Pierce, Sarason, & Sarason, 1991; Sarason, Pierce, & Sarason, 1992). In some studies, the interaction was related to a somewhat stressful task assigned to the student (preparing a speech); in other instance, the child and parent(s) discussed selected aspects of family conflict. These interactions were videotaped and then analyzed by disinterested observers whose ratings of family interactions were compared with those of the family members. Observers who viewed the videotapes rated several characteristics of the interactions, including the following:

- dyadic cooperation ("How well did the mother and student communicate?")
- dyadic support ("To what extent does the mother [student] really know and understand the student [mother] as a person?")
- student sensitivity ("To what extent did the student really listen to what the mother had to say?")
- parental warmth ("How much did the mother [father] like and enjoy being with the mother?")

Observers' ratings of the videotaped interactions were much more strongly related to the participants' perceptions of each other than to their general perception of overall support available to them. That is, the interaction between a student and parent was much more successfully predicted by the students' ratings of that parent's supportiveness (made prior to and independent of the laboratory session) than by general perceived support as assessed by the SSQ. Our measure of parental support was the Quality of Relationships Inventory (QRI), a specially constructed instrument designed to assess support and conflict in the context of particular relationships (Pierce et al., 1991). There were substantial associations between parent and child's perceptions of their relationship as assessed by the QRI, on the one hand, and ratings of their interactions as observed during moderately stressful situations, on the other (Keeker et al., 1992). These findings suggest that, as we mentioned earlier, a comprehensive definition of social support cannot focus simply on either objective or subjective features of supportive interactions. Instead, researchers need to recognize that social support is a complex process involving both observable social behavior and cognitive appraisals of interpersonal behavior. Our research suggests that an especially important determinant of recipients' attributions about supportive behavior is the expectations they have developed concerning their relationship with the support provider (e.g., expectations for social support and conflict; Pierce et al., 1991). We are currently conducting a series of experimental studies to delineate further the roles of general and relationship-specific expectations for social support and conflict in recipients' appraisals of supportive behavior in the context of family and peer relationships.

Several theorists have noted that the individual's world is made up to a significant extent of social situations as they are cognitively represented (Magnusson, 1990, Sarason, 1977). An especially important feature of social situations appears to be the set of interpersonal relationships in which social interactions take place. More attention needs to be paid to what actually goes on and what is perceived to go on in settings that, at least potentially, provide opportunities for social support.

There is growing evidence of the importance of the relational context of social support. Taylor and Dakof (1988) found that support from the spouse is particularly critical in enhancing well-being and encouraging healthy behaviors in cancer patients. Coyne and DeLongis (1986) found that inappropriate, poorly timed, or oversolicitous support from the spouse may prove to be quite stressful for chronically ill patients. Revenson and Majerovitz (1990) studied supportive interactions between rheumatoid arthritis patients and their spouses and found that although spouses are important sources of support for the patients, the amount and quality of extrafamilial support available to the spouses influenced how supportive they were able to be toward the patients. Both specific relational support and general perceptions of support play roles in clinical status and personal adjustment outcomes.

The importance of determining the independent contributions to clinical and adjustment outcomes of various types of support (either general or from particular others) is suggested by studies of emotional support provided by a companion while women are undergoing labor and delivery. Kennell, Klaus, McGrath, Robertson, and Hinkley (1991) found that the presence of a supportive companion (another woman) had a significant positive effect on clinical outcomes. The companions met the study participants for the first time after hospital admission. Each companion stayed at her assigned patient's bedside from admission through delivery, soothing and touching her patient and giving encouragement. In addition, she explained to her patent what was occurring during labor and what was likely to happen next. The provision of social support had a number of effects, including many fewer cesarian sections being necessary in the supported as contrasted with the control group. The supported group also had significantly fewer forceps deliveries than did the control group, and fewer infants born to mothers in the supported group required a prolonged hospital stay.

Bertsch, Nagashima-Whalen, Dykeman, Kennell, and McGrath (1990) have found significant differences in clinical outcomes when either male partners of obstetrical patients or female companions (who were strangers) were present. The female companions touched the laboring women much more than the male partners; male partners chose to be present for less time during labor and to be close to the mother less often than the female companions. Further study is needed of the most active ingredients of the supportive process in this type of situation. Does a supportive companion reduce catecholamine levels? Does this happen because maternal anxiety is reduced and uterine contractions and uterine blood flow are facilitated? A companion's constant presence, physical touch, reassurance, explanations, and anticipatory guidance all probably play roles and may contribute to the laboring woman feeling safer and calmer and needing less obstetrical intervention for labor to proceed smoothly.

The results of laboratory and clinical studies suggest that perceptions of available support from specific relationships are sufficiently distinct from general perceptions of available support to merit independent investigation. These two aspects of perceived support may have different impacts on personal adjustment and clinical status. We believe that the individual's perception of support within a specific relationship reflects unique experiences with the other person that give rise to distinctive expectations regarding the likelihood of receiving support from that person. It is important to compare generalized perceptions of available support and relationship-based perceptions, because each may have impacts on outcome measures through different pathways. Integrated theories of social support that specify these causal pathways are needed to account for observed associations reported in the literature. Experimental and observational studies are needed to clarify the nature of the causal effects of support and to determine the role personality characteristics and specific aspects of relationships might play in promoting adaptive behavior.

AN INTERACTIONAL-COGNITIVE VIEW OF SOCIAL SUPPORT

Early work on social support was stimulated by the observation that the presence of others appeared to facilitate adjustment to life stress and to contribute to health and well-being. This observation, in turn, sparked an interest in the ingredients of support and effective ways of providing support to those in need. Though this topic continues to be popular, the empirical focus seems to be shifting in the direction of assessing interpersonal perceptions. How social support is measured and by what criteria the measurements are evaluated have come to be important foci of research. This is likely to lead to a variety of instruments with which various aspects of support can be measured and may explain how concordant indices of relationships are with psychometrically and observationally assessed measures of social support. Extensive inquiry into the nature of support processes, however, continues to be needed. Careful study is required to determine how particular types of interpersonal transactions relate to outcomes and how the elements of these transactions relate to assessed indices of support. A better picture is needed of the role that interpersonal conflict, either in the presence or absence of support, plays in personal adjustment.

We recently developed a model of social support that emphasizes the interactive roles of the situational, interpersonal, and intrapersonal contexts of social transactions (Pierce, Sarason, & Sarason, 1990; see Figure 1). The situational context includes not only the event to which response is required but also the interpersonal setting, which includes the social behavior of the support provider. The event may range from minor to major and simple to complex—a bruise from a minor fall, a disappointing academic grade, the breakup of a relatively new relationship, the loss of a job, and the death of a loved one are only a few of the possibilities. For example, the impact of losing a job is likely to be complex, because it involves a multitude of factors (e.g., how much money is in the bank account of the person who loses a job; whether the job loss resulted from poor performance, product phase-out, or a company move; and the current state of the job market). Although the aspect of the situational context that has received most attention from researchers concerns whether or not situations are stressful, a broader perspective of situations might be productive.

The interpersonal context includes not only the distinctive qualitative (e.g., support, conflict) and quantitative (e.g., network size, density) features of specific relationships but also those of the larger social networks in which social support takes place. There are several features of relationships that in all likelihood strongly influence the impact of social support on health and well-being. These include interpersonal conflict, the sensitivity with which one participant responds to the support needs of the other participant, and the structure of their interpersonal connections. Cohen and Lichtenstein (1990) recently showed that the context of a close relationship mediated the impact of specific supportive or nonsupportive behaviors. Accumulating evidence indicates that the impact of social support is reduced strongly by the presence of interpersonal conflict (Coyne & DeLongis, 1986; Zavislak & Sarason, 1992). Support received in the context of conflictive relationships may lead to feelings of indebtedness in the recipient that increase rather than decrease stress (Pierce et al., 1990). Another aspect of the interpersonal context is the extent to which a support provider is aware of and sensitive to the needs of the recipient.

The intrapersonal context is derived from the providers' and recipients' unique, stable patterns of perceiving self, important others, and

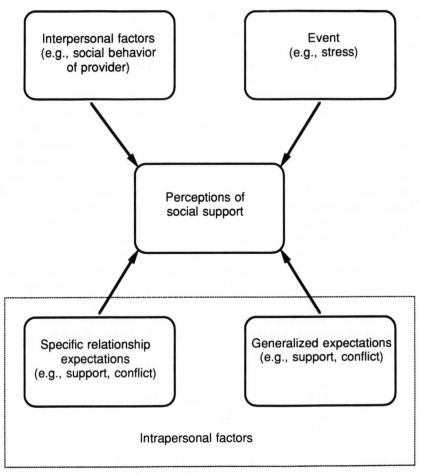

Figure 1. Roles of events and interpersonal and intrapersonal factors in social support.

their relational expectations. Bowlby's (1980) attachment theory has greatly influenced studies of the intrapersonal context of social support (Sarason, Pierce, & Sarason, 1990). It emphasizes the role of working or cognitive models in the formation of an individual's expectations of, appraisals of, and responses to the potentially supportive behavior of others, as well as the provision of support to others. Working models are cognitive representations of self, important others, and the nature of relationships. They are linked to self-esteem, feelings of self-worth, and the perception of being loved, valued, and cared for by others. Working models of others and of relationships lead to distinctive types of expectations and interpretations of others' behavior and interact with situational and social processes. Research using the SSQ and other perceived social support measures has shown that attributions and expectations concerning the global availability of social support reflect a stable personality characteristic, the *sense of support* (Sarason et al., 1990).

We believe that supportive efforts are successful under certain conditions but not necessarily others, and that these conditions interact with the nature of the relationship between the provider and recipient. For example, Dakof and Taylor (1990) found that the effectiveness of supportive intervention depends upon its context, with particular actions being perceived to be helpful from some but not other network members. Dakof and Taylor suggested that future investigations of social support might benefit from identifying the source as well as the type of support. The recipient, the provider, and their interactions need to be studied in an effort to understand better the give-and-take of social support processes.

Mallinckrodt (1991) has found that the outcomes of counseling sessions are related both to clients' current appraisals of their social support and to their recollections of the support parents provided to them during childhood. This suggests that past support, as retained in memory, combines with current perceptions of support in influencing the working alliance between a client and a counselor. The complexity of the dynamics of social support are reflected in Mallinckrodt's finding that the counseling process was influenced particularly by clients' recollections of the supportiveness of their fathers. Though he assessed present and past support only for clients, it would be interesting to examine the client–counselor working alliance as a product of the counselor's sense of present and past support as well.

The effect of support given to individuals varies as a function of providers and recipients' histories of reciprocal supportive relationships. Sarason, Pierce, Bannerman, and Sarason (1993) investigated how parents' assessments of their children's positive and negative characteristics are related to each child's generalized and relationship-specific perceptions of social support. One of their findings was that students' perceptions of support from each of several family members predicted whether specific family members would participate in a research project that required family involvement; that is, students' perceptions of the supportiveness of particular family members predicted whether the members would actually help the student. The researchers also found that mothers', but not fathers', perceptions of students' personal characteristics were predictive of students' generalized perceptions of support availability. The results of this study were consistent with an interactional view of social support in which characteristics of both the recipient and support provider are important determinants of perceptions of social support and outcome measures.

The family environment would appear to be a productive setting in which to study the nature of specific relationships. Although general family environmental factors play important roles in perceptions of support availability, specific family relationships make additional contributions (Gurung, Sarason, Keeker, & Sarason, 1992). It seems likely that for some types of questions, relationship-specific measures of social support might be better predictors than measures of general perceived support.

We see great potential in a broadened theoretical perspective of social support. Such a perspective probably requires attention not only to contemporaneous interactional processes but also to their origins and development. Social support is a personal resource that evolves throughout life. Taking this fact into account, Newcomb (1990) has argued for abandonment of the conception of social support as a unidirectional provision of resources from the external social environment to the individual.

Personality and Working Models of Self and Others

Several studies suggesting the importance of the intrapersonal context have shown that personality characteristics interact with and contribute to the effects of social support (Sarason, Pierce, Shearin, et al., 1991). Elliott and Gramling (1990) have found that how much socially supportive relationships help people cope with stress depends upon their characteristic levels of assertiveness, with assertiveness augmenting the beneficial effects of specific social relationships. Holahan and Moos (1991) obtained similar results regarding the personality characteristic of self-confidence.

Of the three contexts of social support (situational, interpersonal, and intrapersonal) that we have described, the greatest challenges may come from the need to specify the intrapersonal factors that are not readily objectified. In a sense, perceived social support is a cognitive adaptation that individuals make given the constraints and opportunities, both real and imagined, that are placed upon them by a history of experiences. This history molds personal working models of self and others. These models incorporate self-identity and expectations about the nature of relationships both in terms of what individuals have to offer others and what others have to offer them. In this way, perceived social support is not an isolated perception that comes into play only when individuals are confronted by a stressful situation that demands coping behavior. It is part of a constellation of cognitions that drive social behavior and account for differences in interpretations of situations, the motives of others, and beliefs about what others are really like. Attention to this wide range of inner phenomena related to the construct of perceived social support may contribute to a better understanding of both clinical conditions and the events of everyday life.

There is a great need for theory that incorporates the complexity of those situational, interpersonal, and intrapersonal processes that contribute to individuals' perceptions of their relationships with the people who play roles in their lives. The study of social support requires a focus not only on general perceptions of social support, but also on the diversity of cognitions and behaviors associated with specific personal relationships that shape behavior and well-being under diverse circumstances. We believe that although the study of social support is a field still in its infancy, its researchers have demonstrated the creativity and resourcefulness needed to further our understanding of an important aspect of human life.

REFERENCES

Abbey, A., Abrams, D. J., & Caplan, R. (1985). Effects of different sources of social support and social conflict on emotional well-being. *Basic and Applied Social Psychology, 6*, 111–129.

Antonucci, T. C., & Israel, B. A. (1986). Veridicality of social support: A comparison of principal and network members' responses. *Journal of Consulting and Clinical Psychology, 54*, 432–437.

Baron, R. S., Cutrona, C. E., Russell, D. W., Hicklin, D., & Lubaroff, D. M. (1990). Social support and immune function among spouses of cancer patients. *Journal of Personality and Social Psychology, 59*, 344–352.

Barrera, M., Jr., Sandler, I. N., & Ramsey, T. B. (1981). Preliminary development of a scale of social support: Studies on college students. *American Journal of Community Psychology, 9*, 435–447.

Berkman, L. F., & Syme, S. L. (1979). Social networks, host resistance, and mortality: A nine-year follow-up study of Alameda County residents. *American Journal of Epidemiology, 109*, 186–204.

Bertsch, T. D., Nagashima-Whalen, L., Dykeman, S., Kennell, J. H., & McGrath, S. (1990). Labor support by first-time fathers: Direct observations. *Journal of Psychosomatic Obstetric Gynecology, 11*, 251–260.

Blazer, D. (1982). Social support and mortality in an elderly community population. *American Journal of Epidemiology, 115*, 684–694.

Bowlby, J. (1969). *Attachment and loss, vol. 1. Attachment.* New York: Basic Books.

Bowlby, J. (1979). The making and breaking of affectional bonds. *British Journal of Psychiatry, 130*, 201–210.

Bowlby, J. (1980). *Attachment and loss; vol. 3: Loss, sadness and depression.* New York: Basic Books.

Cassel, J. (1976). The contribution of the social environment to host resistance. *American Journal of Epidemiology, 104,* 107–123.

Cobb, S. (1976). Social support as a moderator of life stress. *Psychosomatic Medicine, 38,* 300–314.

Cohen, S., & Lichtenstein, E. (1990). Partner behaviors that support quitting smoking. *Journal of Consulting and Clinical Psychology, 58,* 304–309.

Cohen, S., Mermelstein, R., Kamarck, T., & Hoberman, H. N. (1985). Measuring the functional components of social support. In I. G. Sarason & B. R. Sarason (Eds.), *Social support: Theory, research and applications* (pp. 73–94). Dordrecht, Netherlands: Martinus Nijhoff.

Cohen, S., & Williamson, G. M. (1991). Stress and infectious disease in humans. *Psychological Bulletin, 109,* 5–24.

Cohen, S., & Wills, T. A. (1985). Stress, social support, and the buffering hypothesis. *Psychological Bulletin, 98,* 310–357.

Cook, T. M., Novaco, R. W., & Sarason, I. G. (1982). Military recruit training as an environmental context affecting expectancies for control of reinforcement. *Cognitive Therapy and Research, 6,* 409–428.

Coyne, J. C., & DeLongis, A. M. (1986). Going beyond social support: The role of social relationships in adaptation. *Journal of Consulting and Clinical Psychology, 54,* 454–460.

Coyne, J. C., & Smith, D. A. F. (1991). Couples coping with a myocardial infarction: A contextual perspective on wives' distress. *Journal of Personality and Social Psychology, 61,* 404–412.

Cutrona, C. E., & Russell, D. (1987). The provisions of social relationships and adaptation to stress. In W. H. Jones & D. Perlman (Eds.), *Advances to personal relationships, vol. 1* (pp. 37–67). Greenwich, CT: JAI Press.

Cutrona, C. E., & Russell, D. W. (1990). Type of social support and specific stress: Toward a theory of optimal matching. In B. R. Sarason, I. G. Sarason, & G. R. Pierce (Eds.), *Social support: An interfactional view* (pp. 319–366). New York: Wiley.

Dakof, G. A., & Taylor, S. E. (1990). Victims' perceptions of social support: What is helpful from whom? *Journal of Personality and Social Psychology, 58,* 80–89.

Dunkel-Schetter, C., & Bennett, T. L. (1990). Differentiating the cognitive and behavioral aspects of social support. In B. R. Sarason, I. G. Sarason, & G. R. Pierce (Eds.), *Social support: An interactional view* (pp. 267–296). New York: Wiley.

Elliott, T. R., & Gramling, S. E. (1990). Personal assertiveness and the effects of social support among college students. *Journal of Counseling Psychology, 37,* 427–436.

Gottlieb, B. (1985). Theory into practice: Issues that surface in planning interventions which mobilize support. In I. G. Sarason & B. R. Sarason (Eds.), *Social support: Theory, research and applications.* (pp. 417–438). Dordrecht, Netherlands: Martinus Nijhoff.

Gottlieb, B. H. (1988). Support interventions: A typology and agenda for research. In S. W. Duck (Eds.), *Handbook of personal relationships* (pp. 519–542). New York: Wiley.

Graham, S., & Barker, G. P. (1990). The down side of help: An attributional-developmental analysis of helping behavior as a low-ability cue. *Journal of Educational Psychology, 82,* 7–14.

Gurung, R. A. R., Sarason, B. R., Keeker, K. D., & Sarason, I. G. (1992). *Family environments, specific relationships, and general perceptions of adjustment.* Paper presented at the annual meeting of the American Psychological Association, Washington, DC.

Heller, K. (1979). The effects of social support: Prevention and treatment implications. In

A. P. Goldstein & F. H. Kanfer (Eds.), *Maximizing treatment gains: Transfer enhancement in psychotherapy* (pp. 253–382). New York: Academic Press.

Heller, K., & Swindle, R. W. (1983). Social networks, perceived social support, and coping with stress. In R. D. Felner, L. A. Jason, J. N. Moritsugu, & S. S. Farber (Eds.), *Preventive psychology: Theory, research and practice* (pp. 87–103). Elmsford, NY: Pergamon.

Hirsch, B. J., & Rapkin, B. D. (1986). Multiple roles, social networks, and women's well-being. *Journal of Personality and Social Psychology, 51,* 1237–1247.

Holahan, C. J., & Moos, R. H. (1991). Life stressors, personal and social resources, and depression: A 4-year structural model. *Journal of Abnormal Psychology, 100,* 31–38.

House, J. S., Landis, K. R., & Umberson, D. (1988). Social relationships and health. *Science, 241,* 540–545.

Jacobson, D. (1990). Stress and support in stepfamily formation: The cultural context of social support. In B. R. Sarason, I. G. Sarason, & G. R. Pierce (Eds.), *Social support: An interactional view* (pp. 199–218). New York: Wiley.

Kamarck, T. W., Manuck, S. B., & Jennings, J. R. (1990). Social support reduces cardiovascular reactivity to psychological challenge: A laboratory model. *Psychosomatic Medicine, 52,* 42–58.

Kaplan, R. M., & Hartwell, S. L. (1987). Differential effects of social support and social networks on physiological and social outcomes in men and women with Type II diabetes mellitus. *Health Psychology, 6,* 387–398.

Keeker, K. D., Sarason, B. R., & Sarason, I. G. (1992). *Marital quality and students' social and personal adjustment.* Paper presented at the annual meeting of the American Psychological Association, Washington, DC.

Kennell, J., Klaus, M., McGrath, S., Robertson, S., & Hinkley, C. (1991). *Journal of American Medical Association, 265,* 2197–2201.

King, K. B., Reis, H. T., Porter, L. A., & Norsen, L. H. (1991). *Social support and long-term recovery from coronary artery surgery: Effects on patients and spouses.* Unpublished manuscript, University of Rochester.

Lakey, B., & Heller, K. (1988). Social support from a friend, perceived support, and social problem solving. *American Journal of Community Psychology, 16,* 811–824.

Lehman, D. R., Ellard, J. H., & Wortman, C. B. (1986). Social support for the bereaved: Recipients' and providers' perspectives on what is helpful. *Journal of Personality and Social Psychology, 54,* 438–446.

Lindner, K. C., Sarason, I. G., & Sarason, B. R. (1988). Assessed life stress and social support and experimentally provided social support. In C. D. Spielberger & I. G. Sarason (Eds.), *Stress and anxiety, vol. 11* (pp. 231–240). Washington, DC: Hemisphere.

Magnusson, D. (1990). Personality development from an interactional perspective. In L. A. Pervin (Ed.), *Handbook of personality: Theory and research* (pp. 193–222). New York: Guilford.

Mallinckrodt, B. (1991). Clients' representations of childhood emotional bonds with parents, social support, and formation of the working alliance. *Journal of Counseling Psychology, 4,* 401–409.

May, H. J., & Revicki, D. A. (1985). Professional stress among family physicians. *Journal of Family Practice, 20,* 165–171.

McCormick, I. A., Siegert, R. J., & Walkey, F. H. (1987). Dimensions of social support: A factorial confirmation. *American Journal of Community Psychology, 15,* 73–77.

Newcomb, M. D. (1990). Social support and personal characteristics: A developmental and interactional perspective. *Journal of Social and Clinical Psychology, 9,* 54–68.

Pierce, G. R. (1990). *Predicting perceptions of social support: An experimental study of behavioral, personality, relationship and situational variables.* Unpublished Ph.D. dissertation, University of Washington.

Pierce, G. R., Sarason, B. R., & Sarason, I. G. (1990). Integrating social support perspectives: Working models, personal relationships, and situational factors. In S. Duck (Ed.), *Personal relationships and social support* (pp. 173–189). Newbury Park, CA: Sage.

Pierce, G. R., Sarason, I. G., & Sarason, B. R. (1991). General and relationship-based perceptions of social support: Are two constructs better than one? *Journal of Personality and Social Psychology, 61,* 1028–1039.

Procidano, M. E., & Heller, K. (1983). Measures of perceived social support from friends and from family: Three validation studies. *American Journal of Community Psychology, 11,* 1–24.

Revenson, T. A., & Majerovitz, D. (1990). Spouses' support provision to chronically ill patients. *Journal of Social and Personal Relationships, 7,* 575–586.

Rivera, P. A., Rose, J. M., Futterman, A., Lovett, S. B., & Gallagher-Thompson, D. (1991). Dimensions of perceived social support in clinically depressed and nondepressed female caregivers. *Psychology and Aging, 6,* 232–237.

Sandler, I. N., & Barrera, M., Jr. (1984). Toward a multimethod approach to assessing the effects of social support. *American Journal of Community Psychology, 12,* 37–52.

Sarason, B. R., Pierce, G. R., Bannerman, A., & Sarason, I. G. (1993). Clarifying the concept of perceived social support: Direct and indirect contributions of family relationships, *Journal of Personality and Social Psychology, 65,* 1071–1085.

Sarason, B. R., Pierce, G. R., & Sarason, I. G. (1990). Social support: The sense of acceptance and the role of relationships. In B. R. Sarason, I. G. Sarason, & G. R. Pierce (Eds.), *Social support: An interactional view* (pp. 97–128). New York: Wiley.

Sarason, B. R., Pierce, G. R., & Sarason, I. G. (1992). *Personality and situational variables in parent-child interactions: Two observational studies.* Unpublished manuscript, University of Washington.

Sarason, B. R., Pierce, G. R., Shearin, E. N., Sarason, I. G., Waltz, J. A., & Poppe, L. (1991). Perceived social support and working models of self and actual others. *Journal of Personality and Social Psychology, 60,* 273–283.

Sarason, B. R., Sarason, I. G., Hacker, T. A., & Basham, R. B. (1985). Concomitants of social support: Social skills, physical attractiveness, and gender. *Journal of Personality and Social Psychology, 49,* 469–480.

Sarason, B. R., Shearin, E. N., Pierce, G. R., & Sarason, I. G. (1987). Interrelations of social support: Social skills, physical attractiveness, and gender. *Journal of Personality and Social Psychology, 49,* 469–480.

Sarason, I. G. (1977). The growth of interactional psychology. In D. Magnusson & N. S. Endler (Eds.), *Personality at the crossroads: Current issues in interactional psychology* (pp. 261–272). Hillsdale, NJ: Erlbaum.

Sarason, I. G. (1981). Test anxiety, stress, and social support. *Journal of Personality, 49,* 101–114.

Sarason, I. G., Levine, H. M., Basham, R. B., & Sarason, B. R. (1983). Assessing social support: The Social Support Questionnaire. *Journal of Personality and Social Psychology, 44,* 127–139.

Sarason, I. G., & Sarason, B. R. (1986). Experimentally provided social support. *Journal of Personality and Social Psychology, 50,* 1222–1225.

Sarason, I. G., Sarason, B. R., & Shearin, E. N. (1986). Social support as an individual difference variable: Its stability, origins, and relational aspects. *Journal of Personality and Social Psychology, 50,* 845–855.

Sarason, I. G., Sarason, B. R., Shearin, E. N., & Pierce, G. R. (1987). A brief measure of social support: Practical and theoretical implications. *Journal of Social and Personal Relationships, 4,* 497–510.

Schuster, T. L., Kessler, R. C., & Aseltine, R. H. (1990). Supportive interactions, negative interactions, and depressed mood. *American Journal of Community Psychology, 18,* 423–438.

Schwarzer, R., & Leppin, A. (1991). Social support and health: A theoretical and empirical overview. *Journal of Social and Personal Relationships, 8,* 99–127.

Shulman, N. (1976). Network analysis: A new addition to an old bag of tricks. *Acta Sociologica, 23,* 307–323.

Taylor, S. E., & Dakof, G. A. (1988). Social support and the cancer patient. In S. Spacapan & S. Oskamp (Eds.), *The social psychology of health* (pp. 95–116). Newbury Park, CA: Sage.

Thoits, P. (1983). Multiple identities and psychological well-being: A reformulation and test of the social isolation hypothesis. *American Sociological Review, 48,* 174–187.

Weiss, R. S. (1974). The provisions of social relationships. In Z. Rubin (Ed.), *Doing unto others.* Englewood Cliffs, NJ: Prentice-Hall.

Wethington, E., & Kessler, R. C. (1986). Perceived support, received support, and adjustment to stressful life events. *Journal of Health and Social Behavior, 27,* 78–89.

Zavislak, N., & Sarason, B. R. (1991, August). *Predicting parent–child relationships: Influence of marital conflict and family behavior.* Paper presented at the annual meeting of the American Psychological Association, Washington, DC.

7

Psychosocial Resources and the Stress Process

R. JAY TURNER and PATRICIA ROSZELL

This chapter addresses that domain of theory and research concerned with personal characteristics relevant for either instrumental or socio-emotional adaptation to unexpected, ambiguous, or severe events or circumstances. Our goal is to present a selective review of that subset of personal resources for which relevance to the stress-mediating process has been demonstrated or might reasonably be anticipated. In pursuing this modest objective, we attempt to identify the more significant stress mediators and to specify some promising directions for future research.

SOME PRELIMINARY CONSIDERATIONS

A major impetus for much of the work that has considered social stress and related issues has been the consistently observed associations between psychological distress or disorder and such variables as socio-economic status (Dohrenwend & Dohrenwend, 1969; Hollingshead & Redlich, 1958), marital status (Gove, 1972; Turner, Dopkeen, & La-breche, 1970) and minority status (Kessler & Neighbors, 1986; Ulbrich, Warheit, & Zimmerman, 1989). Based on the assumption that there are

R. JAY TURNER and PATRICIA ROSZELL • Department of Sociology, University of Toronto, Toronto, Ontario, Canada M5T 1P9.
Stress and Mental Health: Contemporary Issues and Prospects for the Future, edited by William R. Avison and Ian H. Gotlib. New York, Plenum Press, 1994.

important etiological messages involved, these linkages have represented a major source of compelling hypotheses and have stimulated research aimed toward the identification of relevant social factors and mechanisms. Much of this research has focused on the effort to identify social and environmental experiences, as well as relevant personal and social resources, that are plausible contributors to the occurrence of distress or illness on the one hand, and that also vary systematically across statuses that locate the individual within the social system on the other. The most obvious such factor, of course, is social stress, which importantly matters for health and well-being and which is clearly differentially distributed across social positions.

Interest in personal and social resources as potential mediators in the stress process appears to derive substantially from two related considerations. The first is associated with the fact that the persistently observed associations between life stress and psychological distress have been disappointingly modest in magnitude, on average accounting for less than 10% of the variation in distress (Rabkin & Struening, 1976). Although this circumstance may arise from the inadequacy of stress measurement, it has also encouraged the hypothesis that various factors may mediate the stress–distress connection. This hypothesis has also been encouraged by the assumption derived from everyday experience that even if stressors were comprehensively and reliably measured, we would still observe cases where individuals are relatively unaffected in the face of substantial stress and cases of distress where the magnitude of exposure to stressors appears minimal. Clearly, individuals differ importantly in their experience of, and how effectively they deal with, given environmental occurrences and circumstances.

A second consideration that has focused attention on personal resources involves the assumption that the availability of such resources varies according to social statuses. Though it is obvious that such availability varies substantially within social categories, there is also basis for assuming systematic differences across risk statuses such as those defined by social class and, perhaps, gender and marital status. Evidence on this point was provided nearly three decades ago in Langner and Michael's (1963) report from their midtown Manhattan study. Although they found stress differences to be an important factor in accounting for class differences in mental health, they stated that "there is a residual mental health variation between the socioeconomic groups which cannot be accounted for by stress factors alone" (p. 152). Moreover, they found that the higher the stress level, the greater the class differences in mental health risk. This suggested, as Kohn (1972) has noted, that "there must be important class differences in how effectively people deal with stress" (p. 299).

Langner and Michael (1963, p. 396) themselves indicated that one possible explanation for the sharper increase in risk in the lower socio-economic status (SES) grouping with increases in stress is that lower-class persons may simply suffer more from the impact of stress. This issue of class differences in vulnerability or responsiveness to stress has, of course, been treated by several contemporary researchers (e.g., Dohrenwend, 1973; Kessler & Cleary, 1980; Turner & Noh, 1988), all of whom have supported this contention. Thus social class, and perhaps such other risk factors as gender and marital status, may matter for psychological well-being partly because of differences in the nature and availability of personal resources. The question at issue is which characteristics, attributes, attitudes, or beliefs are most likely to prove relevant to the stress process and/or directly to mental health outcome.

Our selection of constructs for consideration was influenced by the assumption that the most important factors to identify are those that are linked to position in the social structure in much the same way as are differential stress experiences. This strategy is based on the view that the ultimate objective of research on personal mediators is to identify relevant factors that are potentially socially or programmatically modifiable. We believe that variations in personal resources that at least partially arise from differences in the conditions of life to which the individual has been and/or is being subjected may represent the more malleable of mental health contingencies. Only information on such contingencies can inform judgments about the appropriateness of intervention targets or programs that might be proposed.

PERSONAL AGENCY

Of the various personal resources that have been actively considered by stress researchers, by far the most prominent in terms of attention received has been the issue of perceived causal relevance. This construct has been variously addressed in terms of a sense of powerlessness (Seeman, 1959), effectance motivation (White, 1959), locus of control (Lefcourt, 1976; Rotter, 1966), personal control (Bandura, 1977, 1982; Gurin, Gurin, & Morrison, 1978), helplessness, (Seligman, 1975; Seligman & Maier, 1967), hopelessness (Abramson, Alloy, & Metalsky, 1989), mastery (Pearlin & Schooler, 1978), and fatalism (Wheaton, 1983). Although these concepts may not be identical, they share a focus upon the relevance and significance of personal agency as a contingency in human development and functioning.

One of the earliest modern expressions of this focus was provided by Seeman (1959), who conceptualized a sense of powerlessness as "the expectancy or probability, held by the individual, that his own behavior cannot determine the occurrence of the outcomes, or reinforcements, he seeks" (p. 784). This definition corresponds closely to Rotter's (1966) description of an external locus of control as a learned generalized expectation that outcomes are determined by forces external to oneself (e.g., luck, fate, or powerful others). Internality, in contrast, refers to the belief or expectation that outcomes are contingent on one's own choices, efforts, and actions. Similarly, mastery "concerns the extent to which one regards one's life-chances as being under one's own control in contrast to being fatalistically ruled" (Pearlin & Schooler, 1978, p. 5), and fatalism refers to "a tendency to believe in the efficacy of environmental rather than personal forces in understanding the causes of life outcomes" (Wheaton, 1983, p. 211).

With respect to the construct of learned helplessness, Seligman (1975, 1991) sees it as the opposite of mastery and a sense of control. A program of animal studies led Seligman and his collaborators to the conclusion that the helplessness response resulted from actively learning that response and reward (or effort and outcome) are wholly independent. Subsequent research demonstrated that helplessness can be produced or taught in humans and that it can importantly influence expectations as well as behavior. Experiences in which subjects learned that nothing they did mattered "taught them to expect that, in the future and in new situations, their actions would once again be futile" (Seligman, 1991, p. 67).

Notwithstanding the obvious parallels in these concepts, certain theoretical distinctions have been offered. Thus, Mirowsky and Ross (1986) note that "learned helplessness" represents powerlessness from a behaviorist's point of view, whereas external control is a cognitive construct. A similar kind of distinction has been offered by Gecas (1989) who points to conceptualizations that have been offered in motivational terms in contrast to those involving cognitive theories that describe variations in expectancies and perceptions of control.

In our view, such distinctions are largely of historical interest, having little practical utility in the context of the effort to understand the role and significance of causal agency for psychological well-being or for psychological distress and disorder. Our review of the literature suggests that cognitive explanations arose rather early within efforts to account for the behavior of animals who had been subjected to uncontrollable shocks. Moreover, the revised helplessness theory is explicitly cognitive in nature (Abramson, Seligman, & Teasdale, 1978), focusing as it does on the crucial significance of explanatory dispositions or attributional style.

With respect to the idea that it is useful to make a distinction between motivational and cognitive theories, we need only note the obvious motivational elements within the cognitive view. These are embodied in the implication that effort and action are only rational and only likely to occur in the context of some belief that one can influence relevant events and outcomes in one's life. Correspondingly, White's (1959) explicitly motivational theory, centered around the concept of effectance motivation, also contains a major cognitive element. White argued that the reinforcement associated with effectance motivation was embodied in observing the environmental consequences of one's own actions. According to White, such experiences grow to the conviction (or, presumably, the expectation) that one can act and by acting make a difference in the material or social world.

Because we see no strong arguments to the contrary, we assume that the various constructs just reviewed represent alternative labels for the same personal attribute or resource. Accordingly, our brief consideration of evidence bearing upon the significance of causal agency for psychological distress and disorder will treat these concepts as largely interchangeable.

In addition to these concepts, there are also several broader constructs within which mastery or personal control represents one of several important elements. These include world view constructs such as Antonovsky's (1979, 1987) "sense of coherence," Kobasa's "hardiness" (Kobasa, 1979, 1982a, b; Kobasa, Maddi, & Corrington, 1981), and Ben-Sira's (1985) concept of "potency." By *sense of coherence,* Antonovsky refers to the extent to which one perceives stimuli deriving from one's internal and external environments as comprehensible, as manageable according to available resources, and as meaningful and worthy of investment. Although control represents a significant element within this formulation, Antonovsky argues that the relevant issue may be more a matter of whether control is perceived as properly placed than of whether the individual experiences personal control. Kobasa's *hardiness* construct—which, according to Antonovsky (1987), overlaps with "sense of coherence"—is composed of commitment and challenge, along with personal control. Similarly, *potency* is defined as "a person's enduring confidence in his own capacities as well as confidence in and commitment to his/her social environment, which is perceived as being characterized by a basically meaningful and predictable order and by a reliable and just distribution of rewards" (Ben-Sira, 1985, p. 399).

Despite the obvious similarities across these complex formulations, the differences among them and their differences from concepts described earlier would merit prolonged debate. For present purposes, therefore, we will restrict consideration to those concepts within which variations in the experience of personal agency represents the core and primary element. One such concept, as Gecas (1989) has emphasized, is that of competence. Although the term *competence* has been used to refer to elaborate multidimensional constructs (e.g., Adler, 1982; Dodge & Murphy, 1984; Spivack & Shure, 1982), it has also been used to specify social and personal effectiveness, along with factors that affect and are affected by such effectiveness. This theme was developed by Smith (1968) in his formulation of the competent self. In his view, competence is embodied in distinctive features in the person's attitudes toward self and world: "The self is perceived as causally important, as effective in the world . . . as likely to be able to bring about desired effects, and as accepting responsibility when effects do not correspond to desire" (p. 281). Though competence also implies at least a moderately favorable self-evaluation, including self-respect, this is seen as less important than a sense of efficacy or potency.

Personal Agency and Psychological Distress

A substantial and rather consistent body of evidence has accumulated on the connection between mastery or control and the occurrence of psychological distress. This evidence indicates a fairly strong association such that the greater the sense of control, the lower the level of distress. The brief overview of relevant research findings that follows concentrates on recent research that bears upon the significance of personal control in the context of the stress process model.

Research involving widely differing populations has repeatedly demonstrated that perceived loss of control or helplessness has a strong positive relationship with depressive symptomatology (Seligman, 1975) and, correspondingly, that higher mastery is associated with lower levels of depression or distress (Holahan & Holahan, 1987; Rosenfield, 1989; Wheaton, 1980). Similarly, locus of control has been shown to have a direct relationship to psychological distress and well-being (Johnson & Sarason, 1978; Lefcourt, 1981), and personal and social competence have been found to be related to the development and maintenance of a sense of well-being (Headey, Holmstrom, & Wearing, 1985; Kennedy, 1989). Furthermore, longitudinal analyses conducted by Turner and Noh (1988) have revealed that both level of mastery and changes for either better or worse in mastery over time are independently predictive of depressive symptomatology.

Despite the apparent relevance of helplessness for distress and depression, identified shortcomings of the model, including the argument that it could not adequately account for self-esteem losses associated with depression, led to a significant reformulation centered around explanatory or attributional style (Abramson et al., 1978). According to this revised theory, the tendency to attribute negative outcomes to internal, stable, and global factors increases vulnerability to depression, as does the tendency to attribute positive outcomes to external, transient, and specific factors. Thus, the crucial difference in terms of depression is between individuals who "tend to believe that bad events will last a long time, will undermine everything they do, and are their own fault . . . [and those who] tend to believe defeat is just a temporary setback, that its causes are confined to this one case [and that it] . . . is not their fault" (Seligman, 1991, pp. 4–5). In the face of significant adversity, "*learned helplessness* is the giving-up reaction, the quitting response that follows from the belief that whatever you do doesn't matter. *Explanatory style* is the manner in which you habitually explain to yourself why events happen. It is the great modulator of learned helplessness" (Seligman, 1991, p. 15; emphasis in original).

Evidence on the significance of explanatory style has accumulated rapidly, although interpretations of this body of evidence are not entirely uniform. Relationships have been reported with such variables as divorce outcome among females (Barron, 1987), coping efforts and behaviors (Rosenberg, Peterson, & Hayes, 1987), mortality in ischemic heart disease (Kaplan, 1985), health in general and the immune system in particular (Peterson, Seligman, & Vaillant, 1988; Seligman, 1991), and depression (Riskind, Rholes, Brannon, & Burdick, 1987; Rizley, 1978). Peterson and Seligman (1984) reviewed a number of studies that had employed various designs and methods as well as different populations, concluding that "severity of depressive symptoms is often correlated with the habitual use of internal, stable and global causes to explain bad events involving the self" (p. 359). They also indicated that longitudinal investigations confirm that this depressive explanatory style precedes depression rather than being caused by it. Based on an extensive meta-analysis, Sweeney, Anderson, and Bailey (1986) reached similar conclusions: "As attributions for negative outcomes become more internal, stable, and global, depression increases" (p. 984). They also interpreted research as indicating that depression decreases as attributions for positive outcomes become more internal, stable, and global, although the effects of attributions for positive events were found to be smaller than for negative events. These reviewers further suggested that with corrections for measurement error, the small to medium effects typically reported may actually represent medium to large effects.

This view that explanatory style has both reliable and substantial effects on depression contrasts sharply with the result of Barnett and Gotlib's (1988) careful review of the issue. Limiting consideration to studies that specifically addressed depressive symptomatology, they examined investigations within which state dependence could be ruled out as a competing explanation for observed associations. They found support for the possible prognostic value of attributional style among the depressed, as well as evidence of a predictive relationship between attributional style and negative affect among both children and nondepressed adults. Barnett and Gotlib (1988) conclude, however, that adult research "that has controlled for the effects of concurrent symptoms has, by and large, failed to support the causal hypotheses of the reformulated learned helplessness model" (p. 103).

Though the question of the relevance of explanatory style for distress and depression may remain unsettled, the issue with respect to the general dimension of control or mastery is surely not. This evidence is clearly abundant and compelling. It may or may not be that some part of the process by which the experience of causal relevance is protective involves the way individuals explain negative outcomes to themselves. It is difficult to see attributional style, however, as inherently able to bear more than a portion of the explanatory burden. There are too many other ways in which it is possible, and even likely, that mastery may play a role within the stress process.

In the first instance, variations in mastery may affect the number and type of potentially stressful events and circumstances the individual confronts. Because differences in the sense of mastery must be at least substantially a product of one's history of successes and failures in social and environmental encounters, this sense must also at least reflect gross differences in social and instrumental effectiveness. Accordingly, individuals high in mastery may effectively avoid or prevent the occurrence of some potentially stressful events and circumstances. Moreover, assuming an individual's appraisal of an event depends importantly on the perception of ability or inability to manage or adapt to the situation, those high in mastery may experience a narrower range of life events or circumstances as problematic and thus as having stress potential.

As we emphasized earlier, motivational elements are inextricably involved because effort is only rational in the context of some belief that what one does can make a difference. Thus, a sense of personal agency is also believed to represent an important mediator of outcomes of adverse events because of its implications for the initiation and persistence of efforts to resolve problematic situations. Mirowsky and Ross (1989; Ross & Mirowsky, 1989) suggest that a sense of control reduces depression because it encourages active problem solving, whereas powerlessness is

both demoralizing in itself and decreases effective coping. The consequence is increased vulnerability to the deleterious effects of environmental stressors. Similar conclusions have been drawn from studies of
self-efficacy (Bandura, Adams, Hardy, & Howells, 1980) and fatalism
(Wheaton, 1983). With respect to explanatory style, evidence has been
presented suggesting that it affects depression partly via its impact on
coping efforts and behaviors (Rosenberg et al., 1987).

Control or mastery may also matter for distress and depression
because those high in mastery are, as previously noted, more likely to
possess the skills and abilities required to resolve difficult circumstances
that do occur. In addition, a strong sense of causal relevance may be
more resilient in the face of challenging and disconfirming events. Such
resiliency, of course, may well be at least partially a function of the extent
to which one's explanatory style functions to enhance or diminish the
personal implications, and thus the consequences, of adverse experiences. Whatever mechanism or mechanisms may be involved, available
evidence allows the confident conclusion that a greater sense of mastery
is associated with reduced risk of psychological distress and depression
following exposure to negative life events and role-related stressors
(Pearlin, Lieberman, Menaghan, & Mullan, 1981; Pearlin & Schooler,
1978).

Social Status and Personal Agency

In his discussion of the importance of a sense of efficacy or potency,
Smith (1968, p. 282) introduced the crucial insight that such attitudes
are closely and reciprocally linked to a perception of the world as trust-
able and reasonably fair: "Coordinate with the feeling of efficacy is an
attitude of hope—the world is the sort of place in which, given appropriate efforts, I can expect good outcomes." Because the perception of
oneself as causally important and as effective in the world derives substantially from one's history of successes and failures within social and
instrumental encounters, variations in the responsiveness of the social
environment clearly set at least broad limits on the acquisition of competence. For Smith, competence is differentially distributed in the social
system because opportunity, respect, and power are differentially distributed. Although Smith sees power as the crucial element, it is clear
that he does not mean power over others or over social institutions, but
over the day-to-day contingencies in one's own life.

Yet another formulation with implications that seem complementary to those just described has been provided by Kohn and Schooler
(Kohn, 1972, 1977; Kohn & Schooler, 1978, 1983). In a series of investi-

gations, they observed a relationship between social class position and conforming orientations and concluded that men in lower class positions are more likely to value conformity to external authority and to perceive such conformity as the only option allowed by environmental constraints and by the individual's own capacities.

Kohn (1972) applied these insights in an effort to explicate the origins of class differences in mental illness. Although this formulation was specific to schizophrenia, it is clear that, in large part, it applies equally well to class-related variations in psychiatric disorder and psychological distress generally. He persuasively argued that an important source of heightened vulnerability among the lower class involves conceptions of the external world and of self that serve to define a person's stance toward reality. The lower one's social position, the more likely one is to hold a characteristic conception of social reality that includes "a fatalistic belief that one is at the mercy of forces beyond one's control, often beyond one's understanding" (p. 300).

Perhaps the central contribution of Kohn and Schooler's subsequent work (Kohn, 1977; Kohn & Schooler, 1978, 1983) has been the elaboration and specification of the mechanisms by which the workplace contributes in crucial ways toward conditioning relevant conceptions of reality. The greater the opportunity for self-direction on the job and the more substantively complex the work, the more likely the worker is to value individual freedom and to possess a sense of personal efficacy.

This issue of the connection between social structure and self-efficacy has been a major thrust of sociological research (Gecas, 1989). When parallel concepts such as mastery, internality, personal control, and fatalism are considered, relationships with socioeconomic status have been consistently observed (Gurin et al., 1978; Mirowsky & Ross, 1983; Wheaton, 1980). Thus, both theory and evidence converge on the conclusion that causal agency represents a personal resource that is linked to position in the social structure in much the same way as are differential stress experiences. It is not clear whether the same can be said with confidence in relation to the risk factors of marital or minority status. What evidence can be found, however, encourages such a conclusion. Both Pearlin and colleagues (Pearlin & Schooler, 1978; Pearlin et al., 1981) and Kessler and Essex (1982) report higher levels of mastery among married than nonmarried subjects. With respect to minority status, both Gurin et al. (1978) and Lachman (1985) observed higher scores on personal control among whites than among blacks. Thus, there is some evidence consistent with the hypothesis that differences in the experience of personal control may be implicated in observed elevations in distress or disorder among nonmarried and minority groups.

Since the 1980s considerable attention has been focused on another persistently observed relationship: that between gender and psychological distress and disorder (Nolen-Hoeksema, 1987; Weissman & Klerman, 1977). There is also evidence that females are more likely than males to exhibit learned helplessness in achievement situations (Dweck, Goetz, & Strauss, 1980) and that males are more likely to focus on control of external events than are females (Gunnar-Von Gnechten, 1978). Although most available evidence on gender differences in mastery or control derives from studies of children (Block, 1983), similar results have also been reported for adults (Gurin et al., 1978; Ross, Mirowsky, & Cockerham, 1983). In a large study of physically limited adults resident in the community, however, we found no sex differences in mastery scores, either in general or within subgroups of young, middle-aged, and older subjects (Turner & Noh, 1988). Other studies that have failed to find a sex difference in either control or expectancies for future success have been reviewed by Miller and Kirsch (1987), who question the legitimacy of concluding that males characteristically show higher levels of control or mastery than do females.

Acknowledging that the evidence with respect to gender is equivocal, the hypothesis remains tenable that the status of being female, like lower class status, defines circumstances in which the typical environment may be less responsive and thus less generative with respect to the acquisition of a sense of mastery or control. Indeed, there appears to be no compelling basis for challenging the conclusions of several researchers that elevated levels of depressive symptomatology among females, nonmarried individuals, and persons of lower socioeconomic status may be partially explained by findings that males, the currently married, the better educated, and those who earn higher incomes have higher levels of personal mastery (Pearlin & Schooler, 1978; Peterson & Seligman, 1984). Further support for this hypothesis is provided by direct evidence that variations in personal control account for part of the class–distress relationship (Turner & Noh, 1983) and by findings suggesting the significance of mastery in accounting for the greater distress and morbidity observed among women (Mirowsky & Ross, 1984; Rosenfield, 1989; Verbrugge, 1989).

Thus, evidence makes clear that the sense of powerlessness is firmly linked to the high-risk category of low socioeconomic status, and perhaps to those of female, unmarried, and minority group member. There is also some indication that personal control can be facilitated and that such facilitation results in improvement in well-being (Langer & Rodin, 1976; Seligman, 1991). It appears that the dimension of mastery or control represents a highly promising target for prevention or intervention efforts in relation to subclinical distress and depression, and perhaps to clinically significant disorders as well.

SELF-ESTEEM

The term *mediator* has been used to refer to those factors that have been shown to be associated with differential responses to social stress (Pearlin et al., 1981). As Pearlin (1989, p. 250) has observed, the mediators of coping style and social support, which are the subjects of other chapters in this volume, have received the most attention in the research literature. As we have seen, however, the dimension of mastery or personal control has also attracted considerable scientific interest and effort. We believe that the next most important variable, in terms of both interest and credibility as a mediator of the effects of stressors on stress outcomes, is self-esteem.

That the broader construct of self-concept has been the subject of a truly vast number of papers and studies is witnessed by the fact that more than a decade and a half ago Wylie (1979) was able to assemble a nonexhaustive bibliography covering 86 pages. Moreover, the majority of these studies have focused on self-esteem (McGuire & Padawer-Singer, 1976). Accordingly, our consideration of this construct will in no sense be representative of the available literature and will be limited to conceptualizations and evidence that link self-esteem to elements of the stress process.

One of the most influential and enduring conceptualizations of self-esteem is that provided by Rosenberg (1965, 1979, 1986) whose research has clarified both the meaning and significance of this construct. According to Rosenberg (1965), self-esteem is "the evaluation which the individual makes and customarily maintains with regard to himself or herself: it expresses an attitude of approval or disapproval toward oneself" (p. 5). The process of self-esteem formation is said to involve the principles of "reflected appraisal," "social comparison," and "self-attribution" (Rosenberg, 1986). *Reflected appraisal* involves the individual's interpretation of how he or she is viewed by others, whereas *social comparison* holds that "in the absence of objective information about themselves people judge themselves on the basis of comparison with others" (Rosenberg, Schooler, & Schoenbach, 1989, p. 1006). *Self-attribution* refers to the tendency to draw conclusions about oneself from observing one's own actions, including the success or failure of efforts. Thus conceived, it is clear that self-esteem is potentially modifiable by future social experience. Accordingly, to the extent it is relevant to psychological distress and disorder, it represents one obvious target for prevention and early intervention efforts in the service of mental health. The goal of such efforts would be to increase the individual's capacity to maintain self-esteem in the face of adversity and, especially, loss events.

The hypothesis underlying this latter suggestion is that a positive and resilient self-image (in contrast to a negative or labile self-esteem) represents a crucial resource for combating the negative implications for self that are the frequent accompaniments of stressful events. Presumably, the stability and extent of self-esteem are determined by the nature and consistency of one's cumulative experiences of reflected appraisals, social comparisons, and self-attributions. In this connection, it seems important to note the apparent relevance of the resources of social support and personal control for self-esteem.

In what has come to be accepted as a classic definition, Cobb (1976) described social support as composed of information leading the individual to believe that he or she is loved, wanted, valued, and esteemed and able to count on others should the need arise. Thus, reflected appraisal represents an element of both social support and self-esteem, and experiences that foster or challenge one of these constructs must also be relevant for the other. Moreover, there is basis for assuming a degree of reciprocal causation. Surely the experience of being supported by others contributes toward more stable and positive self-esteem, whereas one's level of self-esteem must set at least broad limits on level of perceived social support. It is clear that individuals vary in their tendency or capacity to derive meaning and sustenance from a given amount of evidence of positive regard and affection. Everyone has encountered individuals who cannot seem to incorporate messages of social and emotional support, no matter how frequently or clearly they are delivered. Self-esteem presumably contributes to such differences in receptiveness because one's capacity to experience the esteem of others must require some minimal level of esteem of self.

The conceptual connection between self-esteem and personal control seems equally fundamental. Because the principles of self-esteem formation include self-attribution, one's history of successes and failures in social and environmental encounters that underlie personal control are also crucial contingencies for self-esteem. The now-common view that self-esteem is based in part on mastery or control (Gecas & Schwalbe, 1983; Pugliesi, 1989) was emphasized by Ryan (1967), who suggested that self-esteem differences represent a significant element in the linkage between poverty and mental health problems and that the experience of power is essential for self-esteem:

> Self-esteem is partially dependent on the inclusion of a sense of power within the self concept, that an effective—if you will, a mentally healthy—person must be able to perceive himself as at least minimally powerful, capable of influencing his envi-

ronment to his own benefit, and, further, that this sense of minimal power has to be based on the actual experience of, and exercise of, power. (p. 50)

Among the disadvantaged, powerlessness results in "significantly lowered self-esteem . . . and significantly higher levels of emotional disorder and other forms of social pathology" (Ryan, 1967, p. 51).

The argument that self-esteem is contingent on some minimal level of experienced self-efficacy seems intuitively compelling given the difficulty in imagining an attitude of self-value and approval in the context of a belief in one's causal irrelevance. From this perspective, Seligman's (1975) original helplessness theory may adequately account for self-esteem loss, at least at the extreme of helplessness. Thus, positive and stable self-esteem may have mediating functions similar to those of mastery (i.e., affecting the number and type of potentially stressful events and circumstances confronted, the initiation and persistence of efforts expended to resolve problematic situations, and greater resiliency in the face of challenge) and may also have implications for other psychosocial resources (e.g., social support and personal control).

Self-Esteem and Psychological Distress

As Rosenberg et al. (1989) have noted, self-esteem theory leads to the expectation of a connection with depression: "If the desire for positive self regard is a major motive of human beings, then the frustration of such a motive would almost inevitably be experienced as depressing" (p. 1007). Evidence consistent with this expectation has been widely reported. Kaplan (1975, 1980), who has systematically attended to the significance of self-esteem for behavior and well-being, reviewed available evidence that suggested a relationship with mental disorder and such related problems as alcoholism, drug abuse, aggressive behavior, and suicidal behavior (Kaplan, 1975), as well as depression (Kaplan & Pokorny, 1969). Since that time research has continued to accumulate indicating a significant inverse correlation between self-esteem and depressive symptomatology (Pearlin & Lieberman, 1979; Rosenberg, 1985; Wylie, 1979).

From the well-known research program of Brown and his colleagues (Brown, 1987; Brown, Harris, & Bifulco, 1986) has come evidence indicating that low self-esteem represents a vulnerability factor that increases risk of depression threefold in the presence of stress (see also Kaplan, Robbins, & Martin, 1983) and that, in this way, it plays a significant mediating role in the relationship between parental depression and vulnerability. In a similar vein, Robertson and Simons (1989) report that perceived parental rejection among adolescents has a direct effect on symptoms of depression and an indirect effect through diminished self-esteem.

The significance of self-esteem as a mediator of the impact of unemployment on psychological distress has been demonstrated by Pearlin et al. (1981). Subsequent studies involving diverse populations and designs have supported this conclusion. Both Shamir (1986) and Kessler, Turner, and House (1988) have reported evidence that individuals high in self-esteem appear to be more resistant to the negative effects of unemployment than individuals low in self-esteem.

Despite the abundance of evidence for a linkage between esteem and distress, especially depression, the conclusion that low self-esteem represents a risk factor for depression, rather than the reverse, requires consideration. As Feather (1987, p. 26) has noted, "Low self-esteem is generally taken as a key defining characteristic of depression." This view is associated with the cognitive theory of depression, which suggests that low esteem may be state dependent, arising out of depressive affect rather than contributing to it (Beck, Rush, Shaw, & Emery, 1979).

In our view, evidence derived from longitudinal studies and studies that have suggested a differential relationship between esteem and depression depending on stress level make it unlikely that the causality involved in this linkage goes entirely from depression to self-esteem. Moreover, a direct test of this issue has recently been provided by Rosenberg et al. (1989). These investigators applied linear structural equation–based reciprocal effects analysis to data from a two-wave panel study of adolescent boys in which self-esteem and depressive symptomatology were examined. The data revealed compelling evidence for reciprocal causation. Interestingly, observed relationships were found to be stronger among lower SES than higher SES subjects.

Thus, it seems safe to conclude that some important part of the causation involved in the self-esteem–depression relationship goes from esteem to depression, and that self-esteem may be especially significant among the disadvantaged and in high-stress circumstances generally. One implication of this conclusion is that prevention or intervention efforts that succeed in enhancing self-esteem can be expected to reduce the risk of psychological distress in general and depressive symptomatology in particular.

Social Status and Self-Esteem

As Gecas and Seff (1990) have noted, the principles of self-esteem theory lead to the clear expectation of a positive relationship between self-esteem and social class: "Those in the higher classes typically have greater power, resources, and prestige, all of which should increase self-esteem" (p. 165). Rosenberg and Pearlin (1979) speculated that the relative paucity of evidence on this relationship may indicate "that investigators have considered it pointless to attempt to establish a conclusion too obvious to require confirmation" (p. 53). In addition to the relative shortage of available evidence, studies reporting on this relationship have presented inconsistent and even contradictory results. Rosenberg and Pearlin (1978) reexamined these results and presented new data, drawing the conclusion that class and self-esteem are unrelated among children, modestly associated among adolescents, and moderately associated among adults. Subsequent reviews (Wylie, 1979) and research (Gecas & Seff, 1989, 1990; Kohn & Schooler, 1983; Mortimer & Finch, 1986) have confirmed a moderate positive relationship between self-esteem and social class position.

With respect to marital status, available evidence indicates that the currently married display higher levels of self-esteem (Pearlin & Schooler, 1978; Pearlin et al., 1981; Kessler & Essex, 1982). Either individuals with a more developed and positive sense of self-worth are more likely to get and remain married or the status and correlates of being married contribute to, or are protective of, self-esteem, or both. In any event, it appears that the higher levels of self-esteem that characterize the married contribute to the lower level of depression they experience (Kessler & Essex, 1982, p. 501).

Although a substantial number of studies have reported that women tend to report lower self-esteem than do men (Maccoby & Jacklin, 1974; Pearlin & Schooler, 1978; Pearlin et al., 1981), researchers have not always observed a difference (e.g., Zuckerman, 1989). Indeed, a review that considered evidence on gender differences in positive and negative self-evaluations led Miller and Kirsch (1987) to conclude that the evidence is both weak and inconsistent.

Though expressing similar doubts about the existence of meaningful gender differences in self-esteem, Gore and Colten (1991) nevertheless argue that it may constitute a highly significant variable relevant to understanding gender differences in depression. Accepting the view that self-esteem may represent an important mediator of the stress–depression relationship, they hypothesize that the relevant gender differences "might lie in the intensity of the interplay between social ties and self-esteem" (p. 149). An important part of the foundation for this view is provided by accumulated evidence (e.g., Bush, 1987; Gilligan, 1982) that aspects of the socialization process result in a dependency among women "on the opinions and evaluations of others in making their own judgements of how they are doing, that is, in maintaining self-image and self-esteem" (Gore & Colten, 1991, p. 150). This evidence suggests that males, in contrast to females, tend to develop sources of esteem in addition to reflected appraisals derived from the interpersonal context—sources associated with judgments of personal value based on achievements in the wider world. Without socialization experiences that foster independent sources of esteem, females must depend entirely on interpersonal experiences for self-evaluation and hence are especially responsive to the nature and strength of emotional ties and social connections.

The application of these insights in relation to the stress process leads to two predictions for which at least some evidence is available. First, because social support involves expressions of regard and value, the experience of social support should represent a more effective stress buffer for women than for men. We are aware of only two studies that have directly examined this expectation; both found evidence that social support represents a more significant stress-mediating variable for women than men (Dean & Lin, 1979; Husaini, Newbrough, Neff, & Moore, 1982).

A second prediction is that stressful events or ongoing difficulties in the interpersonal domain, including threats to or loss of relationships or significant others, should affect females more powerfully than males. Evidence consistent with this prediction has been provided by Kessler and McLeod (1984) and confirmed by Turner and Avison (1989). In both analyses women were found to be more influenced than men by events occurring to significant others, and this differential responsiveness was observed to have important mental health implications. These findings may reflect a cost to women that is associated with a wider domain of concern and a greater sensitivity to the well-being of others, as Kessler and McLeod (1984) suggest. They may also represent, however, the inevitable outcome of a greater dependence among women on social connections and relationships for the maintenance and defense of self-esteem.

Whether the phenomenon demonstrated by Kessler and McLeod (1984) is best conceptualized as a vulnerability factor or as indicating the need to calibrate estimates of stress exposure differentially for women, as Gore and Colten (1991) prefer, need not concern us here. What is clear is that these findings and those on social support are consistent with Gore and Colten's compelling suggestion that in considering the role of self-esteem in the stress process, it is important to focus upon the profoundly interpersonal nature of stressful experiences, especially for women.

This view converges with one expressed by Barnett and Gotlib

(1988) who have recommended that future research on social/developmental risk factors for depression consider the possible role of interpersonal dependency. Reviews of clinical studies have identified *interpersonal dependency* as characteristic of people prone to depression (Chodoff, 1972; Masserman, 1970), and Barnett and Gotlib (1988) have interpreted available evidence as indicating that this relationship does not only or largely reflect state dependence. The central hypothesis associated with this construct is that individuals who rely almost exclusively on the love and attention of others for the maintenance of their self-esteem are more vulnerable to depression (Hirschfeld, Klerman, Chodoff, Korchin, & Barrett, 1976).

> High dependency is hypothesized to develop among people who experienced difficulties in establishing adequate secure relationships early in life. As a result of this developmental disruption, these individuals are thought to become overly preoccupied with interpersonal security and to experience problems in maintaining positive feelings about themselves without external support. (Barnett & Gotlib, 1988, p. 119)

Though such developmental disruptions presumably occur as frequently among boys as among girls, differences in role demands and socialization experiences may well produce circumstances in which girls are more likely to develop interpersonal dependency, as the Gore and Colten (1991) formulation appears to suggest.

OTHER RELEVANT AND PROMISING CONSTRUCTS

As important as mastery and self-esteem may be for understanding the obvious variability in the mental health consequences of stress experiences, their sufficiency, even when combined with assessments of coping style and social support, is hard to argue. In response to this circumstance, a growing number of researchers have hypothesized the relevance of more complex self-representational structures. Although self-image or esteem remains a central theme within most of these conceptualizations, each sees the relevant self-representations as inadequately or incompletely captured by estimates of the quantity of self-esteem. These more complex structures provide explications of hypothesized determinants of variations in vulnerability to negative change (and, in some cases, openness to positive changes) in self-esteem in the face of life stress.

Rosenberg (1965, 1967; Rosenberg & Pearlin, 1978) long ago introduced the concept of "psychological centrality," which posited that some self values are critically important, whereas others are relatively trivial. "Thus, the impact of any given component on global self-esteem will depend on its importance or unimportance, centrality or peripherality, in the individual's cognitive structure" (Rosenberg & Pearlin, 1978, p. 67). From this it follows that the magnitude of the impact on self-esteem, and hence on psychological distress, occasioned by a given stressful event will depend on the importance or centrality of the dimension or component of self that is challenged or disconfirmed by the event. Evidence for the role and significance of psychological centrality has been provided by Rosenberg (1965, 1976) and recently confirmed by Gecas and Seff (1990).

A similar formulation has been offered by Stryker (1980; Stryker & Serpe, 1982) who suggests that identities tend to be organized in a "salience hierarchy." Salience refers to the level of commitment an individual has to an identity and determines the likelihood that a given identity will be invoked across differing situations. Presumably, the more salient the identity that is called into question, the greater will be the impact of a serious negative event on the self-image and well-being of the individual. Given the traditional assumption that work tends to be more salient for the male identity while interpersonal relations tend to be more central for the female identity, the finding by Wheaton (1990) that "work related stress has more contextual relevance for men experiencing job loss or retirement, whereas relationship stress has more contextual relevance for women experiencing the interpersonal role events of recent divorce and marriage" (p. 211) provides additional evidence consistent with the centrality and salience hypotheses.

Thoits (1986) has argued that "the self can be conceptualized as a set of *social identities,* where identities refer to positional designations assigned by others and accepted by the individual himself or herself (e.g., spouse, parent, employee, student, church member)" (p. 259; emphasis in original). She suggests that role identities are important for self-definition and that "one's sense of self as a meaningful, purposeful entity is derived in part from the social roles one accepts and enacts" (p. 259). Because social identities give meaning and guidance to behavior, the more identities an individual possesses, the less psychological distress or depression he or she should exhibit. This hypothesis was tested by Thoits (1983, 1986) in two secondary data analyses. She found "that symptoms of distress vary inversely with the number of role-identities possessed, and that changes in identities over time are psychologically beneficial or harmful, depending upon the direction of the change" (1986, p. 260). Though confirming the observation that possession of multiple role identities significantly reduces distress among both men and women, the second study also suggests the possibility that structural inequalities in role occupancy by gender may contribute to observed differences in distress.

The idea that role acquisition can be psychologically protective is one of the propositions associated with the more complex conceptualization that Thoits (1983) calls the "identity accumulation hypothesis." Briefly, this hypothesis assumes an inverse relationship between the degree of commitment to a particular identity and the number of identities constituting the self. As the number of identities increases, the individual's commitment to any single identity will decrease, and vice versa, in part because of differences in the availability of energy for investment. Thus, how much the individual has at stake when confronted by an identity-challenging circumstance or event is thought to depend on the number of other identities that make up the self. Fewer identities therefore are associated with increased vulnerability to stress, whereas a greater accumulation represents a significant resistance resource.

Writing at about the same time, Linville (1982, 1985, 1987) describes a construct called "self-complexity" that shares much with Thoits's conceptualization. She proposes that "individual differences in vulnerability to stress are due, in part, to differences in cognitive representations of the self; more specifically, to differences in the complexity of self representations" (1987, p. 663). Self-complexity involves a greater number of perceived or experienced self-aspects and the maintenance of clearer distinctions among such aspects. The major result of such complexity is that stressful events in one aspect are less likely to spill over and negatively affect other aspects. As self-complexity increases, the proportion of self-aspects challenged by an emotionally salient event decreases, and the more likely it is that thoughts and feelings that are evoked will be confined to immediately salient self-aspects. Although some supporting evidence for the relevance of self-complexity has been provided (Linville, 1987), here, as with the more complex aspects of Thoits's (1982a, b) conceptualization, more data are required before a confident scientific judgment can be made in relation to the utility of these conceptualizations.

Relationships with Social Status

The question of whether identity accumulation, self-complexity, or availability of secondary roles can be linked to social statuses that describe differences in risk for mental health problems cannot be empirically supported or disconfirmed. Relevant data are simply not yet available. It seems likely, however, that relationships will eventually be observed between such constructs and marital status, gender, and social class position. Married individuals obviously hold the additional role of spouse and are more likely than the currently nonmarried to be filling the role of parent. That men are still somewhat more likely than women to be paid workers suggests the likelihood of a more extensive role set and greater self-complexity for men. Moreover, the structural inequalities that characterize the workplace also suggest that men are more likely than women to hold such self-relevant statuses as foreman, supervisor, manager, or chief executive officer. A similar case can be made for the expectation of relationship with social class position. The higher one's education and occupational prestige, the more likely one is to accumulate roles and identities, and the more complex the self is likely to become.

If such relationships can be confirmed, the hypothesis would follow that differences in the richness of role sets or in self-complexity may contribute to the well-established relationships between mental health problems and gender, marital status, and socioeconomic position. In considering this possibility it may be important to take account of the negative side of role occupancy. That there are potential costs associated with additional roles has been illustrated in a recent study on gender differences in depression. Turner and Avison (1989) confirmed the usual observation that gender differences are minimized in comparisons where employment status is controlled and found the mental health advantage of employment to be about equal for men and women. Among women, however, unlike for men, differences in stress did not contribute toward explaining employment-related depression differences:

> On the contrary, control of such differences would significantly increase, rather than decrease, the depression difference observed. That employed women tend to be less depressed than unemployed women despite the increased burden of depression-relevant stress associated with employment suggests that, overall, the paid worker role must have especially powerful beneficial effects for women. (p. 454).

Clearly, other major roles also carry increased risk of exposure to both eventful stressors and chronic strains. Only parents can have children who get sick, have other enduring problems, or die. Only married individuals can experience a legal separation or divorce, and only the employed can be fired, laid off, or demoted. Thus, there is good news and bad news about role accumulation—increases in numbers of roles are associated with decreases in psychological distress, but such increases are accompanied by increased risk of experiencing life stress as typically indexed. It appears that the psychological rewards of additional roles and complexity may be substantially greater than the observed relationships with distress suggest, given the offsetting influence of additional sources of stress.

If these arguments are correct, the process of role accumulation tends to carry with it both improvement in mental health status and increases in stress exposure—an anomalous circumstance that may help explain other difficult to accept observations from stress research. We have in mind research reviewed by Thoits (1983) suggesting that "undesirable events are distributed more equally among groups than might be expected; certain advantaged groups (the married, those of higher income) actually report equal or even higher numbers of undesirable events than their disadvantaged counterparts" (p. 85).

It is our view that stress and social class cannot be unrelated or positively related; there is just too much contrary demographic and social evidence. One explanation for such findings may be the tendency to focus on recent life events, ignoring major domains such as chronic stressors and life traumas. Another explanatory factor, as we have noted, may lie in the simultaneous opposing consequences of additional roles. It might be that the relevant stress burden is better estimated by something like a per-role stress average than by a raw summation of negative life events and/or chronic stressors.

SOCIAL STRESS AND PERSONAL RESOURCES

The idea that stressful events can have implications for such resources as personal control and self-esteem has been the subject of considerable research, all suggesting that stress experiences affect these resources adversely (Bandura, 1982; Brown & Harris, 1978; Folkman, 1984; Kaplan, 1980; Seligman, 1975). Pearlin et al. (1981) have also presented evidence of the negative impact of stressors on self-esteem and mastery and offer the following interpretation of their findings:

> Persistent role strains can confront people with dogged evidence of their own failures—or lack of success—and with inescapable proof of their inability to alter the unwanted circumstances of their lives. Under these conditions, people become vulnerable to the loss of self-esteem and to the erosion of mastery. (p. 340)

Although it seems both well established and well recognized that stressful life events can result in a diminished self-esteem and sense of mastery, the hypothesis that the outcome of stressful experiences can sometimes include positive changes has not been seriously entertained within modern stress research. It is in this regard that the assumptions that have tended to inform research on both eventful stress and chronic strains have been most discrepant from those associated with "crisis theory." The central propositions associated with this frame of reference can be traced to the work of Erik Erikson (1950, 1959). Erikson conceptualized personality growth as occurring through the resolution of normative developmental crises. He saw developmental stages as systematically interrelated, with each one depending on the successful resolution of those preceding. When crises are successfully resolved, the individual emerges from these encounters with new skills and confidence (or other enabling self-attitudes) that increase the probability that future crises will be handled well. This developmental process thus involves both a synthesizing of new experiences into an evolving self-perception and the accumulation of skills or strategies for instrumental or emotional response.

Although Erikson specifically used the term *vulnerability* to characterize the major corollary of crisis experiences, he implied a meaning that might better be described as openness, both to harm and to enhancement. This is evident from his contention that personality growth occurs through the resolution of normative crises and hence that the disequilibria characterizing these crises offer potential for forward developmental leaps as well as for harm.

Although Erikson's conceptualization considers only developmental and normative crises, it is obvious that the occurrence of events and/or circumstances that may constitute crises are an almost existential accompaniment to the whole life process. It thus followed to writers such as Caplan (1961) that unscheduled crises or life events, when successfully resolved, may also promote personality growth or effectiveness. During the 1950s and 1960s, this view was expressed in research reports on natural disasters (Baker & Chapman, 1962; Lindemann, 1944), in studies of responses to war and combat (Glass, 1955; Janis, 1951), and in investigations on the adaptational consequences of personal crises (Klein & Lindemann, 1961).

These earlier investigations shared with contemporary stress research the assumption that events or circumstances involving adverse change and/or novelty or ambiguity could have profound implications for the health, well-being, and development of those involved. Unlike the general contemporary habit, however, it was not assumed that even profound events were always and in all aspects negative in their effects. For example, it has been observed that civilian populations under repeated stress make increasingly effective adaptations (Janis, 1951), and that the experience of disaster helps equip populations to handle extreme situations better (Beach & Lucas, 1960). Wilson (1962) summarized the implications of these and other consistent findings by stating that "research has demonstrated repeatedly that disaster is not necessarily and in all ways damaging to either individual health or social organizations and . . . many indeed have curiously beneficial implications" (p. 131). Similar observations have been made in relation to the personal consequences of experienced crises. For example, Klein and Lindemann (1961) concluded that "it is clear that hazards provide opportunity for promotion of emotional growth as well as occasions for preventive measures" (p. 305).

Thus, in contrast to the dominant assumption of contemporary stress researchers, the crisis theory perspective recognizes life events as representing opportunities as well as hazards. Although unresolved or poorly resolved events are viewed as uniformly negative in their consequences, successfully resolved events are hypothesized to be enhancing and growth producing. It is further suggested that the likelihood of successfully resolving a present crisis or event depends crucially upon one's history of successes and failures in confronting similar and dissimilar life events.

In our view, contemporary stress research might be advantaged by seriously entertaining the central alternative hypothesis provided by crisis theory. At a minimum, this means examining the possibility that successfully resolved events or circumstances should not be counted when estimating an individual's burden of stress; at a maximum, it means considering the hypothesis that such events may have positive effects on such resources as mastery, self-esteem, self-complexity, or some other identity-relevant construct.

The results of some preliminary efforts to test these ideas have been reported elsewhere (Turner & Avison, 1992a, b). Although available data warrant the conclusion that event resolution should be taken into account when estimating stress burden, compelling evidence that the outcomes of stressful life events can have positive, rather than only negative, implications for constructs such as mastery and self-esteem is lacking. In our view, however, such evidence is likely to be forthcoming. We wonder if it can be otherwise, given that self-esteem and mastery are clearly forged in environmental encounters and conditioned by successes as well as failures within such encounters. To the extent that such resources remain modifiable, stressful circumstances—both discrete and enduring—must constitute opportunities for self-confirmation and discovery as well as sources of threat and personal damage.

CLOSING COMMENTS

In concluding this chapter, we omit a summary because the chapter as a whole has done little more than summarize evidence and issues relevant to the stress process roles of the personal resources we have examined. Given space limitations and because we have already expressed our own judgments about the meanings of available evidence, we also omit a listing of conclusions. Our closing comments are thus restricted to an enumeration of several promising and sometimes neglected research topics that, in our view, are suggested by current theory and evidence.

First, we urge increased attention to potential causal interrelationships among stress process variables. Although negative events and circumstances may be inevitable life accompaniments, exposure to stressors is clearly not a random phenomenon. In addition to social structural influences, variations in level of mastery, self-esteem, and social support may also condition exposure. Research is required to address the hypothesis that these resources, which are assumed to index variations in vulnerability to stressors, may also influence exposure. More generally, what is needed is research in which the quantity and type of potentially stressful experiences is taken as the dependent variable. Evidence on the epidemiology and psychosocial determinants of social stress would provide a more adequate basis for estimating the potential for intervening in the stress process at the exposure level. Similarly, the substantial evidence that has been reviewed suggesting both the direct and stress-buffering significance of personal resources for mental health indicates the importance of understanding the factors (developmental and contemporaneous) that influence one's status on these variables. Though self-esteem has been widely treated as a dependent variable, the same cannot be said of mastery or such other promising dimensions as self-complexity. Moreover, consideration of the significance of stress experiences for personal resources has been largely limited to negative implications. As suggested earlier, the possibility of positive effects on self-esteem and mastery of certain outcomes of stressful experience is worthy of research attention.

Second, although roles and role requirements have been prominent topics within efforts to understand gender differences in distress, variations in the quantity and nature of roles and role sets—within as well as across gender—have received only limited attention. In our view, identity accumulation, self-complexity, availability of secondary roles, or similar constructs that elaborate the self system may well be essential for advancing our understanding of variations in vulnerability or resistance to stressful experiences. In this connection, we have also suggested the need to take account of the negative side of role occupancy. Although number of roles is negatively associated with distress, it seems apparent that increases in role occupancy are associated with elevations in risk for exposure to stressors as typically measured. Factors that are associated simultaneously with lower distress and higher stress exposure may help explain why observed associations between stress exposure and distress tend to be modest in magnitude. Moreover, achievement of a clear understanding of the role and significance of elements of the self system within the stress process requires an understanding of the bad news as well as good news that may be associated with these elements.

Finally, we would like to underline Gore and Colten's (1991) hypothesis that the profoundly interpersonal determinants of self-esteem among women may result in increased vulnerability to esteem loss in the face of interpersonal disruptions which tend to characterize eventful stress and strains as typically measured. This compelling hypothesis deserves research attention, along with the question of gender differences in (and the psychosocial determinants of) risk for interpersonal dependency. It may also be useful to consider the possibility of differential responsiveness of self-esteem to life stresses in relation to other risk statuses (e.g., being poor or unmarried). The sense of this hypothesis may also be extended to such other resources as mastery and social support. Could it be that women, the unmarried, and those of low SES are at increased risk for psychological distress partly because crucial adaptive resources such as self-esteem, mastery, and social support tend to be more adversely affected by negative or disconfirming events and circumstances among these groups? Answers to these questions seem worthy of our time and effort.

REFERENCES

Abramson, L. Y., Alloy, L. B., & Metalsky, G. I. (1989). Hopelessness depression: A theory-based subtype of depression. *Psychological Review, 96*, 358–372.

Abramson, L. Y., Seligman, M. E. P., & Teasdale, J. D. (1978). Learned helplessness in humans: Critique and reformation. *Journal of Abnormal Psychology, 87*, 49–74.

Adler, P. T. (1982). An analysis of the concept of competence in individuals and social systems. *Community Mental Health Journal, 18*, 34–45.

Antonovsky, A. (1979). *Health, stress, and coping.* San Francisco: Jossey-Bass.

Antonovsky, A. (1987). *Unraveling the mystery of health: How people manage stress and stay well.* San Francisco: Jossey-Bass.

Baker, G. W., & Chapman, D. W. (Eds.). (1962). *Man and society in disaster.* New York: Basic Books.

Bandura, A. (1977). Self-efficacy: Toward a unifying theory of behavioral change. *Psychological Review, 84*, 191–215.

Bandura, A. (1982). Self-efficacy mechanism in human agency. *American Psychologist, 37*, 122–147.

Bandura, A., Adams, N., Hardy, A., & Howells, G. (1980). Tests of the generality of self-efficacy theory. *Cognitive Therapy and Research, 4*, 39–66.

Barnett, P. A., & Gotlib, I. H. (1988). Psychosocial functioning and depression: Distinguishing among antecedents, concomitants, and consequences. *Psychological Bulletin, 104*, 97–126.

Barron, C. R. (1987). Women's causal explanations of divorce: Relationships to self-esteem and emotional distress. *Research in Nursing and Health, 10*, 345–353.

Beach, H. D., & Lucas, R. A. (1960). *Individual and group behavior in a coal mine disaster* (Disaster Study No. 13). Washington, DC: National Academy of Sciences.

Beck, A. T., Rush, A. J., Shaw, B. F., & Emery, G. (1979). *Cognitive therapy of depression: A treatment manual.* New York: Guilford.

Ben-Sira, Z. (1985). Potency: A stress-buffering link in the coping–stress–disease relationship. *Social Science and Medicine, 21*, 397–406.

Block, J. H. (1983). Differential premises arising from differential socialization of the sexes: Some conjectures. *Child Development, 54*, 1335–1354.

Brown, G. W. (1987). Social factors and the development and course of depressive disorders in women: A review of a research programme. *British Journal of Social Work, 17*, 615–634.

Brown, G. W., & Harris, T. (1978). *Social origins of depression: A study of psychiatric disorder in women.* New York: Free Press.

Brown, G. W., Harris, T. O., & Bifulco, A. (1986). Long-term effects of early loss of parent. In M. Rutter, C. E. Izard, & P. B. Read (Eds.), *Depression in young people: Developmental and clinical perspectives* (pp. 251–296). New York: Guilford

Bush, D. M. (1987). The impact of family and school on adolescent girls' aspirations and expectations: The public–private split and the reproduction of gender inequality. In J. Figueira-McDonough & R. Sarri (Eds.), *The trapped women* (pp. 258–295). Beverly Hills, CA: Sage.

Chaplan, G. (Ed.). (1961). *Prevention of mental disorders in children: Initial explorations.* New York: Basic Books.

Chodoff, P. (1972). The core problem in depression: Interpersonal aspects. In J. H. Messerman (Ed.), *Science and psychoanalysis, vol. 17* (pp. 56–65). New York: Grune & Stratton.

Cobb, S. (1976). Social support as a moderator of life stress. *Psychosomatic Medicine, 38*, 300–314.

Dean, A., & Lin, N. (1977). The stress buffering role of social support. *Journal of Nervous and Mental Disease, 165*, 403–413.

Dodge, K., & Murphy, R. (1984). The assessment of social competence in adolescents. In P. Karoly, J. Steffan, & J. Lexington (Eds.), *Advances in child behavioral analysis and therapy, vol. 3. Adolescent behavior disorders: Foundations and contemporary concerns.* Lexington, MA: Heath.

Dohrenwend, B. P., & Dohrenwend, B. S. (1969). *Social status and psychological disorder: A causal inquiry.* New York: Wiley.

Dohrenwend, B. S. (1973). Social status and stressful life events. *Journal of Personality and Social Psychology, 28*, 225–235.

Dweck, C. S., Goetz, T. E., & Strauss,'N. L. (1980). Sex differences in learned helplessness: IV. An experimental and naturalistic study of failure generalization and its mediators. *Journal of Personality and Social Psychology, 38*, 441–452.

Erikson, E. (1950). *Childhood and society.* New York: Norton.

Erikson, E. (1959). Identity and the life cycle. *Psychological Issues, 1*, 1–171.

Feather, N. T. (1987). The rosy glow of self-esteem: Depression, masculinity, and causal attributions. *Australian Journal of Psychology, 39*, 25–41.

Folkman, S. (1984). Personal control and stress and coping processes: A theoretical analysis. *Journal of Personality and Social Psychology, 46*, 839–852.

Gecas, V. (1989). The social psychology of self-efficacy. *Annual Review of Sociology, 15,* 291–316.

Gecas, V., & Schwalbe, M. L. (1983). Beyond the looking glass self: Social structure and efficacy-based self-esteem. *Social Psychology Quarterly, 43,* 77–88.

Gecas, V., & Seff, M. A. (1989). Social class, occupational conditions, and self-esteem. *Sociological Perspectives, 32,* 353–365.

Gecas, V., & Seff, M. A. (1990). Social class and self-esteem: Psychological centrality, compensation, and the relative effects of work and home. *Social Psychological Quarterly, 53,* 165–173.

Gilligan, C. (1982). *In a different voice: Psychological theory and women's development.* Cambridge, MA: Harvard University Press.

Glass, A. (1955). *Psychological considerations in atomic warfare* (Report No. 560). Washington, DC: Army Medical Service Graduate School, Walter Reed Army Medical Center.

Gore, S., & Colten, M. E. (1991). Gender, stress, and distress. In J. Eckenrode (Ed.), *The social context of coping* (pp. 139–163). New York: Plenum.

Gove, W. (1972). The relationship between sex roles, mental illness and marital status. *Social Forces, 51,* 34–44.

Gunnar-Von Gnechten, M. R. (1978). Changing a frightening toy into a pleasant toy by allowing the infant to control its actions. *Developmental Psychology, 14,* 157–162.

Gurin, P., Gurin, G., & Morrison, B. M. (1978). Personal and ideological aspects of internal and external control. *Social Psychology Quarterly, 41,* 275–296.

Headey, B., Homstrom, E., & Wearing, A. (1985). Models of well-being and ill-being. *Social Indicators Research, 17,* 211–234.

Hirschfeld, R., Klerman, G., Chodoff, P., Korchin, S., & Barrett, J. (1976). Dependency–self-esteem–clinical depression. *Journal of the American Academy of Psychoanalysis, 4,* 373–388.

Holahan, C. K., & Holahan, C. J. (1987). Self-efficacy, social support, and depression in aging: A longitudinal analysis. *Journal of Gerontology, 42,* 65–68.

Hollingshead, A. B., & Redlich, F. C. (1958). *Social class and mental illness: A community study.* New York: Wiley.

Husaini, B. A., Newbrough, J. R., Neff, J. A., & Moore, M. C. (1982). The stress-buffering role of social support and personal competence among the rural married. *Journal of Community Psychology, 10,* 409–426.

Janis, I. L. (1951). *Air war and emotional stress: Psychological studies of bombing and civil defense.* New York: McGraw-Hill.

Johnson, J. W., & Sarason, I. G. (1978). Life stress, depression and anxiety: Internal–external control as a moderator variable. *Journal of Psychosomatic Research, 22,* 205–208.

Kaplan, G. A. (1985). Psychosocial aspects of chronic illness: Direct and indirect associations with ischemic heart disease mortality. In R. M. Kaplan & M. H. Criqui (Eds.), *Behavioral epidemiology and disease prevention* (pp. 237–267). New York: Plenum.

Kaplan, H. B. (1975). *Self-attitudes and deviant behavior.* Pacific Palisades, CA: Goodyear.

Kaplan, H. B. (1980). *Deviant behavior in defense of self.* New York: Academic Press.

Kaplan, H. B., & Pokorny, A. D. (1969). Self-derogation and psychosocial adjustment. *Journal of Nervious and Mental Disease, 149,* 421–434.

Kaplan, H. B., Robbins, C., & Martin, S. S. (1983). Antecedents of psychological distress in young adults: Self-rejection, deprivation of social support, and life events. *Journal of Health and Social Behavior, 24,* 230–243.

Kennedy, C. (1989). Community integration and well-being: Toward the goals of community care. *Journal of Social Issues, 45,* 677.

Kessler, R. C., & Cleary, P. D. (1980). Social class and psychological distress. *American Sociological Review, 45*, 463–478.

Kessler, R. C., & Essex, M. (1982). Marital status and depression: The role of coping resources. *Social Forces, 61*, 484–507.

Kessler, R. C., & McLeod, J. D. (1984). Sex differences in vulnerability to undesirable life events. *American Sociological Review, 49*, 620–631.

Kessler, R. C., & Neighbors, H. W. (1986). A new perspective on the relationships among race, social class, and psychological distress. *Journal of Health and Social Behavior, 27*, 107–115.

Kessler, R. C., Turner, J. B., & House, J. S. (1988). Effects of unemployment on health in a community survey: Main, modifying, and mediating effects. *Journal of Social Issues, 44*, 69–85.

Klein, D. C., & Lindeman, E. (1961). Preventive intervention in individual and family crisis situations. In G. Caplan (Ed.), *Prevention of mental disorders in children* (pp. 265–283). New York: Basic Books.

Kobasa, S. C. (1979). Stressful life events, personality, and health. *Journal of Personality and Social Psychology, 37*, 1–11.

Kobasa, S. C. (1982a). Commitment and coping in stress resistance among lawyers. *Journal of Personality and Social Psychology, 42*, 707–717.

Kobasa, S. C. (1982b). The hardy personality: Toward a social psychology of stress and health. In G. S. Sanders & J. Suls (Eds.), *Social psychology in health and illness* (pp. 3–32). Hillsdale, NJ: Erlbaum.

Kobasa, S. C., Maddi, S. R., & Corrington, S. (1981). Personality and constitution as mediators in the stress–illness relationship. *Journal of Health and Social Behavior, 22*, 368–378.

Kohn, M. L. (1972). Class, family and schizophrenia: A reformulation. *Social Forces, 50*, 295–313.

Kohn, M. L. (1977). *Class and conformity: A study in values* (2nd ed.). Chicago: University of Chicago Press.

Kohn, M. L., & Schooler, C. (1978). The reciprocal effects of the substantive complexity of work and intellectual flexibility: A longitudinal assessment. *American Journal of Sociology, 84*, 24–52.

Kohn, M. L., & Schooler, C. (1983). *Work and personality.* Norwood, NJ: Ablex.

Lachman, R. (1985). Kuhn and cognitive psychology: A response to Gibson. *New Ideas in Psychology, 3*, 273–275.

Langer, E. J., & Rodin, J. (1976). The effects of choice and enhanced personal responsibility for the aged: A field experiment in an institutional setting. *Journal of Personality and Social Psychology, 34*, 191–198.

Langner, T. S., & Michael, S. T. (1963). *Life stress and mental health.* New York: Free Press.

Lefcourt, H. M. (1976). *Locus of control: Current trends on theory and research.* New York: Erlbaum.

Lefcourt, H. M. (1981). Locus of control and stressful life events. In B. S. Dohrenwend & B. P. Dohrenwend (Eds.), *Stressful life events and their contexts* (pp. 157–166). New York: Wiley.

Lindemann, E. (1944). Symptomatology and management of acute grief. *American Journal of Psychiatry, 101*, 141–148.

Linville, P. W. (1982). The complexity-extremity effect and age-based stereotyping. *Journal of Personality and Social Psychology, 42*, 193–211.

Linville, P. W. (1985). Self-complexity and affective extremity: Don't put all of your eggs in one cognitive basket. *Social Cognition, 3*, 94–120.

Linville, P. W. (1987). Self-complexity as a cognitive buffer against stress-related illness and depression. *Journal of Personality and Social Psychology, 52*, 663–676.

Maccoby, E., & Jacklin, C. (1974). *The psychology of sex differences.* Stanford, CA: Stanford University Press.

Masserman, J. H. (1970). Preface: An historical review of the psychodynamic theories of affect. In J. H. Masserman (Ed.), *Science and psychodynamics, vol. 17* (pp. viii–xviii). New York: Grune & Stratton.

McGuire, W. J., & Padawer-Singer, A. (1976). Trait salience in the spontaneous self-concept. *Journal of Personality and Social Psychology, 33*, 743–754.

Miller, S. M., & Kirsch, N. (1987). Sex differences in cognitive coping with stress. In R. C. Barnett, L. Biener, & G. K. Baruch (Eds.), *Gender and stress* (pp. 278–307). New York: Free Press.

Mirowsky, J., & Ross, C. E. (1983). The multidimensionality of psychopathology in a community sample. *American Journal of Community Psychology, 11*, 573–591.

Mirowsky, J., & Ross, C. E. (1984). Mexican culture and its emotional contradictions. *Journal of Health and Social Behavior, 25*, 2–13.

Mirowsky, J., & Ross, C. E. (1986). Social patterns of distress. *Annual Review of Sociology, 12*, 23–45.

Mirowsky, J., & Ross, C. E. (1989). Psychiatric diagnosis as reified measurement. *Journal of Health and Social Behavior, 30*, 11–25.

Mortimer, J. T., & Finch, M. D. (1986). The development of self-esteem in the early work career. *Work and Occupation, 13*, 217–239.

Nolen-Hoeksema, S. (1987). Sex differences in unipolar depression. *Psychological Bulletin, 101*, 259–282.

Pearlin, L. I. (1989). The sociological study of stress. *Journal of Health and Social Behavior, 30*, 241–256.

Pearlin, L. I., Lieberman, M., Menaghan, E., & Mullan, J. (1981). The stress process. *Journal of Health and Social Behavior, 22*, 337–356.

Pearlin, L. I., & Lieberman, M. A. (1979). Social sources of emotional distress. In R. G. Simmons (Ed.), *Research in community and mental health, vol. 1*, (pp. 217–248). Greenwich, CT: JAI Press.

Pearlin, L. I., & Schooler, C. (1978). The structure of coping. *Journal of Health and Social Behavior, 19*, 2–21.

Peterson, C., & Seligman, M. E. P. (1984). Causal explanations as a risk factor for depression: Theory and evidence. *Psychological Review, 91*, 347–374.

Peterson, C., Seligman, M. E. P., & Vaillant, G. E. (1988). Pessimistic explanatory style is a risk factor for physical illness: A thirty-five-year longitudinal study. *Journal of Personality and Social Psychology, 55*, 23–27.

Pugliesi, K. (1989). Social support and self-esteem and intervening variables in the relationship between social roles and women's well-being. *Community Mental Health Journal, 25*, 87–100.

Rabkin, J. G., & Struening, E. L. (1976). Life events, stress, and illness. *Science, 194*, 1013–1020.

Riskind, J. H., Rholes, W. S., Brannon, A. M., & Burdick, C. A. (1987). Attributions and expectations: A confirmation of vulnerabilities in mild depression in a college student population. *Journal of Personality and Social Psychology, 53*, 249–354.

Rizley, R. (1978). Depression and distortion in the attribution of causality. *Journal of Abnormal Psychology, 87*, 32–48.

Robertson, J. F., & Simons, R. L. (1989). Family factors, self-esteem, and adolescent depression. *Journal of Marriage and the Family, 51*, 125–138.

Rosenberg, M. (1965). *Society and the adolescent self-image*. Princeton, NJ: Princeton University Press.

Rosenberg, M. (1967). On accidents and incidents: A study of self-destruction. *Comprehensive Psychiatry, 8*, 108–118.

Rosenberg, M. (1976, September). Beyond self-esteem: Some neglected aspects of the self-concept. Paper presented at the annual meeting of the American Sociological Association, New York City.

Rosenberg, M. (1979). The self concept: Source, product and social force. In M. Rosenberg & R. H. Turner (Eds.), *Social psychology: Sociological perspectives*. New York: Basic Books.

Rosenberg, M. (1985). Self-concept and psychological well-being in adolescence. In R. L. Leahy (Ed.), *The development of the self* (pp. 205–246). Orlando, FL: Academic Press.

Rosenberg, M. (1986). *Conceiving the self*. Melbourne, FL: Academic Press.

Rosenberg, M., & Pearlin, L. I. (1978). Social class and self-esteem among children and adults. *American Journal of Sociology, 84*, 53–77.

Rosenberg, S. J., Peterson, R. A., & Hayes, J. R. (1987). Coping behaviors among depressed and nondepressed medical inpatients. *Journal of Psychosomatic Research, 31*, 653–658.

Rosenberg, M., Schooler, C., & Schoenbach, C. (1989). Self-esteem and adolescent problems: Modeling reciprocal effects. *American Sociological Review, 54*, 1004–1018.

Rosenfield, S. (1989). The effects of women's employment: Personal control and sex differences in mental health. *Journal of Health and Social Behavior, 30*, 77–91.

Ross, C. E., & Mirowsky, J. (1989). Explaining the social patterns of depression: Control and problem solving—or support and talking? *Journal of Health and Social Behavior, 30*, 206–219.

Ross, C. E., Mirowsky, J., & Cockerham, W. C. (1983). Social class, Mexican culture and fatalism: Their effects on psychological distress. *American Journal of Community Psychology, 11*, 383–399.

Rotter, J. B. (1966). Generalized expectancies for internal vs. external control of reinforcement. *Psychological Monographs, 80*, 1–28.

Ryan, W. (1967). Preventive services in the social context: Power, pathology, and prevention. In *Proceedings of a Mental Health Institute (Salt Lake City)* (pp. 49–58), Western Interstate Commission for Higher Education, Boulder, CO.

Seeman, M. (1959). On the meaning of alienation. *American Sociological Review, 24*, 783–791.

Seligman, M. E. P. (1975). *Helplessness: On depression, development, and death*. San Francisco: Freeman.

Seligman, M. E. P. (1991). *Learned optimism*. New York: Knopf.

Seligman, M. E. P., & Maier, S. F. (1967). Failure to escape traumatic shock. *Journal of Experimental Psychology, 74*, 1–9.

Shamir, B. (1986). Self-esteem and the psychological impact of unemployment. *Social Psychology Quarterly, 49*, 61–72.

Smith, B. (1968). Competence and socialization. In J. A. Clausen (Ed.), *Socialization and society* (pp. 270–320). Boston: Little, Brown.

Spivack, G., & Shure, M. (1982). The cognition of social adjustment: Interpersonal cognitive problem-solving thinking. In B. Lahey & A. Kazdin (Eds.), *Advances in clinical child psychology*. New York: Plenum.

Stryker, S. (1980). *Symbolic interactionism: A social structural version*. Palo Alto, CA: Benjamin/Cummings.

Stryker, S., & Serpe, R. T. (1982). Commitment, identity salience, and role behavior. In W. Ickes & E. S. Knowles (Eds.), *Personality, roles and social behavior* (pp. 199–218). New York: Springer-Verlag.

Sweeney, P. D., Anderson, K., & Bailey, S. (1986). Attributional style in depression: A meta-analytic review. *Journal of Personality and Social Psychology, 50,* 974–991.

Thoits, P. A. (1982a). Conceptual, methodological, and theoretical problems in studying social support as a buffer against life stress. *Journal of Health and Social Behavior, 23,* 145–158.

Thoits, P. A. (1982b). Life stress, social support and psychological vulnerability: Epidemiological considerations. *Journal of Community Psychology, 10,* 341–362.

Thoits, P. A. (1983). Dimensions of life events that influence psychological distress: An evaluation and synthesis of the literature. In H. Kaplan (Ed.), *Psychosocial stress: Trends in theory and research* (pp. 33–103). New York: Academic Press.

Thoits, P. A. (1986). Multiple identities: Examining gender and marital status differences in distress. *American Sociological Review, 51,* 259–272.

Turner, R. J., & Avison, W. R. (1989). Gender and depression: Assessing exposure and vulnerability to life events in a chronically strained population. *Journal of Nervous and Mental Disease, 177,* 443–455.

Turner, R. J., & Avison, W. R. (1992a). Innovations in the measurement of life stress: Crisis theory and the significance of resolution. *Journal of Health and Social Behavior, 33,* 36–50.

Turner, R. J., & Avison, W. R. (1992b). Sources of attenuation in the stress–distress relationship: An evaluation of modest innovations in the application of event checklists. *Research in Community and Mental Health, 7,* 259–294.

Turner, R. J., Dopkeen, L. S., & Labreche, G. P. (1970). Marital status and schizophrenia: A study of incidence and outcome. *Journal of Abnormal Psychology, 76,* 110–116.

Turner, R. J., & Noh, S. (1983). Class and psychological vulnerability among women: The significance of social support and personal control. *Journal of Health and Social Behavior, 24,* 2–15.

Turner, R. J., & Noh, S. (1988). Physical disability and depression: A longitudinal analysis. *Journal of Health and Social Behavior, 29,* 23–37.

Ulbrich, P. M., Warheit, G. J., & Zimmerman, R. S. (1989). Race, socioeconomic status, and psychological distress: An examination of differential vulnerability. *Journal of Health and Social Behavior, 30,* 131–146.

Verbrugge, L. M. (1989). The twain meet: Empirical explanations of sex differences in health and mortality. *Journal of Health and Social Behavior, 30,* 282–304.

Weissman, M. M., & Klerman, G. L. (1977). Sex differences and the epidemiology of depression. *Archives of General Psychiatry, 34,* 98–111.

Wheaton, B. (1980). The sociogenesis of psychological disorder: An attributional theory. *Journal of Health and Social Behavior, 21,* 100–124.

Wheaton, B. (1983). Stress, personal coping resources, and psychiatric symptoms: An investigation of interactive models. *Journal of Health and Social Behavior, 24,* 208–229.

Wheaton, B. (1990). Life transitions, role histories, and mental health. *American Sociological Review, 55,* 209–223.

White, R. W. (1959). Motivation reconsidered: The concept of competence. *Psychological Review, 66,* 297–333.

Wilson, R. N. (1962). Disaster and mental health. In G. W. Baker & D. W. Chapman (Eds.), *Man and society in disaster* (pp. 124–150). New York: Basic Books.

Wylie, R. C. (1979). *The self-concept, vol. 2: Theory and research on selected topics.* Lincoln: University of Nebraska Press.

Zuckerman, P. (1989). Stress, self-esteem, and mental health: How does gender make a difference? *Sex Roles, 20,* 429–444.

V

Vulnerability to Stress

8

Life Stressors and Mental Health
Advances in Conceptualizing Stress Resistance

CHARLES J. HOLAHAN and RUDOLF H. MOOS

The last two decades have witnessed a growing societal concern with stress and its psychological toll. In fact, research on stress has grown exponentially during this period; the issues examined touch almost every specialization in basic and applied social science (Coyne & Downey, 1991). Researchers have examined a wide range of stressors, including general stressors involving acute life events (Thoits, 1983), role strains (Pearlin, 1989), and chronic difficulties (Lazarus & Folkman, 1984), and such specific stressors as technological disaster (Baum, Gatchel, & Schaeffer, 1983).

Despite strong evidence that life change is associated with psychological distress, stress research has been characterized by persistent anomalies. The amount of variance predicted in distress is small, and many persons remain healthy despite high exposure to stressors. By the early 1970s these anomalies encouraged a new approach to conceptualizing and studying the stress process that has been described varyingly as "stress resistance," "resilience," and "invulnerability." Stress re-

CHARLES J. HOLAHAN • Department of Psychology, University of Texas at Austin, Austin, Texas 78712. **RUDOLF H. MOOS** • Department of Veterans Affairs, and Stanford University Medical Centers, Palo Alto, California 94304.
Stress and Mental Health: Contemporary Issues and Prospects for the Future, edited by William R. Avison and Ian H. Gotlib. New York, Plenum Press, 1994.

sistance research examines the personal and social resources and types of coping strategies that help individuals to maintain healthy functioning when stressors occur (see Coyne & Smith, 1991; Kessler, Price, & Wortman, 1985).

Here we review the current state of research on stress resistance. We begin with an overview of the nature of stress resistance research, emphasizing how the approach evolved in an historical perspective. We then describe emerging research directions in contemporary work on stress resistance, using findings from our recent work as illustrations. We conclude by highlighting some broader conceptual and practical implications of the stress resistance approach in social science and contemporary society.

REVIEW OF STRESS RESISTANCE RESEARCH

Historical Context

Early Stress Research

Early stress research was characterized by two profoundly influential exemplars that share a guiding assumption that all changes, whether positive or negative, involve adaptive risks that are predictably related to pathological outcomes. The first exemplar is the General Adaptation Syndrome (for a historical overview, see Selye, 1982), which describes a stereotypical pattern of physiological response elicited by any adaptive demand. The second exemplar is the Social Readjustment Rating Scale (Homes & Rahe, 1967), which uses weighted units to measure the amount of life change an individual experiences during a given period of time. In combination, they have molded the tacit understanding of scientist and layperson alike in approaching the phenomenon of stress: Life change causes people to become sick.

These exemplars provided an investigative framework that has fostered thousands of studies. Findings with diverse population groups have shown that life change (particularly negative change) is associated with stress reactions that involve anxiety and depression as well as psychosomatic symptoms (Dohrenwend & Dohrenwend, 1981). More recent work has identified links between life stressors and infectious disease (Cohen & Williamson, 1991) and immune suppression more generally (O'Leary, 1990). Despite the consistency of stressor effects, the amount of variance predicted in distress is typically less than 10% (Cohen & Edwards, 1989). Moreover, individuals show highly variable reactions to stressors; many persons remain healthy despite being exposed to stressful circumstances, and some people mature more rapidly after effectively managing stressful events (Stewart, Sokol, Healy, & Chester, 1986).

Stress Resistance Research

At first researchers assumed that these anomalies reflected measurement error, but eventually they came to be seen as important findings in their own right. The relatively poor empirical predictions of early stress–illness studies led researchers to focus increasingly on moderating variables, such as personal and social resources and appraisal and coping responses. By the early 1970s a new approach, focusing on *stress resistance*, was beginning to emerge. A guiding assumption of stress resistance research is that personal and environmental resources and adaptive coping strategies can help individuals to manage stressful circumstances effectively and to remain healthy when stressors occur (Coyne & Downey, 1991; Kessler et al., 1985).

Lazarus's (1981) psychologically based conception of the process of coping with stress was an initial exemplar for stress resistance research. An appreciable body of research within the stress resistance paradigm has accumulated since the early 1970s. Lazarus and his colleagues' continuing work on coping (Folkman, Lazarus, Dunkel-Schetter, DeLongis, & Gruen, 1986; Lazarus & Folkman, 1984) and Kobasa and her associates' work on the personality construct of hardiness (Kobasa, 1982; Kobasa, Maddi, & Kahn, 1982) are representative of this trend. In addition to work on coping and adaptive personality characteristics, an extensive body of research has examined the role of social support in stress resistance (Cohen & McKay, 1984; Thoits, 1985).

Rahe and Arthur (1987) characterized the assumptions underlying early stress studies as simple and straightforward, presuming a powerful link between life change and pathology that ignored individual variability in response. Lamentably, they reflected, "It has seemed to some as if there is as close and immediate a relationship between life change and illness as is the relationship between staphylococcus endotoxin and acute dysentery" (p. 121). Stress resistance research fundamentally changed the underlying assumptions that guided the way investigators conceptualized and studied the stress process. Illness, which had been the figure in stress research, became the ground; health, which had been the ground, became the figure.

Reflecting this shift in perspective, Antonovsky (1979, 1987) proposed a neologism, *salutogenesis*, to characterize the emergent study of health. He emphasized the importance of generalized resistance resources in confronting a wide array of stressors. Similarly, after initially focusing on factors associated with psychological vulnerability in childhood, developmental psychopathologists have been increasingly impressed by children's resilience and the psychosocial resources that protect them from adversity (Luthar & Zigler, 1991).

From initially placing an emphasis on people's deficits and vulnerabilities, contemporary stress research has evolved to placing increasing emphasis on individuals' adaptive strengths and capacity for resilience, constructive action, and personal growth in the face of challenge. Stress resistance researchers view the individual as active and resourceful. Moreover, they assume that the human stress response is inherently complex and reflects a dynamic interplay among stressors, personal and social resources, and coping efforts (Kessler et al., 1985; Lazarus & Folkman, 1984). These changes have been accompanied by historical shifts in social science that require a fuller understanding of adaptive functioning in everyday contexts; these shifts include emerging interests in behavioral medicine (Rodin & Salovey, 1989), life span development (Dutan, Rodeheaver, & Hughes, 1987), and preventive interventions (Heller, 1990).

Stress Moderators

Personal and Social Resources

An extensive body of research has examined the role of personal and social resources in stress resistance (Cohen & McKay, 1984; Cohen & Edwards, 1989; Thoits, 1985). A variety of dispositional factors that relate to self-confidence and personal control may protect an individual from the negative effects of stressors, including hardiness (Kobasa, 1982; Kobasa et al., 1982), optimism (Scheier, Weintrraub, & Carver, 1986), a sense of coherence (Antonovsky, 1979, 1987), and learned resourcefulness (Rosenbaum & Ben-Ari, 1985). A calm and easygoing disposition, in contrast to one characterized by impatience and irritability, may also provide resistance to stress (Rhodewalt, Hays, Chemers, & Wysocki, 1984; Suls, Gastorf, & Witenberg, 1979). The array of personal factors that have been shown to relate to stress resistance may operate through a common mechanism, such as generalized expectancies of control (see Lefcourt, Miller, Ware, & Sherk, 1981) or perceived self-efficacy (see Wiedenfeld et al., 1990).

Social resources can provide emotional support that bolsters feelings of self-esteem and belonging, informational guidance that aids in assessing threat and in planning coping strategies, and tangible assistance (Cohen & McKay, 1984). Social support is associated with mental and physical health, with speedier recovery from illness, and with the likelihood of remaining healthy when stressors occur (see Cohen &

Wills, 1985; House, Landis, & Umberson, 1988; Wallston, Alagna, De-Vellis, & DeVellis, 1983).

Some aspects of social support, such as social companionship, may relate to health in a direct way regardless of the level of stressors experienced. Others, such as informational support, may function in an interactional way, with their health-enhancing effects greater under high stressors (Wills, 1985). Although social support generally is conceptualized as an environmental provision, data demonstrating considerable stability in social support and links to developmental precursors suggest that social support also may operate as an individual difference variable (Sarason, Sarason, & Shearin, 1986).

Coping Strategies

The conceptualization of coping processes is a central aspect of contemporary theories of stress. Coping is a stabilizing factor that can help individuals maintain psychosocial adaptation during stressful periods (Lazarus & Folkman, 1984; Moos & Schaefer, 1993). Fleishman (1984) defines coping as cognitive or behavioral responses "that are taken to reduce or eliminate psychological distress or stressful conditions" (p. 229). Although coping responses may be classified in many ways (Moos & Schaefer, 1993), most approaches distinguish between strategies oriented toward *approaching* and confronting the problem and those oriented toward *avoiding* dealing directly with the problem (Roth & Cohen, 1986).

Approach coping strategies, such as problem solving and seeking information, can moderate the potential adverse influence of both negative life change and enduring role stressors on psychological functioning (Pearlin & Schooler, 1978). A higher proportion of problem-focused coping relative to total coping efforts also has been associated with reduced depression (Mitchell, Cronkite, & Moos, 1983). Moreover, coping strategies involving negotiation and optimistic comparisons have been linked to reductions in concurrent distress and to fewer future role problems (Menaghan, 1982).

In contrast, avoidance coping (e.g., denial and withdrawal) is associated with psychological distress, particularly when adjustment is assessed beyond the initial crisis period (Holmes & Stevenson, 1990; Suls & Fletcher, 1985). Menaghan (1982) explained that efforts to manage unpleasant feelings by resignation and withdrawal may increase distress and thus amplify future problems. For example, among lawyers who experienced life stressors, Kobasa (1982) found that those who used more avoidance-coping strategies showed more symptoms of psychological and physical strain. A coping strategy of "selective ignoring" may exacerbate distress in the areas of marriage and parenting (Pearlin & Schooler, 1978). Among elderly persons, the use of avoidance coping (avoidance, wishful thinking, and self-blame) in dealing with negative life events predicted psychological disturbance 4 months later (Smith, Patterson, & Grant, 1990).

Summary

Despite the consistency of stressor effects, the amount of variance predicted in distress is typically less than 10%, and individuals show highly variable reactions to stressors. The relatively poor empirical predictions of early stress–illness studies led researchers to focus increasingly on moderating variables, such as personal and social resources and appraisal and coping responses. A variety of dispositional factors may protect an individual from the negative effects of stressors, including hardiness, optimism, a sense of coherence, learned resourcefulness, and an easygoing disposition. In addition, social support is associated with mental and physical health, with speedier recovery from illness, and with the likelihood of remaining healthy when stressors occur. Approach coping strategies, such as problem solving and seeking information, also can moderate the potential adverse influence of both negative life change and enduring role stressors on psychological functioning. In contrast, such avoidance coping techniques as denial and withdrawal are associated with psychological distress, particularly when adjustment is assessed beyond the initial crisis period.

EMERGING RESEARCH DIRECTIONS

Here we identify areas where more research is needed to refine and broaden our understanding of the nature and operation of stress resistance. We discuss the need to refine predictive models of stress resistance to provide an integrative picture of predictive factors and to reflect the dynamic interplay among stressors and resources. We also discuss the value of conceptually extending the stress resistance concept to clarify related adaptive processes involving recovery from illness, coping in a family context, and crisis growth. We use examples of findings from our recent work as illustrations of emerging findings in each of these areas. Our research serves as a useful model of emerging stress resistance research in that it (a) integrates the various types of stress resistance factors identified in earlier research, (b) employs a longitudinal predictive framework, and (c) cross-validates initial findings across several broadly representative community and clinical samples.[1]

Integrative Predictive Models

Further research is needed to provide an integrative picture of how resources, coping, and mental health are related to one another. For example, personal and social resources may be linked to health under high stressors primarily because they encourage more adaptive coping strategies. Lazarus and Folkman (1984), defining resources as what an individual "draws on in order to cope," argue that resources "precede and influence coping" (p. 158).

Thoits (1986) views social support as a source of coping assistance. Information or advice provided by a confidant may increase the likelihood that a person will rely on logical analysis, information seeking, or active problem solving. In fact, individuals in supportive families engage in more active, problem-focused coping and in less avoidance coping than do individuals in less supportive families (Cronkite & Moos, 1984; Manne & Zautra, 1989). For example, we found that increases in family support over a 1-year interval were related to increases in problem-solving coping among women and to a decline in emotional discharge among men (Fondacaro & Moos, 1987).

Kobasa et al. (1982) speculated that a positive association between hardiness (personality dispositions of commitment, control, and challenge) and adaptive coping may explain why hardiness operates as a psychological buffer when stressors occur. An internal locus of control has been associated with more active coping strategies in dealing with a wide range of stressors (e.g., see Lefcourt, 1985). In addition, Carver, Scheier, and Weintraub (1989) found that optimists tend to use problem-focused coping strategies, whereas pessimists prefer emotion-based strategies, such as denial. The association between personal factors and coping responses may depend on appraisals about the controllability of the stressor; optimists are especially inclined to use problem-focused coping when they construe stressors as controllable (Scheier et al., 1986).

Research also is needed to identify the psychological mechanisms through which personal and social resources foster adaptive coping. An

[1]Detailed descriptive and psychometric information on our measures is available in the Health and Daily Living Form Manual (Moos, Cronkite, & Finney, 1990), the Family Environment Scale (Moos & Moos, 1986) and Work Environment Scale (Moos, 1986) manuals, the Life Stressors and Social Resources Inventory—Adult form Manual (Moos & Moos, 1992), and the Coping Responses Inventory—Adult Form Manual (Moos, 1992).

especially promising construct in this regard is perceived self-efficacy, that is, people's belief in their capability to execute the behaviors necessary to exercise control over adaptive demands (Bandura, 1982). For example, self-efficacy for coping has been shown to mediate the effect of perceived social support on psychological adjustment among women under stress (Cutrona & Troutman, 1986; Major et al., 1990).

A Coping-Based Model of Stress Resistance

In a series of longitudinal studies of two community samples, we examined personal and social stress resistance resources (Holahan & Moos, 1981, 1986, 1987b). We began with an initial representative sample of more than 500 adults, and then used a second representative sample of more than 400 adults to cross-validate and extend our findings. Self-confidence and an easygoing disposition, family support, and less reliance on avoidance coping strategies predicted lower levels of depression over a 1-year period, even when prior depression was controlled. Examining the interrelationships among the predictive factors, we found that individuals with more personal and social resources were more likely to rely on approach coping and less likely to use avoidance coping (Holahan & Moos, 1987a).

Based on these and related findings (e.g., Cronkite & Moos, 1984), we proposed a predictive framework that unifies earlier work on predicting adjustment and on predicting coping responses (Holahan & Moos, 1990). In the framework, shown in Figure 1, personal and social resources relate to subsequent depression both directly and indirectly through approach coping responses. The relative strength of the predictive associations is presumed to vary with the level of intervening stressors. Because coping is a stabilizing factor that helps maintain psychological adjustment during stressful periods, the advantage of approach coping should be greatest under high stressors. Thus, under high stressors, resources should relate to functioning primarily indirectly through coping efforts. Under low stressors, where coping is less necessary, resources should relate to depression primarily in a direct way (Okun, Sandler, & Baumann, 1988).

We tested these hypotheses with a sample of more than 400 respondents in a 4-year structural equation model (Holahan & Moos, 1991). LISREL VI (Jöreskog & Sörbom, 1986) was used to estimate the parameters and overall goodness of fit of the model in a two-group analysis, in which respondents were divided into high- and low-stressor groups. The high-stressor group experienced multiple (2 or more) negative life events during the year prior to the follow-up assessment; the low-stressor group experienced no negative life events during the year.

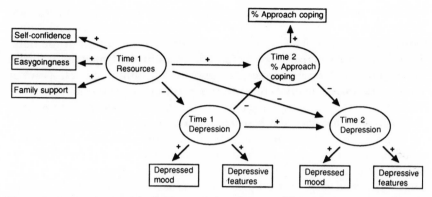

Figure 1. Integrative model of the associations between life stressors, stress resistance factors, and psychological functioning (from Holahan & Moos, 1991).

These conservative models remove the influence of prior depression from both coping and depression at follow-up.

Self-confidence, an easygoing disposition, and family support operated prospectively over 4 years, either directly or indirectly through coping responses, to protect individuals from becoming depressed. As hypothesized, the pattern of predictive associations differed under high and low stressors. Under high stressors, resources related to future psychological health indirectly through their link to more approach coping strategies. Under low stressors, resources related directly to psychological health. The findings under high stressors demonstrate the central role of coping in integrative predictive models of stress resistance. Under high stressors, adaptive personality characteristics and family support function prospectively as coping resources; coping, in turn, mediates between initial resources and later health status.

Interplay among Stressors and Resources

In addition, more fine-tuned assessment of personal and social resources is needed to increase predictive power and to test mediating mechanisms. For example, measures of distinct supportive behaviors from specific providers predict perceptions of being helped more accurately than do general indices of social support (Cutrona & Russell, 1990; Dakof & Taylor, 1990; Dean, Kolody, & Wood, 1990). Similarly, multidimensional indices of coping (Carver et al., 1989) can facilitate the examination of coping effectiveness in the context of contrasting types of adaptive demands (McCrae, 1984).

More research also is needed for a fuller understanding of how different types of life stressors and social resources influence each other. For example, the work environment can amplify the impact of the family, as when supportive coworkers help an individual manage a health crisis. The work environment can also inhibit family impact, as when coworkers reward alcohol consumption rather than abstention. Or it can compensate for a lack of impact, as when young adults learn coping skills at work that they have not learned in the family.

In addition, the conceptualization of stressors needs to be broadened to reflect the complex interplay between acute and enduring demands. For example, Pearlin (1989) has argued that the concept of stressors needs to go beyond the conventional focus on separate stressor domains to encompass constellations of stressors that make up events and more enduring strains that transact with each other across contexts and roles. The conceptual connections among acute stressors, chronic stressors, and social resources indicate that these domains should be measured in a coordinated way.

With these concerns in mind, we developed the Life Stressors and Social Resources Inventory (LISRES; Moos & Moos, 1992) to provide a comprehensive picture of the various interrelated stressors and social resources in a person's life. The inventory includes nine indices of life stressors (e.g., work stressors, spouse or partner stressors). It also includes seven indices of social resources (e.g., work resources, spouse or partner resources).

We recently applied the LISRES to a sample of 500 older adults who were problem drinkers (Brennan & Moos, 1990). Across diverse functioning criteria, chronic stressors accounted for more variance than did negative life events. In addition, chronic stressors were more closely associated with social resources than were negative life events. These findings highlight the importance of separately assessing chronic and acute stressors; it seems likely that the effects of chronic stressors are more cumulative and enduring than those of acute events (see Avison & Turner, 1988).

Results also underscored the importance of assessing individual domains of stressors and resources. Stressors from spouse and friends were more strongly linked to increased drinking problems than were other types of stressors. Similarly, support from spouse and friends was more strongly associated with fewer drinking problems than was support from other sources. These findings suggest that interventions that reduce stress and enhance support from spouse and friends may be especially helpful in improving functioning among problem drinkers.

In terms of mutual influences between stressors and resources, results indicated that stressors and lack of support may often be closely connected in domains where there is a single source of both stressors and support. For example, ongoing difficulties involving finances, spouse, and children were associated with fewer resources in these domains. In contrast, in life domains where there are multiple sources of problems and assistance (e.g., friends), stressors and social resources were more independent.

In a longitudinal assessment with a functionally diverse sample of 80 adults (Moos, Fenn, & Billings, 1988), LISRES data from an initial assessment were used to predict changes in stressors and resources over an 18-month interval. Respondents who experienced more stressful events during this interval had initially reported more ongoing stressors and fewer ongoing resources. New stressful events foreshadowed increases in ongoing stressors in the financial, work, spouse, child, and extended family domains. They also led to a decline in spouse or partner resources. Thus ongoing stressors and a lack of social resources can predict new stressful events; in turn, such events can contribute to a rise in chronic stressors and an erosion of social resources.

A comprehensive picture of the overall balance of stressors and resources in a person's life also can provide a prognostic index of longer-term outcome. For example, Figure 2 shows an illustrative LISRES profile for a 60-year-old married woman (scores are standardized, with a mean of 50 and a standard deviation of 10). Because she was not employed, she has no ongoing stressors or resources in the work area. She reported several negative life events in the past year, including her own hospitalization and her husband's increased alcohol abuse and his involvement in an automobile accident. In addition, she experienced well above-average chronic stressors in most life domains. For example, she had serious ongoing health problems, including cancer, high blood pressure, and severe back pain. Moreover, her spouse, children, and extended family were a source of arguments and excessive demands. Although she had moderate support from friends and slightly above-average spouse support and financial resources, she had few resources from her children and other relatives. Overall, these data show that this woman had an unfavorable balance of high stressors and only low to moderate resources, and they are consistent with her low self-confidence and many symptoms of depression 1 year later (Moos & Moos, 1992).

In contrast are the circumstances of a 66-year-old woman with rheumatoid arthritis. As expected, she reported well above-average physical health stressors. She had below-average stressors, however, in six of the other seven domains. Moreover, she also had above-average social resources in her work setting and in her relationships with her spouse,

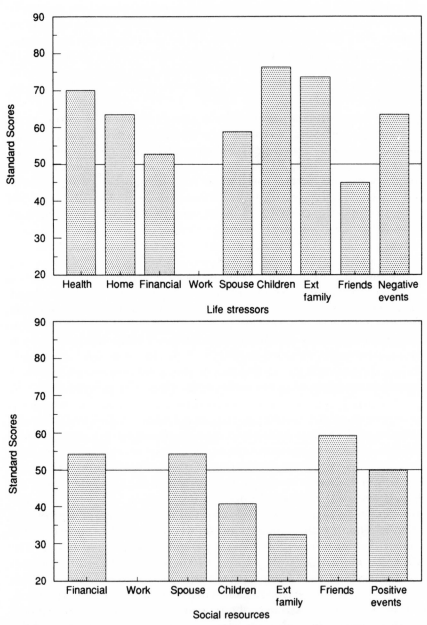

Figure 2. Life stressors and social resources profiles for a depressed woman (from Moos & Moos, 1992).

extended family, and friends. At an 18-month follow-up, this favorable balance of only moderate stressors and high resources enabled her to manage quite well; she reported high self-confidence and below-average depression (Moos & Moos, 1992).

Recovery from Psychological Disorder

The adaptive resources and mechanisms identified in stress resistance research can be extended to broaden our understanding of the process of recovery form psychopathology and addiction. Treatment for behavioral and psychiatric disorders has short-term beneficial effects, but many patients relapse over time (Brownell, Marlatt, Lichtenstein, & Wilson, 1986). In studying clinical populations, we have found that the same factors that protect normally adjusted persons from psychological dysfunction under stress are also related to remission and relapse among clinically ill individuals after treatment. Accordingly, we extended our program of research to examine the role of these factors in the process of recovery and relapse among depressed and alcoholic patients after treatment. We studied two groups of patients: a group of more than 400 patients who entered psychiatric treatment for unipolar depression, and a group of more than 100 patients who underwent residential treatment for alcohol abuse (Moos, 1991; Moos, Finney, & Cronkite, 1990).

Depressed Patients

Compared to a demographically matched normal group, the group of depressed patients at intake reported more stressful life circumstances and less family and work support. Depressed persons also were more likely to use avoidance coping and less likely to use problem-solving coping responses. Moreover, patients who experienced more life stressors and reported fewer social resources tended to be more severely depressed and to report more physical symptoms and less self-confidence. Avoidance coping was also linked to more severe depression, whereas patients who employed more problem-solving coping strategies reported higher self-confidence and less severe depression (Moos, 1991; Billings & Moos, 1984).

In terms of recovery, posttreatment life stressors and social resources were predictably related to patients' posttreatment functioning, even when intake functioning and social background were controlled. Patients who experienced more life stressors (both life events and chronic strains) after treatment reported more severe depression and more physical symptoms at a 1-year follow-up. Life stressors predicted almost

13% additional variance in depression and 10% additional variance in physical symptoms beyond that accounted for by intake functioning and social background. The links between chronic strains in the areas of health, housing, family, and work and the outcome criteria were somewhat stronger and more consistent than those for negative life events.

Conversely, patients who enjoyed more family and work support after treatment experienced less depression and fewer physical symptoms. Social resources added almost 18% incremental variance in predicting depression and 5% incremental variance in predicting physical symptoms after accounting for intake functioning and social background (Billings & Moos, 1985). In a 4-year follow-up, after controlling for initial functioning and social background, family conflict at intake continued to predict patients' depression and physical symptoms 4 years later (Swindle, Cronkite, & Moos, 1989).

Alcoholic Patients

In the group of treated alcoholic patients, we found that patients who experienced more stressful life circumstances (life events and family strains) at 6 to 8 months after treatment showed poorer health and adjustment 2 years after treatment. Conversely, the quality of family relationships and the extent of family social integration were predictively related to better health and adjustment 2 years subsequent to treatment. These relationships remained after intake functioning and patient background characteristics were controlled. Moreover, alcoholic patients who maintained their remission were more self-confident, higher on social competence, and less likely to rely on avoidance coping (Moos, Finney, & Cronkite, 1990).

Posttreatment factors (life stressors and family resources) assessed 6 to 8 months after treatment accounted for almost as much variance in alcoholic patients' 2-year treatment outcome as did intake functioning and patient background. These factors accounted for almost 11% of the variance in physical symptoms and 15% of the variance in depression beyond that accounted for by intake functioning and background factors. In a 10-year follow-up, life context and coping factors assessed 2 years after treatment provided significant increments in accounting for 10-year patient functioning over that provided by intake functioning and demographic characteristics. For example, both family cohesion and the use of active cognitive coping strategies predicted less alcohol consumption and lower depression over the 8-year interval (Finney & Moos, 1991; Moos, Finney, & Cronkite, 1990).

At the same time, the causal links between posttreatment experiences and outcome are dynamic and reciprocal. A patient may resume heavy drinking after treatment as a way of dealing with a bad family situation; family relationships may deteriorate further as a consequence of the increased drinking.

Interdependencies among Family Members

To extend findings showing the dynamic interplay among stressors and resources, family-oriented research is needed to examine how vulnerability and resistance factors in the life of a family member can influence other members of the family. For example, Coyne and Smith (1991) reported that wives were at considerable risk for psychological distress 6 months after their husbands suffered a heart attack. A wife's distress was significantly related to her husband's distress and was at least as pronounced. In studying children and families, we discovered that factors that predict the health of one family member operate indirectly in affecting the health of his or her spouse and children. We examined these issues in both community and clinical samples.

Risk and Resistance among Spouses

One issue involves the mutual influence of spouses on each other. In longitudinal analyses (controlling for prior functioning) with a community sample, we found that being married to a woman who was distressed was more closely associated with a husband's own subsequent depressed mood when he relied more heavily on avoidance coping. This adverse effect strengthened as his wife's reliance on avoidance coping increased. In contrast, self-esteem had a stronger influence in reducing subsequent depression among women whose husbands also experienced high self-esteem (Cronkite & Moos, 1984).

A key facet of the stress process in married couples is the interplay among the functioning, personal resources, and coping responses of the partners. Not only are one spouse's symptoms stressful for the other, but the personal resources and coping strategies of each partner affect the other partner's reaction to and selection of coping responses. These relationships are complex and may be influenced by a tendency for people to select persons similar to themselves as partners.

Similarly, in cross-sectional analyses on our sample of depressed patients, we found that negative events and chronic stressors experienced by a spouse were positively related to the severity of the partner's depression; high family support was associated with less depression. Additional analyses controlling for a married individual's own negative events and strains suggested that the link between their partner's stressors and their own depression may be mediated by a reduction in family support. Spouses in stressful conditions, however, were less prone to depression when they used more problem-focused coping (Mitchell et al., 1983).

The risk factors of stressful life conditions and avoidance coping were also linked to poorer current functioning among spouses of alcoholic patients, whereas the resistance factor of family support was related to better functioning among them. Follow-up analyses over a 2-year period demonstrated that spouses of relapsed alcoholics experienced more negative events and less family support than spouses of either remitted alcoholics or community controls. Moreover, in a longer-term assessment, initial spouse drinking and depression were predictively related to patient alcohol consumption and depression, respectively, 8 years later (Finney & Moos, 1991; Moos, Finney, & Cronkite, 1990).

Risk and Resistance among Children

In work with a second community sample, we also found that risk and resistance factors in parents' lives predicted emotional and physical health problems in their children. In examining children's distress, we broadened our concept of risk to include parental functioning. The strongest findings emerged for family support and maternal risk— depression, physical symptoms, and avoidance coping—each of which was predictably associated with children's concurrent psychological health. Family support and mothers' physical symptoms also were tied to children's concurrent physical health.

Family support and parental risk together accounted for between 20% and 30% of the variance in children's concurrent psychological and physical health problems. Family support also was linked to children's subsequent psychological and physical health 1 year after the initial assessment, but these relationships did not hold when children's initial distress was controlled. Compared to adults, children may be more resilient to past adversity, though also less protected by past environmental support (Holahan & Moos, 1987b).

When we compared the children of parents in our sample of depressed patients with children of nondepressed parents in our initial community sample, we identified specific risk and resistance factors associated with the likelihood of a family having a child with multiple problems. Two groups of risk factors were identified: the presence and acuteness of parental depression, and high family stressors. We also examined the resistance value of a supportive family climate. In cross-sectional analyses, fewer than 3% of the families with no risk factors had a multiproblem child. Among depressed-parent families, the prevalence of multiproblem children rose to 26%. This rate increased to 38% in the presence of high levels of stressors, but it dropped to 22% among depressed-parent families with few stressors, and to less than 11% among those with few stressors and high support (Billings & Moos, 1983). Family support was as strongly associated with children's functioning at a 1-year follow-up, as was the severity of the parents' depressive symptomatology (Billings & Moos, 1986). Similarly, emotional disturbance among children in alcoholic families was associated with their parents' health, as well as with parents' use of avoidance coping, high conflict and lack of cohesion in the family, and negative life change (Moos, Finney, & Cronkite, 1990).

Psychological Growth under Stress

Stress resistance research also needs to be broadened conceptually to examine how life stressors sometimes can create an opportunity for psychological growth. Antonovsky (1979, 1987) has pointed out that stress resistance research remains partially tied to a pathological orientation, because its focus is on *not becoming sick*. A next step in the stress resistance paradigm's focus on health is to understand psychological growth under stress. In fact, many people are remarkably resilient in the face of adversity. They may emerge from a crisis with more self-confidence, new coping skills, closer relationships with family and friends, and a richer appreciation of life (Haan, 1982; Moos & Schaefer, 1986).

This broader view of stressor outcomes suggests conceptual parallels between contemporary stress research and a long-standing psychiatric interest in crisis resolution (Linemann, 1979). According to crisis theory, crisis resolution involves adaptive challenges that can result in a strengthening of resources and personal growth. For example, in a 10-year follow-up of divorce, Wallerstein (1986) found that about 50% of women who experienced a marital breakup showed long-term improvements in psychological functioning. These women became more assertive, developed more realistic views of themselves, and experienced increased self-esteem with successful new careers (see also Bursik, 1991). Similarly, Taylor (1983) reported that some cancer patients are able to view the threat posed by their illness as a "catalytic agent for restructuring their lives" (p. 1163). For many cancer patients, their illness brought a new attitude toward life and reordered priorities, emphasizing relationships, personal projects, and the enjoyment of life.

Research is needed to learn more about how the type and degree of adaptive challenge are linked to psychological growth. Perhaps more manageable stressors promote growth more readily than less manageable ones do (Ruch, Chandler, & Harter, 1980). Also, life stressors may ultimately foster enhanced resilience when they provide an opportunity to learn new coping skills (Caspi, Bolger, & Eckenrode, 1987). In addition, longitudinal research across a sufficient time period is needed to describe the patterned course of psychological growth. Beneficial outcomes to life crises and transitions may emerge only after a process of emotional assimilation that follows an initial stage of emotional distress and disorganization (Stewart et al., 1986).

Moreover, research is needed to examine the parallels between the growth-promoting aspects of life crises and developmental transitions. Like sudden life crises, normative transitions (e.g., beginning college, marriage, parenthood) can facilitate personal growth by stimulating changes in cognition and behavior, a review of life goals, and a reassessment of values and beliefs (see Cantor & Langston, 1989; Stewart et al., 1986).

Models of Prototypic and Crisis Growth

In an integrative review of crisis literature, Schaefer and Moos (1992) propose an organizing framework for the positive outcomes that may stem from confronting stressful experiences. Table 1 lists 10 types of positive changes they identify within three general categories: enhanced personal resources, enhanced social resources, and the development of new coping skills. Central to their view is the long-standing

Table 1. Major Types of Positive Outcomes From Confronting Crises

Enhanced personal resources
Cognitive and intellectual differentiation
Self-reliance and self-understanding
Changes in basic values and priorities
Empathy, altruism, and maturity

Enhanced social resources
Better relationships with family members and friends
Development of a confidant relationship
Formation of new support networks

Development of new coping skills
Problem-solving and help-seeking skills
Cognitive coping skills
Ability to regulate and control affect

Source: Schaefer & Moos (1992).

belief of crisis theory (Lindemann, 1979) that stressors provide an opportunity for people to develop and mature. Personal and social resources provide the context within which crises occur; successful resolution of crises fortifies these resources. As Schaefer and Moos explain, "Resilience develops from confronting stressful experiences and coping with them effectively. . . . Novel crisis situations . . . promote new coping skills and lead to new personal and social resources" (p. 150).

We applied this framework in a 1-year test of two models of improved psychological functioning in a community sample of more than 400 respondents (Holahan & Moos, 1990). First, extending our earlier stress resistance research, we proposed a model for *prototypic growth* under low stressors and predicted that factors that maintain stable functioning during stressful periods would help to improve health during less stressful times. Second, applying crisis theory (Lindemann, 1979; Schaefer & Moos, 1992), we proposed a model for *crisis growth* under high stressors and predicted that improvement in functioning under high stressors would be related to a strengthening of resources during the year.

As hypothesized, the way personal and social resources related to improved functioning differed under low and high stressors. Seventy percent of individuals whose functioning improved had experienced no or only one negative event during the year. Results supported Antonovsky's (1987) contention, however, that the "negative resource" of avoiding stressors may not foster improved functioning without being accompanied by positive personal or social resources. The prototypic pattern of improved functioning involved high personal and social resources combined with low risk from negative life change.

The findings also supported the prediction that stressors can provide an opportunity for psychological growth. One third of respondents whose functioning improved over the year experienced two or more stressors, and more than half of this multiple-stressor group experienced three or more stressors. Growth occurred despite the fact that many stressors involved profound adaptive demands, such as serious financial setbacks and the deaths of friends or family members.

Especially significant, and also consistent with crisis theory, was that the individuals under high stressors whose functioning improved were the only group of respondents whose resources increased significantly during the year. The increase in resources for these individuals reflected increases in self-confidence, easygoingness, and family support. In further support of crisis theory, correlational analyses demonstrated that the increase in resources during the year was significantly related to improved functioning. Positive feedback from effective coping with stressors appeared central to the increase in resources during the year (see Bandura, 1990; Turner & Avison, 1992).

CONCLUSIONS

Stress resistance research is the predominant approach to studying life stressors today and is among the most active research areas in contemporary social science (Coyne & Downey, 1991). Although much remains to be learned about the stress process, the research we have reviewed provides a basic foundation for further understanding of stress resistance. Effective coping strategies are central to stress resistance. Under stressful demands, personality strengths and social support function as coping resources; coping, in turn, mediates between available resources and subsequent health. Although the effects of chronic stressors are more enduring than those of acute events, chronic and acute stressors and social resources are dynamically interrelated. Ongoing stressors and a lack of social resources predict new stressful events; such events, in turn, contribute to a rise in chronic stressors and an erosion of social resources.

Stress resistance research also has served to identify broadly applicable adaptive variables and mechanisms. As we have shown, these factors affect functioning in representative community groups, as well as among depressed and alcoholic patients. They are relevant as well to the health of spouses and the resilience of children in each of these groups. Moreover, conceptual extensions of the stress resistance construct are beginning to provide an empirical foundation to help understand the process of psychological growth during life crises and developmental transitions.

At an applied level, stress resistance research provides a comprehensive framework that encourages innovations in mental health care appropriate to a variety of populations. The findings we have described have implications for intervention at both the environmental and individual levels. Our results emphasize that treatment is part of an open system, where an intervention program is only one of multiple factors that influence psychiatric disorders and other aspects of adaptation. Such a conception of treatment can broaden the conventional psychotherapeutic framework by focusing attention on the interactive relationships among the individual, the family, and related social settings. Recognizing that stressful or relapse-inducing life situations inevitably occur, clinicians can identify coping resources and family and social supports that clients can acquire to help them deal with these situations more effectively.

Our findings pertaining to children and families are especially relevant to prevention programs. Across community and clinical groups, a family member's stressors and maladaptive functioning present a health risk for his or her spouse and children. Even more important, our results demonstrate the potential health-promoting value of preventive interventions directed toward coping skills training for spouses and toward enhancing family support for children.

At a broader level, the most significant contribution of our program of research on stress resistance has been a realization of the general value of a renewed focus on health and adaptive personal and social resources. Social science traditionally has focused much of its attention on pathological processes. Consequently, its view of the person often has emphasized problems and dysfunction. We understand vulnerabilities and illness better than adaptive strengths and health; we are better prepared to treat disorder than to promote well-being and personal growth (see Antonovsky, 1987; Seeman, 1989).

For social science to broaden its vision so it encompasses positive, growth-oriented functioning that is more than the simple absence of disorder, it needs a better conceptualization of adaptive process. Contemporary stress resistance research is playing a key role in efforts to conceptualize adaptive functioning. After conducting a comprehensive review of research on life stressors, Kessler et al. concluded, "Diverse strands of research are beginning to converge on a common conception of the stress process. . . . At its center is the notion that stress exposure sets of a process of adaptation" (p. 565).

Broader developments both within and outside of social science are likely to encourage continued progress in the study of adaptive functioning. Within social science, for instance, increasing interest in life span development (Datan et al., 1987), behavioral medicine (Rodin & Salovey, 1989), and preventive interventions (Heller, 1990) promise a sustained need for empirical knowledge about adaptive processes in the context of a variety of life demands. In medical science, special attention is being devoted to the resistance value of the body's immune system (O'Leary, 1990).

In society more broadly, national policy objectives in the areas of education, aging, drug abuse, and health care call for new social science knowledge that emphasizes competent coping with adaptive challenges and goes beyond traditional illness explanations (see Brickman et al., 1982). As stress resistance research continues to mature, it can play an important role in fostering the development of new knowledge in each of these areas. The stress resistance construct can help us pursue a fuller understanding of adaptive strengths and of the individual capacity for resilience and constructive action in the face of life challenges.

ACKNOWLEDGMENTS

Preparation of this manuscript was supported in part by NIAAA grant AA02863 and AA06699 and by Department of Veterans Affairs Health Services Research and Development Service research funds.

REFERENCES

Antonovsky, A. (1979). Health, stress, and coping. San Francisco: Jossey-Baas.

Antonovsky, A. (1987). Unraveling the mystery of health: How people manage stress and stay well. San Francisco: Jossey-Bass.

Avison, W. R., & Turner, R. J. (1988). Stressful life events and depressive symptoms: Disaggregating the effects of acute stressors and chronic strains. Journal of Health and Social Behavior, 29, 253–264.

Bandura, A. (1982). Self-efficacy mechanism in human agency. American Psychologist, 37, 122–147.

Bandura, A. (1990). Conclusion: Reflections on nonability determinants of competence. In R. J. Sternberg & J. Kolligian (Eds.), Competence considered (pp. 315–362). New Haven, CT: Yale University Press.

Baum, A. G., Gatchel, R. J., & Schaeffer, M. A. (1983). Emotional, behavioral, and physiological effects of stress at Three Mile Island. Journal of Consulting and Clinical Psychology, 51, 565–572.

Billings, A. G., & Moos, R. H. (1983). Comparisons of children of depressed and nondepressed parents: A socio-emotional perspective. Journal of Abnormal Child Psychology, 11, 463–485.

Billings, A. G., & Moos, R. H. (1984). Coping, stress, and social resources among adults with unipolar depression. Journal of Personality and Social Psychology, 46, 877–891.

Billings, A. G., & Moos, R. H. (1985). Life stressors and social resources affect posttreatment outcome among depressed patients. Journal of Abnormal Psychology, 94, 140–153.

Billings, A. G., & Moos, R. H. (1986). Children of parents with unipolar depression: A controlled one-year follow-up. Journal of Abnormal Child Psychology, 14, 149–166.

Brennan, P. L., & Moos, R. H. (1990). Life stressors, social resources, and late-life problem drinking. Psychology and Aging, 5, 491–501.

Brickman, P., Rabinowitz, V. C., Karuza, J., Coates, D., Cohn, E., & Kidder, L. (1982). Models of helping and coping. American Psychologist, 37, 368–384.

Brownell, K. D., Marlatt, G. A., Lichtenstein, E., & Wilson, G. T. (1986). Understanding and preventing relapse. American Psychologist, 41, 765–782.

Bursik, K. (1991). Adaptation to divorce and ego development in adult women. Journal of Personality and Social Psychology, 60, 300–306.

Cantor, N., & Langston, C. A. (1989). Ups and downs of life tasks in a life transition. In L. A. Pervin (Ed.), Goal concepts in personality and social psychology (pp. 127–167). Hillsdale, NJ: Erlbaum.

Carver, C. S., Scheier, M. F., & Weintraub, J. K. (1989). Assessing coping strategies: A theoretically based approach. *Journal of Personality and Social Psychology, 56,* 267–283.

Caspi, A., Bolger, N., & Eckenrode, J. (1987). Linking person and context in the daily stress process. *Journal of Personality and Social Psychology, 52,* 184–195.

Cohen, S., & Edwards, J. R. (1989). Personality characteristics as moderators of the relationship between stress and disorder. In R. W. J. Neufeld (Ed.), *Advances in the investigation of psychological stress* (pp. 235–283). New York: Wiley.

Cohen, S., & McKay, G. (1984). Social support, stress, and the buffering hypothesis: A theoretical analysis. In A. Baum, J. E. Singer, & S. E. Taylor (Eds.), *Handbook of psychology and health, vol. 4* (pp. 253–267). Hillsdale, NJ: Erlbaum.

Cohen, S., & Williamson, G. M. (1991). Stress and infectious disease in humans. *Psychological Bulletin, 109,* 5–24.

Cohen, S., & Wills, T. A. (1985). Stress, social support, and the buffering hypothesis. *Psychological Bulletin, 98,* 310–357.

Coyne, J. C., & Downey, G. (1991). Social factors and psychopathology: Stress, social support, and coping processes. *Annual Review of Psychology, 42,* 401–425.

Coyne, J. C., & Smith, D. A. F. (1991). Couples coping with a myocardial infarction: A contextual perspective on wives' distress. *Journal of Personality and Social Psychology, 61,* 404–412.

Cronkite, R. C., & Moos, R. H. (1984). The role of predisposing and moderating factors in the stress–illness relationship. *Journal of Health and Social Behavior, 25,* 372–393.

Cutrona, C. E., & Russell, D. W. (1990). Type of social support and specific stress: Toward a theory of optimal matching. In I. G. Sarason, B. R. Sarason, & G. R. Pierce (Eds.), *Social support: An interactional view* (pp. 319–366). New York: Wiley.

Cutrona, C. E., & Troutman, B. R. (1986). Social support, infant temperament, and parenting self-efficacy: A mediational model of postpartum depression. *Child Development, 57,* 1507–1518.

Dakof, G., & Taylor, S. E. (1990). Victims' perceptions of social support: What is helpful from whom? *Journal of Personality and Social Psychology, 58,* 80–89.

Datan, N., Rodeheaver, D., & Hughes, F. (1987). Adult development and aging. *Annual Review of Psychology, 38,* 153–180.

Dean, A., Kolody, B., & Wood, P. (1990). Effects of social support from various sources on depression in elderly persons. *Journal of Health and Social Behavior, 31,* 148–161.

Dohrenwend, B. S., & Dohrenwend, B. P. (1981). *Stressful life events and their contexts.* New York: Neale Watson.

Finney, J. W., & Moos, R. H. (1991). The long-term course of treated alcoholism: II. Predictors and correlates of 10-year functioning and mortality. *Journal of Studies on Alcohol, 53,* 1–12.

Fleishman, J. A. (1984). Personality characteristics and coping patterns. *Journal of Health and Social Behavior, 25,* 229–244.

Folkman, S., Lazarus, R. S., Dunkel-Schetter, C., DeLongis, A., & Gruen, R. J. (1986). Dynamics of a stressful encounter: Cognitive appraisal, coping, and encounter outcomes. *Journal of Personality and Social Psychology, 50,* 992–1003.

Fondacaro, M., & Moos, R. H. (1987). Social support and coping: A longitudinal analysis. *American Journal of Community Psychology, 15,* 653–673.

Haan, N. (1982). The assessment of coping, defense, and stress. In L. Goldberger & S. Breznitz (Eds.), *Handbook of stress: Theoretical and clinical aspects* (pp. 254–269). New York: Free Press.

Heller, K. (1990). Social and community intervention. *Annual Review of Psychology, 41,* 141–168.

Holahan, C. J., & Moos, R. H. (1981). Social support and psychological distress: A longitudinal analysis. *Journal of Abnormal Psychology, 90,* 365–370.

Holahan, C. J., & Moos, R. H. (1986). Personality, coping, and family resources in stress resistance: A longitudinal analysis. *Journal of Personality and Social Psychology, 51,* 389–395.

Holahan, C. J., & Moos, R. H. (1987a). Personal and contextual determinants of coping strategies. *Journal of Personality and Social Psychology, 52,* 946–955.

Holahan, C. J., & Moos, R. H. (1987b). Risk, resistance, and psychological distress: A longitudinal analysis with adults and children. *Journal of Abnormal Psychology, 96,* 3–13.

Holahan, C. J., & Moos, R. H. (1990). Life stressors, resistance factors, and psychological health: An extension of the stress-resistance paradigm. *Journal of Personality and Social Psychology, 58,* 909–917.

Holahan, C. J., & Moos, R. H. (1991). Life stressors, personal and social resources, and depression: A four-year structural model. *Journal of Abnormal Psychology, 100,* 31–38.

Holmes, T. H., & Rahe, R. H. (1967). The Social Readjustment Rating Scale. *Journal of Psychosomatic Research, 11,* 213–218.

Holmes, J. A., & Stevenson, C. A. (1990). Differential effects of avoidant and attentional coping strategies on adaptation to chronic and recent-onset pain. *Health Psychology, 9,* 577–584.

House, J. S., Landis, K. R., & Umberson, D. (1988). Social relationships and health. *Science, 241,* 540–545.

Jöreskog, K. G., & Sörbom, D. (1986). *Analysis of linear structural relationships by maximum likelihood, instrumental variables, and least squares methods* (4th ed.). Mooresville, IN: Scientific Software.

Kessler, R. C., Price, R. H., & Wortman, C. B. (1985). Social factors in psychopathology: Stress, social support, and coping processes. *Annual Review of Psychology, 36,* 531–572.

Kobasa, S. C. (1982). Commitment and coping in stress resistance among lawyers. *Journal of Personality and Social Psychology, 42,* 168–177.

Kobasa, S. C., Maddi, S. R., & Kahn, S. (1982). Hardiness and health: A prospective study. *Journal of Personality and Social Psychology, 42,* 168–172.

Lazarus, R. S. (1981). The stress and coping paradigm. In C. Eisdorfer, D. Cohen, A. Kleinman, & P. Maxim (Eds.), *Models for clinical psychopathology* (pp. 177–214). New York: Spectrum.

Lazarus, R. S., & Folkman, S. (1984). *Stress, appraisal, and coping.* New York: Springer.

Lefcourt, H. M. (1985). Intimacy, social support, and locus of control as moderators of stress. In I. G. Sarason & B. R. Sarason (Eds.), *Social support: Theory, research, and applications* (pp. 155–172). The Hague, Netherlands: Martinus Nijhoff.

Lefcourt, H. M., Miller, R. S., Ware, E. E., & Sherk, D. (1981). Locus of control as a modifier of the relationship between stressors and moods. *Journal of Personality and Social Psychology, 41,* 357–369.

Lindemann, E. (1979). *Beyond grief: Studies in crisis intervention.* New York: Aronson.

Luthar, S. S., & Zigler, E. (1991). Vulnerability and competence: A review of research on resilience in childhood. *American Journal of Orthopsychiatry, 61,* 6–22.

Major, B., Cozzarelli, C., Sciacchitano, A. M., Cooper, M. L., Testa, M., & Mueller, P. M. (1990). Perceived social support, self-efficacy, and adjustment to abortion. *Journal of Personality and Social Psychology, 59,* 452–463.

Manne, S. L., & Zautra, A. J. (1989). Spouse criticism and support: Their association with coping and psychological adjustment among women with rheumatoid arthritis. *Journal of Personality and Social Psychology, 56,* 608–617.

McCrae, R. R. (1984). Situational determinants of coping responses: Loss, threat, and challenge. *Journal of Personality and Social Psychology, 46,* 919–928.

Menaghan, E. (1982). Measuring coping effectiveness: A panel analysis of marital problems and coping efforts. *Journal of Health and Social Behavior, 23,* 220–234.

Mitchell, R. E., Cronkite, R. C., & Moos, R. H. (1983). Stress, coping, and depression among married couples. *Journal of Abnormal Psychology, 92,* 433–448.

Moos, R. H. (1986). *Work Environmental Scale manual* (2nd ed.). Palo Alto, CA: Consulting Psychologists Press.

Moos, R. H. (1991). Life stressors, social resources, and the treatment of depression. In J. Becker & A. Kleinman (Eds.), *Psychosocial aspects of depression* (pp. 187–214). Hillsdale, NJ: Erlbaum.

Moos, R. H. (1992). *Coping Responses Inventory—adult form manual.* Palo Alto, CA: Center for Health Care Evaluation, Department of Veterans Affairs and Stanford University Medical Centers.

Moos, R. H., Cronkite, R. C., & Finney, J. W. (1990). *Health and Daily Living form manual* (2nd ed.). Palo Alto, CA: Center for Health Care Evaluation, Department of Veterans Affairs and Stanford University Medical Centers.

Moos, R. H., Fenn, C., & Billings, A. (1988). Life stressors and social resources: An integrated assessment approach. *Social Science and Medicine, 27,* 999–1002.

Moos, R. H., Finney, J. W., & Cronkite, R. C. (1990). *Alcoholism treatment: Process and outcome.* New York: Oxford University Press.

Moos, R. H., & Moos, B. S. (1986). *Family Environment Scale manual* (2nd ed.). Palo Alto, CA: Consulting Psychologists Press.

Moos, R. H., & Moos, B. S. (1992). *Life Stressors and Social Resources Inventory—adult form manual.* Palo Alto, CA: Center for Health Care Evaluation, Department of Veterans Affairs and Stanford University Medical Centers.

Moos, R. H., & Schaefer, J. (1986). Life transitions and crises: A conceptual overview. In R. H. Moos (Ed.), *Coping with life crises: An integrated approach* (pp. 3–28). New York: Plenum.

Moos, R. H., & Schaefer, J. A. (1993). Coping resources and processes: Current concepts and measures. In L. Goldberger & S. Breznitz (Eds.), *Handbook of stress: Theoretical and clinical aspects* (2nd ed., 234–257). New York: Free Press.

Okun, M. A., Sandler, I. N., & Baumann, D. J. (1988). Buffer and booster effects as event-support transactions. *American Journal of Community Psychology, 16,* 435–449.

O'Leary, A. (1990). Stress, emotion, and human immune function. *Psychological Bulletin, 108,* 363–382.

Pearlin, L. I. (1989). The sociological study of stress. *Journal of Health and Social Behavior, 30,* 241–256.

Pearlin, L. I., & Schooler, C. (1978). The structure of coping. *Journal of Health and Social Behavior, 19,* 2–21.

Rahe, R. H., & Arthur, J. (1987). Life change and illness studies: Past history and future directions. In F. Lolas & H. Mayer (Eds.), *Perspectives on stress and stress-related topics* (pp. 108–125). New York: Springer-Verlag.

Rhodewalt, F., Hays, R. B., Chemers, M. M., & Wysocki, J. (1984). Type A behavior, perceived stress, and illness: A person–situation analysis. *Personality and Social Psychology Bulletin, 10,* 149–159.

Rodin, J., & Salovey, P. (1989). Health psychology. *Annual Review of Psychology, 40,* 533–579.

Rosenbaum, M., & Ben-Ari, K. (1985). Learned helplessness and learned resourcefulness: Effects of noncontingent success and failure on individuals differing in self-control skills. *Journal of Personality and Social Psychology, 48,* 198–215.

Roth, S., & Cohen, L. J. (1986). Approach, avoidance, and coping with stress. *American Psychologist, 41,* 813–819.

Ruch, L., Chandler, S., & Harter, R. (1980). Life change and rape impact. *Journal of Health and Social Behavior, 21,* 248–260.

Sarason, I. G., Sarason, B. R., & Shearin, E. N. (1986). Social support as an individual difference variable: Its stability, origins, and relational aspects. *Journal of Personality and Social Psychology, 50,* 845–855.

Schaefer, J. A., & Moos, R. H. (1992). Life crises and personal growth. In B. N. Carpenter (Ed.), *Personal coping: Theory, research, and applications* (pp. 149–170). New York: Praeger.

Scheier, M. F., Weintraub, J. K., & Carver, C. S. (1986). Coping with stress: Divergent strategies of optimists and pessimists. *Journal of Personality and Social Psychology, 51,* 1257–1262.

Seeman, J. (1989). Toward a model of positive health. *American Psychologist, 44,* 1099–1109.

Selye, H. (1982). History and present status of the stress concept. In L. Goldberger & S. Breznitz (Eds.), *Handbook of stress: Theoretical and clinical aspects* (pp. 7–17). New York: Free Press.

Smith, L. W., Patterson, T. L., & Grant, I. (1990). Avoidant coping predicts psychological disturbance in the elderly. *Journal of Nervous and Mental Disease, 178,* 525–530.

Stewart, A. J., Sokol, M., Healy, J. M., & Chester, N. L. (1986). Longitudinal studies of psychological consequences of life changes in children and adults. *Journal of Personality and Social Psychology, 50,* 143–157.

Suls, J., & Fletcher, B. (1985). The relative efficacy of avoidant and nonavoidant coping strategies: A meta-analysis. *Health Psychology,* 249–288.

Suls, J., Gastorf, J. W., & Witenberg, S. H. (1979). Life events, psychological distress, and the type A coronary-prone behavior pattern. *Journal of Psychosomatic Research, 23,* 315–319.

Swindle, R. W., Cronkite, R. C., & Moos, R. H. (1989). Life streessors, social resources, coping, and the four-year course of unipolar depression. *Journal of Abnormal Psychology, 98,* 468–477.

Taylor, S. E. (1983). Adjustment to threatening events: A theory of cognitive adaptation. *American Psychologist, 38,* 1161–1173.

Thoits, P. A. (1983). Dimensions of life stress that influence psychological distress: An evaluation and synthesis of the literature. In H. R. Kaplan (Ed.), *Psychosocial stress: Trends in theory and research* (pp. 33–103). New York: Academic Press.

Thoits, P. A. (1985). Social support and psychological well-being: Theoretical possibilities. In I. G. Sarason & B. R. Sarason (Eds.), *Social support: Theory, research, and applications* (pp. 51–72). The Hague, Netherlands: Martinus Nijhoff.

Thoits, P. A. (1986). Social support as coping assistance. *Journal of Consulting and Clinical Psychology, 54,* 416–423.

Turner, R. J., & Avison, W. R. (1992). Innovations in the measurement of life stress: Crisis theory and the significance of event resolution. *Journal of Health and Social Behavior, 33,* 36–50.

Wallerstein, J. S. (1986). Women after divorce: Preliminary report from a ten-year follow-up. *American Journal of Orthopsychiatry, 56,* 65–77.

Wallston, B. S., Alagna, S. W., DeVellis, B. M., & DeVellis, R. F. (1983). Social support and physical health. *Health Psychology, 2,* 367–391.

Widenfeld, S. A., O'Leary, A., Bandura, A., Brown, S., Levine, S., & Raska, K. (1990). Impact of perceived self-efficacy in coping with stressors on components of the immune system. *Journal of Personality and Social Psychology, 59,* 1082–1094.

Willis, T. A. (1985). Supportive functions of interpersonal relationships. In S. Cohen & S. L. Syme (Eds.), *Social support and health* (pp. 61–82). New York: Academic Press.

9

The Disaggregation of Vulnerability to Depression as a Function of the Determinants of Onset and Recurrence

RONALD C. KESSLER and WILLIAM J. MAGEE

The investigation of stress and stress-buffering effects has been central to research on psychosocial determinants of mental illness since at least the early 1960s. Most of the early work in this tradition focused on the gross effects of life events (Dohrenwend & Dohrenwend, 1974). There was little interest in stress-buffering effects, although some consideration was given to the modifying effects of social class (Langner & Michael, 1963). More recent research has broadened this focus to consider a much larger range of individual differences and processes that might play a part in modifying the effect of stress on mental health, including personality (Cohen & Edwards, 1989), social support (House, Landis, & Umberson, 1988) and coping (Eckenrode, 1991).

The predictor variables in studies of stress-buffering effects have usually been aggregate measures of recent life events (e.g., Dohrenwend, Krasnoff, & Dohrenwend, 1978). The outcome variables have

RONALD C. KESSLER • Department of Sociology and Institute for Social Research, University of Michigan, Ann Arbor, Michigan 48106-1248. WILLIAM J. MAGEE • Department of Psychiatry, University of Wisconsin, Madison, Wisconsin 53706.
Stress and Mental Health: Contemporary Issues and Prospects for the Future, edited by William R. Avison and Ian H. Gotlib. New York, Plenum Press, 1994.

usually been screening scales of nonspecific psychological distress (e.g., Derogatis, Lipman, Rickels, Uhlenhuth, & Covi, 1974). The relationship between life events and psychological distress has typically been weak in these studies, with life events usually explaining less than 10% of the variance in distress (Thoits, 1983). It is this fact, perhaps more than anything else, that has led to the enormous amount of interest that currently exists in stress-buffering effects. The gross effect of differential exposure to stress on mental health is weak, according to the stress-buffering argument, because some people are more vulnerable than others to the distress-provoking effects of stressful life experiences. The relationship between negative events occurring to others and depression, for example, is much stronger among women than among men (Kessler & McLeod, 1984; Turner & Avison, 1989), whereas the relationship between economic pressures and depression is much stronger among husbands than wives (Elder, Conger, Foster, & Ardelt, 1992). Differences in vulnerability across roles and statuses must therefore be taken into consideration in order to understand the full impact of stress on mental health (Kessler, Price, & Wortman, 1985).

A second influential argument about the weak relationship between life events and psychological distress is based on the observation that scores on symptom screening scales have high stabilities over time (Myers, Lindenthal, Pepper, & Ostrander, 1974: Pearlin, Menaghan, Lieberman, & Mullan, 1981; Srole & Fischer, 1989; Wheaton, 1978). This has been taken to mean that most of the reliable variance in these scales is attributable to chronic psychological distress. If this is the case, it is little wonder that the acute stresses measured either as dummy variables indicating the recent occurrence of specific negative life events or in life-event scales in which recent events are summed or weighted are not strong predictors of these outcome measures (Depue & Monroe, 1986).

The observation that symptom screening scales are insensitive measures of acute distress has stimulated two recent developments in the stress literature. First, researchers who continue to be interested in explaining variation in screening scales have begun to expand their predictor variables to include scales of chronic role-related stress (Pearlin et al., 1981) and daily hassles (Lazarus, DeLongis, Folkman, & Gruen, 1985). This is a difficult area of research because of problems in measuring chronic stress in a way that avoids confounding between the stress and the outcome (Barnett & Gotlib, 1988; Dohrenwend, Dohrenwend, Dodson, & Shrout, 1984) and because of statistical problems in sorting out cause and effect when the stress and distress measures both represent chronic conditions (Kessler, 1987). It is a very important area of research, though, because there is good reason to believe that chronic stress is a much more important cause of emotional distress than has traditionally been thought (McGonagle & Kessler, 1990; Pearlin, 1991). A challenge for stress research in the future is to develop new methods of data collection (e.g., Stone, Kessler, & Haythornthwaite, 1991) and data analysis (e.g., Bolger, DeLongis, Kessler, & Schilling, 1989; Kessler, 1987) capable of accurately measuring chronic stress and assessing its effects on distress.

A second recent development, stimulated in part by the recognition of confounding between chronic and acute distress in symptom screening scales, has been the adoption of diagnostic measures of clinically significant episodes of depression (Brown & Harris, 1978) and anxiety (Blazer, Hughes, & George, 1987) as outcome measures in studies of stress effects. Despite ongoing controversy over the validity of dichotomous distinctions between cases and noncases (Mirowsky & Ross, 1989; see also Chapter 10) and evidence from epidemiological research that more and less severe diagnostic classifications may represent nothing more than successively more extreme cut points on a continuous latent liability (Kessler, Kendler, Heath, Neale, & Eaves, 1992), the use of diagnostic measures is still useful in focusing attention on clinically significant levels of distress. Furthermore, the fact that diagnostic measures are discrete means that they can be retrospectively dated for onset, thus making it possible to discriminate between chronic and acute "cases." When this is done, the evidence is clear and consistent that exposure to severe life events has a much more powerful effect on the acute onset of extreme distress than on standard symptom screening scales (e.g., Brown & Harris, 1986).

The purpose of this chapter is to explore opportunities for elaborating our understanding of life-event stress-buffering effects based on the use of diagnostic outcome measures. We begin by discussing how the use of diagnostic measures makes it possible to decompose stress and stress-buffering effects into components that influence initial onset and recurrence of episodes. We then argue that this type of decomposition can be useful in pinpointing the processes involved in stress-buffering effects. We also argue that decomposition of stress-buffering effects can help minimize biases that exist in more highly aggregated analyses. At an operational level, we suggest that researchers discriminate the predictors of lifetime occurrence of disorder from the predictors of recent onset and recent recurrence, and we show how these distinctions can clarify several causal processes that have been the focus of attention in recent research. The implications of these arguments are illustrated with data analyses based on a recently completed national survey. We focus on clinical depression as the outcome variable, although similar arguments could be made for other types of clinically significant outcomes.

CONCEPTUAL ISSUES

Life Stress and Episode Onset

A good deal of progress has been made since the early 1980s in general population research on the relationship between life stress and episodes of clinically significant depression. The seminal work of Brown and Harris (1978) had an enormous influence on this area of research because of its important substantive results as well as its methodological innovations. The former include the documentation of strong effects of severe life events and difficulties on episodes of clinical depression in community samples, as well as powerful stress-buffering effects associated with both current life circumstances (e.g., access to a confiding relationship) and early life experiences (e.g., early parental loss). The methodological innovations include the use of a sophisticated method of assessing stress severity and of information about the timing of events and episodes of disorder to help sort out cause and effect. Much subsequent work on stress and depression can trace its intellectual origins to the work of Brown and Harris.

The basic logic of research in the Brown-Harris tradition has been to obtain data about the occurrence of severe life events and difficulties and about episodes of clinically significant anxiety or depression using retrospective methods that reconstruct the timing of both the stresses and the episodes of disorder, typically over a 12-month recall period (e.g., Bebbington, Sturt, Tennant, & Hurry, 1984; Campbell, Cope, & Teasdale, 1983; Costello, 1982; Solomon & Bromet, 1982). The information about timing is used to create a case-control (Schlesselman, 1982) data file comparing the stresses that occurred in the months before the onset of the depression to those that occurred in the same months to respondents who did not become depressed.[1] Stratified cross-tabulations (e.g., Brown & Harris, 1978) or loglinear/logistic regression

---

[1]The logic of this method is described by Brown and Harris (1978). It should be noted that a more comprehensive approach would use a discrete-time survival model, treat person-months as the unit of analysis, and include in the control sample all the months prior to the onset of disorder for persons who subsequently became anxious or depressed, as well as all the person-months observed for persons who did not become anxious as depressed. This latter approach is discussed in more detail by Kessler (1987).

equations with interactions (e.g., Brown, Harris, & Eales, 1993) are then used to estimate the effects of stress and stress buffers.

Some of the stress-buffering variables included in these studies have been based on retrospective reports of early childhood experiences (e.g., McLeod, 1991; Rutter, 1989). Concerns have been raised that current depression may color these reports in a way that leads to bias in the estimated relationships between early life experiences and vulnerability to adult stress (Brewin, Andrews, & Gotlib, 1993). Based on these concerns, several recent studies have adopted a panel design that uses measures of stress-buffering variables assessed in the baseline interview to predict variations in the effects of life stress on episode onset during a later follow-up period (e.g., Brown, Bifulco, & Harris, 1987; Lewinsohn, Hoberman, & Rosenbaum, 1988).

The Importance of History as a Control Variables

A critical limitation of research in this tradition is that history of depression has not been considered in a serious way. Recent data from the Epidemiologic Catchment Area (ECA) program indicate that the typical person with a history of clinical depression has a first episode by his or her early 20s (Sorenson, Rutter, & Aneshensel, 1991), which means that most episodes of depression that occur in the adult years are recurrences rather than first onsets. Our own analysis of the ECA public use data tape showed that 91% of the respondents who reported an episode of depression in the 12 months prior to the baseline ECA interview had a history of depression.

An obvious question is whether prior depression should be thought of as a predictor variable in risk-factor analyses of the sort carried out by Brown and Harris and those who have built on their work. It is clear that such a variable would be a powerful predictor of subsequent episode onset. In our analysis of the ECA data, for example, we found that history of depression had an odds ratio close to 40.0 in predicting episode onset in the 12 months prior to the baseline ECA interview. We are not aware of any other risk factor in the literature on depression that comes close to having a predictive effect nearly this large. Despite this fact, however, it is not clear that prior depression should be used as a control variable in risk-factor analyses. Indeed, a good argument could be made that it should not if the purpose of the analysis is to evaluate the gross effects of long-term risk factors. For example, the use of history of depression as a control variable leads to a reduction in the estimated effect of childhood loss on adult depression, because part of the total effect of childhood loss is indirect through history. As discussed in more detail below, our analyses of data from a recent national survey show that the net effects of some childhood adversities on recent depression become insignificant when we control for history of depression. It would be a mistake to conclude from this exercise that these adversities had no effect on depression; rather, their effects are largely mediated by history. Yet it would be impossible to discover this mediating process if all analyses investigating the long-term effects of childhood adversity controlled for history of depression.

Conversely, a good case could be made that failure to control for history of depression can lead to incorrect inferences about the importance of seemingly significant mediator variables. The critical consideration is whether these mediators could themselves be influenced by history. A useful illustration of the issues involved is provided by Parker and Hadzi-Pavlovic's (1984) investigation of women whose mothers died in the subjects' childhoods. Retrospective reports about lack of care from fathers and stepmothers after the death of the mother were significantly associated with high adult scores on screening scales of both state depression and trait depression. These associations were attenuated among respondents with supportive spouses, however, leading the authors to conclude that success in forming intimate relationships "largely corrected any diathesis to greater depression exerted by uncaring parenting" (p. 125). Yet this conclusion ignores the equally plausible hypothesis that lack of success in forming a supportive marriage and current depression could both be attributable, at least in part, to a history of depression prior to marriage. If so, there might be no causal effect of success in forming a supportive marriage on subsequent depression, even though these variables are significantly related to each other. The only way to control for the existence of this potential bias is to include history of depression (before the age of marriage) as a predictor variable in analyses of the effects of marriage.

We are not aware of any published research that has explicitly tested the hypothesis that history of depression explains, either in whole or in part, the effects of variables that intervene between childhood adversity and adult depression. The plausibility of this hypothesis, however, can be inferred from research showing that many forms of childhood adversity are associated with increased risk of depression in late adolescence (Fleming & Offord, 1990; Goodyear, 1990; Kandel & Davies, 1986) and that early-onset depression is associated with high recurrence risk later in life (Clarizio, 1988; Harrington, Fudge, Rutter, Pickle, & Hill, 1990; Lavori, Keller, & Klerman, 1984; Lewinsohn et al., 1988). Recent research, in fact, suggests that there is specificity in the continuation of depression between childhood and adulthood (Harrington et al., 1990).

These results imply that the relationship between childhood adversity and adult depression could be attributable to the mediating influence of earlier depression.

The question does not stop with a consideration of mediators of the long-term effects of childhood adversity. It can also be raised with regard to the direct effects on depression in adulthood of such contemporary risk factors as social class, social support, and personality (Barnett & Gotlib, 1988). History of depression might influence these risk factors, in which case failure to control for history would lead to an overestimation of their effects on adult depression. We are not aware of any prior research that has directly examined this possibility, but there is a great deal of evidence consistent with the possibility that prior depression is an important explanatory variable. We know, for example, that the interactional styles of depressed people provoke others to act toward them in ways that are nonsupportive (Coyne, 1976; Monroe & Steiner, 1986). Based on this research, it is reasonable to assume that history of depression is one cause of low social support. This possibility, in turn, implies that a risk-factor analysis that includes history of depression as a control variable would find that social support is a less powerful predictor of episode onset than would an analysis that failed to control for history. In the extreme, one might hypothesize—as Henderson, Byrne, and Duncan-Jones (1981) did in a related context—that what appears to be an effect of social support is entirely attributable to history of depression. Even without embracing this extreme form of the argument, it is clear that any analysis of the direct effects of risk factors that could plausibly be considered under the influence of prior depression will yield biased estimates unless history of depression is included as a control variable.

The Importance of History as a Modifier

Up to now we have considered prior depression only as a control variable, but it is clear that it can also be a modifier of the effects of other risk factors. We noted earlier that the vast majority of people who report recent episodes of depression in adulthood have a history of depression. This means that history is a powerful risk factor for episode onset. It might also be the case, though, that the effects of other risk factors are more powerful in the subsample of people with a history of depression. For example, it might be that a stressful life event is more likely to provoke a recurrence of depression in a person with a history of depression than to provoke a first onset of depression in a person who has never before been depressed. This could occur because history of depression is correlated with unmeasured heterogeneity in vulnerability to depression (Flinn & Heckman, 1982). Persons with a history of depression may, for example, have less adequate coping resources available to them, or they may be biologically predisposed to become depressed in the face of certain types of stress. It is frequently not possible to measure the actual factors responsible for vulnerability, but history of depression is one indicator of greater vulnerability to other risk factors.

As we show later in the chapter, our own analyses of data from a large national survey found that history of depression modified the effects of many significant predictors of depression. In fact, the significant effects of some predictors were entirely confined to the subsample of respondents with a history of depression. This means that as a practical matter, the most sensible way to analyze the effects of risk factors for depression is to carry out separate analyses of first onset and recurrence. In general population surveys of adults, the number of people with recent first onsets will be so small that powerful investigation of the predictors of first onset will be impossible. This means that the major focus for most studies of risk factors for recent episodes of depression will be on recurrence in the subsample of respondents with a history.

The Determinants of Lifetime History

It is important to remember that a full understanding of the factors that influence prevalence of depression requires the researcher to investigate the determinants of prior depression as well. This is because a risk factor that affects history of depression will have a gross effect on prevalence through history, even if it does not affect recurrence directly. The literature on sex differences in depression provides an interesting illustration of this situation. Lifetime prevalence of depression among women is much higher than it is among men (Weissman et al., 1988). There is evidence, however, that there is no sex difference in recurrence of depression (Coryell, Endicott, & Keller, 1991), which means that the higher rates of recent depression typically found among women (Eaton et al., 1989; Weissman et al., 1988) stem from the strong relationship between sex and prior depression. An analysis that focused entirely on the predictors of recurrence would incorrectly lead to the conclusion that sex is not an important risk factor for depression.

A decomposition of risk-factor effects on lifetime history and recurrence can be very informative, particularly when age of onset is taken into consideration in the analysis of history. In the case of sex differences in depression, for example, we know that average age of onset for both men and women is in the early 20s (Sorenson et al., 1991). The sex difference in prevalence of depression is more pronounced in midlife, however, because the density of episodes of depression (mostly recurrences) is greatest in this period of the life cycle. This midlife bulge in the sex difference in depression has been taken by many commentators as evidence that chronic life stresses associated with sex roles explain the sex difference in depression (e.g., Ensel, 1982). A consideration of sex differences in first onset and in recurrence risk, however, shows that the midlife sex difference in depression is in fact largely caused by a sex difference in lifetime onset of depression that occurs by the early 20s. The implications of this observation for current ideas about the relationship between sex roles and depression are profound.

EMPIRICAL ILLUSTRATIONS

Data are presented in this section of the chapter to illustrate some of the arguments made above. All the data come from a longitudinal survey entitled Americans' Changing Lives (ACL) carried out by the Survey Research Center at the University of Michigan. The ACL is a survey of noninstitutionalized persons aged 25 or older in the continental United States based on a multistage, stratified area probability sampling design. The purpose of the survey was to study productivity and successful aging in midlife and the later years of life. The baseline survey was carried out in 1986; the sample size was 3,617, and the response rate was 70%. The follow-up survey, carried out in 1989, reinterviewed 2,867 of the baseline respondents, representing 83% of those who were surviving at the time of recontact. For more details on the ACL design, see House et al. (1988).

The follow-up ACL interview included a reworded version of the stem question from the depression section of the Diagnostic Interview Schedule (DIS) version III-A (Robins, Helzer, Croughhan, & Ratcliff, 1981), along with questions about age of first onset, lifetime number of episodes, and Family History Research Diagnostic Criteria symptoms (Endicott, Andreasen, & Spitzer, 1978). Responses to the symptom questions were used to make best-estimate diagnoses of major depression (MD) based on the A criterion of the DSM-III-R diagnostic system (American Psychiatric Association, 1987). ACL respondents who reported dysphoric affect or anhedonia; feeling sad, blue, or depressed; or loss of interest or pleasure nearly every day for at least 2 weeks were asked whether they also experienced a list of other symptoms during the same period. These other symptoms ranged from diminished ability to concentrate to weight loss or weight gain to recurrent thoughts of death or attempted suicide. Those who reported affective disturbance and four other symptoms out of a list of nine for 2 weeks or more were considered to have suffered an episode of major depression. Consistent with our previous analysis of the ECA public use tapes, we found that approximately 90% of ACL respondents with an episode of MD in the 12 months prior to the follow-up ACL interview had a history of depression prior to that time.

The Importance of History as a Control Variable

We argued above that history of depression is a powerful predictor of subsequent depressive episodes and that the inclusion of history as a control variable in risk-factor analysis will importantly affect the conclusions drawn about the role of other predictors. This is only true, though, if history is also significantly associated with these other risk factors. In an effort to determine whether this is the case, we assembled a set of risk factors to predict episode onset of MD in the interval between the baseline and follow-up interviews in the ACL panel data. Four broad sets of predictors were used from the baseline interview: (a) basic demographic characteristics (age, sex, race); (b) social roles (marital status, number/ages of children, employment status, income, education); (c) social networks and support (access to a confidant, positive support from friends and relatives, negative interactions with friends and relatives); and (d) personality (neuroticism, extroversion, self-esteem, mastery). We also included measures of stress (separate summary measures of life events and chronic role-related stresses) obtained in the follow-up interview. There were a total of 20 predictor variables in the final model.

Consistent with the results of previous research, the analysis documented significant relationships between most of these 20 predictors and subsequent episodes of MD. In particular, risk of depression was significantly elevated among women, blacks, persons in lower socioeconomic positions, the previously married, the unemployed, and those with weak social support systems. There was a significant positive association between depression and neuroticism and negative associations between depression and self-esteem and mastery. Stressful life events and chronic role-related stresses, finally, were significantly related to increased risk of depression.

We then estimated a series of models to determine whether history of depression significantly predicted these risk factors. The results were striking; 14 of the 20 risk factors were significantly associated with history of depression. Controlling for age, sex, race, and childhood socioeconomic status, respondents with a history of depression were much more likely than other respondents to have low income, to be separated or divorced, to be unemployed, to have weak social support networks, to have low self-esteem and mastery and high levels of neuroticism, and to have high exposure to both stressful life events and chronic role-related stresses. Furthermore, when history of depression was added as a control variable to the risk-factor analysis predicting 12-month episode onset of MD, there were substantial reductions in the estimated effects of 13 of the 20 risk factors.

The Importance of History as a Modifier

We next investigated the possibility of interactions between history and the risk factors. As noted above, we expected the risk factors to predict episode onset of MD more powerfully in the subsample of people with a history of depression than in the subsample of those who were never before depressed. The results of the analysis were consistent with this expectation. Of the 20 interactions between the risk factors and history in predicting subsequent-episode onset of MD, 10 were significant, and the vast majority of these were stronger among respondents with a history than among those without a history of depression.

At the same time, it is important to appreciate that the estimated effects of the risk factors were usually smaller, not larger, in the subsample of respondents with a history of depression than in the total sample. This occurred because the total-sample analyses, unlike the subsample analyses, failed to control for history of depression. As a result, the effects of history were confounded with the effects of the risk factors in the total-sample analyses, and this inflated the estimated effects of the risk factors.

The estimated effects of stress buffers were also substantially reduced when analyses were carried out in the separate subsamples rather than in the total sample. In total-sample analyses that ignored the effect of history, we found 10 significant interactions among baseline risk factors and follow-up life events in predicting onset of MD between the interviews.[2] Of these 10, 4 became clearly insignificant when the analyses were replicated in the subsample of respondents with a history of depression. There were also eight significant stress-buffering effects

[2]The coding of the life events measure was based on the case-control strategy described above in the discussion of Brown and Harris. For respondents who reported an episode of MD at Time 2, the events scale was made up of the events that occurred in the 12 months prior to the onset of the episode. For respondents who did not report an episode of MD, the scale was made up of the events that occurred in the 12 months prior to a random month prior to the Time 2 interview that was selected to match the aggregate distribution of onset times in the subsample of people who had episodes of MD.

that involved chronic role-related stress in the total-sample analyses. Six of these eight became clearly insignificant in analyses of the subsample with a history of depression.

The reason for these stress-buffering effects disappearing in subsample analyses is that history of depression (which was strongly related to all of the stress buffers) was the vulnerability factor. That is, it was people with a history of depression who were vulnerable to the effects of life stress on MD; the other risk factors only appeared to be stress buffers because they were associated with history. When history was, in effect, controlled in the subsample analyses, the evidence of stress-buffering effects of the risk factors disappeared. Though it is true that the dichotomous variable discriminating people with a prior history of depression from those with no such history is controlled by subsample analyses of this sort, it is important to recognize that variations in more subtle aspects of prior history are not controlled. Variations in number of prior episodes, length and severity of these episodes, age at first onset of depression, and other aspects of the person's history of depression might be important predictors of subsequent risk of recurrence and should be introduced as controls in substantive analyses aimed at exhaustively evaluating the effects of prior depression. This was not done in the ACL analysis because we lacked detailed information about these other aspects of the respondents' history of depression.

The Determinants of Lifetime History

As noted above, a complete understanding of the factors that influence prevalence of depression requires the researcher to investigate the determinants of history as well as the determinants of recurrence. This is so because a risk factor that affects history will have an indirect effect on prevalence through history even if it does not affect recurrence directly. One way in which this situation can be analyzed is by using survival analysis methods to study the predictors of first onset of depression. Our favored approach in this regard is to use respondents' reports about age at first onset of depression to construct a discrete-time survival file with person-years as the unit of analysis.[3] This method is described in an accessible way by Allison (1984) and is illustrated in studies of depression by McLeod, Kessler, and Landis (1992) and Kessler and Magee (1993). The

---

[3]A limiting condition in this type of work is the respondent's ability to provide accurate retrospective reports about age at first onset. Recent work by cognitive psychologists provides some hope that data collection procedures can be developed to improve this sort of memory (Loftus, Smith, Klinger, & Fiedler, 1991), but this is likely to remain the weakest link in this area of investigation for some time to come.

main virtue of this approach is that it allows the researcher to utilize more adequately information on the timing of events and reduces bias that can be introduced into conventional analyses which fail to take into consideration that some persons have not been observed long enough for the event of interest to happen. We prefer the discrete-time approach over more conventional continuous-time survival analysis methods because they give the researcher considerable flexibility in the use of time-varying predictor variables and in the analysis of nonproportionality in the hazards.

We used this approach to study the effects of basic ascriptive characteristics (age, sex, and race) and eight measures of childhood adversity on life history of depression in the ACL survey. The results showed quite clearly that women, nonwhites, and persons born in more recent cohorts were all at increased risk of a lifetime history of depression compared to men, whites, and persons born in earlier cohorts. We also found that childhood adversity is associated with increased risk of lifetime depression. Variation in these effects as a function of age at first onset were also examined, and we discovered that most of the effects were more strongly related to early-onset depression (defined as a first onset prior to the age of 20) than to later-onset depression. Some of the effects were totally confined to early-onset depression. For example, the odds of becoming depressed by the age of 20 were close to three times higher among people whose mother died when the respondent was a child than among people from intact families. This elevated risk, however, totally disappeared in the analysis of first onset after the age of 20.

We also estimated equations for the effects of these same predictors on recurrence of depression among people with a history. This analysis showed quite clearly that most childhood adversities did not significantly predict recent recurrence. There were significant associations between childhood adversity and recent prevalence of MD, but these were attributable to the mediating effects of history of depression, and they disappeared when history was controlled in subsample analyses.

Decomposition of Lifetime Effects

A decomposition of risk-factor effects through lifetime history and recurrence can be very informative, particularly when age of onset is taken into consideration in the analysis of history. In the case of childhood adversity, for example, we found that the effect on lifetime history of depression is, for the most part, an effect on early-onset depression. The main exception to this general pattern was family violence, which not only had the strongest effect on early-onset depression of any dimension of childhood adversity considered in our analysis but also continued to affect first onset after the age of 20. Furthermore, people who experienced family violence during their childhoods were at increased risk of recurrence of MD compared to other people with an earlier onset of depression.

Although the ACL design did not allow us to trace out the causal pathways linking childhood violence to first onset of depression, we were able to decompose the long-term effects of childhood violence on recurrence of MD between the baseline and follow-up interviews through mediators measured at baseline. In particular, we found that chronic interpersonal difficulties measured at baseline were significantly more common among respondents with a history of childhood violence and that this led to increased risk of recurrence of MD. In fact, the significant effect of childhood violence on recurrence of MD was confined to the subsample of respondents with severe interpersonal difficulties in their adult social networks at the time of the first interview. This finding is consistent with evidence suggesting that chronic depression is associated with disturbed interpersonal networks (Keitner & Miller, 1990) in adulthood, although it goes beyond previous literature in this area to suggest that both outcomes are associated with exposure to violence earlier in life.

DISCUSSION

The argument presented above has been a fairly simple one: Most episodes of depression in adulthood are recurrences, and history of depression should be taken into consideration in analyses of risk factors for these episodes. We showed that history of depression is significantly associated with a wide range of psychosocial risk factors and illustrated this with data from a recent national survey showing that failure to control for history can lead to biased conclusions about the importance of these risk factors. We argued that the most sensible way of carrying out risk-factor analyses of this sort is to do separate analyses of first onset and recurrence. We illustrated how this might be done and discussed how it is possible to trace out the long-term effects of early life predictors of adult depression through disaggregated analyses of first onset and recurrence.

We believe that this line of thinking provides an elegant way of addressing the problem of confounding that has heretofore plagued research on risk factors for depression. We suspect that the broad application of our approach to risk-factor analysis will yield important insights that are currently obscured by the confusing ways in which researchers in this area work with risk-factor data. A great deal of research will be required to investigate this issue because even very basic associations are largely unexplored, as illustrated earlier by the discussion of sex differences in onset and recurrence.

We also recognize that our thinking about the distinctions made here is still fairly primitive. In particular, we need to increase the subtlety with which we conceptualize and measure history of disorder. The coarse dichotomous distinction between people who had a previous episode of depression and those who did not needs to be elaborated into a more detailed set of distinctions between people with and without subclinical manifestations of disorder (in the no-history subsample) and between people who vary in the number, length, and intensity of prior episodes (in the history subsample).

This kind of elaboration is particularly important for the analysis of risk factors for recurrence. Though it is true that the exclusive focus on the subsample of respondents with a history controls for the worst kind of confounding in analyses of recurrence, there is still important variation in the recurrence subsample in the number of prior episodes and other aspects of history that might affect recurrence risk and introduce confounding with other risk factors. For example, our finding that the long-term effect of childhood violence on recurrence of depression in adulthood is modified by baseline interpersonal conflicts could reflect an underlying influence of severity of history of depression on both quality of interpersonal networks and risk of recurrence between the baseline and follow-up interviews. The only way to examine this possibility is to include controls for these more detailed aspects of history in analyses of risk factors for recurrence. More fine-grained information about number of prior episodes might also be important in analyses of stress effects on recurrence, given that several clinical studies report that patients with a large number of prior episodes are at increased risk of subsequent recurrences in the absence of precipitating life events (Ezquiaga, Gutierrez, & Lopez, 1987; Ghaziuddin, Ghaziuddin, & Stein, 1990; Perris, 1984).

A related issue involves the possibility of expanding the survival analysis framework to include the analysis of recurrence. This could be done by conceptualizing number of episodes as a progression in much the same way as in survival analyses of educational or occupational transitions (e.g., Mare, Winship, & Kubitschek, 1984), recognizing that there may be nonproportionalities in the predictions as a function of number of prior episodes. These nonproportionalities could involve differences in the risk of recurrence over a given interval of time as a function of number or timing of prior episodes (e.g., having a previous depression in the past 6 months may be a more powerful predictor of recurrence than having been depressed years ago). They could also involve differences in the effects of other risk factors in provoking recurrence as a function of number or timing of prior episodes. The relationship between recent negative life events and the onset of second or third lifetime episodes of depression, for example, may be stronger than the relationship of recent life events to the onset of a tenth or twelfth episode.

A related issue involves the way we deal with unmeasured heterogeneity in vulnerability to disorder. The notion of unmeasured heterogeneity was devised to make sense of the empirical observation that many risk-factor effects become smaller over time in analyses of first onset, presumably because unmeasured risk factors become more and more attenuated among survivors as time goes on, and because the remaining survivors are increasingly made up of not-at-risk people (Flinn & Heckman, 1982). More thought is required to conceptualize unmeasured heterogeneity, theorize about possible variables that explain its effect, and evaluate the part it plays in the analysis of both first onset and recurrence. Although biostatisticians have developed strategies to control for unmeasured heterogeneity in analyses of first onset (Heckman & Singer, 1984), these methods are rather inflexible and provide no substitute for a clear understanding of the substantive reasons for changing risk of onset and recurrence over time (Clogg, 1986).

ACKNOWLEDGMENTS

Preparation of this chapter was supported by MERIT Award R37-MH42714, Training Grant T32 MH16806, and Research Scientist Development Award K02 MH00507 from the National Institute of Mental Health and by the John D. and Catherine T. MacArthur Foundation Research Network On Successful Midlife Development. The data used to illustrate the arguments made in this chapter come from the Americans Changing Lives (ACL) Survey. Data collection for the ACL was supported by Program Project Grant P01 AG05561 from the National Institute of Aging. We thank James House, Director of the ACL, for allowing us to use these data here. A previous version of this paper was presented at the Michigan Training Seminar in Psychosocial Factors in Mental Health and Illness. We thank the seminar participants for helpful comments.

REFERENCES

Allison, P. D. (1984). *Event history analysis: Regression for longitudinal event data.* Beverly Hills, CA: Sage.

Barnett, P., & Gotlib, I. (1988). Psychosocial functioning and depression: Distinguishing among antecedents, concomitants, and consequences. *Psychological Bulletin, 104,* 97–126.

Bebbington, P. E., Sturt, E., Tennant, C., & Hurry, J. (1984). Misfortune and resilience: A community study of women. *Psychological Medicine, 14,* 347–364.

Blazer, D., Hughes, D., & George, L. K. (1987). Stressful life events and the onset of a generalized anxiety syndrome. *American Journal of Psychiatry, 144,* 1178–1183.

Bolger, N., DeLongis, A., Kessler, R. C., & Schilling, E. (1989). The effects of daily stress on negative mood. *Journal of Personality and Social Psychology, 57,* 808–818.

Brewin, C. R., Andrews, B., & Gotlib, I. H. (1993). Psychopathology and early experience: A reappraisal of retrospective reports. *Psychological Bulletin, 113*(1), 82–98.

Brown, G. W., Bifulco, A., & Harris, T. O. (1987). Life events, vulnerability and onset of depression: Some refinements. *British Journal of Psychiatry, 150,* 30–42.

Brown, G. W., & Harris, T. O. (1978). *Social origins of depression.* New York: Free Press.

Brown, G. W., & Harris, T. O. (1986). Stressor, vulnerability and depression: A question of replication. *Psychological Medicine, 16,* 739–744.

Brown, G. W., Harris, T. O., & Eales, M. J. (1993). Etiology of anxiety and depressive disorders in an inner-city population: II. Comorbidity. *Psychological Medicine, 23*(1), 155–165.

Campbell, E., Cope, S., & Teasdale, J. (1983). Social factors and affective disorder: An investigation of Brown and Harris's model. *British Journal of Psychiatry, 143,* 548–553.

Clarizio, H. F. (1988). Continuity in childhood depression. *Adolescence, 24,* 253–267.

Clogg, C. C. (1986). Invoked by RATE. *American Journal of Sociology, 92,* 696-706.

Cohen, S., & Edwards, J. R. (1989). Personality characteristics as moderators of the relationship between stress and disorder. In R. W. J. Neufeld (Ed.), *Advances in the investigation of psychological stress.* New York: Wiley.

Coryell, W., Endicott, J., & Keller, M. B. (1991). Predictors of relapse into major depressive disorder in a nonclinical population. *American Journal of Psychiatry, 148,* 1353–1358.

Costello, C. G. (1982). Social factors associated with depression: A restrospective community study. *Psychological Medicine, 12,* 329–339.

Coyne, J. C. (1976). Depression and the response of others. *Journal of Abnormal Psychology, 85,* 186–193.

Depue, R., & Monroe, S. (1986). Conceptualization and measure of human disorder in life stress research: The problem of chronic disturbance. *Psychological Bulletin, 99,* 36–51.

Derogatis, L., Lipman, R., Rickels, K., Uhlenhuth, E. H., & Covi, L. (1974). The Hopkins symptom checklist. *Canadian Journal of Psychiatry, 35,* 239–242.

Dohrenwend, B. S., & Dohrenwend, B. P. (1974). A brief historical introduction to research on stressful life events. In B. S. Dohrenwend & B. P. Dohrenwend (Eds.), *Stressful life events: Their nature and effects* (pp. 1–5). New York: Wiley-Interscience.

Dohrenwend, B. S., Dohrenwend, B. P., Dodson, M., & Shrout, P. (1984). Symptoms, hassles, social supports and life events: The problem of confounding measures. *Journal of Abnormal Psychology, 93,* 222–230.

Dohrenwend, B. S., Krasnoff, L., & Dohrenwend, B. P. (1978). Exemplification of a method for scaling life events: The PERI life events scale. *Journal of Health and Social Behavior, 19,* 205–229.

Eaton, W. W., Kramer, M., Anthony, J. C., Dryman, A., Shapiro, S., & Locke, B. Z. (1989).

The incidence of specific DIS/DSM-III mental disorders: Data from the NIMH Epidemiologic Catchment Area program. *Acta Psychiatrica Scandinavica, 79,* 163–178.

Eckenrode, J. (Ed.). (1991). *The social context of coping.* New York: Plenum.

Elder, G. H., Conger, R. D., Foster, E. M., & Ardelt, M. (1992). Families under economic pressure. *Journal of Family Issues, 13*(1), 5–37.

Endicott, J., Andreasen, N., & Spitzer, R. L. (1978). *Family History Research Diagnostic Criteria.* New York: Biometrics Research, New York State Psychiatric Institute.

Ensel, W. M. (1982). The role of age in the relationship of gender and marital status to depression. *Journal of Nervous and Mental Disease, 170,* 536–543.

Ezquiaga, E., Gutierrez, J. L. A., & Lopez, A. G. (1987). Psychosocial factors and episode number in depression. *Journal of Abnormal Disorders, 12,* 135–138.

Fleming, J. E. & Offord, D. R. (1990). Epidemiology of childhood depressive disorders: A critical review. *Journal of the American Academy of Child and Adolescent Psychiatry, 29,* 571–580.

Flinn, C. J., & Heckman, J. J. (1982). New methods for analyzing individual event histories. In S. Leinhardt (Ed.), *Sociological methodology 1982* (pp. 99–140). San Francisco: Jossey-Bass.

Ghaziuddin, M., Ghaziuddin, N., & Stein, G. S. (1990). Life events and the recurrence of depression. *Canadian Journal of Psychiatry, 35,* 239–242.

Goodyear, I. M. (1990). Family relationships, life events and childhood psychopathology. *Journal of Child Psychology and Psychiatry, 31,* 161–192.

Harrington, R., Fudge, H., Rutter, M., Pickle, A., & Hill, J. (1990). Adult outcomes of childhood and adolescent depression. *Archives of General Psychiatry, 47,* 465–473.

Heckman, J. J., & Singer, B. (1984). A method for minimizing the impact of distributional assumptions in econometric models for duration data. *Econometrica, 52,* 271–320.

Henderson, S., Byrne, D. G., & Duncan-Jones, P. (1981). *Neurosis and the social environment.* New York: Academic Press.

House, J. S., Landis, K., & Umberson, D. (1988). Social relationships and health. *Science, 241,* 540–545.

Kandel, D. B., & Davies, M. (1986). Adult sequelae of adolescent depressive symptoms. *Archives of General Psychiatry, 43,* 255–262.

Keitner, G. I., & Miller, I. W. (1990). Family functioning and major depression: An overview. *American Journal of Psychiatry, 147,* 1128–1137.

Kessler, R. C. (1987). The interplay of research design strategies and data analysis procedures in evaluating the effects of stress on health. In S. V. Kasl & C. L. Cooper (Eds.), *Stress and health: Issues in research methodology* (pp. 113–139). New York: Wiley.

Kessler, R. C., Kendler, K. S., Heath, A., Neale, M. C., & Eaves, L. J. (1992). Social support, depressed mood, and adjustment to stress: A genetic epidemiologic investigation. *Journal of Personality & Social Psychology, 62,* 257–272.

Kessler, R. C., & Magee, W. J. (1993). Childhood adversity and adult depression: Basic patterns of association in a U.S. national survey. *Psychological Medicine, 23,* 679–690.

Kessler, R. C., and McLeod, J. (1984). Sex differences in vulnerability to undesireable life events. *American Sociological Review, 49,* 620–631.

Kessler, R. C., Price, R. H., & Wortman, C. B. (1985). Social factors in psychopathology: Stress, social support, and coping processes. *American Journal of Psychology, 36,* 531–572.

Langner, T. S., & Michael, S. T. (1963). *Life stress and mental health: The midtown Manhattan study.* New York: Free Press.

Lavori, P. W., Keller, M. B., & Klerman, G. L. (1984). Relapse in affective disorders: A reanalysis of the literature using life table methods. *Journal of Psychiatric Research, 18,* 13–25.

Lazarus, R. S., DeLongis, A., Folkman, S., & Gruen, R. (1985). Stress and adaptational outcomes: The problem of confounding measures. *American Psychologist, 40,* 770–779.

Lewinsohn, P. M., Hoberman, H. M., & Rosenbaum, M. (1988). A prospective study of risk factors for unipolar depression. *Journal of Abnormal Psychology, 97,* 251–264.

Loftus, E. F., Smith, K. D., Klinger, M. R., & Fiedler, J. (1992). Memory and mismemory for health events. In J. M. Tanur (Ed.), *Questions about questions: Inquiries into the cognitive bases of surveys.* New York: Russell Sage Foundation.

Mare, R. D., Winship, C., & Kubitschek, W. N. (1984). The transition from youth to adult: Understanding the age pattern of employment. *American Journal of Sociology, 90,* 326–358.

McGonagle, K. A., & Kessler, R. C. (1990). Chronic stress, acute stress, and depressive symptoms. *American Journal of Community Psychology, 18,* 681–705.

McLeod, J. (1991). Childhood parental loss and adult depression. *Journal of Health and Social Behavior, 35,* 205–220.

McLeod, J. D., Kessler, R. C., & Landis, K. R. (1992). Speed of recovery from major depressive episodes in a community sample of married men and women. *Journal of Abnormal Psychology, 101*(2), 277–286.

Mirowsky, J., & Ross, C. E. (1989). Psychiatric diagnosis as reified measurement. *Journal of Health and Social Behavior, 30,* 11–40.

Monroe, S. M., & Steiner, S. C. (1986). Social support and psychopathology: Interrelations with preexisting disorder, stress, and personality, *Journal of Abnormal Psychology, 95,* 29–39.

Myers, J. K., Lindenthal, J. J., Pepper, M. P., & Ostrander, D. R. (1974). Social class, life events and psychiatric symptoms: A longitudinal study. In B. S. Dohrenwend & B. P. Dohrenwend, (Eds.), *Stressful life events: Their nature and effects* (pp. 191–206). New York, Wiley.

Parker, G., & Hadzi-Pavlovic, D. (1984). Modification of levels of depression in mother-bereaved women by parental and marital relationships. *Psychological Medicine, 14,* 125–135.

Pearlin, L. I., Menaghan, E., Lieberman, M., & Mullan, J. (1981). The stress process. *Journal of Health and Social Behavior, 22,* 337–356.

Pearlin, L. I. (1991). The study of coping: An overview of problems and directions. In J. Eckenrode (Ed.), *The social context of coping* (pp. 261–277). New York: Plenum.

Perris, H. (1984). Life events and depression: Part 2. Results in diagnostic subgroups, and in relation to the recurrence of depression. *Journal of Affective Disorders, 7,* 25–36.

Robins, L. N., Helzer, J. E., Croughhan, J., & Ratcliff, K. L. (1981). National Institute of Mental Health Diagnostic Interview Schedule: Its history, characteristics and validity. *Archives of General Psychiatry, 38,* 381–389.

Rutter, M. (1989). Pathways from childhood to adult life. *Journal of Child Psychology and Psychiatry, 30,* 23–51.

Schlesselman, J. J. (1982). *Case-control studies: Design, conduct, analysis.* New York: Oxford University Press.

Solomon, Z., & Bromet, E. (1982). The role of social factors in affective disorder: An assessment of the vulnerability model of Brown and his colleagues. *Psychological Medicine, 12,* 123–130.

Sorenson, S. B., Rutter, C. M., & Aneshensel, C. S. (1991). Depression in the community: An investigation into age of onset. *Journal of Consulting and Clinical Psychology, 59,* 541–546.

Srole, L., & Fischer, A. K. (1989). Changing lives and well-being: The midtown Manhattan panel study 1954–1976. *Acta Psychiatrica Scandinavica, 79*(Suppl.), 35–44.

Stone, A. A., Kessler, R. C., & Haythornthwaite, J. A. (1991). The measurement of daily events and experiences. *Journal of Personality, 148,* 1501–1504.

Thoits, P. A. (1983). Dimensions of life events that influence psychological distress: An evaluation and synthesis of the literature. In H. B. Kaplan (Ed.), *Psychosocial stress: Trends in theory and research* (pp. 33–103). New York: Academic Press.

Turner, R. J., & Avison, W. R. (1989). Gender and depression: Assessing exposure and vulnerability to life events in a chronically strained population. *Journal of Nervous and Mental Disease, 177*(8), 443–455.

Weissman, M. M., Leaf, P. J., Tischler, G. L., Blazer, D. G., Karno, M., Bruce, M. L., & Florio, L. P. (1988). Affective disorders in five United States communities. *Psychological Medicine, 18,* 141–153.

Wheaton, B. (1978). The sociogenesis of psychological disorder: Reexamining the causal issues with longitudinal data. *American Sociological Review, 43,* 383–403.

VI

The Dependent Variable in Stress Research

10

The Advantages of Indexes over Diagnoses in Scientific Assessment

JOHN MIROWSKY

INDEXES CLARIFY WHAT DIAGNOSES CONFOUND

The power of an index flows from its unity and simplicity. Researchers can choose to assess troublesome thoughts, moods, and behaviors using either indexes or diagnoses. Both forms of assessment represent syndromes, which are groups of signs and symptoms that collectively characterize a disorder; however, these forms embody two opposite views of proper representation. This chapter argues for the use of indexes in research on stress and mental, emotional, or behavioral problems. It begins by contrasting the concepts and procedures that distinguish indexes from diagnoses. Then it illustrates several ways that results based on indexes differ from those based on diagnoses. First, indexes reveal patterns of correlation that are obscured by the diagnostic discounting of symptoms in people with coincident traits. The case of depression in old age illustrates this point. Second, indexes help reduce the surface complexity of appearances to the most concise useful set of distinctions and assessments. Diagnostic categories proliferate because each factor

JOHN MIROWSKY • Department of Sociology, Ohio State University, Columbus, Ohio 43210-1353.

Stress and Mental Health: Contemporary Issues and Prospects for the Future, edited by William R. Avison and Ian H. Gotlib. New York, Plenum Press, 1994.

261

taken into consideration varies in intensity and the factors coincide in an extremely large number of combinations, each of which appears distinctive. Third, indexes minimize the attenuation of correlations and significance tests, and they minimize bias from stereotypes and other sources of diagnostic preconception. By using indexes, stress researchers can distinguish effects on thoughts, feelings, and behaviors from effects on the likelihood of getting a diagnosis net of, or adjusting for, the symptoms. Indexes avoid the confounding of diagnostic preconception with empirical correlation.

Indexes and Diagnoses: Contrasting Forms of Assessment

An index represents an attribute distinct from others by pattern of correlation and place in a causal structure. Indexes get refined through the dissection of nodes and connections in a causal structure, as when the mood of depression is distinguished from the personal losses and the endocrine dysfunctions that may cause it. Table 1 summarizes the properties of indexes. The elements of an index correlate more highly among themselves than with other things. They also share a distinct profile of correlations with other things. One element does not cause or result from the others; the elements correlate because they share a single common factor, which is the extent or intensity of the attribute they reflect. Thus indexes represent syndromes defined as empirically distinct patterns of correlation.

In contrast to an index, a diagnosis binds distinct attributes into a distinctive pattern. Table 1 contrasts the qualities of indexes with those of diagnoses. Diagnoses get refined through differentiation of whole patterns on multiple levels, as when otherwise identical emotional states are defined as grief if the person's spouse died recently or as melancholia if a cortisol nonsuppression test is positive. Together, the elements create a distinctive impression; changing one element changes the overall impression. Diagnoses categorize persons based on combinations of attributes, labeling accordingly. Often diagnoses draw information from more than one causal level, looking for distinctive sequences of cause and effect, or separating similar presentations that have different apparent origins. Thus diagnoses represent syndromes defined as noticeably different combinations of attributes.

Etiological research creates representations of the causal relationships among attributes. Measuring with indexes enhances the detail and precision of those representations. Much of the reason is that an index represents the degree of a single attribute. It does not embody inferences about what caused the attribute to be present to such a degree, nor

Table 1. Indexes Compared to Diagnoses

	Index	Diagnosis
Definition	A composite of information assessing the degree of an attribute.	A categorical judgment based on the assessment of one or more attributes.
Basic operation	Individuals are assigned scores representing their standing relative to others on the magnitude of the attribute.	Individuals are sorted into classes, based on the similarity of assessed attributes to category descriptions.
Level of measurement	Ordinal, interval, or ratio.	Nominal (dichotomous).
Use	Gauging the relative degree of an attribute, and ordering persons according to the assessment.	Categorizing persons based on their attributes, and labeling them accordingly.
Component information	Can be self-reports, informant reports, observer appraisals, and mechanical or chemical measures.	Can be self-reports, informant reports, observer appraisals, and mechanical or chemical measures.
Proper construction	The parts of an index correlate more highly among themselves than with other things, and share a distinctive profile of correlations with other things.	The rules of a diagnosis embody and prescribe someone's (or some group's) informed judgment about the proper response to specified information.
Standardization	Standard indexes can be developed and adopted.	Standard diagnoses can be developed and adopted.
Level of generality	Indexes can be designed to represent general factors, or distinct specific factors.	Diagnoses can be designed to represent broad classes, or sets of specific subclasses.
Exclusiveness	Distinct idexes are not mutually exclusive. The correlation between specific indexes can be positive, null, or negative. By construction, distinct indexes have reproducible independent variance. Whatever the direction and size of the correlation between two distinct indexes, *some* individuals score high on one and low on the other, some score high on both, and some score low on both.	Distinct diagnoses are mutually exclusive on some level. Sometimes the categories are defined as mutually exclusive. Sometimes the categories are ranked by precedence. Sometimes one of a person's possible categories is designated as central or original. Ultimately, each individual is placed in a single or primary category.

(*continued*)

Table 1. (*Continued*)

	Index	Diagnosis
Validation	By empirical correlations of the parts.	By conformance of the whole with a concept.
As syndrome	Represents a syndrome defined as an empirically distinct set of correlated symptoms and signs.	Represents a syndrome defined as a set of symptoms and signs that appear distinctive in combination.
Level of causality	A proper index consists of parts on the same causal level. One element does not cause or result from the others. The elements covary because of a common factor, which is the extent or intensity of the attribute they measure.	A proper diagnosis may draw information from many causal levels. Often, diagnosis looks for a train of causes and effects thought characteristic of a specific type of problem. Often, diagnosis categorizes by inferred cause.
Refinement	Indexes get refined through the dissection of nodes and connections in a causal structure, as when the mood of depression is distinguished from the personal losses and the endocrine dysfunctions that may cause it.	Diagnoses get refined through differentiation of whole patterns on multiple levels, as when otherwise identical emotional states are defined as grief if the person's spouse died recently or as melancholia if a cortisol nonsuppression test is positive.
Reliability	Evaluated by the degree of inter-item and item-total correlation. An index cannot be reliable if composed of uncorrelated items.	Evaluated by the amount of inter-rater agreement in excess of chance agreement. A diagnosis *can* be reliable even though based on uncorrelated phenomena, *if* the phenomena are obvious and the rules are clear and observed.
Decision rules	Indexes do not embody decision rules. They provide information on the degree or extent of a factor in the decision. Separating decision rules from assessment allows the rules to be varied, evaluated, or adjusted to circumstances.	Diagnoses embody rules about which factors to consider, and what amounts and combinations to require. The built-in rules may not be optimum.

does it mix the assessments of correlationally distinct attributes. In contrast, diagnoses fuse elements that have different profiles of correlation with other variables, thus confounding each one's pattern with that of the others. Diagnoses also fuse inferred causes with presentation, thus collapsing the causal structure that analysis seeks to model.

No matter how clever, data analysis cannot recover or clarify information abandoned or confounded at the stage of measurement. Psychiatric diagnoses discount some problems captured by indexes and emphasize others. Diagnosis begins by noting symptoms that must be present to a stated degree for at least a stated period, then it rules out people whose symptoms are discounted for various reasons. The discounting process builds preconceptions into diagnostic data that confound the patterns of symptom factors with patterns of discounting.

The Example of Depression in Old Age

The current literature on depression in old age provides an example of a relationship revealed by an index but obscured by diagnostic discounting. The following paragraphs will show that the probability of qualifying for a diagnosis of depression and the indexed levels of sadness and malaise have opposite age patterns. Contrary to what some researchers think, the difference does not reflect physiogenic bias in the index. Rather, it reflects diagnostic rules excluding people whose sadness and malaise seems to have an obvious or mundane explanation. In other words, it reflects diagnostic rules excluding problems that appear to be common responses to stress.

Opposite Age Patterns of Symptoms and Diagnoses

Although average levels of sadness and malaise climb in old age, the probability of qualifying for a clinical diagnosis of depression drops to near zero (Kennedy et al., 1989; Newmann, 1989; Mirowsky & Ross, 1992). Figure 1 graphs the results of logistic regressions fitted by Newmann (1989) to the results of two sets of studies relating depression to age. (see Appendix A; Newmann, 1989, for details.) The unbroken line summarizes the results of five studies that measure depression using the Center for Epidemiologic Studies depression index (CES-D). The figure shows the overall age pattern of "severe" depression, defined as CES-D scores of 16 or greater. (A curve fitted to mean scores by age has the same basic shape. I show the categorical version to simplify comparison with the diagnostic studies.) As measured using the index, the prevalence of serious depression drops in successively older adults up to mid-

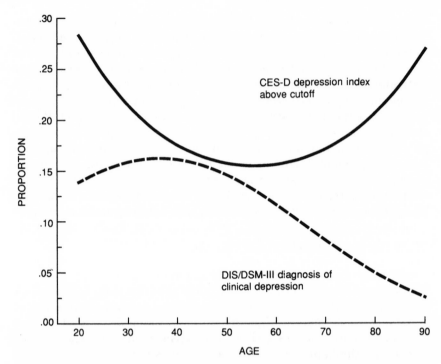

Figure 1. The rules for diagnosing clinical depression reverse the age pattern of depressed feelings. The curves represent quadratic logistic regressions fitted by Newmann (1989) to published data on age-specific proportions, as described in Appendix A.

dle age, and then rises into old age. By this definition, the oldest adult age groups are among the *most* depressed.

In contrast, the broken line in Figure 1 summarizes the results of four studies that measure depression using the Diagnostic Interview Schedule (DIS) based on the American Psychiatric Association's diagnostic and statistical manual (DSM-III). The figure shows the overall age pattern of "clinical" depression, defined as qualifying for a diagnosis of affective disorder other than bipolar (manic) depression sometime within 6 months of the survey. As measured by diagnosis, the prevalence of clinical depression rises in successively older adults up to middle age, then drops. By this definition, the oldest adult age groups are among the *least* depressed.

Malaise and Potential Physiogenic Bias

Some researchers think the difference in age patterns of depression found using indexes and diagnoses result from measurement bias attributable to infirmity and poor health among the elderly (Newmann, 1989). Indexes and diagnoses both reflect malaise and lassitude, as well as sadness and despondency, but in different ways. Indexes *sum* malaise and sadness, whereas diagnoses *require* both malaise and sadness. Average index scores go up with one, the other, or both; rates of diagnoses go up only if malaise and sadness both go up. The different constructions suggest an explanation of the divergent results: Malaise may rise in old age while sadness declines.

The physiological-bias argument appears in two forms. One says indexes overestimate depression among the elderly, by mistaking disease and infirmity for depression (e.g., Blazer, 1982). The other says diagnoses underestimate depression among the elderly, because depression presents as malaise without sadness in the elderly more than in other adults (e.g., Blazer & Williams, 1980; Salzman & Shader, 1978). Both forms of the argument are incorrect, as shown below.

Uniform Age Patterns of Malaise and Sadness

Indexes of depression refer to malaise as well as sadness because the two correlate positively and share the same profile of correlations with other factors, including age. Figure 2 shows average scores by age on two subsets of items from the CES-D. The data come from a 1990 nationwide U.S. telephone survey (for details, see Appendix A; Mirowsky & Ross, 1992). The figure shows the same age pattern of depressed vitality as of depressed mood. The parallel exists because psychometric techniques for constructing and refining indexes combine items that have similar patterns of correlation. If psychometricians had found a major difference in the correlational profiles of sadness and malaise, they would have indexed the two separately and treated them as distinct nodes in the causal structure. Of course, it was possible that such a difference had been overlooked. Figure 2, however, shows that the index correctly treats malaise and sadness as interchangeable aspects of depression in their relation to age.

A psychometric covariance model confirms that sadness and malaise share the same profile of correlations with age, education, minority status, family income, and perceived control of one's own life (Mirowsky & Ross, 1991, p. 139). Figure 3 diagrams the model, which has both latent and observed variables. The presence of a latent variable (also called a "factor") is inferred from correlations among observed ones. In the model, depression is a latent variable. (So are agreement orientation and the sense of control.) Its presence is inferred from the correlations of sadness and malaise subindexes with other measured variables, such as age or agreement with statements claiming responsibility for the bad

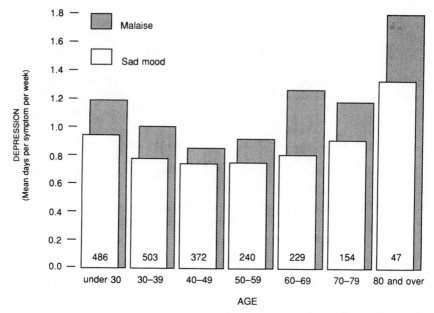

Figure 2. Malaise and sad mood both show the same age pattern. The late-life rise in scores on the depression index (CES-D) cannot be attributed to a rise in malaise alone. The data come from the 1990 U.S. Survey of Work, Family, and Well-Being (described in Appendix A).

events or outcomes in one's life (I_B). (Variables labeled e or U are random components, like the residual in a regression.) Each arrow in the model represents a statistically significant regression coefficient, shown in its standardized (normalized) form.

A path is a connection between two variables formed by traveling in the direction of the arrows from one to the other. Some paths are direct, such as the one from family income to the sense of control. Other paths are indirect, such as the one from family income to depression *through* the sense of control. Notice that all paths to sadness and malaise are indirect, going through the depression factor. (The only exceptions are the paths from random measurement error, e, which affect the observed subindexes directly).

The hypotheses embodied in the model illustrated in Figure 3 are tested by comparing actual correlations with ones implied by the model. For example, the model says the correlation of the malaise subindex with family income is $(.262)(-.347)(.759) = -.071$ after adjusting for age, education, and minority status. It says the correlation of the sadness

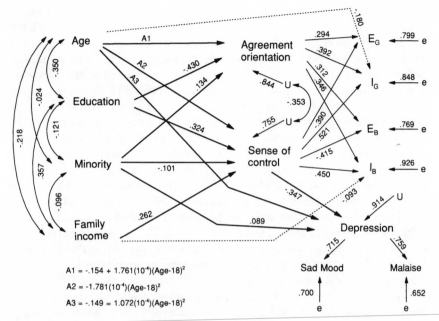

Figure 3. A psychometric covariance model shows that age does not affect malaise apart from its impact through depression (Mirowsky & Ross, 1991, reproduced with the permission of the American Sociological Association). The data come from the 1985 Illinois Survey of Well-Being described in Appendix A. Depression, the sense of control, and agreement orientation are latent factors implied by correlations among the other variables. The indexes E_G, I_G, E_B and I_B represent agreement with statements about the control of events and outcomes in one's own life. E represents external (fatalistic) statements, and I represents internal (instrumental) ones. G refers to good outcomes, and B to bad ones.

subindex with family income is $(.262)\,(-.347)\,(.715) = -.065$ after the adjustments. Notice that the implied correlation with malaise differs from that with sadness by a ratio of $.759/.715 = 1.062$. In other words, the model says the correlation with malaise equals 1.062 times the correlation with sadness. The model says the same ratio holds for correlations of sadness and malaise with all observed variables. including age.[1]

Significance tests indicate that the correlations implied by the model

[1] Age correlations are more complex than others because many are not linear. (Note that several paths from age in Figure 3 have coefficients—A1, A2, and A3—that change with age.) In the case of depression, the correlation is low around age 45, where being 10 years older or younger makes little difference. The correlation is high around age 75, where being 10 years older or younger makes a large difference. Nevertheless, the impact of greater age on average levels of malaise remains proportional to the impact on average levels of sadness.

in Figure 3 fit the data quite well. A psychometric covariance model is tested by comparing the matrix of correlations implied by the model to the actual observed correlations (Bentler, 1989). If the model neglects to specify *any* direct path that actually exists, the implied correlation matrix will be significantly different from the observed one. For the model in Figure 3, a chi-square test says the probability is .212 that the implied correlations differ from the observed ones solely by chance. A Lagrange multiplier test (Bentler, 1989) says that none of the direct paths to malaise (bypassing depression) that could be added to the model would significantly improve the fit between implied and observed correlations.

All the paths to sadness and malaise go through their common factor of depression. No path from age (or from any other variable) runs directly to malaise, bypassing general depression. Apart from its effect on depression, age does not significantly effect malaise; neither does education, minority status, family income, or the sense of control.

If advanced age increases malaise solely in proportion to increased sadness, then what accounts for the discrepant age curves in Figure 1? The rules for diagnosing major clinical depression empirically rule out much of the sadness and despair found among the elderly. As Figure 1 shows, the low and declining odds of qualifying for a psychiatric diagnosis of major clinical depression among older age groups does not result from low and declining feelings of depression. As Figures 2 and 3 show, it does not result from diagnostic elimination of bias attributable to infirmity and sickness, because no such bias exists. Most likely, it results from diagnostic discounting.

Discounting for Grief, Sickness, and Dysfunction

Current psychiatric philosophy views clinical depression as essentially endogenous—springing from the organism rather than from its environment and history (Newmann, 1989, p. 160). Sadness and malaise are necessary, but not sufficient, to qualify for the diagnosis (Boyd, Weissman, Thompson, & Myers, 1982). No matter how badly they feel, people with apparent, mundane reasons for feeling depressed often get excluded from a diagnosis of clinical depression. Weissman and Klerman (1980) argue that "without some diagnostic criteria for who is 'in' or 'out' of a diagnostic class, such as depression, it is not possible to decide whether a given person or group of persons are clinically depressed as distinct from unhappy and discontented because of social deprivation or the frustration of their personal wishes" (p. 1424). Newmann (1989) says diagnosis tries to "distinguish between persons . . . experiencing a normal distress reaction to the vagaries of everyday life and others whose symptom experiences suggest an abnormal or clinical depression"

(p. 160). Notably, people who are disabled or sick, grieving the death of a spouse, or taking drugs often get excluded.

Discounting corrupts the pure correlation profiles of indexed attributes. Censored measures hide patterns that should be revealed through analysis. In the example of depression, censoring hides the age pattern of sadness and malaise *and* the reasons for the pattern from analytic recovery. Figure 4 illustrates the effect of censoring the sick, disabled, or widowed, using the 1990 U.S. data mentioned above. (The data do not contain information on drug use, so drug takers are not censored in the example.) A whole bar represents the proportion of an age group reporting sadness and malaise in the top 20% of the total sample. The

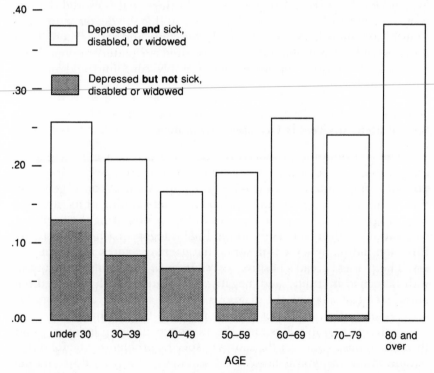

Figure 4. Because sickness, disability, and widowhood rise in late life, depressed vitality and mood in their absence decline. The pattern suggests that clinical depression declines in late life because diagnostic rules exclude those with obvious or mundane reasons for feeling depressed. The data come from the 1990 U.S. Survey of Work, Family, and Well-Being described in Appendix A.

open part of the bar represents those who are both depressed *and* sick, disabled, or widowed. The filled part represents those who are depressed *but not* also sick, disabled, or widowed. The edited prevalence of depression decreases with age because the proportion cut increases.

Diagnostic discounting purges information sought in data analysis. Imagine parallel incremental regression analyses using data on people over the age of 40. The first regression analysis uses the uncensored measure represented by the whole bars in Figure 4, and the second uses the censored measure represented by the filled parts. Both analyses begin by regressing the depression measure on age, then adjust for sickness, disability, and widowhood. The first regression would show that uncensored depression rises with age for those over 40, but that it declines with age after adjustment for sickness, dysfunction, and widowhood. Thus the uncensored analysis reveals both the age pattern and its explanation. The second regression would show that censored depression decreases with age for those over 40, and that the decrease does not vanish with adjustment for sickness, dysfunction, and widowhood. Thus the censored analysis would show the censored age pattern and mask the explanation. Censored measures irretrievably confound and obscure patterns of correlation.

Simple Elements versus Layered Distinctions

The confounding produced by censoring gets worse as diagnostic categories get more refined. Partitioning a diagnostic category into progressively finer subcategories creates the impression of convergence on the essence of a problem, and thus on an understanding of its cause. In fact, progressive subdivision obscures causes by obscuring the source of correlations with membership in the final category. Each diagnostic bifurcation indirectly screens in some characteristics and screens out others. The process creates positive correlations of the resulting diagnosis with screened-in traits, and negative correlations with screened-out ones.[2] Correlations with the diagnosis hide the specific trait responsible for the correlation in the set of traits required for the diagnosis.

A simple example illustrates the advantage of using indexes rather than diagnoses to uncover the causes of specific problems. The following outline mimics a typical nosological scheme.[3] The procedure defines

[2]Metaphorically, if a club's membership rules discourage women from joining, then membership will correlate negatively with being female.

[3]The example is much more orderly and straightforward than actual current diagnostic systems.

melancholia as sadness and enervation with no apparent cause such as grief or illness, but with definite signs of cortisol dysregulation:

POPULATION
Very sad?
I. No > affective normality
II. *Yes* > affective distress
   Enervated?
   A. No > blue mood
   B. *Yes* > affective disorder
      Has an apparent reason for depression, such as grief or illness?
      1. Yes > dysthymia
      2. *No* > clinical depression
      Wakes early, feels worst in the morning, and gets agitated?
      a. No > essential depression
      b. *Yes* > *melancholia*

Suppose an epidemiologist finds that the proportion of males is greater in people classified as melancholic than in the population as a whole. Which step screens out the females? Are females less sad? Less lethargic? More likely to have an apparent reason for feeling bad? Less likely to wake too early, feel worst in the morning, or get markedly agitated? To find out, the epidemiologist needs indexes of sadness, enervation, reasons for feeling depressed, and signs of cortisol dysregulation.

Null findings highlight the need for indexes even more. Suppose the epidemiologist finds no association between education and melancholia. Is education uncorrelated with each and every distinction that leads to the diagnosis? Or is screening out on some levels (e.g., educated people feel less sad and enervated) countered by screening in on others (e..g, educated people have fewer apparent reasons for feeling depressed)?

The clinical researcher needs indexes, too, for much the same reason the epidemiologist does. Suppose a clinical researcher finds that one particular treatment seems to work better than others for people classified as melancholic. Why? Does it ease the sadness? The lethargy? The cortisol dysregulation? Or is there an interaction? Does it reduce sadness and lethargy more, the greater the degree of cortisol dysregulation present at baseline? Indexes of each factor make it possible to answer such questions. Whatever the type of research, indexes provide the clarity and specificity lost in diagnosis.

EFFICIENT ASSESSMENT

Indexes Allow Concise Sets of Concepts

Indexes help reduce the surface complexity of appearances to the most concise useful set of distinctions. Diagnostic categories proliferate because each assessed attribute varies in intensity, and because distinct attributes can coincide in an extremely large number of distinctive combinations. Diagnostic schemes change endlessly, with drifting trends in the intensities and combinations seen as noticeably different. The proliferation and drift of categories can seem like progress. Large numbers of categories make knowledge seem detailed; new categories make knowledge seem advanced. Unlike diagnoses, indexes progress toward simplicity—toward the smallest useful set. In physics, measures are defined as functions of four elementary properties: time, distance, density, and charge. In color theory, all colors blend three primaries plus black in varying saturations and combinations. To paraphrase Einstein, we need a set of measures that is as small as possible, but not smaller.

Obviously, we do not know yet the minimum number of dimensions needed to describe adequately all mental, emotional, and behavioral problems. By using indexes rather than diagnoses, though, one can greatly reduce the set of measures without yet knowing how small the smallest workable set will be. DSM-III describes over 160 psychiatric diagnoses applicable to adults; DSM-IV describes even more. Yet correlations among the symptoms of psychiatric patients reveal only about 16 distinct factors: inappropriate or bizarre appearance or behavior, belligerence and negativism, agitation and excitement, retardation and emotional withdrawal, speech disorganization, suspicion or a sense of persecution, hallucinations and delusions, grandiosity, depression and anxiety, tendency to suicide or self-mutilation, somatic concerns, social isolation, disorientation and memory problems, antisocial impulses or acts, drug abuse, and alcohol abuse (Endicott & Spitzer, 1972; Spitzer, Endicott, Fleiss, & Cohen, 1970; Spitzer, Fleiss, Endicott, & Cohen, 1967). Indexes representing the 16 factors provide efficiency an order of magnitude greater than 160 diagnoses.

The indexes provide greater precision, as well as greater efficiency. The precision of 16 indexes exceeds that of 160 diagnoses because the number of combinations of 16 ordinal variables is very large. Suppose researchers and clinicians score each symptom factor as absent or low (1), moderate (2), or intense (3). The 16 trichotomized factors produce $3^{16} =$ 43,046,721 distinctive categories. Rather than iterate toward a ponderous DSM, we should iterate toward a more efficient and precise set of indexes.

Indexes Solve Combination and Boundary Problems

Indexes sidestep the endless shuffling of combinations and boundaries. When properly constructed, an index represents a single, correlationally distinct attribute on an ordered scale. In contrast, the defining features of a diagnostic category typically refer to several correlationally distinct factors that, when seen together, seem different from other combinations. The separate factors assessed in a diagnosis have considerable independent variance. In fact, a diagnosis can require a combination of factors that have null or negative correlations, so long as the combination appears distinctive. More commonly, a diagnosis may require a combination of factors whose correlations are spurious as a result of common origins in threatening and disorganized family and socioeconomic environments. In either case, the variety of real combinations exceeds the number of available diagnoses by many orders of magnitude.

A relatively small set of indexes can describe an enormous variety of mixes and blends with great precision, and with no need for cobbled types. Diagnostic schemes attempt to cope with the variety of possible combinations by making very broad distinctions, and by defining some categories as in between, just short of, or left over from others (Mirowsky, 1990). In DSM-III, schizoaffective disorder blends schizophrenia and depression. Schizophreniform personality is just short of schizophreniform disorder, which is just short of schizophrenia. Cases that cannot be classified as just short of any particular category are diagnosed as "unspecified" if the case does not provide sufficient information for making a judgment, "residual" if the case does not fit any of the defined subcategories in a larger class, and "atypical" if a case does not quite meet the minimum criteria for one class and blends aspects of others.

Indexes sidestep confusion created by shared attributes. By design, no two indexes may share the same indicator. For example, if "no hope for the future" is part of the depression index, it cannot be part of any other index. A diagnostic category often refers to one or more attributes also specified by other diagnostic categories; for example, grandiosity and agitation are taken as signs of bipolar depression if the person also has bouts of sadness and dejection, but as signs of schizophrenia if the person also has delusions or hallucinations. Likewise, suicidal impulses may be taken as signs of unipolar depression or of schizophrenia. To some extent, all psychiatric diagnoses refer to either emotional distress, cognitive dysfunction, or social dysfunction. Shared attributes cloud distinctions and thus obscure the meaning of research results.

By design, one index does not share components with another, separate index. As a consequence, the correlation between two indexes reflects the natural covariance of the assessed factors, not the percentage of items the two indexes have in common. In contrast, shared attributes spuriously magnify the correlations between diagnoses. For example, the distinction between depression and schizophrenia is among the most basic. Nevertheless, the odds of qualifying for a diagnosis of schizophrenia are 28.5 times greater for those who also qualify for a diagnosis of major depression than for those who do not (Boyd et al., 1984). To put this multiple in perspective, the odds of getting lung cancer are only 14 times greater for those who smoke than for those who do not, even though more than 90% of all lung cancer is attributable to smoking (Mausner & Bahn, 1974). In fact, qualifying for one major psychiatric diagnosis increases the odds of qualifying for all the others; the multiples range from 1.6 for alcoholism and somatization to 89.1 for schizophrenia and manic (bipolar) depression, with a geometric mean of 10.3. It seems likely that substantial portions of the correlations between diagnostic categories result from the sharing of attributes rather than from the empirical correlation of attributes.

Indexes make it possible to assess the correlation attributable to shared causes or cascading effects without bias resulting from shared components. Some causal factors contribute to a variety of problems. In particular, a variety of mental, emotional, and behavioral problems concentrate in people in low socioeconomic positions or with family histories of psychiatric problems (e.g., Coryell & Zimmerman, 1988; Holzer et al., 1986). Also, problems may cascade from one factor to another, as when alcohol abuse leads to belligerence and memory problems, and then to social isolation and depression. Diagnostic surveys cannot distinguish artificial correlation caused by shared attributes from substantive correlation as a result of shared causes or cascading problems. Indexes solve that problem.

MINIMIZING ATTENUATION AND PRECONCEPTION

Attenuation and preconception make the results found with diagnostic measures different from those found with indexes. Diagnostic assessment weakens correlations by ignoring the differences in symptoms within diagnostic categories; this is called *diagnostic attenuation*. Diagnostic assessment also shapes correlations to conform with ideas about them; this is called *diagnostic preconception*.

Diagnostic attenuation produces uniform differences, making its effects simpler to assess than those of preconception. The first of the following subsections describes the causes and consequences of diagnostic attenuation. Briefly, it reduces the size of correlations and the power of statistical tests, making larger samples necessary for studies that diagnose rather than index.

The second subsection describes the manifestations and sources of diagnostic preconception. Briefly, preconception produces correlation of a trait with the likelihood of diagnosis that is not explained by the trait's correlation with symptoms. Diagnostic preconceptions reflect stereotypes, discounting rules, communication gaps, and clinical realities that contradict social realities.

Diagnostic Attenuation: Reduced Correlation and Statistical Power

Diagnostic attenuation results from dichotomizing ordinal, interval, or ratio assessments. Inherently, diagnosis abandons information on differences in symptoms among those who qualify for the diagnosis, and it likewise abandons information on differences in symptoms among those who do not qualify (Mirowsky & Ross, 1989). The total correlation of symptoms with an attribute such as age or chronic economic strain has two parts: (a) the mean difference in the attribute between those who qualify for the diagnosis and those who do not, and (b) the correlation within diagnostic categories between symptoms and the attribute. Diagnostic assessment attenuates correlations by ignoring the correlation remaining within diagnostic categories (Mirowsky & Ross, 1989).

Using a complete symptom index minimizes attenuation, thus producing clearer results with smaller samples. Where the psychiatric problem appears as a dependent variable, attenuation exhibits predictable and uniform manifestations: smaller mean differences, correlation and regression coefficients nearer to zero, and larger standard errors (Bohrnstedt & Carter, 1971). Together, these limit the ability to detect small but true effects (Mirowsky & Ross, 1991). Thus attenuation reduces the *number* of significant results while increasing the *proportion* of all positive tests that are false positives.[4] Generally speaking, attenuation increases as the number of persons qualifying for the diagnosis decreases. To compensate, diagnostic surveys must enlist much larger samples, and sometimes they must combine two or more diagnostic categories into one in order to get enough respondents in the "case" group (e.g., Aneshensel, Rutter, & Lachenbruch, 1991).

[4]The choice of an alpha level fixes the conditional probability of a false positive *t*-test given a true correlation of zero. Attenuation does not change the number of associations that truly are zero, so it does not change the expected number of false positives. Attenuation does, however, reduce the ability to detect a true nonzero association as significant. Thus dichotomization increases the proportion of all significant effects that are false positive.

Table 2 illustrates diagnostic attenuation. It shows the correlations of 25 variables with a diagnosis of major or minor depression (SADS-RDC) and with an index of depression (CES-D; Lewinsohn, Hoberman, & Rosenbaum, 1988; Radloff, 1977; Spitzer & Endicott, 1978). (Nineteen percent of the sample qualified for a diagnosis of depression. Appendix A describes the survey.) Of the 25 variables, 19 (76%) correlate more strongly with the index score than with the diagnosis. On average, the correlation of a variable in Table 2 with the index score is 36.7% larger than its corresponding correlation with the diagnosis (the geometric mean ratio of $r_{x,Ix}/r_{x,Dx} = 1.367$). The general pattern of smaller correlations with the diagnosis than with the index results from diagnostic attenuation.

Diagnostic Preconception: Extrafactual and Counterfactual Correlation

Preconceptions affect diagnostic correlations through practices such as stereotyping or discounting. The effect of a variable on diagnosis, *adjusting for the level of symptoms,* reveals the preconception. Diagnostic preconception produces less uniform and predictable effects than those of diagnostic attenuation. Whereas attenuation always reduces the size of a correlation, preconception can enlarge, reduce, or even reverse the sign of a correlation. Figure 5 illustrates two opposite types of diagnostic preconception. Extrafactual preconceptions emphasize a correlate of sadness and malaise; counterfactual preconceptions de-emphasize one.

The diagram on the left of Figure 5 shows the extrafactual effect of sex on the likelihood of qualifying for a SADS-RDC diagnosis of major depression. The values for *a, b,* and *c* are standardized regression coefficients. They represent, respectively, (a) the effect of being female (rather than male) on the indexed level of sadness and malaise; (b) the effect of being female on the likelihood of qualifying for a diagnosis, *adjusting for the level of sadness and malaise;* and (c) the effect of sadness and malaise on the likelihood of qualifying for a diagnosis, adjusting for sex. The diagram shows that females feel more depressed than males (*a* = .089). It also shows that, at any given level of sadness and malaise, females are more likely to qualify for a diagnosis of depression than males (*b* = .256). The direct effect is 5.8 times greater than the indirect effect through symptoms.

The diagram on the right of Figure 5 shows the counterfactual effect of externalizing success on the likelihood of qualifying for a SADS-RDC diagnosis of major depression. Externalizing success means

Table 2. Correlations with Depression:
Diagnostic Attenuation and Preconception

Correlate X	$(r_{x,Dx} =)$ $b + ac$	$(r_{x,Ix} =)$ a	b	c	$(DPR =)$ b/ac
Extrafactual					
1. Interviewer-judged chronicity	.780	.134	.724	.419	12.8
2. Female	.300	.089	.256	.493	5.8
3. Prior 2 week episode	.396	.235	.291	.448	2.5
4. Age	−.142	−.090	−.096	.507	2.1
5. Other psychopathology	.535	.783	.389	.251	2.0
6. Self-reported severity	.524	.633	.329	.308	1.7
7. Interpersonal discomfort	.201	.176	.114	.496	1.3
8. Social contact rate	−.136	−.128	−.017	.509	1.1
Perifactual					
9. Minor daily stressors	.318	.360	.152	.461	0.9
10. Self dissatisfaction	.420	.595	.175	.412	0.7
11. Expect good outcomes	−.371	−.508	−.147	.442	0.7
12. Unemployed	.057	.067	.023	.514	0.7
13. Low self-esteem	.363	.501	.139	.446	0.6
14. Income	−.123	−.157	−.043	.509	0.5
15. Irrational beliefs	.240	.329	.079	.490	0.5
16. Major life events	.091	.128	.025	.513	0.4
17. Marriage difficulties	.228	.374	.041	.501	0.2
18. Externalize failure	.120	.210	.012	.513	0.1
19. Pleasant activities	−.126	−.228	−.009	.514	0.1
Counterfactual					
20. Expects bad outcomes	.135	.287	−.014	.520	−0.1
21. Paranoia	.180	.387	−.023	.525	−0.1
22. Perception of control	−.119	−.339	.063	.537	−0.3
23. Education	−.033	−.100	.019	.519	−0.4
24. Divorced or separated	.020	.099	−.031	.519	−0.6
25. Externalize success	.020	.200	−.087	.533	−0.8

Note: Each row represents a 3-variable path model, like the ones illustrated in Figure 5. The column $r_{x,Dx}$ shows the correlation with a diagnosis of depression (SADS-RDC). In the model, it represents the total effect of X on the diagnosis $(b + ac)$. The column $r_{x,Ix}$ shows the correlation with an index of symptoms (CES-D). In the model, it represents the effect of X on depressed mood and vitality (a). (The larger correlation is underlined.) The column b represents the effect of X on a diagnosis, adjusting for the level of symptoms. The column c represents the effect of symptoms on a diagnosis, adjusting for the level of X. (The implicit correlation between index and diagnosis $[c + ab]$ is .516 in all rows.) The final column shows the diagnostic preconception ratio (DPR), which represents the ratio of X's direct effect on a diagnosis (b) to its indirect effect through symptoms (ac). Diagnostic correlates with direct and indirect effects of the same sign are labeled "extrafactual" if the DPR is greater than 1.0, and as "perifactual" otherwise. Diagnostic correlates with direct effects on diagnosis opposite in sign from the indirect effect through symptoms are labeled "counterfactual." The correlations were reported by Lewinsohn, Hoberman, and Rosenbaum (1988; see Appendix A).

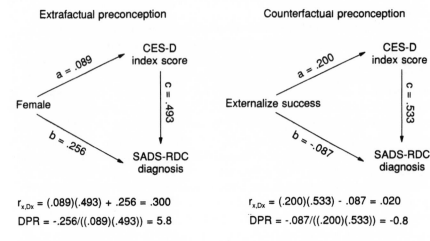

$r_{x,Dx} = (.089)(.493) + .256 = .300$

DPR = -.256/((.089)(.493)) = 5.8

$r_{x,Dx} = (.200)(.533) - .087 = .020$

DPR = -.087/((.200)(.533)) = -0.8

Figure 5. Diagnostic preconceptions augment or diminish effects on diagnosis through symptoms. Extrafactual preconceptions enlarge a correlation expected based on symptoms. Counterfactual preconceptions reduce, cancel, or reverse a correlation expected based on symptoms. The path diagrams correspond to rows 2 and 25 of Table 2. The data are from a study by Lewinsohn, Hoberman, and Rosenbaum (1988) described in Appendix A.

attributing the good events and outcomes in one's life to fate, chance, and the grace of others rather than to one's own effort and ability. The diagram shows that sadness and malaise increase with the tendency to externalize success ($a = .200$). It also shows that at any given level of sadness and malaise, externalizing success *reduces* the likelihood of qualifying for the diagnosis ($b = -.087$). Externalizing success has little overall correlation with the likelihood of diagnosis because the direct effect negates the impact of greater sadness and malaise. The direct effect cancels about 80% of the correlation through symptoms.

Table 2 lists the coefficients *a, b,* and *c* for each of 25 correlates of depression. The last column shows the diagnostic preconception ratio (DPR), which represents the ratio of a variable's direct effect on diagnosis, adjusting for symptoms, to its indirect effect through symptoms. The DPR is positive if the direct effect on diagnosis and the indirect effect through symptoms have the same sign. By definition, an *extrafactual* diagnostic correlation has a DPR greater than 1.0; a *perifactual* diagnostic correlation has a DPR between 1.0 and 0; and a *counterfactual* diagnostic correlation has a negative DPR. The DPR is negative if the direct effect on diagnosis is opposite in sign from the indirect effect through symptoms.

Some diagnostic preconception effects are explicit and intended, but many are unspecified or unintended. For example, the rules for diagnosing clinical depression explicitly emphasize chronicity, prior episodes, and severity, so those factors increase the odds of qualifying for a diagnosis at any given level of sadness and malaise. In contrast, the diagnostic rules do not explicitly recommend discounting the sadness and malaise of older persons, but they have that effect. In the somewhat young sample of Table 2, the linear correlation of sadness and malaise with age is negative. Age, however, also decreases the likelihood of qualifying for a diagnosis of depression at any given level of symptoms. (In row 4 of Table 2, a and b are both negative.) Implicitly, the older the person reporting the symptoms, the more diagnostic judgment discounts sadness and malaise. Note that in an older sample, age's diagnostic correlation would become counterfactual: In an older sample, the linear correlation of symptoms with age (column a) would become positive, but the direct effect of age on diagnosis net of symptoms (column b) would remain negative.

Most diagnostic preconceptions probably are implicit and unknown. Table 2 reveals a number of preconceptions about depression implicit in the SADS-RDC diagnosis. Among the implicit extrafactual correlations, that of sex has the largest DPR. As noted earlier, women report more symptoms of depression than men; however, women also are more likely to get a diagnosis of clinical depression than men reporting the same level of symptoms. To put it another way, diagnosis implicitly discounts men's reported feelings of depression compared to women's. This might reflect the assignment of despondent men to alternative diagnostic classes, such as substance abuse or antisocial personality. It also might reflect stereotyping.

Because women generally report more depression than men, clinicians may tend to see being female as a sign of depression, and being male as a sign of some other problem. When in doubt, an intuition of prior probability will sway the clinician to categorize a person as depressed if the person is female and as something else if the person is male. Although such stereotypes accrete around empirical correlations, they become self-reinforcing. The more that clinicians categorize women's problems as depression and men's problems as something else, the more they see that people classified as depressed are women rather than men, and thus guess that a woman's problem is depression and a man's problem is something else.

The other implicit extrafactual correlations in Table 2 reflect the impact of coincident problems on diagnostic judgments. Persons with forms of psychopathology other than depression report more sadness and malaise than others do, but also get a diagnosis of depression more frequently than others who feel equally despondent (row 5 of Table 2). Interpersonal discomfort and low rates of social contact increase the predicted level of symptoms, too, but they also increase the likelihood of diagnosis more than expected based on the symptoms alone (rows 6 and 7). As with the effect of sex, stereotyping may produce these effects on the diagnosis net of sadness and malaise. Because people with other mental and behavioral problems feel more depressed on average, clinicians see such problems as signs of depression. Because shy or isolated people feel more sad and lonely on average, clinicians see shyness and isolation themselves as signs of depression.

Some implicit diagnostic preconceptions are counterfactual. In such cases, the attribute's correlation with symptoms is opposite to its effect on the likelihood of getting the diagnosis at a given level of symptoms. Counterfactual correlations in Table 2 suggest that the SADS-RDC diagnosis treats emotionally healthy instrumentalism as pathological. For example, externalizing success has the largest negative DPR in Table 2. As noted earlier, people who attribute personal successes to luck, fate, or others tend to feel more depressed than those who claim responsibility for personal success. At any given level of sadness and malaise, however, disclaiming responsibility for success implicitly reduces the likelihood of getting a diagnosis of depression. In contrast, a general perception of control over one's life reduces the level of sadness and malaise, but increases the likelihood of getting the diagnosis at any given level of symptoms (row 22). It may be that instrumental people are more effective at getting their problems recognized. Or it may be that clinicians see instrumental beliefs as delusional, and thus as a sign of problems.

Some counterfactual effects reflect the exclusion or discounting of sadness and malaise with an obvious, mundane cause. For example, divorce and marital separation increase the level of depression (a in row 24), but slightly decrease the likelihood of getting a diagnosis adjusting for symptoms (b is negative). Other counterfactual effects may reflect the assignment of cases to other preemptive diagnostic categories. For example, paranoia increases the level of depression, but slightly decreases the likelihood that a given level of sadness and malaise will be diagnosed as depression.

Some counterfactual diagnostic correlations reflect the difference between social reality and clinical reality. Such effects project stereotypes from clinical experiences that distort the reality of the larger social order. Notably, in clinics treating mental, emotional, and behavioral problems, education increases the likelihood that the problem is emotional rather than cognitive or behavioral (Hollingshead & Redlich, 1958). In the general population, education decreases the average levels of emotional problems, as well as of cognitive and behavioral ones (Holzer et al., 1986; Mirowsky & Ross, 1989).

People with low levels of education generally do not seek professional treatment for depression and anxiety, but they often get sent for problems such as hallucinations, delusions, substance abuse, and bizarre behavior. Education increases self-referral for treatment of emotional distress, as well as the ability and willingness to pay for it. Thus, in the experience of many clinicians, patients whose problems are solely depression or anxiety are better educated than patients whose problems include hallucinations, delusions, bizarre behavior, aggression, or substance abuse. "When-in-doubt" stereotyping thus can produce counterfactual effects of education on the diagnosis of depression. The study reported in Table 2 took steps to minimize such clinical population bias (Lewinsohn et al., 1988). Nevertheless, education increases the likelihood of qualifying for a diagnosis of depression at any given level of sadness and malaise.

IMPLICATIONS FOR STRESS RESEARCH

Indexes provide advantages over diagnoses in research on stress. The most important is that indexes do not discount symptoms that coincide with stressors that might have caused the symptoms. The more that diagnoses try to distinguish clinical cases from cases of discontent, frustration, and deprivation, the more they eliminate the very information stress researchers seek. Also, the more that diagnoses eliminate the predictable cases, the less information the data based on them can yield. Indexes assess the level of symptoms without discounting those that coincide with sickness, disability, loss, or other possible causes. Thus indexes allow researchers to measure, test, and explain the correlations of those possible causes with symptoms.

A diagnostic measure would not be any better if it required the presence of a known stressor, rather than the absence of one. The problem is not just that diagnoses often eliminate the very cases stress researchers most want to study; it is that diagnoses often build ideas about correlations and causes into measures of the dependent variable. Some of those ideas are explicit in the diagnostic rules. One might find the rules and then make an educated guess about which results are artifacts (although few reports of diagnostic studies state the rules used), but some diagnostic preconceptions are implicit or indirect. For example, the SADS-RDC rules for diagnosing depression do not say to count women's sadness and malaise more than men's, or young persons' more than old persons', even though they have that effect.

The hidden preconceptions behind diagnostic rules can make interpretations uncertain. Suppose a researcher hypothesizes that women and men respond differently to stressors: Women get depressed and anxious, men get drunk and disorderly. Now suppose the researcher's diagnostic survey finds that a stressor correlates with the diagnosis of depression for women but not men, and with the diagnosis of alcoholism for men but not women. How much of this reflects the stereotypes implicit in diagnostic rules, and how much reflects differences in emotional and behavioral response? Clearly the researcher wants to measure the responses, not implicit diagnostic preconceptions. By design, indexes avoid confounding preconceptions with results. Using indexes, the researcher can be more certain that the results reflect subject response rather than observer presupposition.

Another important advantage of indexes for stress research is that they assess the full range of symptoms, not just the extremes that justify clinical action. At heart, stress research provides information meant to help people avoid those extremes. Most differences in mental, emotional, and behavioral problems occur within the large majority of people not qualified for a psychiatric diagnosis. Those differences provide most of the information available and relevant to prevention. This is true even of problems not traditionally studied across their full spectrum, such as paranoia and schizophrenia. For example, only about 1% of the general population has symptoms that qualify for a clinical diagnosis of schizophrenia (Holzer et al., 1986). Thus, typical community samples of 500 to 2000 might find about 5 to 20 persons qualified for the diagnosis, which is not enough to study. Nevertheless, even a sample of less than 500 finds scores of people who, at some time in the previous year, felt their minds dominated by outside forces, heard voices, had visions, felt possessed, felt they had special powers, felt nonexistent, heard their own thoughts as if spoken aloud, or felt their thoughts were being broadcast. Even in such a small sample, an index of schizophrenia provides rich information on the effects of stressors and of moderators such as mastery and flexibility on the commonness and intensity of these problems (Wheaton, 1985).

The final advantage of indexes for stress research lies in their efficiency, precision, and specificity. Perhaps the strongest claim made by proponents of diagnostic assessment is that diagnoses distinguish different types of problems better than indexes do (e.g., Eaton & Kessler, 1985). In fact, just the opposite is true. Diagnoses typically combine several distinct attributes into a single nominal, dichotomous variable. Thus correlations with the diagnosis do not show which diagnostic attribute is responsible for the correlation. In addition, two different diagnostic categories often share one or more defining attributes. Correlations between diagnoses reflect the proportion of attributes shared, and the more that two diagnostic categories (e.g., schizophrenia and depression) share the same defining attributes, the less one can distinguish findings and statements about one from those about the other.

By classifying symptoms rather than people, indexes distinguish, rather than blend, different types of problems. By design, each index represents one, and only one, distinct attribute. Two distinct indexes do not share elements. Thus indexes minimize confusion about the type of mental, emotional, or behavioral problem that arises. Appendix B lists symptoms that form indexes of depression, anxiety, delusions and hallucinations, and mistrust and paranoia. With the addition of questions about alcohol and drug abuse (e.g., Seeman, Seeman, & Budros, 1988), the indexes represent the range of problems related to stress that, when extreme or persistent, warrant attention. By using these or similar indexes, stress researchers maximize statistical power and analytic clarity. The strength of an index flows from its simplicity and unity.

ACKNOWLEDGMENTS

My thanks go to Catherine E. Ross for her advice and feedback, and for her work on Appendix B.

APPENDIX A: DATA

Figure 1: Contrasting CES-D and DIS/DSM-III Age Curves

The age curves in Figure 1 graph Newmann's (1989) quadratic logistic regressions. The formula for the logged odds of a CES-D index score above the cutoff is taken from Newmann's Table 5, model 2 (p. 158): $\text{logit}_{\text{CES-D}} = .169 + .067 \, (\text{Age}) + .0006 \, (\text{Age}^2)$. The regression is fit to the results of five studies that published proportions above the cutoff by age category. The formula for the logged odds of a DIS/DSM-III diagnosis is taken from Newmann's Table 6, model 2 (p. 160): $\text{logit}_{\text{DIS/DSM-III}} = -2.565 + .051 \, (\text{Age}) - .0007 \, (\text{Age}^2)$. The regression is fit to the results of four studies that published diagnostic prevalence by age category. The proportions are calculated by reversing the logit transformation: $P = e^{logit} / (1 + e^{logit})$.

Figures 2 and 4: Symptoms of Depression by Age

The data for Figures 2 and 4 are from the 1990 National Survey of Work, Family, and Well-Being, a telephone survey of a national probability sample of U.S. households. Random digit dialing ensured the inclusion of unlisted numbers. Within each household, the person 18 years or older with the most recent birthday was selected as the respondent. The response rate of 82.3% yielded a total of 2,031 respondents, ranging in age from 18 to 90.

The National Science Foundation supported this research with a grant (SES-8916154) to Catherine E. Ross. Sampling, pretesting, and interviewing were conducted by the Survey Research Laboratory of the University of Illinois.

"Sickness" is measured as self-reported poor health. "Disability" is difficulty walking, using stairs, kneeling or stooping, lifting or carrying things (e.g., a bag of groceries), using hands or fingers, hearing, or seeing. A respondent is considered "widowed" if his or her spouse died and he or she did not remarry.

Figure 3: Psychometric Covariance Model

The data for Figure 3 are from the 1985 Illinois Survey of Well-Being, a telephone survey of a statewide probability sample of households. Random digit dialing ensured the inclusion of unlisted numbers. Within each household, the person 18 years or older with the most recent birthday was selected as the respondent. The response rate of 79% yielded a total of 809 respondents, ranging in age from 18 to 85. The model in Figure 4 is based on the reports of the 713 respondents who provided complete information (including family income).

The Research Board of the University of Illinois supported the study. Sampling, pretesting, and interviewing were conducted by the Survey Research Laboratory of the University of Illinois.

Figure 5 and Table 2: Diagnostic Attenuation and Preconception

The correlations in Table 2 were reported by Lewinsohn, Hoberman, and Rosenbaum (1988) in their Table 1. The data are based on a 1978 panel survey of adults in Eugene and Springfield, Oregon. Depressive symptoms were assessed at intake using the Center for Epidemiologic Studies depression scale (CES-D; Radloff, 1977). Information collected in the same time period using the semistructured Schedule for Schizophrenia and Affective Disorder was used to make diagnoses according to the Research Diagnostic Criteria (SADS-RDC; Spitzer & Endicott, 1978). Details are given in the original report.

APPENDIX B: SHORT INDEXES

Respondents are asked, "How often in the past 12 months have you _____?" Responses are recorded as never (0), almost never (1), sometimes (2), fairly often (3), or often (4). Alternatively, respondents are asked, "Now I'm going to read a list of different feelings that people sometimes have. After each one I would like you to tell me on how many days you have felt this way during the last week. On how many days have you _____?" (0–7).

I. Distress
  A. Depression
    1. Mood
      Felt sad[a]
      Felt lonely[a]
      Felt you couldn't shake the blues[a]
      Felt depressed[b]
      Been bothered by things that don't usually bother you[b]
      Wondered if anything was worthwhile anymore[c]
      Felt that nothing turned out for you the way you wanted it to[c]
      Felt completely hopeless about everything
      Felt worthless
      Thought about taking your own life
    2. Malaise
      Felt that everything was an effort[a]
      Felt you just couldn't get going[a]
      Had trouble keeping your mind on what you were doing[a]
      Had trouble getting to sleep or staying asleep[a]
      Didn't talk to anyone or talked less than usual[b]
      Felt no interest in anything or anybody
      Felt tired all the time
      Had poor appetite
    3. Positive affect
      Enjoyed life[b]

Felt hopeful about the future[b]
Felt happy[b]
B. Anxiety
1. Mood
Worried a lot about little things[c]
Felt anxious, tense, or nervous[c]
Felt restless or fidgety[c]
2. Malaise
Had dizziness[c]
Had shortness of breath when you were not exercising or working hard[c]
Had your hands tremble[c]
Had your heart beating hard when you were not exercising or working hard[c]
Suddenly felt hot all over[c]

II. Cognitive
A. Delusions and Hallucinations
Felt that your mind was dominated by forces beyond your control[d]
Heard voices without knowing where they came from[d]
Had visions or seen things other people say they cannot see[d]
Felt that you were possessed by a spirit or devil[d]
Felt you had special powers[d]
Felt that you did not exist at all, that you were dead, dissolved[d]
Seemed to hear your thoughts spoken aloud—almost as if someone standing nearby could hear them[d]
Felt that your unspoken thoughts were being broadcast or transmitted, so that everyone knew what you were thinking[d]
B. Mistrust/Paranoia
Felt it was safer to trust no one[e]
Been very suspicious[e]
Believed you were being plotted against[e]
Felt that people were saying all kinds of things about you behind your back[e]
Felt you had enemies who really wished to do you harm[e]
Been sure that everyone was against you[e]

[a]From the short version of the Center for Epidemiological Studies depression scale (Modified CES-D) (Mirowsky & Ross, 1990).
[b]From the CES-D (Radloff, 1977).
[c]Modified version of symptoms from the Langner (1962) index.
[d]From the schizophrenia scale (Wheaton, 1985).
[e]From the mistrust and paranoia scales (Mirowsky & Ross, 1983).

Researchers can use the level of generality or specificity relevant to their research question. At a general level, for example, a distress index can include depression and anxiety, mood and malaise, and positive affect (scored in reverse). At more specific levels, researchers can distinguish between depression and anxiety, and further between depressed (or anxious) mood and malaise. Cognitive symptoms can also be distinguished or combined.

REFERENCES

Aneshensel, C. S., Rutter, C. M., & Lachenbruch, P. A. (1991). Social structure, stress, and mental health: Competing conceptual and analytic models. *American Sociological Review, 56,* 166–178.

Bentler, P. M. (1989). *EQS: Structural equations program manual.* Los Angeles: BMDP Statistical Software.

Blazer, D. G. (1982). *Depression in late life.* St. Louis: Mosby.

Blazer, D. G., & Williams, C. (1980). Epidemiology of dysphoria and depression in an elderly population. *American Journal of Psychiatry, 137,* 439–444.

Bohrnstedt, G. W., & Carter, T. M. (1971). In H. L. Costner (Ed.), *Sociological methodology 1971* (pp. 118–146). San Francisco: Jossey-Bass.

Boyd, J. H., Burke, J. D., Gruenberg, E., Holzer, C. E., Rae, D. S., George, L. K., Karno, M., Stolzman, R., McEnvoy, L., & Nestadt, G. (1984). Exclusion criteria of DSM-III: A study of co-occurrence of hierarchy-free syndromes. *Archives of General Psychiatry, 41,* 983–989.

Boyd, J. H., Weissman, M. M., Thompson, D., & Myers, J. K. (1982). Screening for depression in a community sample: Understanding the discrepancies between depression symptom and diagnostic scales. *Archives of General Psychiatry, 39,* 1195–1200.

Coryell, W., & Zimmerman, M. (1988). The heritability of schizophrenia and schizoaffective disorder: A family study. *Archives of General Psychiatry, 45,* 323–327.

Eaton, W. W., & L. G. Kessler. (1985). *Epidemiologic field methods in psychiatry: The NIMH Epidemiologic Catchment Area program.* New York: Academic Press.

Endicott, J., & Spitzer, R. L. (1972). What! Another rating scale? The Psychiatric Evaluation Form. *Journal of Nervous and Mental Disease, 154,* 88–104.

Hollingshead, A. B., & Redlich, F. C. (1958). *Social class and mental illness: A community study.* New York: Wiley.

Holzer, C. E., III, Shea, B. M., Swanson, J. W., Leaf, P. J., Myers, J. K., George L., Weissman, M. M., & Bednarski, P. (1986). The increased risk for specific psychiatric disorders among persons of low socioeconomic status: Evidence from the Epidemiologic Catchment Area surveys. *American Journal of Social Psychiatry, 6*(4), 259–271.

Kennedy, G. J., Kelman, H. R., Thomas, C., Wisniewski, W., Metz, H., & Bijur, P. E. (1989). Hierarchy of characteristics associated with depressive symptoms in an urban elderly sample. *American Journal of Psychiatry, 146,* 220–225.

Langner, T. S. (1962). A twenty-two item screening score of psychiatric symptoms indicating impairment. *Journal of Health and Human Behavior, 3,* 269–276.

Lewinsohn, P. M., Hoberman, H. M., & Rosenbaum, M. (1988). A prospective study of risk factors for depression. *Journal of Abnormal Psychology, 97,* 251–264.

Mausner, J. S., & Bahn, A. K. (1974). *Epidemiology: An introductory text.* Philadelphia: Saunders.

Mirowsky, J. (1990). Subjective boundaries and combinations in psychiatric diagnoses. *Journal of Mind and Behavior, 11*, 407–424.
Mirowsky, J., & Ross, C. E. (1983). Paranoia and the structure of powerlessness. *American Sociological Review, 48*, 228–239.
Mirowsky, J., & Ross, C. E. (1989). *Social causes of psychological distress.* New York: Aldine de Gruyter.
Mirowsky, J., & Ross, C. E. (1990). Psychiatric diagnosis as reified measurement. *Journal of Health and Social Behavior, 30*, 11–25.
Mirowsky, J., & Ross, C. E. (1991). Eliminating defense and agreement bias from measures of the sense of control: A 2 × 2 index. *Social Psychology Quarterly, 54*, 127–145.
Mirowsky, J., & Ross, C. E. (1992). Age and depression. *Journal of Health and Social Behavior, 33*, 187–205.
Newmann, J. P. (1989). Aging and depression. *Psychology and Aging, 4*, 150–165.
Radloff, L. (1977). The CES-D scale: A self-report depression scale for research in the general population. *Applied Psychological Measurement, 1*, 385–401.
Salzman, C., & Shader, R. I. (1978). Depression in the elderly: I. Relationships between depression, psychologic defense mechanisms and physical illness. *Journal of the American Geriatrics Society, 26*, 253.
Seeman, M., Seeman, A. Z., & Budros, A. (1988). Powerlessness, work, and community: A longitudinal study of alienation and alcohol use. *Journal of Health and Social Behavior, 29*, 185–198.
Spitzer, R. L., & Endicott, J. (1978). *Schedule for Affective Disorders and Schizophrenia.* New York: Biometric Research Division, Evaluation Section, New York Psychiatric Institute.
Spitzer, R. L., Endicott, J., Fleiss, J. L., & Cohen, J. (1970). The Psychiatric Status Schedule: A technique for evaluating psychopathology and impairment of role functioning. *Archives of General Psychiatry, 23*, 41–55.
Spitzer, R. L., Fleiss, J. L., Endicott, J., & Cohen, J. (1967). Mental status schedule: Properties of factor-analytically derived scales. *Archives of general Psychiatry, 16*, 479–493.
Weissman, M. M., & Klerman, G. L. (1980). In reply. *Archives of General Psychiatry, 37*, 1423–1444.
Wheaton, B. (1985). Personal resources and mental health: Can there be too much of a good thing? In J. R. Greenley (Ed.), *Research in community and mental health, vol. 5* (pp. 139–184). Greenwich, CT: JAI Press.

11

Psychophysiological and Behavioral Measurement of Stress
Applications to Mental Health

NAOMI LESTER, LINDA E. NEBEL, and ANDREW BAUM

Stress is a pervasive and familiar phenomenon. Because it reflects a biobehavioral pattern that cuts across disease states, settings, and other traditional categories, it has generated an enormous amount of research and theory. Measurement problems, conceptual and operational inconsistencies across studies, and reliance on single-discipline perspectives on stress, however, have hindered our understanding of the stress process and contributed to confusion regarding the stress construct. For example, some studies define stress in terms of events that require change, others as self-reported emotional distress, others as behavioral change, and still others in terms of blood pressure change or hormone levels. Further complicating this picture is the tendency for prior studies to

The opinions and assertions expressed herein are those of the authors and should not be construed as reflecting those of the Uniformed Services University of the Health Sciences or the Department of Defense.

NAOMI LESTER, LINDA E. NEBEL, and ANDREW BAUM • Department of Medical Psychology, School of Medicine, Uniformed Services University of the Health Sciences, Bethesda, Maryland 20814-4799.
Stress and Mental Health: Contemporary Issues and Prospects for the Future, edited by William R. Avison and Ian H. Gotlib. New York, Plenum Press, 1994.

measure stress in only one or two ways, rather than assessing it as a multilevel process. Since the early 1970s, research has approached stress more broadly, examining patterns of response within and across different levels (e.g., Frankenhauser, 1975; Mason, 1975). At the same time, slow conceptual development and inconsistent assessment approaches have led to confusion in the field.

Integrated biobehavioral models of stress have gradually become the predominant view of stress in the field. Early attempts to integrate the biological traditions of Cannon (1935) and Selye (1976) with the concepts of cognitive appraisal and coping (e.g, Lazarus, 1966) were concerned, of necessity, with demonstrating that cognitive and behavioral factors could determine hormonal patterns and physiological arousal (Elliott & Eisdorfer, 1982; Mason, 1975). More recent advances in this field have included the development of assessment models that tap several levels of response during stress and simultaneous measurement of multiple levels of response (Baum, Grunberg, & Singer, 1982; Fleming & Baum, 1986; Frankenhauser, 1973).

In this chapter we will describe multilevel assessment approaches that partition stress into four different levels of response: self-report, behavioral, physiological, and biochemical. We will then outline potential applications and implications of this assessment model for mental health research on disorders such as substance abuse, anxiety disorders (including posttraumatic stress disorder), and depression. Stress appears to contribute to the etiology, progression, and relapse of several psychological disorders. Consequently, a better understanding of how stress affects these disorders at all possible levels is important for mental health research.

MEASUREMENT OF STRESS

Past definitions of stress describe it as an event or a response: Stress is either a situation that places demand on an organism or the organism's response to this demand. Current definitions emphasize the importance of viewing stress as a process. For the purposes of this chapter, we will define stress as the process through which organisms respond to internal or external stimuli that are perceived as threatening or dangerous. This process-oriented definition emphasizes the ways in which environmental events are perceived and evaluated (Baum, 1990; Lazarus & Folkman, 1984; Selye, 1976). With a process-oriented definition of stress, it is important to consider both the stressor—the environmental event viewed as taxing or requiring adjustment—and the cognitive, affective, behavioral, physiological, and biochemical changes that occur when stress is experienced.

Because stress is a complex process affecting many bodily systems and modes of experience, it can be measured in many ways. For example, the occurrence of stressful stimuli or events can be measured, or the individual's recollections of responses to those events can be assessed. Measurement of events has included assessment of the frequency of typical stressors and estimates of the amount of change required of each (e.g., Holmes & Rahe, 1967; Rahe, 1975). Depending on one's research questions and orientation, self-report measures of a variety of feelings or behaviors can be obtained, as with symptom reporting or problem solving. In this way affective and cognitive aspects of stress can be measured, and one's experiences assessed. Coping, task performance changes, and other overt changes are also measurable, as are physiological and biochemical changes in several systems.

Multilevel measurement of stress has clear advantages, the most obvious of which is that it provides more information about the situation and the experience of it. Relationships among various bodily responses, mood changes, or other stress-related changes are more likely to be detected using multilevel assessment. In addition, specific stress-related changes may not always be present whenever stress is experienced, and measurement of several indicators increases chances of convergence or, in some cases, detection (Fleming, Baum, & Singer, 1984). Given the complex and largely unexplored relationships between stress and mental health or between stress-related physiological and biochemical changes and emotional disturbance, this multilevel approach may be of considerable value in studying stress as a factor in mental health.

Levels of Measurement

The different levels of measurement that can be used when studying stress depend on how one views the stress process or level of response. By categorizing levels along types of measures, one taps not only a methodological class but also different levels of experience and response. Measures can reflect the *stressor* (the causal agent, with characteristics such as regular or irregular occurrence, intensity, and duration), *appraisal* (thoughts about the stressor or its characteristics, assets, judgments of predictability and controllability, and coping), *response* (directed at the stressor or stressful experience, including emotional changes, changes in behavior, sympathetic arousal), and *consequences* (changes not directly related to coping, including immune system changes and post-stressor performance effects). Assessment of only one level tells us relatively little, whereas multiple assessment not only affords more information and a greater possibility for discovery but also allows greater accuracy for prediction. If one is interested in the psychobiological changes that occur during stress and how they contribute to mental health problems, measurement of only stressors does not allow distinction between those who experience stress and those who do not. It assumes a universal response and fails to measure the specific processes of interest. Far greater precision can be gained by tapping into several phases in the stress process.

The same is true of measures across levels or modes of response. Traditionally, stress has been measured by capturing reactions at four different levels: *self-report* (responses/changes of which we are aware, many accessible only through self-report), *behavioral* (overt behavior, task performance), *physiological* (systemic changes in endocrine, nervous, cardiovascular, and other systems) and *biochemical* (neuropeptides, neurotransmitters, hormones, and other chemical messengers). Though some measures may not closely correspond, they may measure different components of the stress response, thus making multilevel assessment an even more valuable tool.

Self-Report Measures

Self-report is most often used to assess or infer perceived levels of stress. Such measures include the frequency of life events and the amount of adjustment required, whether a situation is stressful and how threatening or demanding it is, how distressed one becomes, and how one attempts to cope. These measures often reflect responses or reactions that cannot be measured directly, as in measures of symptom experience, attitudes, and mood. Self-reports can be easily obtained through interviews or the use of questionnaires, and a good deal of specificity can be achieved. For example, identification of ongoing levels of stress and evaluation of particular stressors can be accomplished by assessing major life events (Holmes & Rahe, 1967). Because major life events occur relatively infrequently, more recent approaches have focused on alternate sources of stress, including daily hassles—small events or annoyances that by themselves are of little adaptive consequence (Lazarus & Cohen, 1977). Collectively, or if experienced in a chronic manner, hassles may become more stressful and may provide a better prediction of stress. DeLongis and her colleagues found that daily hassles were more strongly related to reports of symptoms than were life events (DeLongis, Coyne, Dakof, Folkman, & Lazarus, 1982).

Mood changes can be assessed with one of several instruments, and other aspects of personal experience (e.g., the way people cope) can be measured with additional instruments or with ad hoc questionnaires. Stress may also result in increases in the number of symptoms reported and complaints of both somatic and emotional distress (Baum, Gatchel, & Schaeffer, 1983). These symptoms can be assessed with instruments such as the 58-item Hopkins Symptom Checklist (Derogatis, Lipman, Rickels, Uhlenhuth, & Covi, 1974) or the expanded Symptom Check List (SCL 90-R; Derogatis, 1977). The SCL 90-R asks respondents to indicate which of 90 listed symptoms they have experienced in the preceding 2 weeks and to indicate how bothersome they found the symptoms to be. Subscales assessing clusters of symptoms such as anxiety and concentration difficulties may also be derived. Other symptoms checklists, such as the Cornell Index, assess symptoms that are more neuropsychiatric in nature (Weider, Wolfer, Brodman, Mittelmann, & Wechsler, 1948). More clinically relevant symptoms may also be assessed using one of several structured interviews. The Diagnostic Interview Schedule (DIS) is an assessment procedure based on the diagnostic and statistical manual (DSM-III-R) of the American Psychiatric Association (1987). A trained interviewer using the DIS is able to record various symptoms and approximate diagnoses of psychopathology. The Structured Clinical Interview (SCID; Spitzer et al., 1987) is also a symptom-based assessment interview based on the DSM-III. Again, the interviewer is able to estimate the severity of many mental health problems.

Self-report measures generally provide information about important processes not accessible in other ways. Because they are easier to administer, less expensive, and often easier to interpret, self-report measures are used more consistently or frequently than are other measures. Self-reports are more easily influenced by unintentional bias and intentional manipulation, however, and sole reliance on self-report measures can pose interpretive difficulties. In addition, the retrospective nature of most measures of life events or hassles may lead to recall and other biases (e.g., Dohrenwend & Dohrenwend, 1974; Rabkin & Struening, 1976). Self-reports of stress have also been criticized because they appear to be influenced by negative affectivity, or neuroticism, inflating the correlation between stress and health outcomes and contributing to spurious findings (McCrae &' Costa, 1986; Watson & Pennebaker, 1989). Similarly, the meaning of changes in symptom reporting and whether they reflect bodily changes, attentional changes, or mood can cloud interpretation of findings. Self-reports may be most useful for creating impressions of peoples' experience rather than conveying specific information, but these measures clearly provide a necessary level of analysis for studying stress. Although self-report data must often be interpreted cautiously when used alone, they are valuable sources of information that should be supplemented with other measures in order to get a more complete and knowledgeable picture.

Behavioral Measures

A second level of measurement of stress is the assessment of behavioral aspects of stress. Coping (often a behavioral response), risk taking, engaging in healthy or unhealthy behaviors (e.g., substance use), maintenance of proper diet, compliance with preventive or curative regimes (e.g., exercise), and a variety of other behaviors affect mental or physical health (Schachter, 1978). These behaviors also vary with stress, and changes in these behaviors can be used as behavioral indices of the stress process. Performance on tasks can be used to assess persistence, narrowing of attention, or other cognitive changes that seem to occur during stress. Not only can performance be examined, but *aftereffects* of stress can also be evaluated (Glass & Singer, 1972). Aftereffects are performance decrements that are found after a stressor has been terminated or resolved; Glass and Singer found that exposure to noise negatively affected task performance after termination of the stressor. Behavioral changes such as reduced tolerance for frustration, impaired problem-solving ability, poorer concentration, and the like may accompany or follow substantive stress experiences (Cohen, 1980).

Physiological and Biochemical Measures

Another level of assessment involves measures of physiological responses. These include such noninvasive measures as blood pressure and heart rate, respiration, and skin conductance. Changes in these measures as a result of stress represent arousal of the sympathetic nervous system; the "fight or flight" response that occurs during stress is largely a sympathetic function (Cannon, 1935). When confronted with stress-provoking stimuli, people exhibit sympathetic arousal characterized by increases in heart rate, blood pressure, respiration, muscle tone, and other systemic changes. The parasympathetic nervous system (e.g., vagal tone) is also involved in the stress response and can be estimated by analyzing heart-rate variability (Porges & Bohrer, 1990). These measures are often relatively easy to obtain and can provide indications of the effects of stress relevant to clinical outcomes. To carry out physiological measurement, however, one may require complex instrumentation that may limit the activities subjects can engage in during monitoring. In addition, though different than the problems with self-report data, there are biases and sources of error for physiological data that can also hinder interpretation. All measures of stress that one can consider share inevitable measurement error.

Other physiological aspects of stress that have been included in assessments of stress are neuroendocrine functioning and biochemical changes. Adrenal hormones are of primary importance in the biochemical changes that occur during stress, as are a number of neurotransmitters or messenger peptides. The adrenals produce both corticosteroids (adrenal cortex), which serve to regulate such bodily functions as metabolism, and catecholamines (adrenal medullae), which affect sympathetic arousal. These biochemicals have been widely studied as they relate to the stress process, and both corticosteroids and catecholamines can be measured fairly easily in urine or plasma.

The connection between corticosteroid changes and stress was first systematically drawn by Selye (1936, 1976), who believed that increased adrenal cortical activity attributable to stress caused such nonspecific physiological responses as enlarged adrenal cortexes, shrinkage of thymic and lymphoid tissue, and ulcers of the gastrointestinal tract. (Selye, 1936; 1976). Various environmental and psychosocial stressors are associated with increased adrenal cortical activity, and psychological stress-mediating variables, such as coping, have been shown to modify corticosteroid levels (Baum et al., 1982; Wolff, Friedman, Hofer, & Mason, 1964).

The catecholamines (epinephrine and norepinephrine) have also been found to increase in response to a variety of stressors. In addition, they are affected by a variety of behaviors such as activity and diet. These chemicals are secreted by the adrenal medullae, which, unlike the adrenal cortex, are innervated by the sympathetic nervous system. This provides a quick and direct neural link by which stress can affect hormonal functioning.

The neurotransmitter serotonin may be useful in the study of stress but shows varying dynamics in different types of stress, with both increases and no significant changes found (Adell, Garcia-Marquez, Armario, & Gelpi, 1988; Paris et al., 1987). Similarly, research on insulin levels during stress also suggests varying results, with decreases frequently observed but increases or no changes reported in some cases (Mason, 1975; Nesse et al., 1985; Selye, 1976). Prolactin has been found to decrease during exposure to stressors (Arnetz, Fjellner, Eneroth, & Kallner, 1985) but not in response to painful stimuli (Bullinger et al., 1984). Endogenous opioid peptides, in contrast, appear to increase with stress in humans (Cohen, Pickar, Dubois, & Bunney, 1982).

One can break stress responding down to more specific levels if desired, but these four serve to illustrate the usefulness of multiple-level assessment and the limitations in using only one or two indicators. When research examines only one or two levels, the whole picture is not being seen, and it may even be obscured. For example, many psychological studies rely solely on self-reports of such things as emotions and stress. By doing this, however, inaccurate information may be obtained. Although subjects may not deliberately deceive the researcher, they can certainly be biased by what they think the researcher wants them to say. All of the potential measurement areas that have been described contain limitations when they are used alone; when used in combination, however, these limitations can be overcome.

In addition to the benefits associated with multilevel assessment noted above, this approach allows for measurement *convergence:* cases in which measures of different levels come together to provide strong evidence of a phenomenon. Measurement convergence can be seen in a series of studies examining residents of the Three Mile Island (TMI) area after the nuclear accident there (e.g., Baum et al., 1983; Davidson & Baum, 1986). For several years, residents of the TMI area reported more symptoms, more anxiety and depression, and more somatic distress than did comparable control subjects, and also showed poorer performance on a concentration task, higher blood pressures, and higher catecholamine levels than did the control groups (Baum, Fleming, & Reddy, 1986; Baum et al., 1983; Davidson & Baum, 1986). There were times at which some measures showed differences between TMI and control subjects and times when these measures were not different, but the overall picture of most measures showing differences between groups most of the time allowed more confident conclusions and indicated that TMI area residents experienced chronic stress. This research was strengthened by convergence across measures; the stressors, responses to these stressors, and the consequences of this distress were all part of the stressful experience for people living near TMI (e.g., Baum, 1990; McKinnon, Weisse, Reynolds, & Bowles, 1989).

STRESS AND MENTAL HEALTH

A growing body of research suggests that psychophysiological processes are important in the development and progression of several mental disorders. One cannot disregard the strong genetic component of health in general, but research suggests that stress can interact with genetic predispositions to produce disease. The similarities of psychophysiological responses seen during stress and a number of disorders may provide researchers and clinicians with further clues concerning the etiology, progression, and treatment of many mental health problems. Using a multilevel assessment approach when investigating the connections between stress and mental health problems should prove useful. We have chosen four types of disorders for illustrative purposes and will briefly review evidence supporting links between stress and substance use disorders, anxiety (including posttraumatic stress disorder), and depression.

Psychoactive Substance Use

Multilevel assessment has proven helpful in research on stress and substance use problems. The commonalities between stress and the use of psychoactive substances are apparent at many levels. Research has suggested that stress is closely linked to the initiation and maintenance of drug and alcohol use at both the psychological and biobehavioral levels (Grunberg & Baum, 1985; Vaux & Ruggiero, 1983). Several studies have found that increased numbers of stressful life events are correlated with the initiation of drug and alcohol use (Burns & Geist, 1984; Duncan, 1977; Vaux & Ruggiero, 1983). In one such study, Vaux and Ruggiero (1983) obtained measures of stressful life events and reported drug and alcohol use from more than 500 high school students. Positive correlations between stressful life events and reported drug and alcohol use were observed.

Drinking alcohol and the consumption of many drugs is known to reduce the feelings of anxiousness and tension associated with stress (Grunberg & Baum, 1985; McNamee, Mello, & Mendelson, 1968). Sher and Walitzer (1986) reported a study investigating the dose-response relationship between alcohol and its stress-dampening effects. Participants consumed a beverage with either no alcohol (a placebo drink), a low concentration of alcohol, or a higher concentration of alcohol, and their psychological and physiological responses to a stressful social situation were measured. Subjects who received alcohol exhibited diminished stress responses compared with those who consumed the placebo. Those who received drinks with the higher dose of alcohol showed greater dampening of psychological and physiological responses than did those receiving the lower dose.

These findings suggest a tension-reduction role for alcohol, and several tension-reduction models for drug use have been formulated (e.g., Conger, 1956; Cooper, Russel, & George, 1988). Though these models differ slightly, they all suggest that one of the primary reinforcing properties alcohol and drugs is the ability to reduce sensations of tension. The reduction of aversive subjective and physiological aspects of stress reinforces the use of these substances. In addition, alcohol and many addictive drugs produce pleasant emotional experiences. Both the relief from tension and an enhancement of the subjective sense of emotional well-being could work together to make the reinforcement of drug-seeking and drug consumption behaviors more powerful. Because of this potential for double reinforcement of drug and alcohol use, the establishment of drug habits may occur quickly, and extinction may be very difficult (Cohen & Baum, in press).

Application of such models to the study of substance use initiation in young people is difficult. Drugs appear to have unusually strong reinforcing properties during adolescence, however, perhaps because of the pressure generated by rapid physiological, psychological, and social change. During this turbulent period, adolescents look to peers for social support and as models for behavior (Blum & Singer, 1984; Pihl & Smith, 1983). Often substances of abuse are first consumed during periods of tension or as part of peer group activities (Blum & Singer, 1984; Vaux & Ruggiero, 1983). With the tension reduced, the ritual of taking these substances may be strongly reinforced. Additionally, the increased sense of social support and belonging associated with alcohol or drug consumption among peers further reinforces continued use of these substances (Blum & Singer, 1984; Coombs, Paulson, & Risa, 1988). Again, multiple reinforcement should increase the likelihood that in the absence of other ways to reduce tension, alcohol and drug use will increase.

After initiation of drug or alcohol consumption, psychological reinforcement of drug-taking behavior may develop beyond the actual pharmacological effects of these drugs (Grunberg & Baum, 1985). Situations and even objects, such as drug paraphernalia, may become associated with carving. Addicted drug users injected with saline might, for example, experience physiological effects that mimic those seen when the actual drug of abuse (e.g., opium) is injected (Grunberg & Baum, 1985). Coping strategies that an individual previously used in stressful situations may be abandoned in favor of drug taking as the preferred coping method. Also, social supports that existed before the initiation of drug use may become difficult to maintain, and an individual's social group may be composed primarily of other drug users (Litman, Eiser, & Rawson, 1977). Finally, the unpleasant feelings and sensations that occur with withdrawal are stressful, and desire to avoid withdrawal may help perpetuate substance use (Grunberg & Baum, 1985).

Physiologically and biochemically, stress is linked to some of the pharmacological actions of psychoactive substances. Many of these mechanisms have biological origins (Grunberg & Baum, 1985; Levenson, Oyama, & Meek, 1987; Wise, 1984). Research has shown that increases in stress can alter the pharmacological effects of drugs within the body and speed their clearance from the system (Schachter, 1978). Research in animals has suggested that stress-related hormonal changes may affect individual vulnerability to the reinforcing properties of amphetamines (Cole et al., 1990; Piazza et al., 1991). These hormones may also increase symptoms associated with withdrawal from addictive substances (Donegan, Rodin, O'Brien, & Solomon, 1983). Further, substance use disorders appear to precede or accompany other disorders (Rounsaville et al., 1991). Seventy-five percent of nearly 300 cocaine abusers seeking treatment had a lifetime incidence of other disorders. Affective disorders such as depression usually followed the onset of drug use, whereas anxiety disorders, antisocial personality difficulties, and childhood attention-deficit disorder typically preceded problems with cocaine (Rounsaville et al., 1991).

Kosten and Kleber (1988) suggest that the type of drug abused by an individual is an important tool in determining comorbidity. Together with multilevel assessments, a broad view of drug use may prove successful in understanding the independent and joint manifestations of these different disorders. An individual in crisis presenting with cocaine intoxication or withdrawal exhibits symptoms that may mask difficulties with mania or depression. In addition, individuals may initiate using substances to self-medicate underlying psychiatric conditions. This is particularly evident in depression and anxiety, both of which may be masked by drug effects and withdrawal but may persist after withdrawal is completed (Kleber & Gawin, 1986; McLellan & Druley, 1977).

Stress plays an important role in the initiation and maintenance of drug and alcohol use. The physiological effects of stress in combination with pharmacological actions of substances of abuse must also be considered. The examination of these stress effects at the physiological, behavioral, and psychological level is vital to intervention and treatment efforts directed at those with substance use problems.

Anxiety Disorders

Similarities between stress and anxiety can be clearly seen at any level. Anxiety is a feeling of apprehension caused by threatening stimuli, which can be external or intrapsychic (Kaplan & Sadock, 1988). It can be focused on a particular situation or be a pervasive fear of the unknown (Kaplan & Sadock, 1988). As an emotional state, anxiety can be transient and well within the normal bounds of routine affect. When abnormally intense or persistent, however, anxiety may prove to be a more substantial problem. Anxiety disorders develop when the feared situation is of an extreme magnitude (as in posttraumatic stress disorder) or of a chronic nature. Chronic stress may cause prolonged periods of autonomic nervous system activation and psychological stress that can contribute to the development of anxiety disorders (Kaplan & Sadock, 1988).

Physiological and neuroendocrine patterns observed during anxiety closely match those observed during stress. Anxiety is manifest in stresslike symptoms such as heightened cardiovascular responses, intestinal upset, and dizziness (Kaplan & Sadock, 1988). During periods of acute anxiety, increases in norepinephrine have been observed (Charney et al., 1990). In fact, much of the biochemical data about anxiety disorders has been derived from studies of panic disorder and posttraumatic stress disorder (Charney et al., 1990).

Panic disorder is an intensification of the anxiety felt by individuals when they appraise a situation as potentially dangerous. During a panic attack, acute periods of emotional fear and physiological reactivity, including increased heart rate and blood pressure, are experienced. In a paper exploring the role of noradrenergic systems in the development of panic disorder, Charney et al. (1990) have suggested that norepinephrine and its effects on the locus coeruleus are the primary triggering mechanism for panic attacks. These researchers postulate that stimuli in the environment that are appraised as threatening or stressful, as well as some internal physiological events such as a drop in blood glucose or change in body temperature, trigger the norepinephrine and locus coeruleus actions that precipitate panic attacks. Additionally, in animal studies, uncontrollable stress has been shown to alter activity in the locus coeruleus (Charney et al., 1990).

Posttraumatic stress disorder (PTSD) is an anxiety disorder that occurs following a stressful event that falls outside the range of usual human experience (American Psychiatric Association, 1987). Such traumatic events could include military combat experience, being in a disaster, a severe automobile accident, and being physically assaulted. PTSD is characterized by hyperalertness to stimuli associated with the traumatic event, prolonged feelings of guilt, social withdrawal, and intrusiveness of thoughts about the trauma. Frequently individuals with PTSD also have emotional numbing to other experiences and may have difficulty in interpersonal relationships (Kaplan & Sadock, 1988).

The psychological and behavioral elements of PTSD have been investigated by many researchers and clinicians, and their findings confirm an assumed relationship: Many of the symptoms of PTSD are intensified manifestations of stress, and PTSD may be best thought of as a stress disorder (e.g., Davidson & Baum, 1986). Green, Wilson and Lindy (1985) proposed a model of PTSD that includes individual characteristics (e.g., coping), characteristics of the trauma experience (e.g., extent of bereavement), cognitive variables (e.g., intrusiveness of thoughts), and the recovery environment (e.g., social support). Considering PTSD as a combination of these components leads to a much better understanding of the complexities of the disorder. Outcomes, interventions, and treatment efficacy may be jointly determined by several of these levels, and assessment of several helps the researcher or clinician in intervention and treatment efforts.

Recent research has concentrated on identifying possible psychoendocrine markers for the disorder (Kosten, Wahby, Giller, & Mason, 1990; Mason, Giller, Kosten, & Harkness, 1988; Mason, Kosten, Southwich, & Giller, 1990). The identification of these markers has come partially through a greater understanding of the biochemical effects of stress and again helps to illustrate the importance of investigating this disorder from multiple levels. In one such study, veterans with PTSD were compared to individuals suffering from depressive disorders and schizophrenia. Levels of norepinephrine and cortisol showed a different pattern for individuals with PTSD than that among depressed or schizophrenic patients; norepinephrine was significantly higher and cortisol was significantly lower among PTSD patients than among those with comparison disorder. In similar studies, male veterans with PTSD have been found to exhibit heightened levels of testosterone, thyroxine, and epinephrine (Kosten et al., 1990; Mason et al., 1990). The identification of these hormonal patterns is important because they indicate that, physiologically, PTSD is a very different disorder than depression or schizophrenia. Mason suggests that under the conditions of chronic stress seen with PTSD, continued elevations of cortisol may be suppressed. Such suppression does not occur in depression. In addition, low cortisol levels have been linked to modes of coping with stress that rely on methods for detaching or denying the stressful situation (Mason et al., 1990).

Recent research on the cognitive/emotional components of PTSD has explored the role of intrusive imagery in the maintenance of chronic stress in PTSD. Intrusive images are unwanted or uncontrolled thoughts about past trauma or dreams where the traumatic events are reexperienced (Baum, 1990). The presence of these unbidden thoughts may retrigger some of the physiological and neurobiological reactions originally experienced during the trauma. This continual reexperiencing of feelings associated with severe stress may partially explain the lowered cortisol patterns observed by Mason et al. (1990). In addition, the presence of recurrent reminders of trauma may continually stress the individual and contribute to the emotional numbing and interpersonal difficulties observed in those with PTSD.

Through the example of PTSD we see that the multilevel approach, which has been used to study stress, can also be applied to the investigation of anxiety disorders. This approach can only strengthen the development of intervention and treatment strategies. The value of this integrative approach is also evident for the understanding of depression.

Depression

The chances of developing unipolar depression at some point in one's lifetime are relatively high (20% for women and 10% for men), but bipolar disorders are less common (Kaplan & Sadock, 1988). Depression is characterized by melancholy mood, the inability to experience pleasure, and a number of cognitive distortions or tendencies. Because depression has a relatively high incidence and has clear consequences for job performance, well-being, and health, it constitutes a major health problem. Depressed people often report having decreased levels of energy, decreased appetitive behaviors, and sleep disturbances.

Research on the etiology of depression suggests that stress may be involved. Psychosocial variables such as social support influence the way people perceive stress and may help prevent psychological distress. Research has shown that although depression increases with the number of life events, it decreases when more social support is available (Aneshensel & Stone, 1982). Some research suggests that stress does not cause depression per se, but that it may combine with other variables to precipitate depressive episodes (Breslau & Davis, 1986). Furthermore, social factors, such as the daily possible role conflict problems that face women with multiple roles, can contribute to the development and severity of depression (Brown & Harris, 1978).

There are many reasons to be wary of these findings. The usual problems of retrospective studies are compounded by the nature of depression; a negative view of the world could lead to different appraisals and an increased reporting of negative events. Billings and Moos (1982) developed a longitudinal model that controls for some of these problems. In a study of stress and health, these researchers asked subjects to complete life-events and symptom checklists at two time points. Billings and Moos used peoples' reporting of depressive symptoms and life events at the first time point to control for reporting at the second. They still found a positive relationship between the number of negative events and depressive symptom reporting.

An alternate perspective on the causes of depression is a behavioral one, focusing on learned helplessness. Much of the research in this area has been done with animals. In an early study of this phenomenon, Overmier and Seligman (1967) exposed animals to uncontrollable electric shock and compared them to animals who were not exposed to shock. The animals were then placed in a experimental box and given a task where they had to learn how to escape in order to avoid shock. Those animals that had been previously exposed to electric shock showed deficits in learning the escape response.

Of 18 animal models of depression reviewed by Willner (1984), the learned helplessness model was seen as being one of the most valid. This model focuses on the loss of control that many depressed people feel, and it has a good deal of face validity. Many of the behaviors produced by the learned helplessness paradigm in animals, including decreases in activity, decreases in appetitive behavior, and sleep disturbances, mirror symptoms typically seen in human depression. Animal research has shown that many of the treatments that are successfully used with depression also help to prevent or inhibit the behavioral deficits found in connection with the learned helplessness procedure (e.g., tricyclic antidepressants, monoamine oxidase inhibitors, and electroshock therapy; Dorworth & Overmier, 1977; Leshner, Remler, Biegon, & Samuel, 1979; Petty & Sherman, 1979). Helplessness may also be reflected by passive behavior, negative expectations, and a pervasive sense of hopelessness. Depressed people may have experienced a series of situations in which they failed to live up to their or others' expectations, and this may further contribute to feelings of lack of control and helplessness (Seligman, 1975).

Weiss and his colleagues extended the association of learned helplessness and depression to physiological and biochemical levels, suggesting that "stress-induced behavioral depression" is caused by decreased norepinephrine and locus coeruleus changes in the brain (Weiss & Simson, 1985). Drugs that inhibit this noradrenergic activity in the locus coeruleus, through alpha-2 receptor blockade, lead to behavioral signs of depression similar to the learned helplessness model. Drugs that stimulate these receptors help prevent behavioral depression (Weiss & Simson, 1985).

More recently, researchers have suggested that rather than a decrease, there is excessive activation of norepinephrine in the locus coeruleus during depression. This notion is more consistent with a simpler stress induction model whereby some aspect of stress (e.g., norepinephrine) provides a causal link to depression. Depressed patients exhibit increased levels of both cerebrospinal fluid norepinephrine and plasma norepinephrine (e.g., Lake et al., 1982; Post et al., 1984). In addition, when treating depressed patients with antidepressants, decreased levels of cerebrospinal fluid and plasma MHPG (a norepinephrine metabolite) are observed (Linnoila, Karoum, Calil, Kopin, & Potter, 1982). Animal studies applying the learned helplessness model to produce behavioral depression suggest that norepinephrine may be overactivated by increased activity in the locus coeruleus (Gold, Goodwin, & Chrousos, 1988). These findings highlight the importance of examining hormones that change in response to stress, as these changes might relate to the etiological development of depression.

It is also important to examine biochemical measures along with behavior and self-reports because they can provide explanations for broader clinical findings. For example, women are twice as likely to be diagnosed with depression as are men (Kaplan & Sadock, 1988). In searching for reasons for this difference one must look not only at social and behavioral factors, such as the conflict and pressure of work and family roles, but at constitutional differences as well. People suffering from depression also can exhibit very high levels of cortisol (Gold et al., 1986). Possible gender differences in cortisol response may help explain the greater predominance of female depression. One study, for example, reports differences in adrenocorticotropic hormone (ACTH) response to corticotropin-releasing hormone (CRH) among men and women, and similar but longer-lasting stress-related cortisol responses among women (Gallucci, Baum, Gold, Chrousos, & Kling, 1992).

Serotonin is another neurotransmitter that has been widely studied as a cause or correlate of depression. Research suggests that serotonergic functioning is deficient in depressed people, and that many of the processes that appear abnormal in depression (e.g., appetite, sleep, and mood) are serotonergically mediated (Meltzer & Lowy, 1987). Physiological studies have shown that 5-HIAA (a serotonin metabolite) is lower in the cerebrospinal fluid of depressed patients (Asberg et al., 1984) and that there are fewer serotonin uptake sites found on the blood platelets of depressed patients (e.g., Meltzer, Arora, Baber, & Tricou, 1981). Pharmacological treatment of depression provides further evidence for a theory of serotonergic deficit in this disorder. Many of the treatments successfully used with different forms of depression (e.g., tricyclic antidepressants, monoamine oxidase inhibitors, lithium, and electroshock therapy) also improve serotonergic functioning (Meltzer, 1989). Though depression appears to involve a deficit in serotonergic functioning, chronic stress appears to increase CNS levels of serotonin in animals (Adell et al., 1988).

Changes in tryptophan, the precursor necessary for the production of serotonin, have been linked to basic changes in mood. Decreases in dietary tryptophan are associated with increases in depressed mood (Smith, Pihl, & Young, 1987). Furthermore, seasonal affective disorder, characterized by depressive symptomatology in the late fall and winter months, is associated with dietary changes that may reflect patients' efforts to self-medicate. These dietary changes appear to be attributable to intense craving for carbohydrates. Carbohydrates, when eaten with little or no protein, increase tryptophan and may thereby provide a mechanism by which serotonin levels are increased (Rosenthal et al., 1989; Spring, Chiodo, & Bowen, 1987).

In addition to norepinephrine and serotonin, other neurochemicals have been studied in relation to depression (e.g., dopamine, acetylcholine, GABA). How stress-induced changes in these neurochemicals may relate to altered levels of these compounds among depressed patients, and how these changes relate to the behavioral and psychological processes characteristic of depression, provide the researcher and clinician with potentially useful applications of multilevel assessment in future studies of depression.

Multilevel assessment of stress in examining causes of depression is useful because of the many relationships between depression and stress at different levels. The fact that the reward system of the brain is clearly linked to both stress and depression (Akiskal & McKinney, 1973) and the similarity of symptoms of stress and mood disorders in general suggests the importance of considering multiple levels of analysis. These relationships can be portrayed by measuring life events, by applying behavioral models such as learned helplessness, or by considering physiological correlates of stress and depression (e.g., activation of norepinephrine). Measurement and conceptual elaboration at these different levels may lead to new and important information about the etiology and treatment of illnesses such as depression.

Multilevel Assessment of Gender Differences

Another example of the usefulness of multilevel assessment can be seen in investigations of gender differences in depression. As discussed previously, women are twice as likely as men to be diagnosed with depression (Kaplan & Sadock, 1988). Many factors contribute to the development of depression, but these factors may work differently in men and women. Research designed to investigate the interactions between etiological factors at the psychological, behavioral, physiological, and biochemical levels may help determine the nature of these gender differences.

Research has suggested that women may be more psychologically susceptible to the stressful effects of life events (Dean, 1985), and as mentioned previously, the multiple roles that many women face can lead to a variety of daily stressors that may contribute to the development of depression (Brown & Harris, 1978). The differential incidence rates of depression among men and women may also be partially attributable to differences in the ways men and women seek assistance when feeling distressed. Mechanic (1972) has shown that women are more likely to seek medical help when bothered by symptoms than are men.

Factors such as a greater willingness to reveal feelings or report distress and negative affects, however, have not been adequately ruled out in this regard. Men and women may also react to stress in different ways. In studies examining the stressful effects of challenging tasks, a meta-analysis reported by Stoney, Davis, and Matthews (1987) suggests that men show greater blood pressure responses to challenge, whereas women exhibit larger heart-rate responses. Gender differences in the hormonal patterns of men and women in response to stress may also provide information about the different rates of depression in men and women. In a study comparing the responses of men and women to a physiological challenge that mimics the stress response (a bolus dose of corticotropin-releasing hormone), Gallucci and colleagues found that women showed greater pituitary ACTH responses than men and that cortisol levels remained high longer among women. When ACTH is released in greater quantities, higher levels of cortisol are expected, and higher levels of cortisol are often observed in depressed individuals (Gold et al., 1986). Although, preliminary, these studies suggest one possible hormonal explanation for gender differences in depression. These hormonal data should be examined within the context of gender differences in the ways people experience stressful events and how they cope with these events. Exploration of the interactions between the variables involved in the etiology of depression in men and women may lead to a much greater understanding of gender differences in this area.

The study of gender differences in depression also illustrates how the multilevel assessment approach incorporates both laboratory studies and field work. Gender differences in depression cannot be fully understood if researchers rely only on laboratory research. The work of Gold et al. (1986) indicated that gender differences in cortisol may be partially responsible for the higher incidence of depression in women. Yet without an understanding of how men and women react to stressors in their lives and how they seek to cope with these stressors, the value of the data on gender differences in cortisol reactivity is diminished. Similarly, sole reliance on field studies falls short in addressing many of the possible physiological and biochemical mechanisms at work in depression. A greater understanding of the role of stressful phenomena such as life events and gender role conflicts in the development of depression is important, but a more comprehensive understanding of how these stressors may contribute to health-impairing physiological changes is also vital.

CONCLUSIONS

We have described a multilevel assessment approach that has been used in the study of stress, as well as the potential usefulness of this approach for mental health research on disorders such as drug use problems, anxiety (including posttraumatic stress disorder), and depression. Of course, as with all research approaches, a multilevel assessment design does have several potential limitations. First, this approach may require more funding than a single assessment approach. Not only is support necessary for the materials required for multiple measures, but more personnel are also likely to be needed. For example, biochemical measures need to be assayed, and behavioral data coded and scored. Similarly, because of the increased number of measures, multilevel research may take more time to complete than a simpler approach. Also, because of the multiple measures and analyses required, multilevel research may require that additional subjects be included in a study, adding to the potential increases in time and funding necessary to complete the project. Once the study is completed and analyzed, there is a possibility that the results from the multiple measures will not correspond. If convergence among measures is not found, it may indicate that aspects of the stress response are being differentially affected (e.g., behavioral processes versus self-reports). Lack of convergence may be a problem; however, data can still provide the researcher with valuable clues regarding the phenomena being studied. Nonconverging results may also lead to new research questions.

Although this approach may require more time and funding, the information that can be gained using this method is extensive. Valuable data can be obtained by examining the psychological, behavioral, and biochemical aspects of disorders such as depression, drug use, anxiety and posttraumatic stress disorder, and how stress relates to these complex processes. Stress may contribute to the etiology, progression, and relapse of many mental health problems; therefore knowledge of how stress affects aspects of these disorders or how they may be predisposed is vital for future research and intervention efforts. Furthermore, commonalities between the stress process and these disorders at multiple levels of measurement provide the researcher with underlying clues regarding the nature of these disorders. Promising areas of research include investigation of the locus coeruleus and malfunctions of the noradrenergic system. The disregulation of these systems appears to be important in the etiology of many mental health problems. In addition, the connections between specific behaviors and emotions and their physiological consequences should be explored.

REFERENCES

Adell, A., Garcia-Marquez, C., Armario, A., & Gelpi, E. (1988). Chronic stress increases serotonin and noradrenaline in rat brain and sensitizes their responses to a further acute stress. *Journal of Neurochemistry, 50*(6), 1678–1681.

Akiskal, H. S., & McKinney, W. T. (1973). Depressive disorders: Toward a unified hypothesis. *Science, 182,* 20–29.

American Psychiatric Association (1988). *Diagnostic and statistical manual of mental disorders* (3rd ed., rev.). Washington, DC: Author.

Aneshensel, C. S., & Stone, J. D. (1982). Stress and depression. *Archives of General Psychiatry, 39,* 1392–1396.

Arnetz, B. B., Fjellner, B., Eneroth, P., & Kallner, A. (1985). Stress and psoriasis: Psychoendocrine and metabolic reactions in psoriatic patients during standardized stressor exposure. *Psychosomatic Medicine, 47*(6), 528–541.

Asberg, M., Bertilsson, L., Martensson, B., Scalia-Tomba, G. P., Thoren, P., & Traskman-Bendz, L. (1984). CSF monoamine metabolites in melancholia. *Acta Psychiatrica Scandinavica, 69,* 201-219.

Baum, A. (1990). Stress, intrusive imagery, and chronic distress. *Health Psychology, 9,* 653–675.

Baum, A., Fleming, R., & Reddy, D. M. (1986). Unemployment stress: Loss of control, reactance and learned helplessness. *Social Science and Medicine, 22,* 509–516.

Baum, A., Gatchel, R. J., & Schaeffer, M. A. (1983). Emotional, behavioral, and physiological effects of chronic stress at Three Mile Island. *Journal of Consulting and Clinical Psychology, 51,* 565–572.

Baum, A., Grunberg, N. E., & Singer, J. E. (1982). The use of psychological and neuroendocrinological measurements in the study of stress. *Health Psychology, 1*(3), 217–236.

Billings, A. C., & Moos, R. H. (1982). Stressful life events and symptoms: A longitudinal model. *Health Psychology, 1*(2), 99–117.

Blum, A., & Singer, M. (1984). Substance use and social deviance: A youth assessment framework. *Child and Youth Services, 6,* 7–21.

Brown, G. W., & Harris, T. (1978). *Social origins of depression: A study of psychiatric disorder in women.* New York: Free Press.

Breslau, N., & Davis, G. C. (1986). Chronic stress and major depression. *Archives of General Psychiatry, 43,* 309–314.

Bullinger, M., Naber, D., Pickar, D., Cohen, R. M., Kalin, N. H., Pert, A., & Bunney, W. E. (1984). Endocrine effects of the cold pressor test: Relationships to subjective pain appraisal and coping. *Psychiatry Research, 12,* 227–223.

Burns, C., & Geist, C. S. (1984). Stressful life events and drug use among adolescents. *Journal of Human Stress, 10,* 135–139.

Cannon, W. B. (1985). Stresses and strains of homeostasis (Mary Scott Newbold lecture). *American Journal of Medical Sciences, 189,* 1–14.

Charney, D. S., Woods, S. W., Nagy, L. M., Southwich, S. M., Krystal, J. H., & Heniger, G. P. (1990). Noradrenergic function in panic disorder. *Journal of Clinical Psychology, 51*(12, Suppl. A), 5–11.

Cohen, L., & Baum, A. (in press). Stress, vulnerability, and drug use. In J. H. Jaffe (Ed.), *The encyclopedia of drugs and alcohol.* New York: Macmillan.

Cohen, M. R., Pickar, D., Dubois, M., & Bunney, W. E. (1982). Stress-induced plasma beta-endorphin immunoreactivity may predict postoperative morphine usage. *Psychiatry Research, 6,* 7–12.

Cohen, S. (1980). Aftereffects of stress on human performance and social behavior: A review of research and theory. *Psychological Bulletin, 98,* 310–357.

Cole, B. J., Cador, M., Stinus, L., Rivier, C., Rivier, J., Vale, W., Le Moal, M., & Koob, G. F. (1990). Critical role of the hypothalamic-pituitary-adrenal axis in amphetamine-induced sensitization of behavior. *Life Sciences, 47,* 1715–1720.

Conger, J. J. (1956). Reinforcement theory and the dynamics of alcoholism. *Quarterly Journal of Studies on Alcohol, 17,* 296–305.

Coombs, R. H., Paulson, M. J., & Risa, P. (1988). The institutionalization of drug use in America: Hazardous adolescence, challenging parenthood. *Journal of Chemical Dependency Treatment, 1,* 9–37.

Cooper, M. L., Russel, M., & George, W. H. (1988). Coping expectations, and alcohol abuse: A test of social learning formulations. *Journal of Abnormal Psychology, 97,* 218–230.

Davidson, L. M., & Baum, A. (1986). Chronic stress and posttraumatic stress disorders. *Journal of Consulting and Clinical Psychology, 54*(3), 303–308.

Dean, A. (1985). *Depression in multidisciplinary perspective.* New York: Brunner/Mazel.

DeLongis, A., Coyne, J. C., Dakof, G., Folkman, S., & Lazarus, R. S. (1982). Relationship of daily hassles, uplifts, and major life events to health status. *Health Psychology, 1*(2), 119–136.

Derogatis, L. R. (1977). *The SCL-90 Manual I: Scoring, administration and procedures for the SCL-90.* Baltimore: Johns Hopkins University School of Medicine, Clinical Psychometrics Unit.

Derogatis, L. R., Lipman, R. S., Rickels, K., Uhlenhuth, E. II., & Covi, L. (1974). The Hopkins Symptom Checklist (HSCL): A self-report symptom inventory. *Behavioral Science, 19,* 1–15.

Dohrenwend, B. S., & Dohrenwend, B. P. (Eds.). (1974). *Stressful life events: Their nature and effects.* New York: Wiley.

Donegan, N. H., Rodin, J., O'Brien, C. P., & Solomon, R. L. (1983). A learning theory approach to commonalities. In D. K. Levinson, D. R. Gerstein, & D. R. Maloff (Eds.), *Commonalities in substance abuse and habitual behavior.* Lexington, MA: Heath.

Dorworth, T. R., & Overmier, J. B. (1977). On "learned helplessness": The therapeutic effects of electroconvulsive shocks. *Physiological Psychology, 5,* 355–358.

Duncan, D. F. (1977). Life stress as a precursor to adolescent drug dependence. *International Journal of the Addictions, 12,* 1047–1056.

Elliott, G. R. & Eisdorfer, C. (Eds.). (1982). *Stress and human health: Analysis and implications of research.* New York: Springer.

Fleming, I., & Baum, A. (1986). The role of prevention in technological catastrophe. *Prevention in Human Services, 4,* 139–152.

Fleming, R., Baum, A., & Singer, J. E. (1984). Toward an integrative approach to the study of stress. *Journal of Personality and Social Psychology, 46,* 939–949.

Frankenhauser, M. (1973). *Experimental approaches to the study of catecholamines and emotion.* Stockholm: Psychological Laboratories, University of Stockholm.

Frankenhauser, M. (1975). Sympathetic-adrenomedullary activity, behavior, and the psychosocial environment. In P. H. Venables & M. J. Christie (Eds.), *Research in psychophysiology* (pp. 71–94). New York: Wiley.

Gallucci, W. T., Baum, A., Gold, P. W., Chrousos, G. P., & Kling, M. A. (1992). Sex differences in sensitivity of the hypothalamic-pituitary-adrenal-cortical axis to stress-like stimulation. *Health Psychology, 12*(5), 420–425.

Glass, D. C., & Singer, J. E. (1972). *Urban stress: Experiments on noise and social stressors.* New York: Academic Press.

Gold, P. W., Goodwin, F. K., & Chrousos, G. P. (1988). Clinical and biochemical manifestations of depression: Relation to the neurobiology of stress (part 1). *New England Journal of Medicine, 319,* 348–353.

Gold, P. W., Loriaux, D. L., Roy, A., Kling, M. A., Calabrese, J. R., Kellner, C. H., Nieman, L. K., Post, R. M., Pickar, D., Gallucci, W., Avgerinos, P., Paul, S., Oldfield, E. H., Cutler, G. B., & Chrousos, G. P. (1986). Responses to corticotropin-releasing hormone in the hypercortisolism of depression and Cushing's disease: Pathophysiologic and diagnostic implications. *New England Journal of Medicine, 314,* 1329–1335.

Green, B. L., Wilson, J. P., & Lindy, J. D. (1985). Conceptualizing post-traumatic stress disorder: A psychosocial framework. In C. R. Figley (Ed.), *Trauma and its wake: The study and treatment of post-traumatic stress disorder.* New York: Brunner/Mazel.

Grunberg, N. E., & Baum, A. (1985). Biological commonalities of stress and substance abuse. In S. Shiffman & T. A. Wills (Eds.), *Coping and substance use.* New York: Academic Press.

Holmes, T. H., & Rahe, R. H. (1967). The Social Readjustment Rating Scale. *Journal of Psychosomatic Research, 11,* 213–218.

Kaplan, H. I., & Sadock, B. J. (1988). *Synopsis of psychiatry.* Baltimore: Williams & Wilkins.

Kleber, H. D., & Gawin, F. H. (1984). Cocaine abuse: A review of current and experimental treatments. In J. Grabowski (Ed.), *Cocaine: Pharmacology, effects, and treatment of abuse* (NIDA Research Monograph 50). Washington, DC: Government Printing Office.

Kosten, T. R., & Kleber, H. D. (1988). Differential diagnosis of psychiatric comorbidity in substance abusers. *Journal of Substance Abuse Treatment, 5,* 201–206.

Kosten, T. R., Wahby, V., Giller, E., & Mason, J. (1990). The dexamethasone suppression test and thyrotropin-releasing hormone stimulation test in post-traumatic stress disorder. *Biological Psychiatry, 28,* 657–664.

Lake, C. R., Pickar, D., Ziegler, M. G., Lipper, S., Slater, S., & Murphey, D. L. (1982). High plasma norepinephrine levels in patients with major affective disorder. *American Journal of Psychiatry, 139,* 1315–1318.

Lazarus, R. (1966). *Psychological stress and the coping process.* New York: McGraw-Hill.

Lazarus, R. S., & Cohen, J. B. (1977). Environmental stress. In I. Attman & J. F. Wohwill (Eds.), *Human behavior and the environment: Current theory and research, vol. 2.* New York: Plenum.

Lazarus, R. S., & Folkman, S. (1984). *Stress appraisal and coping.* New York: Springer.

Leshner, A. I., Remler, H., Biegon, A., & Samuel, D. (1979). Effect of desmethylimipramine (DMI) on learned helplessness. *Psychopharmacology, 66,* 207–213.

Levenson, R. W., Oyama, O. N., & Meek, P. S. (1987). Greater reinforcement from alcohol for those at risk: Parental risk, personality risk, and sex. *Journal of Abnormal Psychology, 96,* 242–253.

Linnoila, M., Karoum, F., Calil, H. M., Kopin, I. J., & Potter, W. Z. (1982). Alteration of norepinephrine metabolism with desipramine and zimelidine in depressed patients. *Archives of General Psychiatry, 39,* 1025–1028.

Litman, G. K., Eiser, J. R., & Rawson, N. S. B. (1977). Towards a typology of relapse: A preliminary report. *Drug and Alcohol Dependence, 2,* 157–162.

Mason, J. W. (1975). A historical view of the stress field. *Journal of Human Stress, 1,* 22–36.

Mason, J. W., Giller, E. L., Kosten, T. R., & Harkness, L. (1988). Elevation of urinary norepinephrine/cortisol ratio in post-traumatic stress disorder. *Journal of Nervous and Mental Disease, 176,* 498–502.

Mason, J. W., Kosten, T. R., Southwich, S. M., & Giller, E. L. (1990). The use of psychoendocrine strategies in posttraumatic stress disorder. *Journal of Applied Social Psychology, 20,* 1822–1846.

McCrae, R. R., & Costa, P. T. (1986). Personality, coping, and coping effectiveness in an adult sample. *Journal of Personality, 54,* 385–405.

McKinnon, W., Weisse, C. S., Reynolds, P. C., & Bowles, C. A. (1989). Chronic stress, leukocyte subpopulations, and humoral responses to latent viruses. *Health Psychology, 8,* 389–402.

McLellan, A. T., & Druley, K. A. (1977). Non-random relation between drugs of abuse and psychiatric diagnosis. *Journal of Psychiatric Research, 13,* 179–184.

McNamee, H. B., Mello, V. K., & Mendelson, T. H. (1968). Experimental analysis of drinking patterns of alcoholics: Concurrent psychiatric observations. *American Journal of Psychiatry, 124,* 1063–1071.

Mechanic, D. (1972). Social psychologic factors affecting the presentation of bodily complaints. *New England Journal of Medicine, 286,* 1132–1139.

Meltzer, H. (1989). Serotonergic dysfunction in depression. *British Journal of Psychiatry, 155*(Suppl. 8), 25–31.

Meltzer, H. Y., Arora, R. C., Baber, R., & Tricou, B. J. (1981). Serotonin uptake in blood platelets of psychiatric patients. *Archives of General Psychiatry, 38,* 1322–1326.

Meltzer, H. Y., & Lowy, M. T. (1987). The serotonin hypothesis of depression. In H. Meltzer (Ed.), *Psychopharmacology, the third generation of progress* (pp. 513–526). New York: Raven.

Nesse, R. M., Curtis, G. C., Thyer, B. A., McCann, D. S., Huber-Smith, M. J., & Knopf, R. F. (1985). Endocrine and cardiovascular responses during phobic anxiety. *Psychosomatic Medicine, 47*(1), 320–333.

Overmier, J. B., & Seligman, M. E. P. (1967). Effects of inescapable shock on subsequent escape and avoidance learning. *Journal of Comparative Physiological Psychology, 63,* 23–33.

Paris, J. M., Lorens, S. A., Van de Kar, L. D., Urban, J. H., Richardson-Morton, K. D., & Bethea, C. L. (1987). A comparison of acute stress paradigms: Hormonal responses and hypothalamic serotonin. *Physiology and Behavior, 39,* 33–43.

Petty, F., & Sherman, A. D. (1979). Reversal of learned helplessness by imipramine. *Communication in Psychopharmacology, 3,* 371–373.

Piazza, P. V., Maccari, S., Deminiere, J., Le Moal, M., Mormede, P., & Simon, H. (1991). Corticosterone levels determine individual vulnerability to amphetamine self-administration. *Proceedings of the National Academy of Sciences, 88,* 2088–2092.

Pihl, R. O., & Smith, S. (1983). Of affect and alcohol. In L. A. Pohorecky & J. Brick (Eds.), *Stress and alcohol use* (pp. 203–228). New York: Elsevier.

Porges, S. W., & Bohrer, R. E. (1990). The analysis of periodic processes in psychological research. In J. T. Cacioppo & L. G. Tassinary (Eds.) *Principles of psychophysiology: Physical, social, and inferential elements* (pp. 708–753). Cambridge: Cambridge University Press.

Post, R. M., Jimerson, D. C., Ballenger, J. C., Lake, C. R., Uhde, T. W., & Goodwin, F. K.

(1984). Cerebrospinal fluid norepinephrine and its metabolites in manic-depressive illness. In R. M. Post & J. C. Ballenger (Eds.), *Neurobiology of mood disorders*. Baltimore: Williams & Wilkins.

Rabkin, J. G., & Struening, E. L. (1976). Life events, stress, and illness. *Science, 194*, 1013–1020.

Rahe, R. H. (1975). Life changes and near-future illness reports. In L. Levi (Ed.), *Emotions: Their parameters and measurement* (pp. 511–529). New York: Raven.

Rosenthal, N. E., Genhart, M. J., Caballero, B., Jacobsen, F. M., Skwerer, R. G., Coursey, R. D., Rogers, S., & Spring, B. (1989). Psychobiological effects of carbohydrate- and protein-rich meals in patients with seasonal affective disorder and normal controls. *Biological Psychiatry, 25*, 1029–1040.

Rounsaville, B. J., Anton, S. F., Carroll, K., Buddle, D., Prusoff, B. A., & Gawin, F. (1991). Psychiatric diagnosis of treatment-seeking cocaine abusers. *Archives of General Psychiatry, 48*, 43–51.

Schachter, S. (1978). Pharmacological and psychological determinants of smoking. *Annals of Internal Medicine, 88*, 104–114.

Seligman, M. E. P. (1975). *Helplessness: On depression, development, and death*. San Francisco: Freeman.

Selye, H. (1936). A syndrome produced by diverse noxious agents. *Nature, 138*, 32.

Selye, H. (1976). *The stress of life*. New York: McGraw-Hill.

Sher, K. J., & Walitzer, K. S. (1986). Individual differences in the stress-response dampening effects of alcohol: A dose-response study. *Journal of Abnormal Psychology, 95*, 159–167.

Smith, S. E., Pihl, R. O., & Young, S. N. (1987). A test of possible cognitive and environmental influences on mood lowering effects of tryptophan depletion in normal males. *Psychopharmacology, 91*, 451-457.

Spitzer, R. J., Williams, J. B., & Gibbon, M. (1987). *Structured clinical interview for DSM-III—Non-patient version*. New York: Biometrics Research Department, New York State Psychiatric Institute.

Spring, B., Chiodo, J., & Bowen, D. J. (1987). Carbohydrates, tryptophan, and behavior: A methodological review. *Psychological Bulletin, 102*(2), 234–256.

Stoney, C., Davis, M., & Matthews, K. (1987). Sex differences in physiological responses to stress and in coronary heart disease. A causal link? *Psychophysiology, 24*, 127–131.

Vaux, A., & Ruggiero, M. (1983). Stressful life change and delinquent behavior. *American Journal of Community Psychology, 11*, 169–183.

Watson, D., & Pennebaker, J. W. (1989). Health complaints, stress, and disease: Exploring the central role of negative affectivity. *Psychological Review, 96*(2), 234–254.

Weider, A., Wolfe, H. G., Brodman, K., Mittelmann, B., & Wechsler, D. (1948). *Cornell Index*. New York: Psychological Corporation.

Weiss, J. M., & Simson, P. G. (1985). Neurochemical basis of stress-induced depression. *Psychopharmacology Bulletin, 21*(3), 447–457.

Willner, P. (1984). The validity of animal models of depression. *Psychopharmacology, 83*, 1–16.

Wise, R. (1984). Neural mechanisms of the reinforcing action of cocaine. *National Institute of Drug Abuse Research Monographs, 50*, 15–33.

Wolff, C. T., Friedman, S. B., Hofer, M. A., & Mason, J. W. (1964). Relationship between psychological defenses and mean urinary 17-OHCS excretion rates: A predictive study of parents of fatally ill children. *Psychosomatic Medicine, 26*, 576.

VII

Conclusion

12

Future Prospects for Stress Research

WILLIAM R. AVISON and IAN H. GOTLIB

The chapters in this book present an excellent assessment of the current state of stress research. More importantly, they also provide a rich source of new ideas about the processes through which stressors manifest themselves in terms of various mental health outcomes. In our view, these chapters are representative of the multidisciplinary interest of stress research today. Moreover, they provide excellent examples of the theoretical sophistication and the methodological creativity characteristic of the groundbreaking work in this area. Whereas some authors have focused on a critical review of the research literature and the specification of important new theoretical issues, others have chosen to present compelling empirical analyses to demonstrate significant novel methodological and conceptual directions for stress researchers. Regardless of their approach, these contributors provide not only a clear view of the most pressing research problems in the field but an agenda for future work in this rapidly expanding area of mental health research.

A reading of these chapters reveals a number of emergent themes. Indeed, it is noteworthy that researchers working independently in diverse disciplines should agree on so many issues. In this final section of

WILLIAM R. AVISON • Centre for Health and Well-Being, Department of Sociology, The University of Western Ontario, London, Ontario, Canada N6A 5B9.   **IAN H. GOTLIB** • Department of Psychology, Northwestern University, Evanston, Illinois 60208.

Stress and Mental Health: Contemporary Issues and Prospects for the Future, edited by William R. Avison and Ian H. Gotlib. New York, Plenum Press, 1994.

the book we identify six such themes and briefly discuss their implications for future research agendas. At the same time, it is important to note that there are a number of issues over which the authors in this book clearly disagree. Though the format of this book presents no opportunity for the authors to debate these divergent points of view, we also briefly review these issues. These differences in scientific opinion, of course, constitute rich sources of research questions for future investigation.

EMERGENT THEMES

The Complexity of the Stress Universe

The early conceptual work of Cannon (1932) and Selye (1956) and the development of the Schedule of Recent Experiences by Holmes and Rahe (1967) provided the impetus for a vast body of research on the impact of stress on human experience. Since that time, researchers have become keenly aware of the complexity of the stress domain. This complexity is reflected not only in the challenges that confront the measurement of stressors but also in the complicated issues associated with specifying the universe of stressful experience.

Working from different methodological perspectives, Bruce and Barbara Dohrenwend (Dohrenwend & Dohrenwend, 1974, 1981; Dohrenwend, Krasnoff, Askenasy, & Dohrenwend, 1978) and George Brown and his colleagues (Brown, 1974, 1981; Brown & Harris, 1978) drew attention to the many problems involved in accurately estimating the impact of stressful experience on mental health outcomes. This body of research alerted stress researchers to the problems of inter- and intraevent variability, operational confounding of measures of stress with measures of mental health or illness, and the advantages and disadvantages of interviewer-based versus self-report techniques for assessing life stress. Indeed, the groundbreaking work of Brown and the Dohrenwends set the agenda for methodological developments in the measurement of stress over the 1970s and 1980s.

In this volume, the chapters by McLean and Link (Chapter 2) and by Monroe and McQuaid (Chapter 3) provide an updated assessment of the state of the art in measuring stressful life events. Both chapters alert us to difficulties associated with event linkage and redundancy, the recall of events, the timing of events, the context in which events occur, and the question of causal ordering. These authors suggest strategies for adequately capturing the complexity of stressful life experiences. McLean and Link (Chapter 2) advocate a strategy based upon a theoretically grounded approach directed at a specific research question. Such an approach involves identifying specific circumstances that represent opportunities to test competing theoretical explanations. Given a particular circumstance (e.g., unemployment and its mental health consequences; the impact of fateful loss on depression), the range of measurement issues that can be addressed are constrained by the theoretically important research questions to be answered. This approach provides the researcher with a more limited set of measurement problems to be addressed.

Adopting a somewhat broader perspective, Monroe and McQuaid (Chapter 3) argue for measurement procedures that specify explicit rules and operational criteria for defining events and for assessing linkages and associations among life events, ongoing stressors, and life difficulties. In their view, interviewer- or rater-based techniques such as Brown and Harris's (1978) LEDS hold the most promise for reliable measurement of eventful stress. Of course, in exchange for adopting the type of interviewer-rated procedure advocated by Monroe and McQuaid, with its probable increased validity, one will likely be required to sacrifice the relative ease of administration and greater standardization of self-report life-event checklists.

In our view, one of the challenges that faces contemporary stress researchers is the need to develop measures of stressful life events that take advantage of both the administrative advantages of self-report checklists and the contextual detail that can be derived from rater-based techniques. There are a number of checklist approaches that have developed sophisticated probing techniques to accomplish this. These include modifications of the Psychiatric Epidemiology Research Interview (Dohrenwend, Link, Kern, Shrout, & Markowitz, 1990), Kessler and Wethington's (1991) use of memory and contextual cues to improve the reliability of recall on a life-events checklist, and Turner and Avison's (1992) use of a set of probes to address intraevent variability.

Regardless of the choice of methods, it seems clear that the assessment of stressful experience is fraught with complexity. Future research examining the stress process will require considerable sophistication both in defining the stressors to be studied and in selecting the appropriate measurement techniques. It is clear that methodological investigations will also be warranted. Although there have been limited explicit comparisons of interviewer-based approaches and modified checklist approaches, few attempts have been made to combine the two methodologies. Such an integrative approach might provide an effective trade-off between the ease of administration of checklist methods and the specificity and objectivity of rater-based techniques.

The complexity of the stress domain is not limited to measurement problems. Indeed, several chapters in this book have demonstrated that a fundamental issue confronting researchers in this area is an appreciation of the considerable breadth of the stress universe. In this context, Wheaton (Chapter 4) focuses on the spectrum or continuum of stressors that must be considered in studying the stress process. In Wheaton's mapping of the stress universe, the fundamental classification of stressors is based upon their discreteness. Whereas sudden traumas and life events are among the most discrete stressors, chronic strains are among the most continuous. Crosscutting this array, Wheaton also describes a micro–macro dimension, a life-course dimension, and a dimension of imputed seriousness.

McLean and Link (Chapter 2) and Menaghan (Chapter 5) similarly underscore the considerable range of stressors that individuals may confront. Consistent with Wheaton's perspective, McLean and Link argue that persistent life difficulties or chronic stressors represent an important segment of the stress universe. Both Wheaton and McLean and Link also emphasize the notion that chronic strains include not only role strains but other ongoing stressors as well. Menaghan extends the concept of chronic strain to include stressors in the workplace. Most importantly, perhaps, Menaghan focuses on an aspect of work stress that has largely been ignored by stress researchers. Whereas most studies of work stress focus on work overload or work conflict, Menaghan argues that the absence of self-direction in one's occupation constitutes a significant source of chronic strain. She argues that low levels of occupational complexity or self-direction contribute to a sense of powerlessness and feelings of low self-esteem. Menaghan clearly demonstrates that the "cognitive content" of one's everyday activities likely constitutes a source of ongoing stress. In so doing, she alerts us to yet another layer of complexity in our consideration of the stress universe.

In sum, it is clear from these chapters that stress research has made substantial progress since the early studies of the adverse effects of life events on mental health outcomes. Contemporary researchers have elaborated the stress model to include a variety of often interrelated stressors. It is apparent that a more comprehensive understanding of the complexity of the stress universe will require increasingly sophisticated approaches that take into account the suggestions made by the authors in this book. With theoretically driven research designs and more thoughtful measures of these different stressors, investigators may begin to estimate the relative impact of different types of stressors on mental health outcomes, thereby leading to a better understanding of the complex nature of the stress universe.

Mental Health Outcomes

Throughout many of the chapters in this book, there is clear evidence that stressful experiences manifest themselves in a wide range of mental health outcomes. For example, whereas studies of the effects of stress on psychological distress or depression have tended to dominate the area, McLean and Link (Chapter 2) explicitly advocate the use of an array of outcome measures. Similarly, Monroe and McQuaid's (Chapter 3) consideration of the linkage between different stressors and different disorders or constellations of symptoms is also consistent not only with this position but with several recent developments in stress research (e.g., Aneshensel, 1992; Aneshensel, Rutter, & Lachenbruch, 1991; Brown & Harris, 1989; Dohrenwend et al., 1992). Indeed, Wheaton's analyses of the relative impact of different stressors on an array of outcomes clearly underscore the benefits of considering various manifestations of stress.

Holahan and Moos (Chapter 8) also demonstrate the utility of examining the dynamics of the stress process across a range of disorders. Moreover, they also extend their consideration of outcomes to recovery from problems with depression and alcohol abuse. This focus points to a relatively neglected issue in stress research and, indeed, in research in psychopathology in general: Whereas most studies examine the ability of stressors and their mediators to predict onset or recurrence of illness, substantially fewer investigations have assessed how these factors might predict duration of illness or recovery from disorder. Clearly these are important foci for future work in this area.

Lester, Nebel, and Baum (Chapter 11) extend the domain of potential outcomes even further. Their suggestion for a multilevel measurement approach that includes self-reports from respondents, behavioral assessments, physiological measures, and biochemical outcomes presents at least two major challenges to stress researchers. First, research that considers a range of outcomes will require greater interdisciplinary collaboration among sociologists, psychologists, epidemiologists, physiologists, biochemists, and immunologists. Moreover, if such collaborations are to advance significantly our understanding of the multilevel effects of stressors, careful theoretical development will be required to determine what types of outcomes can be expected to be affected most strongly and by what types of stressors.

The second challenge is that research that crosses so many disciplinary boundaries is likely to be exceedingly difficult to design. Stress research already incorporates a variety of methodological designs, each of which reflects traditional disciplinary domains. For example, whereas

sociologists and community epidemiologists tend to employ population surveys, other epidemiologists often work with retrospective case-
control designs. In contrast, psychologists, psychophysiologists, and biochemists are likely to design and utilize case-comparison and experimental or quasi-experimental designs with smaller samples. It is likely that
research collaborations across these various disciplines will face the challenge of developing multimethod designs that incorporate multiple levels of measurement.

Although these challenges are not insurmountable, they will require
considerably greater interaction among scientists in these disciplines
than has previously been the case. On a positive note, there are encouraging signs that these kinds of projects may already be on the horizon.
Review articles by Baum, Grunberg, and Singer (1982), Cohen and Williamson (1991), and Kaplan (1992) have brought the results of research
on the immunological, biochemical, and physiological effects of stress to
the attention of social scientists. At this point it is imperative that a
similar transmission of social science research on stress be made available
to life scientists interested in collaborative initiatives.

The Pervasive Effects of Stressors

Several chapters in this book have demonstrated that stressors may
have diverse effects on individuals' mental health. There are, however,
other ways in which stressors have a pervasive influence on individuals'
lives. This fact is perhaps most clearly explicated in Menaghan's (Chapter 5) examination of the impact of work stress. Menaghan demonstrates
how stressors associated with one's occupation can influence patterns of
family interaction. Specifically, she documents how work stress creates
tensions in both marital relationships and parenting behaviors. These
strained relationships have consequences in their own right (see Gotlib &
Hammen, 1992).

Menaghan's findings are consistent with one of the original tenets of
the stress process formulation developed by Pearlin, Lieberman, Menaghan, and Mullan (1981): Stressors may generate other ongoing
stressful circumstances. This formulation has been developed more explicitly by Pearlin (1989) in his consideration of primary and secondary
stressors. It is clear that stressful experience in one social role may contribute to stress in other roles and relationships. It is also becoming
recognized that individuals may generate their own stressful environment, rather than simply being a passive recipient of life events (e.g.,
Hammen, 1991). This proliferation and generation of stress throughout
individuals' lives is an issue that warrants, and undoubtedly will receive,
further investigation.

A related area of research concerns the effects of stress on others in the individual's interpersonal environment. Menaghan's account of the impact of parental work stress on children's mental health outcomes is an eloquent example of this pervasive effect of stressors. Similarly, Holahan and Moos (Chapter 8) review their research on the ways in which parents' risk and resistance factors influence their children's emotional health. Indeed, an increasing number of studies have demonstrated how stressors experienced by one family member have consequences for the mental health of others in the family unit. For example, recent reviews of risk factors for children's psychopathology (Gotlib & Avison, 1993) and the impact of divorce and marital conflict on children's well-being (Amato & Keith, 1991; Lee & Gotlib, 1991) are consistent with the notion that stressors may have intergenerational effects within the family.

These considerations suggest the need for investigations of the effects of stressors on family units. Such studies are likely to be most informative when they are designed to assess the impact of particular kinds of stressors on family life. For example, research examining the impact of unemployment on family life or the effects of immigration on parents and children might provide us with important insights concerning the pervasive effects of particular stressful experiences. Moreover, if these studies are designed along the lines advised by McLean and Link (Chapter 2) and Monroe and McQuaid (Chapter 3), stress research will undoubtedly enhance our understanding of the effects of stressors in the family milieu.

The Social Context of Stressful Experience

It is a simple truism to state that the stress process is inherently social in context. There are a number of specific dimensions of this social context, however, that have been emphasized by the authors in this book. First, many of the components and dynamics of the stress process are the products of interpersonal relationships or the currency of interpersonal exchanges. As Wheaton (Chapter 4) and Menaghan (Chapter 5) both point out, many of the stressors that we experience are a function of long-term interpersonal difficulties. These problems in interpersonal relationships constitute an important area of study in stress research. Sarason, Pierce, and Sarason (Chapter 6) provide a convincing argument for the need to consider the relationship between the provider and the recipient of support. Moreover, Turner and Roszell (Chapter 7) clearly describe how social experiences condition one's sense of personal agency and self-esteem. Finally, Holahan and Moos (Chapter 8) firmly anchor their analyses on the assumption that interdependencies among family members are of critical importance for understanding resistance to stressors.

The centrality of interpersonal interactions and exchange in the stress process suggests the need for greater attention to the social psychology of stress. To date, most stress research has not explicitly attempted any theoretical synthesis with this large body of research. An appreciation of the methods and theories that have been applied to the study of interpersonal processes may stimulate some novel approaches to the study of the stress process.

A second aspect of the social context of stress has been addressed by Turner and Roszell (Chapter 7). These authors argue that the most important psychosocial constructs to consider are those that are linked to individuals' positions in the social structure. Turner and Roszell's point of view represents a classic sociological perspective on stress and mental health. For decades, one of the central issues in the sociology of mental health has been to explicate the inverse relation between social class and problems in mental health. Turner and Roszell remind us of the importance of social status in the stress process. Not only do differences in social position expose individuals to greater or lesser numbers of stressful experiences; these differences may also condition the development of psychosocial resources that enable individuals to cope with such stressors. This is the distinctive contribution of the sociological perspective to the stress process (see Pearlin, 1989). To ignore the ways in which social status influences the experience of stressors and their mediation is to assume that human experience is considerably more homogeneous than is the case.

The Chronology of Stressors and Their Outcomes

Individuals' lives can be described in terms of a chronology of experiences. An emerging theme in this volume is the need to date accurately the onset, duration, and conclusion of both stressors and their effects. There are a number of reasons why stress research needs to address these issues. First, temporal sequence is a critical criterion for determining causality, and it is crucial to understand how stressful experiences are causally related to mental health outcomes. Moreover, as Kessler and Magee (Chapter 9) astutely point out, it is important to date the onset of mental health problems because such difficulties may, in turn, generate stressors and affect social support. Such processes may then significantly influence the probability of relapse of psychiatric illness or the reoccurrence of symptoms of distress.

Second, as Wheaton (Chapter 4) notes, the timing of stressors in the life course most certainly has important implications for mental health outcomes. Thus, for example, a stressful experience that occurs in childhood is likely to have a different impact on an individual's mental health than would a similar experience occurring in midlife. In general, it is likely that the onset or recurrence of mental health problems at different stages of the life course have different effects. Research examining the timing of stressors and health outcomes with respect to individuals' life histories will undoubtedly provide us with a better understanding of the stress process.

Researchers who wish to address these issues will need to familiarize themselves with recent analytic techniques that allow for the use of time-varying predictors. Survival/hazard analyses and event history analyses (Allison, 1984; Singer & Willett, 1991) are rapidly becoming the methods of choice in taking into account the timing of stressors and their sequelae (for particularly useful examples, see Aneshensel, Pearlin, & Schuler, 1993; McLeod, Kessler, & Landis, 1992). Such techniques enable researchers to estimate the impact of the timing of stressors in relation to the onset and recurrence of mental health outcomes while avoiding biases resulting from time censoring of data.

There is a third reason why attention should be paid to the chronology of the stress process. In Chapter 6, Sarason, Pierce, and Sarason assert that the effect of social support is likely to vary with providers' and recipients' previous experiences of supportive relationships. This formulation suggests that it may be useful to attempt to document individuals' histories of supportive relationships, because such experiences may influence the subsequent expression of mental health problems. In this regard, some investigators have found that respondents' reports of supportive family relationships as children predict social support in adulthood (Sarason, Sarason, & Shearin, 1986; Sarason, Shearin, Pierce, & Sarason, 1987) and adult psychopathology (Gotlib, Whiffen, Wallace, & Mount, 1991). To date, there has been no widespread attempt to examine how the experience of early supportive exchanges may result in more effective social support later in one's life. In the same way that some studies carefully date the occurrence of stressors and mental health problems, it will likely prove to be informative to date supportive experiences. A similar case might also be made for dating individuals' experiences of success or mastery in life. If Turner and Roszell (Chapter 7) are correct in arguing that personal agency reflects one's personal history of successes and failures, then knowledge of the occurrences of noteworthy positive experiences may assist researchers in predicting subsequent levels of self-efficacy.

We recognize that some readers might object to this preoccupation with recording the chronology of the stress process on the grounds that assessing chronology will be hampered by inaccurate reports from respondents. There are, however, a number of studies and reviews that suggest that individuals can reliably report the key events in their lives (see Brewin, Andrews, & Gotlib, 1993; McLeod, 1991; Robins et al., 1985). Furthermore, recent advances in techniques for obtaining retrospective reports of stressors from respondents could usefully be applied to all kinds of experiences that constitute the stress process. In this way, the timing of important incidents in people's lives will be better specified. The potential dividend to stress research will be a clearer and more comprehensive understanding of the temporal processes that link stressors, mediators, and mental health outcomes.

Integrating Sociological and Psychological Perspectives

As we indicated in our introduction to this volume, one of the distinctive features of stress research has been its interdisciplinary character. Sociologists, psychologists, psychiatrists, and epidemiologists have all made substantive contributions to this field. To some extent, however, the dissemination of empirical results across disciplines has been less common than one might expect. In general, there is still a tendency for sociologists to focus on the work of their disciplinary colleagues, and for psychologists to do the same.

The chapters in this book clearly reveal that there are several research issues for which these various disciplines share substantially similar perspectives. For example, sociologists and psychologists appear to have similar concerns about the measurement of stressors. Though there are certain to be debates over the relative validity of interviewer-rated versus self-report approaches, these different perspectives are not discipline specific. Similarly, interest in understanding the processes by which social support and other psychosocial resources influence the stress process is shared by sociologists and psychologists alike.

In our view, there are other possibilities for greater interdisciplinary exchange. Sociological analyses of the stress process have placed substantial emphases on the ways in which social structure is associated with greater or lesser exposure to stressors. Social characteristics such as age, gender, marital status, social class, and ethnicity affect the probabilities that one will experience various stressors. Indeed, some authors (e.g., Aneshensel et al., 1991; Pearlin, 1989) have argued that a distinctive feature of sociological analyses of stress is a focus on the ways in which social structure gives rise to stress and its various sequelae. In this tradition, sociologists have been interested in how social roles may generate stressful circumstances. We believe that further consideration of the impact of social structure on the stress process will further the inter-disciplinary understanding of the ways in which stressors manifest themselves in various mental health outcomes.

A second possibility relates to the rich tradition in psychology of examining the roles played by personal predispositions or diatheses in the stress process. Monroe and Simons (1991), for example, provide a compelling argument for the need to consider diathesis–stress interactions more carefully. They make a number of important points. First, it is critical that stress researchers be precise in examining the types of stressors that interact with various predispositions. Second, diatheses or predispositions may influence individuals' lives in ways that have important implications for the stress process; for example, diatheses may actually influence individuals' perceptions and experiences of stress. Third, Monroe and Simons argue for the need to examine diathesis–stress interactions for specific mental health outcomes.

We believe that stress researchers will make substantial advances if they simultaneously incorporate social structural considerations with precise attention to potential stress–diathesis interactions. Indeed, many of the chapters in this book are cogent examples of this approach.

EMERGENT ISSUES

In any vibrant field of research, scientists can be expected to disagree; the area of stress research is no exception. Although there is substantial agreement among authors on a number of points, the chapters in this volume also draw attention to some emerging issues that will require further research.

Clarifying the Concept of Stress

As we have seen, the authors in this book extend the domain of stress well beyond a consideration of life events to include various types of chronic or ongoing stressors, childhood and adult traumas, and daily hassles. It might be argued that researchers have extended the concept of stress to the point where it is too broad to be meaningful or useful. We believe that it is important for stress researchers to address this concern both theoretically and empirically.

At a theoretical level, it is important for stress researchers to continue to develop a typology of stressors. By developing clear descriptions of the different kinds of stressors that individuals encounter, stress researchers will be better able to provide rules for classifying different stressful experiences. Careful attention to the defining characteristics of different types of stressors should lead to insights into their potential consequences for mental and physical health.

Empirically, it is incumbent upon researchers to demonstrate that various types of stressors can be measured with validity. In this context, it is also critical that investigators be able to demonstrate that particular stressors are not simply different manifestations of distress or psychopathology, and that different types of stressors are indeed conceptually and empirically distinct. Finally, given the expanding domain of stressors that have been identified, it is clearly important that we estimate their relative impact on different mental health outcomes in different social circumstances.

The chapters in this book have provided important insights concerning the steps that must be taken to address these issues. These examples of theoretical and empirical strategies for defining stressors and estimating their impact should provide a number of useful directions for future research.

The Concept of Vulnerability

In the mid-1970s and early 1980s, explanations of social differences in mental health outcomes emphasized the differential vulnerability of specific social groups to stressful experience. The idea that individuals occupying certain social statuses might be more likely to suffer from the experience of stress can be found in Dohrenwend and Dohrenwend's (1974) and Brown's (1974) discussions of substantial variations in mental health outcomes among individuals experiencing the same stressful event. Examples in the sociological literature include Pearlin and Johnson's (1977) examination of differential responsiveness to stress and Kessler's (1979a,b) explicit examination of the differential vulnerability hypothesis. Just a few years later, research in psychology by Lazarus (1981), Kobasa (1982), and Cohen and McKay (1984) examined concepts such as vulnerability and stress resistance. Since then, research on vulnerability to social stressors has become a dominant theme in stress research across disciplines.

Despite the wealth of research on vulnerability, there continue to be a number of unresolved issues. For example, in the sociological literature, some investigators have suggested that particular social groups (e.g., women, the unmarried, persons of lower socioeconomic status, minorities) are differentially vulnerable to stressors (see, e.g., Kessler & Neighbors, 1986; McLeod & Kessler, 1990). Other researchers have challenged the existence of any pervasive group differences in vulnerability, arguing instead that vulnerability effects are specific to the stressors considered, the outcomes examined, and the interaction of acute stressors and chronic strains (see Aneshensel, 1992). In the psychological literature, the concept of vulnerability to stress, both in children and adults, is often associated with studies of personal resources or coping strategies that alter the distressful consequences of a stressor. In this context, vulnerability seems to be conceived to have strong dispositional or personal qualities, as opposed to being a function of environment or group membership.

In Chapter 9, Kessler and Magee identify yet another source of vulnerability to stressors. Their suggestion that previous episodes of disorder are associated with a range of psychosocial risk factors that predict recurrence is consistent with Monroe and Simons's (1991) diathesis–stress formulations discussed earlier, and it promises to stimulate an important and fruitful new avenue of investigation.

Given the range of issues that appear to be involved in considerations of vulnerability to stressors, it is critical that more conceptual and theoretical work be focused on defining this concept and on identifying various dimensions or levels of vulnerability. This process of specifying the nature of vulnerability has the potential to advance the field in the same manner that has been achieved by theorists defining the stress universe.

Indexes and Diagnoses

Perhaps the most controversial chapter in this book is Mirowsky's (Chapter 10) indictment of the use of diagnostic categories in stress research. His position challenges researchers to consider a number of important issues concerning the use and measurement of "the dependent variable." If, as Mirowsky asserts, some diagnostic rules contain implicit preconceptions about particular social groups, it seems likely that estimates of vulnerability using such outcome measures will yield biased and inaccurate results. Moreover, Mirowsky's observation that different diagnoses may share defining attributes has important implications for examining the specificity of the impact of stressors on different disorders.

There is little doubt that these represent significant issues that researchers need to address. This is especially true for the vast number of studies that employ diagnostic measures as dependent variables in stress research. Mirowsky has raised an important series of challenges to be met by researchers in this tradition.

Given the demands of clinical research and the widespread acceptance of diagnostic systems such as DSM-III-R, it seems unlikely that stress researchers (especially those who are clinical psychologists or psychiatrists) will abandon diagnostic outcomes; nor do we believe they should. For these investigators, however, Mirowsky's chapter must stimulate a greater focus on exactly what outcomes are being assessed and how these outcomes are derived. For example, a diagnosis of depressive disorder can be obtained by a wide range of symptoms, and it is seldom clear exactly which symptoms, if any, are primary as responses to stress. Clinical researchers must attend to this concern if significant progress is to be made in this realm.

In just over a decade, research on the stress process has substantially advanced our understanding of the ways in which socially induced stressors are manifested in mental and physical health problems. The chapters in this book provide not only excellent summaries of progress to date but, equally important, useful directions for further work in this area. They represent superb illustrations of the reciprocal relation between careful theoretical thinking and creative analysis on one hand, and empirical research on the other. The collection of chapters in this book reinforces the notion that an understanding of the stress process involves, first, an appreciation of the breadth of the stress universe, and second, the recognition that stressors manifest themselves in a variety of health outcomes. This process is conditioned by not only the social circumstances in which individuals live but also the psychosocial resources they have available to meet the demands that stressors impose upon them. Moreover, these resources and the stressors themselves affect and are affected by the individual's history of psychological functioning or dysfunction. Faced with such complexity, it is clear that there remains much for stress researchers to do.

REFERENCES

Allison, P. D. (1984). *Event history analysis: Regression for longitudinal event data*. Beverly Hills, CA: Sage.

Amato, P. R., & Keith, R. (1991). Parental divorce and the well-being of children: A meta-analysis. *Psychological Bulletin, 110*, 26–46.

Aneshensel, C. S. (1992). Social stress: Theory and research. *Annual Review of Sociology, 18*, 15–38.

Aneshensel, C. S., Pearlin, L. I., & Schuler, R. H. (1993). Stress, role captivity, and the cessation of caregiving. *Journal of Health and Social Behavior, 34*, 54–70.

Aneshensel, C. S., Rutter, C., & Lachenbruch, P. (1991). Social structure, stress and mental health: Competing conceptual and analytic models. *American Sociological Review, 56*, 166–178.

Baum, A., Grunberg, N. E., & Singer, J. E. (1982). The use of psychological and neuroendocrinological measurements in the study of stress. *Health Psychology, 1,* 217–236.

Brewin, C. R., Andrews, B., & Gotlib, I. H. (1993). Psychopathology and early experience: A reappraisal of retrospective reports. *Psychological Bulletin, 113,* 82–98.

Brown, G. W. (1974). Meaning, measurement and stress of life events. In B. S. Dohrenwend & B. P. Dohrenwend (Eds.), *Stressful life events: Their nature and effects* (pp. 217–244). New York: Wiley.

Brown, G. W. (1981). Life events, psychiatric disorder, and physical illness. *Journal of Psychosomatic Research, 25,* 461–473.

Brown, G. W., & Harris, T. O. (1978). *Social origins of depression: A study of psychiatric disorder in women.* London: Tavistock.

Brown, G. W., & Harris, T. O. (1989). *Life events and illness.* New York: Guilford.

Cannon, W. B. (1932). *The wisdom of the body* (2nd ed.). New York: Norton.

Cohen, S., & McKay, G. (1984). Social support, stress, and the buffering hypothesis: A theoretical analysis. In A. Baum, J. E. Singer, & S. E. Taylor (Eds.), *Handbook of psychology and health, vol. 4* (pp. 253–267). Hillsdale, NJ: Erlbaum.

Cohen, S., & Williamson, G. M. (1991). Stress and infectious disease in humans. *Psychological Bulletin, 109,* 5–24.

Dohrenwend, B. P., Levav, I., Shrout, P., Schwartz, S., Naveh, G., Link, B., Skodal, A., & Stueve, A. (1992). Socioeconomic status and psychiatric disorder: The causation-selection issue. *Science, 255,* 946–952.

Dohrenwend, B. P., Link, B. G., Kern, R., Shrout, P. E., & Markowitz, J. (1990). Measuring life events: The problem of variability within event categories. *Stress Medicine, 6,* 179–188.

Dohrenwend, B. S., & Dohrenwend, B. P. (Eds.). (1974). *Stressful life events: Their nature and effects.* New York: Wiley.

Dohrenwend, B. S., & Dohrenwend, B. P. (1981). *Stressful life events and their contexts.* New York: Prodist.

Dohrenwend, B. S., Krasnoff, L., Askenasy, A. R., & Dohrenwend, B. P. (1978). Exemplification of a method for scaling life events: The PERI life events Scale. *Journal of Health and Social Behavior, 19,* 205–229.

Gotlib, I. H., & Avison, W. R. (1993). Children at risk for psychopathology. In C. G. Costello (Ed.), *Basic issues in psychopathology* (pp. 271–319). New York: Guilford.

Gotlib, I. H., & Hammen, C. L. (1992). *Psychological aspects of depression: Toward a cognitive-interpersonal integration.* Chichester, UK: Wiley.

Gotlib, I. H., Whiffen, V. E., Wallace, P. M., & Mount, J. H. (1991). A prospective investigation of postpartum depression: Factors involved in onset and recovery. *Journal of Abnormal Psychology, 100,* 122–132.

Hammen, C. (1991). Generation of stress in the course of unipolar depression. *Journal of Abnormal Psychology, 100,* 555–561.

Holmes, T. H., & Rahe, R. H. (1967). The Social Readjustment Rating Scale. *Journal of Psychosomatic Research, 11,* 213–218.

Kaplan, H. B. (1992). Social psychology of the immune system: A conceptual framework and review of the literature. *Social Science and Medicine, 33,* 909–923.

Kessler, R. C. (1979a). A strategy for studying differential vulnerability to the psychological consequences of stress. *Journal of Health and Social Behavior, 20,* 100–108.

Kessler, R. C. (1979b). Stress, social status, and psychological distress. *Journal of Health and Social Behavior, 20,* 259–272.

Kessler, R. C., & Neighbors, H. W. (1986). A new perspective on the relationships among race, social class, and psychological distress. *Journal of Health and Social Behavior, 27,* 107–115.

Kessler, R. C., & Wethington, E. (1991). The reliability of life events reports in a community survey. *Psychological Medicine, 21,* 723–738.

Kobasa, S. C. (1982). The hardy personality: Toward a social psychology of stress and health. In G. S. Sanders & J. Suls (Eds.), *Social psychology of health and illness* (pp. 3–32). Hillsdale, NJ: Erlbaum.

Lazarus, R. S. (1981). The stress and coping paradigm. In C. Eisdorfer, D. Cohen, A. Kleinman, & P. Maxim (Eds.), *Models for clinical psychopathology* (pp. 177–214). New York: Spectrum.

Lee, C. M., & Gotlib, I. H. (1991). Family disruption, parental availability, and child adjustment: An integrative review. In R. J. Prinz (Ed.), *Advances in the behavioral assessment of children and families, vol. 5* (pp. 166–199). London: Kingsley.

McLeod, J. D. (1991). Childhood parental loss and depression. *Journal of Health and Social Behavior, 35,* 205–220.

McLeod, J. D. & Kessler, R. C. (1990). Socioeconomic status differences in vulnerability to undesirable life events. *Journal of Health and Social Behavior, 31,* 162–172.

McLeod, J. D., Kessler, R. C., & Landis, K. R. (1992). Speed of recovery from major depressive episodes in a community sample of married men and women. *Journal of Abnormal Psychology, 101,* 277–286.

Monroe, S. M., & Simons, A. D. (1991). Diathesis–stress theories in the context of life stress research: Implications for depressive disorders. *Psychological Bulletin, 110,* 406–425.

Pearlin, L. I. (1989). The sociological study of stress. *Journal of Health and Social Behavior, 30,* 241–256.

Pearlin, L. I., & Johnson, J. S. (1977). Marital status, life strains, and depression. *American Sociological Review, 42,* 704–715.

Pearlin, L. I., Lieberman, M. A., Menaghan, E. G., & Mullan, J. T. (1981). The stress process. *Journal of Health and Social Behavior, 22,* 337–356.

Robins, L. N., Schoenberg, S. P., Holmes, S. J., Ratcliff, K. S., Benham, A., & Works, J. (1985). Early home environment and retrospective recall: A test for concordance between siblings with and without psychiatric disorders. *American Journal of Orthopsychiatry, 55,* 27–41.

Sarason, B. R., Shearin, E. N., Pierce, G. R., & Sarason, I. G. (1987). Interrelations of social support measures: Theoretical and practical implications. *Journal of Personality and Social Psychology, 52,* 813–832.

Sarason, I. G., Sarason, B. R., & Shearin, E. N. (1986). Social support as an individual difference variable: Its stability, origins, and relational aspects. *Journal of Personality and Social Psychology, 50,* 845–855.

Selye, H. (1956). *The stress of life.* New York: McGraw-Hill.

Singer, J. D., & Willett, J. B. (1991). Modeling the days of our lives: Using survival analysis when designing and analyzing longitudinal studies of duration and the timing of events. *Psychological Bulletin, 110,* 269–290.

Turner, R. J., & Avison, W. R. (1992). Sources of attenuation in the stress–distress relationship: An evaluation of modest innovations in the application of event checklists. In J. R. Greenley & P. Leaf (Eds.), *Research in community and mental health, vol. 7* (pp. 269–294). Greenwich, CT: JAI Press.

Index

Adolescence, substance abuse onset during, 300
Adolescents
  parental rejection of, 192–193
  self-esteem of, 194
Adrenal hormones, in stress response, 297
Adrenocorticotropic hormone (ACTH)
  in depression, 306
  in stress response, gender differences in, 308
Affective disorders, comorbidity with drug abuse, 301
Aggression, self-esteem and, 192
Alcohol abuse
  multilevel assessment of, 299–300, 301
  as stress cause, 96
  stress predictors of, 103, 104
Alcoholics
  children of, 229
  self-esteem of, 192
  social support for, 222, 226
  spouses of, 228
  treatment outcome for, 226–227
Alienation, work-related, 118
Americans' Changing Lives survey, 247–252
Amphetamines, reinforcing properties of, 300–301
Antidepressants, 305–306
Antisocial personality, comorbidity with drug abuse, 301
Anxiety/anxiety disorders, 60
  comorbidity with drug abuse, 301
  definition of, 301

Anxiety/anxiety disorders (Cont.)
  multilevel assessment of, 301–304
  predictors of, 99, 100
  rape-related, 35
Appraisal, reflected, 190, 191
Arousal, during fight-or-flight response, 296
Arousal theory, of change-related stress, 81, 89
Assertiveness, 172
Attachment theory, 154, 165, 170–171
Attention-deficit disorder, comorbidity with drug abuse, 301
Attenuation, diagnostic, 276–278, 279
Attributional style, in depression, 184–186
Authority, conformity to, 187–188
Autonomic nervous system, in anxiety disorder, 301–302
Avoidance behavior, as coping strategy, 217–218, 220
  in depression, 225

Bedford College Life Events and Difficulties Schedule. See Life Events and Difficulties Schedule (LEDS)
Bereavement, social support during, 162, 163
Biological model, of stress, 79, 111, 292
Blood pressure
  in panic disorder, 302
  as stress indicator, 296, 308
Brain, reward system of, 307

Cancer patients, psychological growth of, 229

Carbohydrates, as seasonal affective disorder therapy, 307

Cardiovascular responsivity
in anxiety, 302
social support's effect on, 164

Caregiver
depression in, 159
as social support source, 159, 161

Caretaking strain, 25

Catecholamines
during childbirth, 168
in stress response, 297

Causal inference, in life events inventories, 35

Causal relationship, of events, raters' evaluation of, 51, 52–53

Causal relevance, 181, 187, 188. *See also* Personal agency

Census Bureau, occupational codes of, 127, 131

Center for Epidemiologic Studies—Depression Scale (CES-D) 265–266, 267, 268

Change
following life events, 24
psychological meaning of, 20–21
relationship to stress, 79

Checklist approach, of life events inventories, 29, 319
development of, 44
comparison with interview methodology, 21, 56–58
interrelationship of events on, 33
methodological problems of, 19–22, 23, 47–49
subjects' recall on, 34

Child Behavior Checklist, 130

Childbirth, social support during, 167–168

Child care, father's involvement in, 121

Childhood trauma, 18
as depression predictor, 99, 102, 243–245, 251–252, 253
measurement of, 96
interaction with other stressors, 98, 105, 107, 112
relationship to distress, 100, 101, 109, 110

Childhood trauma (*Cont.*)
interaction with other stressors (*Cont.*)
relationship to later-life stressors, 105, 107
relationship to physical health problems, 103–104

Children
adult, relationship with elderly parents, 162, 165
of alcoholics, 229
of depressed parents, 228–229
of divorce, 162
effect of parental work stress on, 135–139, 323
stressors of, 90–91
stress resistance of, 215–216, 228–229, 233

Cocaine abuse, 301

Cognitive impairment, stress-related, 296

Coherence, 183, 216

Communication, parent–child, 166

Communities, chronic strains within, 23, 26–27

Competence, 184, 187
social, as role strain component, 85

Conflict
interpersonal, during social support, 169
role-related, 304, 307, 308–309

Control. *See also* Personal agency
locus of
effect on mental health, 5
external, 182
internal, 219
stress resistance function of, 216

Coping
approach-type, 217
avoidance-type, 217–218
as behavioral index of stress, 296
definition, 217
in depression, 220–221, 225
drug abuse as substitute for, 300
failure of, 155
of married couples, 227
powerlessness and, 186–187
research in, 215
social support relationship, 160
as stress modifier, 3, 5–6, 67, 68, 220–221

Coping-based model, of stress resistance, 220–221
Cornell Index, 295
Coronary artery surgery patients, social support for, 161
Corticosteroids, in stress response, 297
Corticotropin-releasing hormone, in depression, 306
Cortisol
  in depression, 306
    gender differences in, 308
  in posttraumatic stress disorder, 303
Crisis support, during depression, 68
Crisis theory, of psychological growth, 200–201, 202, 230–232
Cultural factors, in stress perception, 44

Daily diary studies, 87–88
Daily hassles, 79, 85–88, 93
  as chronic strain, 23–24
  comparison with life events, 294
  definition, 86, 88
  as depression predictor, 99, 102
  interaction with other stressors, 105, 107, 108, 112
    relationship to distress, 100, 101, 109
    relationship to physical health problems, 103
Daily Hassles Scale, 86–87
"Decay model," of depression, 32
Denial, 218
Depressed patients, stress research with, 48–49
Depression, 69–70
  active problem-solving and, 186
  acute stress and, 32
  age at onset, 246–247, 251
  age factors in, 246–247, 251
  attributional style in, 184–186
  childhood trauma, relationship of, 99, 102, 243–245, 251–252, 253
  chronic strains and, 32
  comorbidity with drug abuse, 301
  coping strategies in, 220–221, 225
  "decay model" of, 32
  diagnostic outcome measurement in, 241–254
  endogenous nature of, 70, 270
  gender differences in, 240, 248, 251
    age factors in, 246–247

Depression (Cont.)
  gender differences in (Cont.)
    diagnostic preconceptions and, 278, 281, 284
    multilevel assessment of, 306, 307–309
    relationship to prior depression, 246
    self-esteem and, 194–196
  helplessness and, 184–185, 304–306
  "hopelessness," 60
  index measurement versus psychiatric diagnoses of, 265–272, 275, 276
    diagnostic preconceptions and, 278–283
  interpersonal dependency and, 195–196
  learned helplessness model of, 184-185, 304–306
  life events relationship, 304
  of married couples, 227–228
  mastery and, 184, 187, 189–190, 248–249
  measurement of, 21, 34–35
  multilevel assessment of, 304–309
    gender differences in, 306, 307–309
  neuroticism and, 248–249
  noisome occupations and, 35
  norepinephrine in, 303, 305–306
  in old-age, index measurement versus psychiatric diagnoses of, 265–272
  onset time of, 61
  in parents, 228–229
  patients' characteristics in, 63
  postpartum, 159
  predictors of, 58, 99, 100, 220
  during pregnancy, 24, 28–29
  prevalence of, 304
  racial factors in, 251
  rape-related, 35
  recurrent, 48–49, 62, 64, 65, 253
  risk-factor analysis of, 239–258
    Americans' Changing Lives survey data, 247–252
    decomposition of prior depression effects, 251–252
    depression history as control variable, 243–245, 248–249
    depression history as risk factor modifier, 245–246, 249–250
    for depression recurrence, 253

Depression (*Cont.*)
  risk-factor analysis of (*Cont.*)
    depression vulnerability and, 245–
      246, 249–250, 254
    determinants of prior depression,
      246–247, 250–251
    life stress/episode onset methodology
      and, 242–243
    self-esteem and, 184–185, 192–193,
      248–249
    social support relationship, 68, 159–
      160, 304
    stressful life events and, 9–10
    stress severity in, 55, 60
    subsyndromal, 61
    survival analysis of, 250–251, 253–254
    treatment
      attrition in, 66–67
      initiation of, 65–66
    treatment outcome, 63–65
      relapse, 64, 65
      social support and, 225, 226
      stressors and, 225–226
      untreated, 65
    vulnerability to, 245–246, 249–250
    unmeasured heterogeneity in, 254
Diagnoses, comparison with index mea-
    surement. *See* Indexes, comparison
    with psychiatric diagnoses
Diagnostic and Statistical Manual-III, 266,
    274, 275, 295
Diagnostic and Statistical Manual-IV, 274
Diagnostic Interview Schedule (DIS), 266,
    295
    version III-A, 247
Diatheses-stress interaction, 327, 329
Dictionary of Occupational Titles (DOT), 97,
    98, 97, 127, 131
Disasters
  beneficial effects of, 201–202
  natural, 90, 92
  nuclear, 26, 37, 90, 298
  as posttraumatic stress disorder cause,
    302
  as stress/strain cause, 26
Discrimination, as chronic strain cause,
    25–26
Distress, 77
  decomposition of stressor effects in,
    108–111

Distress (*Cont.*)
  personal agency and, 184–187
  predictors of, 99–102
  self-esteem and, 192–193
  social status and, 193–196
  variance prediction in, 214, 218
Distress scale, 96
Distress-stress relationship, statistical asso-
    ciation in, 180
Donner party, 152, 153
Drug abuse
  multilevel assessment of, 299–301
  self-esteem and, 192
  stress predictors of, 103, 104
Dual-career couples, 119–120

Educational level, relationship to emotion-
    al problems, 283
Efficacy, 187. *See also* Self-efficacy
Engineering model, of stress, 80–81, 111
Epidemiologic Catchment Area, 243, 248
Epinephrine
  in posttraumatic stress disorder, 303
  in stress response, 297
Ethnic groups, discrimination-related
    chronic strain of, 25
Event history analysis, 325
Explanatory style, 185–186, 187

Family, impact of work-related stressors
    on. *See* Work stressors, intergenera-
    tional effects of
Family History Research Diagnostic Crite-
    ria, 247
Family members, life events occurring to,
    27–28
Fatalism, 181, 182, 187
Father
  supportiveness of, 171
  work-related stress of
    effect on children's well-being, 135–
      138
    relationship to marital problems, 133,
      134–135
Fight-or-flight response, 296
Financial stress
  relationship to depression, 99, 102
  as role strain, 25
Focus of events, as interview rating factor,
    51, 52

Gender role beliefs, work-related influences on, 199–122
General adaptation syndrome, 214
Guidance, as social support function, 154
Guilt, posttraumatic stress disorder-related, 302

Hardiness, 183, 216, 219
Heart attack patients, spouses of, 161, 227
Heart rate
  in panic disorder, 302
  stress-related changes in, 308
Helplessness, 181. *See also* Learned helplessness
  depression and, 184–185
  effect on mental health, 5
  self-esteem and, 192
Holmes and Rahe Schedule of Recent Events. *See* Schedule of Recent Events
HOME scales, 130–131
"Hopelessness" depression, 60
Hopkins Symptom Checklist, 295
Hormonal factors
  in posttraumatic stress disorder, 303
  in substance abuse, 300–301
Housework, couples' shared responsibility for, 120, 121
Husband
  provider role of, 119–120, 122
  shared household responsibilities of, 120, 121

Identity accumulation hypothesis, 198
Imagery, intrusive, 303
Immune system function
  explanatory style and, 185
  of spouses of cancer patients, 161
Independence of events, as interview rating factor, 51, 52–53
Indexes, comparison with psychiatric diagnoses, 261–290, 329–330
  attenuation, 276–278
  boundary problems, 275
  censored measures, 271–272
  combination problems, 275–276
  definitions, 262, 263
  implications for stress research, 283–285

Indexes, comparison with psychiatric diagnoses (*Cont.*)
  null findings, 273
  preconceptions, 276, 278–283
  shared attributes, 275–276, 285
Information seeking, 218
Insulin, in stress response, 297
Interpersonal dependency, 195–196
Interpersonal relationships
  as chronic stress cause, 99, 102
  gender-related reactions to, 195, 197
  of posttraumatic stress disorder patients, 302
  social support and, 164–168
Interpersonal Support Evaluation List, 157
Interview methodology, 21, 22–23, 29, 33, 34, 49–51, 294, 319
  compared with checklist method, 21, 56–58
  combined with checklist approach, 319
  process of, 49
  psychometric data base for, 54–55
  rating of interview data, 49, 51–54
  subjects' fabrication of events in, 50–51
  subjects' recall in, 50
Invulnerability, 213–214

Jobs, "women's," 119

Labeling, of the mentally-ill, 26
Learned helplessness, 182
  in depression, 184–185, 304–306
  sex factors in, 189
Learned resourcefulness, 216
Life-course perspective, on stress, 91
Life cycle, implications for life events inventory measurement, 31
Life events
  assessment of, 294. *See also* Life events inventory
    bias in reporting, 8
    limitations of, 16–17
  chronicity of impact, 101
  chronic stressors relationship, 81–83, 107–108
  comparison with daily hassles, 294
  context of, 54
  definition of, 18
  as depression predictors, 99, 102

Life events (*Cont.*)
  as discrete stressors, 92–93
  distress relationship, 100
  duration of stress related to, 31–33
  earlier-adult, relationship to distress,
    109, 110
  interactive effects of, 4–5, 53
  personal growth through, 200–201,
    202, 230–232
  physical health relationship, 103, 104
  physiological adaptation to, 18
  psychological meaning of, 20–22
  recent, 18
  relationship to distress, 109
  remote, 18
  social context measurement, 29–31
  strategic versus comprehensive ap-
    proach towards, 35–38
  trauma relationship, 92–93
Life Events and Difficulties Schedule
    (LEDS), 319
  comparison with Psychiatric Epidemiol-
    ogy Research Interview, 57–58
  comparison with Schedule of Recent
    Events, 57
  description of, 54
  gender factors in, 63
  predictive validity of, 55, 56
Life events inventories, 17–34, 45–59, 79,
    319
  causal inference of, 35
  checklist approach of, 19–22, 23, 29,
    33, 34
    comparison with interview method,
      56–58
    development of, 44
    interrelated events measurement by,
      46
    methodological problems of, 45–49
  chronic strains measurement, 23–24,
    96–97
    acute stress measures by, 240
    community-related measures, 26–27
    discrimination measures, 25–26
  conceptual development of, 18
  effect on stress research, 111
  for ethnic groups, 19
  event redundancy in, 3–34
  gender-bias of, 19
  inadequacy of, 19, 20

Life events inventories (*Cont.*)
  interview methodology of. *See* Interview
    methodology
  intraevent variability of, 22–23
  issues regarding, 318–319
  limitations of, 44
  narrative probe methodology, 22, 29
  network events measures, 27–29
  "non-events" measures, 19, 21
  outcome focus of, 34–35
  persistent life difficulties measures, 24–
    25
  positive events measures, 19–20
  psychological meaning focus of, 20–22
  recommendations regarding, 35–38
  role strain measures, 25
  self-reports, 34
  social context of stressors measures, 29–
    31
    combination approach, 29–31
    separation approach, 29, 30, 31
  subjects recall on, 34
  timing of measures, 31–33
  traumatic events measures, 90
Life events-distress relationship, weak sta-
    tistical association of, 240
Life Stressors and Social Resources Inven-
    tory (LISRES), 9, 222–225
Locus coeruleus
  in depression, 305, 360
  in panic attacks, 302
  in stress, 309–310
Loss, emotional, 21–22

Macrostressor, 86, 88–89, 91, 93
Malaise, index measurement versus psy-
    chiatric diagnoses of, 265, 267–272,
    278, 279, 280, 281, 282
Marital problems, work stress-related,
    133–135
  effect on children's well-being, 136–
    137
Marital relationship, women's inequality
    in, 119–121
Marital status
  personal control and, 188
  psychological distress and, 179–
    180
  self-esteem and, 194
  social status and, 198

Married couples. *See also* Work stressors, intergenerational effects of
  mutual influence of, 227–228
Mastery, 181, 182, 183, 200
  depression and, 184, 187, 189–191, 248–249
  effect on mental health, 5
  individual variations in, 186
  sex factors in, 189
Maturation, as stress effect, 214–215
Mental illness. *See also* specific types of mental illness
  social class differences in, 188
  untreated, 65
Mentally ill persons, labeling of, 26
Microstressor, 86, 88–89, 91, 93
Minority status
  personal control relationship, 188
  psychological distress relationship, 179–180
Mood changes, assessment of, 294
Mother, employment of, 116–117. *See also* Work stressors, intergenerational effects of
  effect on children's behavior problems, 137–139
  effect on children's well-being, 127, 140, 141
  effect on relationship with children, 124–125
  marital problems and, 133, 134
  occupational complexity and, 138, 139
  working hours, 122–123
Mother-child separation, 18
Motivation, effectance, 181, 183
Myocardial infarction patients, spouses of, 161

Narrative probe, 22, 29, 319
National Longitudinal Surveys of Youth, 126, 128
Network, familial, 27–29
Neuroendocrine function, in stress response, 297
Neuroticism, relationship to depression, 248–249
Neurotransmitters, in stress response, 297
Noisome occupations, 35

Nonevents, 89
  definition, 93, 107
  interaction with other stressors, 98, 105, 107, 108
  relationship to distress, 109, 110
  relationship to physical health problems, 103
  as stress cause, 95
Norepinephrine
  in anxiety, 302
  in depression, 303, 305–306
  in posttraumatic stress disorder, 303
  in schizophrenia, 303
  in stress response, 297
Nuclear accidents, 90
  Three Mile Island, 26, 37, 90, 298
Nurturance, as social support function, 154

Occupational self-direction, 117, 118, 121, 123
  marital problems and, 133–135
Occupational stressors. *See* Work stressors
Opioid peptides, endogenous, in stress response, 297
Optimists, 216, 219

Panic disorder, 302
Parasympathetic nervous system, in stress response, 296
Parent–child relationship
  of adult children, 162, 165
  social support in, 162, 165–166
Parents
  perceptions of children's character by, 171–172
  psychosocial resources of, 127
  work stressors of. *See* Work stressors, intergenerational effects of
Peer factors, in substance abuse, 300
Persistent life difficulties, 24–25
Personal agency, 181–190, 203, 204, 325
  psychological distress and, 184–187
  social stress and, 187–190
Personality factors, in social support, 172
Personality growth, crisis theory of, 200–201, 202, 230–232
Pessimists, coping strategies of, 219
Physical abuse, during childhood, 18

Physical health
  relationship to social support, 160–161
  as stress cause, 96
  stress predictors of, 102–104
Physician, work stress of, 160
Posttraumatic stress disorder, 301, 302–304
Potency, 183, 187
Power, 187
  self-esteem and, 191–192
Powerlessness, 181–182
  of the disadvantaged, 191–192
  effect on coping, 186–187
  factors contributing to, 189
  work-related, 118
Preconceptions, diagnostic, 276, 278–283, 284
  counterfactual, 278, 279, 280, 282–283
  extrafactual, 278, 279, 280, 281, 282
  perifactual, 279, 280
Pregnancy
  depression during, 24, 28–29
  network events during, 28
Problems, 78
  chronic stress relationship of, 82
Problem-solving, 218
  as coping focus, 219
Prolactin, in stress response, 297
Psychiatric Epidemiology Research Interview (PERI), 57–58, 319
Psychiatric patients, stereotyping of, 282–283, 284
Psychiatric symptoms, distinct factors of, 274
Psychoactive substance abuse, multilevel assessment of, 299–301
Psychological analysis, of stress process, 322, 326, 327
Psychological centrality, 196–197
Psychological distress. See Distress
Psychological growth, under stress, 229–232
  crisis theory of, 200–201, 202, 230–232
Psychological resources, 9
Psychosocial resources, 179–210. See also Social support
  interaction with stressors, 221–225
  of parents, 127

Psychosocial resources (Cont.)
  personal agency, 181, 190, 203, 204
    psychological distress and, 184–187
    social status and, 187–190
  psychological centrality, 196–197
  role acquisition, 197–200
  salience hierarchy, 197
  self-complexity, 198
  self-esteem, 190–196, 203
  social stress and, 200–202
  as stress mediator, 3, 4, 5, 216–217

Quality of Relationships Inventory, 166

Racial factors, in depression, 251
Racism, 25
Rape, 35
Rater-based methodology, 49, 51–54, 319
  contextual consideration in, 54
Recall, by interview subjects, 50
Recession, as macrostressor, 93
Recurrence
  of depression, 48–49, 62, 64, 65, 253
  of psychological disorders, 62
Reflected appraisal, 190, 191
Relationship strain, 25
Reliable alliance, 154
Resilience, 213–214
  crisis-related, 231
Resources. See also Social support
  definition, 219
Respiration rate, as stress indicator, 296
Rheumatoid arthritis patients, spousal support for, 167
Role(s), multiple, 25
Role acquisition, 197–200
Role captivity, 84, 85, 89
Role conflict, as depression cause, 304, 307, 308–309
Role occupancy
  as chronic stress cause, 102
  gender differences in, 197
  negative effects of, 199, 203
Role strain
  distinguished from chronic stress, 84–85
  self-esteem and, 200
  types of, 84

Salience hierarchy, 197
Salutogenesis, 215–216
Schedule for Affective Disorders and
    Depression-RDC (SADS-RDC),
    278–280, 281, 284
Schedule of Recent Events (SRE), 19, 44,
    45, 46, 58, 79, 318
  comparison with Life Events and Diffi-
    culties Schedule, 57
  evaluation of, 16
Schizoaffective disorder, 275
Schizophrenia
  index measurement versus psychiatric
    diagnoses of, 275, 276, 284
  noisome occupations and, 35
  norepinephrine in, 303
  prevalence of, 284
  social class factors in, 188
  stress severity in, 60
Schizophreniform personality, 275
Seasonal affective disorder, 306–307
Self-attribution, 190, 191
Self-complexity, 198–199
Self-concept, 190
Self-efficacy, 5, 187, 192, 325
  perceived, 216, 219–220
  social structure and, 9, 188
Self-esteem, 190–196, 203
  depression and, 184–185, 192–193,
    248–249
  of divorced women, 229
  effect on mental health, 5
  gender differences in, 204
  interpersonal dependency and, 204
  psychological distress and, 192–193
  role strain and, 200
  of spouse, 227
Self-help groups, 163
Self-medication, 301
  for seasonal affective disorder, 307
Self-reliance, social support and, 162
Self-reports
  of chronic stress, subjectivity of, 96–97
  of life events, 34
    reliability of, 325–326
  of social support, 154–155
  of stress, 293, 294–296
    advantages of, 295–296
    disadvantages of, 295
  of work stress, 127

Separation, mother-child, 18
Serotonin
  in depression, 306
  in seasonal affective disorder, 307
  in stress response, 297
Severity of life events
  as interview rating factor, 51, 52, 53
  recall of, 55
Sexism, 25
Sex segregation, occupational, 119
Sexual abuse, during childhood, 18, 90
Skin conductance, as stress indicator, 296
Smoking, relationship to stress, 96, 103–
    104
Social class. See Social status
Social identity, 197
Social integration, as social support func-
    tion, 154
Social isolation, as mortality risk factor,
    160
Social network, structure of, 153–154
Social Provision Scale, 157
Social Readjustment Rating Scale, 19,
    214
Social role, relationship to stress, 6
Social status
  depression and, 283 ·
  implications for life events measure-
    ments, 29, 30
  personal agency and, 187–190
  psychological distress and, 179–180,
    193–196
  schizophrenia and, 188
  stress-mental health relationship and,
    180–181, 188
  stress relationship, 6, 198–200, 324
Social structure
  self-efficacy and, 9
  stress relationship, 326–327
Social support, 9, 151–177
  assessment of, 156–158, 162, 168
  during childhood, 325
  coping and, 160, 219
  counseling outcome and, 171
  definition, 156, 191
  as depression modifier, 68, 159–160,
    304
  effect of stress on, 67–68
  functions of, 154
  interactional-cognitive view of, 168–173

Social support (*Cont.*)
  interaction with stressors, 222–225
  interpersonal conflict during, 169
  laboratory studies of, 163–164
  perceived, 158–160
    assessment of, 155–156, 157–158,
      164–165
    as cognitive adaptation, 172–173
    interactional basis of, 171–172
    relationship context of, 166
  personality factors in, 172
  physical health relationship, 160–161
  physiological effects of, 164
  provision of, 162–163
  received, assessment of, 154–155, 156–
    158
  relationships context of, 164–168
    working models of, 169–171, 172–
      173
  social network structure and, 153–154
  as stress mediator, 3, 4, 5, 216–217,
    323–324
    gender differences in, 195
  substance abuse as, 300
Social Support Questionnaire, 157, 159,
  163–164, 165, 166, 171
Sociological analysis, of stress process,
  321–322, 326–327
Spouses
  of alcoholics, 228
  of cancer patients, 161, 167
  of heart attack patients, 161, 227
Stage of life issues, 90–91
Stepfamily, formation of, 163
Stereotyping
  cultural, 25–26
  of psychiatric patients, 282–283, 284
Strain
  ambient, 85
  chronic, 17–18
    community-wide, 23, 26–27
    "daily hassles" as, 23–24
    depression and, 32
    engineering analogy of, 80
    measurement of, 23–24
    persistent life difficulties and, 24–25
    physiological adaptation to, 18
    role strain as, 23, 25
    types of, 23, 320
  definition, 77

Stress
  acute, depression and, 32
  aftereffects of, 296
  arousal theory of, 81, 89
  biological model of, 79, 111, 292
  chronic, 84–85. *See also* Strain, chronic
    as anxiety disorder cause, 301–302
    definition, 85
    distinguished from role strain, 84–
      85
    inventory of, 99
    measurement of, 240–241
    subcomponents of, 85
    subjectivity of reports of, 97
  classification of, 91–94
  cognitive appraisal concept of, 292
  conflict over definition of, 291
  continuum of, 83–94, 320
  definition, 77
  engineering model of, 80–81, 111
  expanded concept of, 327
  indirect effects of, 44
  life events relationship, 78–79
  physiological adaptation to, 18–19
    as stress research focus, 43–44
  physiological basis of, 79
  as process, 292–293
  reciprocal causation with distress,
    98
  relationship to change, 81
  researchers' operationalization of, 47,
    51–53, 58–59
  social context of, 116, 323–324. *See also*
    Social support
  social psychology of, 324
  subjective perception of, 47–48
  variability of response to, 152
Stress assessment, 291–314. *See also* Life
    events inventories
  behavioral measures, 294, 296
  biochemical measures, 294, 297
  definitional problems of, 291
  issues in, 318
  multilevel approach of, 292–310, 321–
    322
    advantages of, 293
    for anxiety disorders, 301–304
    for depression, 304–309
    gender differences in, 307–309
    levels of measurement, 293–298

Stress assessment (*Cont.*)
  multilevel approach of (*Cont.*)
    measurement convergence and, 298
    for psychoactive substance abuse
        problems, 299–301
    physiological measures, 294, 296–298
    problems of, 291–292
    self-reports, 293, 294–296
Stress-buffering, 67–68
  predictor variables in, 239–240
  of social support, 154
Stress-illness relationship. *See also* Stress-
      mental health relationship
  assessment of, 295
  causal association of, criticism of, 15–17
  individual variability in, 214–215
Stress invulnerability, 213–214
Stress mediators, 3, 4
  social support as, 3, 4, 5
Stress-mental health relationship, 321–
      322. *See also* specific types of men-
      tal illness
  assessment instruments for, 294–295
  factors affecting, 59–70
    clinical course of disorder, 62–65
    onset of illness, 59–62, 324
    stress correlates in, 65–69
  multilevel assessment of, 298–310
  outcome measure of, 321
  parental work stress and, 323
  positive events in, 19–20
  socioeconomic factors in, 180–181
  specificity of stressors in, 60
  stressor chronology in, 324–326
  symptom expression in, 60–61
  weak statistical association of, 15- 17,
      69, 240
Stress models, components of, 3, 4
Stressors. *See also* Life events; Strain,
      chronic
  acute, separated from chronic strains,
      24–25
  in childhood, 18, 90–91. *See also* Child-
      hood trauma
  chronic
    associated with social resources, 222,
        232
    chronicity of, 93, 108
    correlation with other stressors, 4–5,
        100–101, 105, 106–107, 109, 110

Stressors (*Cont.*)
  chronic (*Cont.*)
    definition, 111, 115–116
    as depression predictor, 99, 102
    inventory of, 96–97
    life events versus, 81–83
    relationship to distress, 100–101, 109,
        110
    relationship to physical health prob-
        lems, 103–104
  chronology of, 324–326
  classification of, 17, 91–94, 320
  community, 26–27
  cumulative effects analysis of, 8, 95–
      112
    causal model of, 104–108
    data sources, 95
    decomposition of effects in, 108–111
    measures of, 96–98
    outcome measures of, 96
    stress concepts in, 98–104, 112
    stress sources, 96–98
  discrete, 320
  engineering analogy of, 80–81
  interaction with social/personal re-
      sources, 221–225
  macro-level, 86, 88–89, 91, 92
  measurement of, 293
    disadvantages of, 294
  micro-level, 86, 88–89, 91, 93
  multiplicity of, 77–78
  pervasive effects of, 322–323
  positive, 60
  range of, 320
  stage of life of occurrence of, 90–91
  system, 88, 93
  timing of, 31–33
  types of, 77–78, 83–91, 327–328
Stress process paradigm, 3–12
  advantages of, 6–7
Stress-related disorders, implications for
      interviews, 50
Stress research
  development of, 43–44
  emergent issues in, 327–330
    concept of stress, 327–328
    concept of vulnerability, 328–329
    indexes and diagnoses, 329–330
    interdisciplinary, 321–322, 326–327
    methodological designs in, 321–322

Stress resistance research, 9, 213–238
  with children, 215–216, 228–229, 233
  family-oriented, 227–229, 233
  historical background, 214–216
  implications for psychotherapy, 232–
    233
  integrative predictive models, 219–221
  of psychological disorder recovery, 225–
    227
  social support and, 323–324
  of stress moderators, 216–218
  of stressors/resources interaction, 221–
    225
  of stress-related psychological growth,
    229–232
Stress universe, 8
  complexity of, 318–320
  mapping of, 320
Structured Clinical Interview, 295
Suicide, self-esteem and, 192
Survival analysis, 325
  of depression, 250–251, 253–254
Symptom Checklist 90-R (SCL-90-R), 295
System stressor, 88, 93, 112

Tension, alcohol/drug-related reduction
    of, 299–300
Testosterone, in posttraumatic stress dis-
    order, 303
Three Mile Island nuclear accident, 26,
    37, 90, 298
Thyroxine, in posttraumatic stress disor-
    der, 303
Time factors
  in onset of stressors, 324–326
  in stress, 31–33, 51, 53
  in stress-related disorder onset, 61–62
Trauma, 89–90, 92
  life events relationship, 92–93
"Trouble," as stress cause, 79
Tryptophan, in depression, 306–307

Unemployment
  as depression cause, 199
  self-esteem and, 193

Valence, as interview rating factor, 51–
    52
Violence, familial, relationship to later-life
    depression, 251–252, 253
Vulnerability
  definition of, 29
  to depression, 61, 245–246, 249–250,
    254
  Erikson's definition of, 201
  individual variability in, 240, 328–
    329
  psychosocial risk factors and, 329
  to stress, 9–10
  stress response and, 67–68
  stressor-specificity of, 328–329

Wages, gender-related disparities in,
    122
War stress, 90, 93
Withdrawal, 300, 301
  as coping strategy, 218
Women
  divorced, self-esteem of, 229
  employment of. See also Mother, em-
    ployment of
    contribution to family income, 119–
      120
  role strain of, 25
Workers
  personal efficacy of, 188
  social status of, 199
Work strain, 25
Work stressors, 116–147, 320
  effects on individual workers, 117–
    119
  intergenerational effects of, 8–9, 116–
    117, 222, 322, 323
    cross-sectional studies of, 126–127
    example, 125–142
    gender differences in, 119–125
    marital problems, 133–135
  of physicians, 160
  self-reports of, 127
  sex factors in, 197
Worth, reassurance of, 154